Infants, Toddlers, and Caregivers

Seventh Edition

Infants, Toddlers, and Caregivers

A Curriculum of Respectful, Responsive Care and Education

Janet Gonzalez-Mena
Napa Valley College

Dianne Widmeyer Eyer
Cañada College

Boston   Burr Ridge, IL   Dubuque, IA   Madison, WI   New York
San Francisco   St. Louis   Bangkok   Bogotá   Caracas   Kuala Lumpur
Lisbon   London   Madrid   Mexico City   Milan   Montreal   New Delhi
Santiago   Seoul   Singapore   Sydney   Taipei   Toronto

Higher Education

INFANTS, TODDLERS, AND CAREGIVERS: A CURRICULUM OF RESPECTFUL, RESPONSIVE CARE AND EDUCATION
Published by McGraw-Hill, a business unit of The McGraw-Hill Companies, Inc., 1221 Avenue of the Americas, New York, NY, 10020. Copyright © 2007, 2004 by The McGraw-Hill Companies, Inc. All rights reserved. Previous editions © 2001, 1997, 1993, 1989 by Mayfield Publishing Company. No part of this publication may be reproduced or distributed in any form or by any means, or stored in a database or retrieval system, without the prior written consent of The McGraw-Hill Companies, Inc., including, but not limited to, in any network or other electronic storage or transmission, or broadcast for distance learning.

Some ancillaries, including electronic and print components, may not be available to customers outside the United States.

This book is printed on acid-free paper.

2 3 4 5 6 7 8 9 0 DOC/DOC 0 9 8 7

ISBN-13: 978-0-07-313129-0
ISBN-10: 0-07-313129-6

Vice President and Editor-in-Chief: *Emily Barrosse*
Publisher: *Beth Mejia*
Executive Editor: *David Patterson*
Freelance Development Editor: *Terri Wise*
Freelance Permissions Coordinator: *Connie Dowcett*
Executive Marketing Manager: *Pamela S. Cooper*
Lead Media Producer: *Shannon Gattens*
Managing Editor: *Jean Dal Porto*
Project Manager: *Meghan Durko*
Art Director: *Jeanne Schreiber*
Designer: *Srdjan Savanovic*
Cover Designer: *Srdjan Savanovic*

Interior Designer: *Ellen Pettengell*
Art Editor: *Ayelet Arbel*
Senior Photo Research Coordinator: *Alexandra Ambrose*
Photo Researcher: *Judy Mason*
Cover Credit: © *Geri Engberg/The Image Works*
Production Supervisor: *Jason I. Huls*
Media Project Manager: *Michele Borrelli*
Senior Supplement Producer: *Louis Swaim*
Supplement Author: *Alika Hope Despotopoulos*

Composition: 10/12 Janson Text, by Interactive Composition Corporation
Printing: 45 # New Era Matte, R.R. Donnelley/Crawfordsville, IN.

Credits: The credits section for this book begins on page C-1 and is considered an extension of the copyright page.

Library of Congress Cataloging-in-Publication Data
Gonzalez-Mena, Janet.
    Infants, toddlers, and caregivers: a curriculum of respectful, responsive care and education / Janet Gonzalez-Mena, Dianne Widmeyer Eyer.—7th ed.
        p. cm.
    Includes bibliographical references and index.
    ISBN 0-07-313129-6 (softcover: alk. paper)
    ISBN 978-0-07-313129-0
    1. Child care—United States. 2. Child development—United States. 3. Education, Preschool—Activity programs—United States. I. Eyer, Dianne Widmeyer. II. Title.
HQ778.63.G663 2007
362.71'2—dc22   2005052278

The Internet addresses listed in the text were accurate at the time of publication. The inclusion of a website does not indicate an endorsement by the authors of McGraw-Hill, and McGraw-Hill does not guarantee the accuracy of the information presented at these sites.

www.mhhe.com

To Magda Gerber, Emmi Pikler, and Anna Tardos

About the Authors

It was the mid-1970s when the authors, who shared an office at Cañada College in Redwood City, California, became concerned about the quality of training available for infant-toddler caregivers. Babies were coming into child care, and two-year-olds were sometimes enrolled in preschool. Training for early child-hood educators didn't go all the way down to infants and toddlers. So they decided to do something about that. Janet Gonzalez-Mena became an intern in Magda Gerber and Dr. Tom Forrest's program, the Demonstration Infant Program (now called Resources for Infant Educarers—RIE), where she learned the philosophy on which this book is based. Dianne Widmeyer Eyer completed a second master's degree in special education and developed curriculum in early childhood special education, and became the ECE/CD Program Coordinator in 1978.

A few years later both authors became more involved with family child care. As Director of Child Care Services for Family Service Agency in San Mateo County, California, Janet supervised a network of family child-care homes that served infants and toddlers (as well as preschoolers). Under her direction, the agency opened a new infant center and also created a pilot program of therapeutic child care for abused and neglected infants and toddlers. Dianne worked with the Child Care Coordinating Council of San Mateo County to develop a Certificate Training Program for Family Child Care Providers at Cañada College. This curriculum also models the Gerber philosophy of respect and responsiveness for infant-toddler care. Janet went on to teach at Napa Valley College until she retired from there in 1998. Today Janet continues to educate and train infant-toddler caregivers in a variety of settings. She is currently working with WestEd's Program for Infant Toddler Caregivers training trainers. Her latest passion is understanding more about the Pikler Institute in Budapest, Hungary, where Magda Gerber came from. She has made three trips there to study the approach and is convinced that this residential nursery is a model for the world. She is working with a group in Mexico to explore how the approach might fit into their models of residential care for infants and toddlers. She is also exploring how this approach can be adapted for child care in the United States. Dianne has developed several curriculum specializations in early childhood education/ child development (ECE/CD), including "Children with Special Needs," "Family Support," "SAFE START/Violence Intervention & Prevention in the Early Years," and "Home-Based Child Care." She is a member of the National Association for the Education of Young Children and the Child Development Training Consortium. She is Professor Emeritus, Early Childhood Education/ Child Development, at Cañada College, retiring from there fall 2005. She continues to coordinate a grant with First 5 San Mateo County to recruit and retain teachers in the early care and education field. Dianne is also a Professional Growth Advisor for the California Child Development Permit.

Brief Contents

Contents

chapter 2

Infant-Toddler Education 25

chapter 3

Caregiving as Curriculum 47

chapter 11

Social Skills 231

part 3 ## Focus on the Program 253

chapter 12

The Physical Environment 255

chapter 13

The Social Environment 285

chapter 14

Adult Relations in Infant-Toddler Care and Education Programs 307

Preface

The Philosophy of Infants, Toddlers, and Caregivers

Previous editions of this book were based mainly on the philosophy of Magda Gerber, a Los Angeles infant-toddler expert originally from Hungary. This new edition is based on a combination of Gerber's philosophy and that of her colleague, Emmi Pikler. Pikler was a pediatrician who first met Gerber back in the 1930s when their children were very young. Pikler became Gerber's pediatrician and later Gerber became Pikler's colleague. After World War II, Pikler founded an institution for the Hungarian government for war orphans. The residential nursery, nicknamed Lóczy, was where Gerber worked. Gerber brought the philosophy, research, and training from Lóczy to the United States at the time of the Hungarian Revolution in the mid 1950s. She eventually established an organization called Resources for Infant Educarers (RIE), which trains caregivers, parents, and trainers in the Gerber method. The Pikler Institute, as it is now called, continues to this day with its fine work of caring for infants and toddlers whose families cannot care for them. It also continues to be a research and training institution. Much of the Institute's research has been published in languages other than English, so Gerber's contribution has been an enormous benefit to those of us in early care and education in the United States.

Gerber is known for introducing the word *respect* into the vocabulary of infant-toddler care. Respect is one of the themes that runs throughout this book and is a key component of the curriculum. Gerber had a curriculum, but she never called it that. Nobody was talking about curriculum for infants and toddlers back when Gerber started spreading her word. Today, however, *curriculum* has become an important term in the early care and education field, and this text reflects that change. The last edition added the word *curriculum* in the book's subtitle, and two chapters have curriculum in their titles, but in reality, the whole book has always been about curriculum. We use the word to mean "a plan for learning," but we don't mean lessons! Our concept of curriculum is that it is all-inclusive and centers on connections and relationships. Briefly, curriculum is about educating, but in the infant-toddler world *care* and *education* are one and the same. Curriculum has to do with respecting and responding to each child's needs in warm, respectful, and sensitive ways that promote attachment. The term "curriculum" embraces all the sensitive interactions that occur during the day. Those interactions may be part of activities, both planned and unplanned, but they go way beyond. The interactions that occur during caregiving routines are an important part of the curriculum. Even down times during the day when caregivers just hang out with the little ones can include the kinds of interactions that make up curriculum. Every chapter represents what J. Ronald Lally, one of the originators of the Program for Infant/Toddler Caregivers, calls a respectful and responsive curriculum based on relationships.

Perhaps the most important feature of this book is the consistency with which it outlines well-established practices designed to promote infants' and toddlers' total well-being, including physical and mental growth and development, mental health, emotional stability, and human relationships. In order to counterbalance one-sided treatments that do not consider all facets of a child's development, this book also looks at the importance that sensitive care and proper program planning have on the identity formation of infants and toddlers.

The Ten Principles: A Philosophy of Respect

Respect is the foundation of the philosophy on which this book is built. Is respect different from kindness and warmth? The answer is yes. What does it mean to respect infants and toddlers? The answer to that question lies in the Ten Principles on which this book is based, which are introduced in Chapter 1 and integrated throughout the text. (See page 5 for a listing of these principles.) Why are these principles needed? Before the word "respect" came into the vocabulary of those concerned with infants, parents and professionals alike often treated babies like objects at worst or lesser humans at best. Think of the negative connotations of "treating someone like a baby." The message of this book is to treat babies like the human beings they are. So, what does it mean to respect babies? Respect is an attitude, but what counts is when that attitude shows up in behavior. Respectful behaviors are the basis of the Ten Principles and can be quickly explained in terms of how adults respect each other. For example, when adults fall down, nobody rushes over, picks them up, brushes them off, pats them on the head, and says, "You're okay" whether they are or not. If an adult is going into surgery, those involved explain what's going to happen rather than surprising him or her with uncomfortable procedures. Even the statement "This instrument will feel cold" is a sign of respect for the person. The Ten Principles show how respect applies to treating babies as people when changing a diaper, communicating with them, and facilitating their growth, development, and learning. The book refers back to the Ten Principles in every chapter. In addition, a feature, *The Principles in Action*, uses a scenario to further explain the individual principles.

Terminology

In this book the youngest children—those from newborn to walking—are called infants. The children who are walking (from about a year old to two years) are called young toddlers. Children from two to three are called older toddlers. Children from three to five are called preschoolers. Please note that these labels and descriptions apply to typically developing children. When development is not typical the labels and descriptions don't fit as well. For example, a non-walking child who has reached the stage when other children walk, may have many other characteristics of that age group; not all toddlers toddle, but that doesn't mean they should be thought of as infants.

What to call adults in this book was a concern. Adults in the teacher/caregiver role go by different titles, depending on where they work. Magda Gerber coined the term "educarers," which is now used by other people as well. She used the term in relation to the people she trained to work with children under three. Her successors in the program Resources for Infant Educarers (RIE) still use the term. We decided to call the adults in this book "caregivers" to simplify matters and to emphasize the importance of "caring" in programs for the youngest children. The caregiver role incorporates that of teacher, educator, child rearer, and surrogate parent.

Organization of the Text

This book is divided into three parts and is organized in a unique way. Instead of starting with standard child development information and its practical application, Part 1 focuses on the caregivers' actions and relationships with the children. By starting with the *interactive* aspect of caregiving, we highlight the philosophy from the beginning pages of the book. Part 1 is an explanation of how the caregivers' actions and interactions with the children make up the curriculum in infant-toddler programs, both center-based and in family child care.

Part 2 presents basic child development information along with the curriculum implications of that information. Each chapter in Part 2 also has a special section explaining various issues related to children with special needs and challenges. Part 2 reflects the basic philosophy found throughout the book.

Part 3 looks at additional infant-toddler child care components and includes environments as well as adult-adult relationships. These are examined from a programmatic point of view in both center and family child care settings.

Appendix A is a checklist for determining quality in infant-toddler programs. Appendix B includes an environmental chart that combines the information from all three parts into one concise but comprehensive chart designed for practical use in program design and implementation. The chart tells what to do when and with what, based on infants' and toddlers' specific stage-related developmental needs. Appendix C gives a sample set of guiding principles for working in partnership with parents. The principles used as examples are from the Parent Services Project (PSP) headed by Ethel Seiderman.

A Focus on Diversity and Inclusion

As in previous editions, we are concerned about honoring diversity and the inclusion of infants and toddlers with special needs in child care and early education programs. The focus is even greater now because of new immigrants pouring in to child care centers and because children with disabilities and atypical development are also entering at an even greater rate than before. The goal is to place all children regardless of their differing abilities in "natural environments," which means that those with special needs will be in the same environments as their typically-developing peers. This book's focus on inclusion is timely and useful. The skills and sensitivity emphasized here can help caregivers make a difference in the development of all children, including those with special needs.

Responding to diversity is a necessity and we've focused more on cultural differences each edition, even though we still present a cohesive philosophy without confusing it with multiple views on each and every subject. Our emphasis on self-reflection helps caregivers who may feel uncomfortable in the face of differences discover where their "hotspots" lie. Only when caregivers understand themselves can they understand infants and toddlers and their families. Sensitivity is an important qualification for anyone who works with very young children. For that reason, the reader is asked to focus on personal experience throughout this book.

Bilingualism is promoted in the text. An important part of caregiver training is learning to understand, acknowledge, and respond to language and cultural differences. Knowing how to promote home language is also important.

A Focus on Application and Practice

Knowing *about* is different from knowing *how to*. Knowing *about* means learning theory. Knowing *how to* puts theory into action. We purposely organized this book to emphasize action because we know that even people with considerable understanding of infants and toddlers have trouble acting on that understanding unless they have also learned to *apply* theory. Knowledge does not necessarily build skill.

Caregivers who have knowledge but lack confidence in their ability to use it may suffer from "analysis paralysis," which prevents caregivers from making quick decisions, stating their feelings clearly, and taking needed action. A common pattern when analysis paralysis strikes is inaction, then indecision, then overemotional or otherwise inappropriate reaction, followed by more inaction. Take for example an inexperienced caregiver in an infant-toddler center who stands by, watching a toddler throwing sand in the air, unsure whether the child's obvious enjoyment of this new accomplishment is more important than the possibility of getting sand in her (or someone else's) eyes. The caregiver may hang back hesitantly, doing nothing for a time, then say or do nothing until the conflict within grows strong enough to cause another reaction. This time she may laugh and play with the child, enjoying with her the pleasure of her new discovery, until sand gets into someone's eyes, at which time the caregiver may angrily remind that child that she told her to stop a long time ago.

When adults have analysis paralysis and either cannot react or react inconsistently, infants cannot learn to predict what will happen as the result of their own actions. This learning to predict what effect they have on the world is the primary accomplishment of infants in early life. Depriving them of this learning affects their development. Because of internal conflicts, adults may put up with behavior that bothers them. Infants and toddlers can sense adult conflicts. They then continue with behavior that adults disapprove of—testing to see what will happen. They get no clear message about the approved way to behave or about the effects of their behavior.

New to the Seventh Edition

This edition includes a good deal of new information and several new features. If you have used the book in earlier editions, you'll notice right away an addition at the beginning of each chapter—a feature called "What Do You See?" These short scenes show a child or children in a situation related to the material to follow and immediately engage the reader in the chapter's subject matter. The reader is encouraged to think back on these scenes at least once, and sometimes several times, in each chapter. Another new feature is the Video Observation in each chapter. These text features introduce and encourage readers to think about the issues and concepts presented in online video clips related to chapter material. At the book's Online Learning Center, readers can watch these live action examples of what they are reading about and can respond to questions analyzing what they observe in each clip.

We made a special effort in this new edition to make connections to help readers study, understand, review, and retain the material. For example, with a little reorganizing, we have connected the Principles in Action features to the Appropriate Practice boxes through a new heading in Appropriate Practice boxes called "Appropriate Practice in Action." With a little more reorganizing, the Focus Questions at the beginning of each chapter are now aligned with chapter headings, which also match up with the Chapter Summaries.

We have also added references to the Program Standards of the National Association for the Education of Young Children (NAEYC). These references appear in the margins whenever the material relates to those standards, adding to the coverage already given to NAEYC standards in the guidelines for appropriate practice that appear at the end of each chapter. The complete NAEYC Program Standards appear on the endpapers at the front and back of the book.

The new edition also features marginal reflection questions designed to relate the material to the reader's own life experience.

We have added information throughout, and have updated References and Further Reading sections. The new information brings the book right up to the minute and includes:

- More on Magda Gerber and especially Emmi Pikler in Chapter 1.
- Information on the Pikler Institute throughout the book.
- A stronger focus on explaining and defining curriculum in Chapters 1 and 2, plus how to observe and record behavior in Chapter 2.
- A more detailed explanation in Chapter 2 of why infant-toddler education is not scaled-down preschool.
- Added information on nutrition and sanitation issues in Chapter 3.
- More theory and research in Chapter 4.
- Additional information on Ainsworth in Chapter 5, including some questions about the universal applicability of her research.
- Information on sensory integration in Chapter 6 and updated research.
- Added information on dynamic systems approach in Chapter 7.
- Added guidance regarding when to seek assistance for developmental delays in Chapter 7.
- More information on Piaget in Chapter 8.
- New information about fast mapping in Chapter 9 and updated research.
- An exploration of parents' role in the development of social skills and the parent-caregiver relationship in Chapter 11.
- More details in the diapering section in Chapter 12.
- Additional information on safety (in Chapter 12 and elsewhere).
- Discussion of the concept of redirection, revision of the section on time-out, and addition of some of the work of Marian Marion.
- Reorganization of Chapter 14, adding more subheadings; expanding the section on communication; and adding active listening, cross-cultural conflict, and parental involvement.
- Expansion beyond California examples throughout to give the book a broader base.
- Incorporation of key parts from the Conclusion into Chapter 14 and elimination of the separate Conclusion section.

We still prominently feature children with special needs as well as cultural differences, resilience in children, early literacy, and identity development.

The following features from earlier editions have been retained and updated.

Appropriate Practice Feature

This feature lists summarizing points of NAEYC's guidelines for developmentally appropriate practice related to the chapter topics. Each feature has four sections: "Overview of Development," "Developmentally Appropriate Practice," "Individually Appropriate Practice," and "Culturally Appropriate Practice." The latter three sections list points to keep in mind and practical suggestions for interacting with infants and toddlers based on the NAEYC guidelines.

Developmental Pathways Feature

A *Developmental Pathways* feature is included in each of the development chapters in Part 2. Each feature begins with generalizations about stages of development by showing a chart of behaviors related to the chapter topic and then uses examples of two different children to show diverse developmental pathways. The details of each example are explored under the headings.

The Principles in Action Feature

A case study scenario followed by questions helps students analyze the scenario based on the Ten Principles. This feature allows students to apply the content they have learned to a "real life" situation.

Pedagogy

Each chapter contains a pedagogical system designed to provide learning support for students and to encourage students to reflect on and apply what they learn. Pedagogical features include:

- **Focus Questions** that prepare students for the content to follow
- **Boldfaced In-text Key Terms** that highlight key terminology and now define it in context of the paragraph in which it appears
- *The Principles in Action* **Boxes** that allow students to apply the principles to scenarios
- *Appropriate Practice* **Boxes** that provide practical suggestions related to the NAEYC guidelines for developmentally appropriate practice and refer to the Principles in Action Boxes, showing how Appropriate Practice can be applied to the scenarios
- *Developmental Pathways* **Boxes** that list trends in development and variations
- **Online Resources Sections** that list the study and extension resources available to the student on the Online Learning Center
- **Chapter Summaries** that summarize key ideas of the chapters
- **Key Terms Sections** that list all key terms from the chapter and provide page references
- **Thought/Activity Questions** that encourage students to review, reflect, and apply
- **For Further Reading Lists** that suggest additional readings
- **Video Observation** features in each chapter with pedagogy to help readers think about the video clips they view at the Online Learning Center

- **NAEYC Program Standards** found in the margins next to related material
- **Reflection Questions** designed to help readers consider their own feelings and experiences that relate to what they are reading about

Student and Instructor Resources and Supplements

For the Student

- The **Online Learning Center** at www.mhhe.com/itc7e offers a student study guide including quizzes with feedback, video observations, Web links, and additional resources.
- **English-Spanish Early Childhood Glossary:** *Infants, Toddlers, and Caregivers* now offers a complimentary English-Spanish glossary of Early Childhood terms taken from the text. Ofelia Garcia of Cabrillo College developed this glossary to support Spanish-speaking students and students who anticipate working in communities where English is not the first language. The glossary is free to students through the book's website at www.mhhe.com/itc7e.
- *The Caregiver's Companion: Readings and Professional Resources*— Free with new copies of the text, *The Caregiver's Companion* includes practical articles to extend student understanding of important topics, observation guidelines, and a wealth of useful forms to use when becoming a professional caregiver. To purchase separately (ISBN 0-07-313132-6), contact McGraw-Hill Customer Service at 1-800-338-3987.
- *Folio*Live is an online portfolio tool you can use to create an electronic portfolio in three easy steps: (1) Use a template to create a homepage, (2) Choose to create a custom framework or general framework to structure your portfolio, and (3) Add artifacts to build your portfolio by uploading existing files (from Word, PowerPoint, or video), linking to artifacts posted elsewhere on the Web, or creating an artifact through *Folio*Live embedded forms. Go to www.foliolive.com to learn more.

For the Instructor

- An Instructor's Resource CD-ROM with Instructor's Manual and EZ Test electronic testing software is available. McGraw-Hill's EZ Test is a flexible and easy-to-use electronic testing program. The program allows instructors to create tests from book specific items. It accommodates a wide range of question types and instructors may add their own questions. Multiple versions of the test can be created and any test can be exported for use with course management systems such as WebCT,

BlackBoard or PageOut. EZ Test Online is a new service and gives you a place to easily administer your EZ Test created exams and quizzes online. The program is available for Windows and Macintosh environments. Please contact your McGraw-Hill sales representative for more information.

- *Observing Infants, Toddlers, and Caregivers*—This video, free to adopters of this text, includes real-life segments of infants, toddlers, and caregivers. Use this video with students to practice observation techniques and to show the real worlds of young children and their caregivers. The video has been revised for the Seventh Edition to include What to Watch For and Discussion Questions surrounding each observation.
- **PageOut** allows you to easily create your own custom course Web site. Simply plug your course information into a template and click on one of sixteen designs, and you can create your own professional-looking Web site. Powerful features include an interactive course syllabus that allows you to post content and links, an online gradebook, lecture notes, bookmarks, and a discussion board where students can discuss course-related topics.
- More instructor resources are available on the **Online Learning Center** at www.mhhe.com/itc7e.

Acknowledgments

We would like to acknowledge and thank the reviewers who provided feedback on the sixth edition of *Infants, Toddlers, and Caregivers*. These instructors include:

Nancy H. Beaver, *Eastfield College*

Corinne Greenberg, *Santa Fe Community College*

Donna Greene, *Mt. San Jacinto College*

Kere P. Huges, *Iowa State University*

Tamra Keim, *Hesston College*

Michelle Meadows, *Eastern Illinois University*

Michelle B. Morris, *Wor-Wic Community College*

Cheryl Plonka, *U.S. Army Training Program*

Joan Ports, *Towson University*

Teri Rossman, *Illinois Valley Community College*

Debbie Stoll, *Cameron University*

Terri Jo Swim, *Indiana University, Purdue*

Cheryl Williams-Jackson, *Modesto Junior College*

Wayne L. Wolf, *South Suburban College*

Susan Wyatt, *Eastfield College*

Resources for Caregivers

Packaged with your text is *The Caregiver's Companion: Readings and Professional Resources. The Caregiver's Companion* includes twenty-one readings regarding the Ten Principles; curriculum; keeping toddlers safe and healthy; culture, identity, and families; and including infants and toddlers with special needs. Readings include:

"Caring for Infants with Respect: The RIE Approach" by Magda Gerber

"Curriculum and Lesson Planning: A Responsive Approach" by J. Ronald Lally

"Respectful, Individual, and Responsive Caregiving for Infants" by Beverly Kovach and Denise Da Ros

"Facilitating the Play of Children at Loczy" by Anna Tardos

"A Primary Caregiving System for Infants and Toddlers" by Jennifer L. Bernhardt

Excerpt from "Our Moving Bodies Tell Stories, Which Speak of Our Experiences" by Suzi Tortora

"The Development of Movement" by Emmi Pikler

"How Infants and Toddlers Use Symbols" by Karen Miller

"Preparing for Literacy: Communication Comes First" by Ruth Anne Hammond

"Helping a Baby Adjust to Center Care" by Enid Elliot

"Toddlers: What to Expect" by Janet Gonzalez-Mena

"Creating a Landscape for Learning" by Louis Torelli and Charles Durrett

"The Impact of Child Care Policies and Practices on Infant/Toddler Identity Formation" by J. Ronald Lally

"Cross-Cultural Conferences" by Janet Gonzalez-Mena

"Sudden Infant Death Syndrome" by Susan S. Aronson

"Supporting the Development of Infants and Toddlers with Special Health Needs" by Cynthia Huffman

"Breastfeeding Promotion in Child Care" by Laura Dutil Aird

"Cultural Dimensions of Feeding Relationships" by Carol Brunson Phillips and Renatta Cooper

"Cultural Differences in Sleeping Practices" by Janet Gonzalez-Mena and Navaz Peshotan Bhavnagri

"Talking with Parents When Concerns Arise" by Linda Brault and Janet Gonzalez-Mena

"Strategies for Supporting Infants and Toddlers with Disabilities in Inclusive Child Care" by Donna Sullivan and Janet Gonzalez-Mena

The Caregiver's Companion also provides eighteen forms for tracking and relaying information:

Registration Form
Tell Us About Your Child
Identification and Emergency Form
Infant Feeding Plan
Daily Information Sheet
Sign-In Sheet
Diapering Log
Feeding Log
Allergy Notice
Sample Exposure Notice
Medication Schedule

Individual Child's Record of Medications Given
Incident Log
Incident Report
Documentation of Concern for a Child
How Are We Doing? Family Feedback Form
Developmental Health History
Physician's Report Form—Day Care Centers

Additionally, *The Caregiver's Companion* includes observation guidelines, observation forms for use with the video observations on the text's Online Learning Center, and an outline of a parent handbook.

If you purchased a used copy of *Infants, Toddlers, and Caregivers* that did not include *The Caregiver's Companion*, you can order this resource (ISBN 0-07-313132-6) by calling McGraw-Hill Customer Service at 1-800-338-3987.

chapter 1

Principles, Practice, and Curriculum

Focus Questions

After reading this chapter you should be able to answer the following questions:

1 What kinds of interactions grow into the relationships that are so important in infant-toddler care and education?

2 Give an example of at least one adult behavior that shows respect to an infant or toddler.

3 Provide key words or phrases for at least 5 of the 10 principles of infant-toddler care and education.

4 Define the word "curriculum" as it applies to infant and toddler care and education.

5 What are the roles of adults in infant-toddler curriculum?

6 What are the three knowledge bases of developmentally appropriate practice as defined by the National Association for the Education of Young Children (NAEYC)?

What Do You See?

A five-month-old is lying on the floor with several play materials scattered within reach. She is contentedly surveying the five other infants and toddlers who are in the room with her. Reaching now and then, she caresses a toy first with her eyes, then with her hands. As we look more closely, we can see that some moisture has crept onto the infant's outer clothes in the area of her bottom. The infant hears a step, and her eyes travel in the direction of the sound. Then we see a pair of legs and feet traveling along in the direction of the infant. A voice says, "Caitlin, I'm wondering how you are getting along."

The legs move over close to the blanket, and Caitlin looks up at the knees. Her eyes brighten as the rest of the person appears in her visual range. A kind face comes close. Caitlin smiles and makes a cooing noise. The caregiver responds, then notices the dampness of the clothing. "Oh, Caitlin, you need a change," the caregiver says. Caitlin responds by smiling and cooing.

Reaching out her hands, the caregiver says, "I'm going to pick you up now." Caitlin responds to the gesture and the words with an ever-so-slight body movement. She continues to smile and coo. The caregiver picks her up and walks toward the diapering area.

Did you notice that there was a lot more going on here than just a diaper change? This scene illustrates several of the basic principles of this book. Think back on it as you read on. Do you know what it means to respect a baby as a person? We'll answer that question when we return to this scene later.

This book is based on a philosophy of infant-toddler care and education that is summarized in a curriculum or framework of 10 principles for practice. The philosophy comes from the work of two pioneers in infant-toddler care and education: Emmi Pikler and Magda Gerber. Pikler was a Hungarian pediatrician and researcher who got started in group care in 1946 after World War II, by creating an orphanage for children under age three. Called the Pikler Institute today, the program is still running under the direction of her daughter, Anna Tardos. Magda Gerber, friend and colleague of Pikler, brought what she knew to the United States in 1956 and eventually started a program called Resources for Infant Educarers (RIE). Her followers across the United States and elsewhere have been training caregivers and parents since the 1976. Although the Pikler's and Gerber's philosophies are not identical, they are in tune with each other.

Relationships, Interactions, and the Three Rs

Relationship is a key word in infant-toddler care and education. In the opening scene you saw an example of how interactions like the one between Caitlin and the adult caregiver can lead to a close relationship built on respect. Relationships between caregivers[1] and very young children don't just happen. They grow from a number of interactions. So **interactions** is another keyword. But relationships don't grow from just any kind of interactions, they grow from those that are *respectful, responsive,* and *reciprocal.* You can think of them as the three Rs of infant-toddler care and education. The caregiver's interaction with Caitlin was obviously responsive—the caregiver responded to the child and the child to the caregiver. The responses were linked in a reciprocal way, forming a chain of interaction, with each response triggered by the previous one and leading into the next response by the other person. What was respectful about them?

Behaviors indicating respect may not be as obvious as those indicating responsiveness and reciprocation. Did you notice that the caregiver walked up to Caitlin in a way that enabled the child to see her coming? The caregiver consciously slowed her pace and made contact before checking to see if Caitlin needed a diaper change. It's not uncommon to observe caregivers rush over and swoop up a baby unexpectedly and start feeling the diaper without a word of acknowledgment to the person inside the diaper. Imagine how you would feel if you were the baby. That's disrespectful. Instead, Caitlin's caregiver initiated a conversation by talking to Caitlin. She kept it going by responding to Caitlin's smiles and coos. She also talked to Caitlin about what she was going to do before she did it. This scene illustrates a responsive interaction chain that is the basis of effective caregiving. A number of interactions such as this kind of diaper

Reflect

When were you involved in a respectful, responsive, and reciprocal interaction? Describe what that was like. Then contrast that description with an experience you've had with a disrespectful, unresponsive, nonreciprocal interaction. What are the implications of your experiences for working with infants and toddlers?

changing build a partnership. This feeling of being part of a team instead of an object to be manipulated is vital to wholesome development. Reciprocal interactions like these promote attachment between caregiver and child.

Caregiving Routines as Opportunities for Three-R Interactions

It is no coincidence that the first example in this book is of an interaction involving diapering. There's a message here. Relationships develop through all kinds of interactions, but especially during ones that happen while adults are carrying out those essential activities of daily living sometimes called caregiving routines. Think about how diapering is a time when caregivers and children are in a one-on-one situation. If you count all the diaperings in a child's life, the total probably comes to somewhere between 4,000 and 5,000. Imagine the opportunities that will be lost if adults focus only on the activity, regard it as a chore, and don't bother to interact with the child. And that happens a lot, because a common diapering practice is to distract the child somehow—often with a toy or something interesting to look at. Then the caregiver focuses on the chore, manipulating the child's body, and hurrying to get finished. This is the opposite of what we advocate.

It may seem that anyone who is warm and friendly can care for infants and that anyone with patience and nurturing qualities can work with toddlers. Certainly those are valuable characteristics in caregivers, but caring for children under three involves more than just going by instinct or by what seems to work. Going back to that opening scene, perhaps you can see that the caregiver was doing more than just what felt right. She had training in a particular way of caregiving. In fact what you saw was a caregiver whose training was influenced by RIE, the program Magda Gerber created.

Ten Principles Based on a Philosophy of Respect

Now let's look at the 10 principles that underlie this book.

1. Involve infants and toddlers in things that concern them. Don't work around them or distract them to get the job done faster.
2. Invest in quality time, when you are totally available to individual infants and toddlers. Don't settle for supervising groups without focusing (more than just briefly) on individual children.
3. Learn each child's unique ways of communicating (cries, words, movements, gestures, facial expressions, body positions) and teach yours. Don't underestimate children's ability to communicate even though their verbal language skills may be nonexistent or minimal.

NAEYC Program Standards 1, 2, 3
Relationships, Curriculum, Teaching

4. Invest time and energy to build a total person (concentrate on the "whole child"). Don't focus on cognitive development alone or look at it as separate from total development.
5. Respect infants and toddlers as worthy people. Don't treat them as objects or cute little empty-headed people to be manipulated.
6. Be honest about your feelings around infants and toddlers. Don't pretend to feel something that you don't or not to feel something that you do.
7. Model the behavior you want to teach. Don't preach.
8. Recognize problems as learning opportunities, and let infants and toddlers try to solve their own. Don't rescue them, constantly make life easy for them, or try to protect them from all problems.
9. Build security by teaching trust. Don't teach distrust by being undependable or often inconsistent.
10. Be concerned about the *quality* of development in each stage. Don't rush infants and toddlers to reach developmental milestones.

Let's look further into each of the principles.

Principle 1: Involve Infants and Toddlers in Things That Concern Them

Caitlin isn't just the recipient of her caregiver's actions; she's a participant in what happens to her. She and her caregiver do things together. If the caregiver had given Caitlin a toy to play with to keep her occupied while she changed her diaper, the whole tone of the scene would have been different. The partnership would have vanished, and in its place would have been a distracted child and a caregiver dealing with a damp bottom and a wet diaper instead of a whole child. Or if she had distracted Caitlin with other sorts of entertainment, the caregiver still would have had Caitlin's attention, but the focus would have been on fun and games rather than on the task at hand.

The caregiver's primary goal in this scene was to keep Caitlin involved in the interaction as well as focused on her own body and on what was happening to it. Diapering then became an "educational experience," through which Caitlin increased attention span, body awareness, and cooperation. A number of experiences like these give Caitlin an education in human relations from which she can build her whole outlook toward life and people.

There is a rumor that infants and toddlers have short attention spans. Some people say they can't pay attention to anything for very long. You can test that rumor for yourself. Watch an infant or toddler who is actually involved in something that concerns and interests him. Clock the amount of time spent on the task or event. You may be surprised at what a long attention span infants and toddlers have when they are interested, because they are involved. Consider how long Caitlin paid attention to her diapering because she was involved in the task.

Think about a time in your own life when you were involved in a respectful, responsive, reciprocal interaction. You don't have to be an infant to experience the focused attention of someone else. This can happen when someone is teaching you something. Or it can happen when you are in the doctor's office. Can you use your own experience to help you understand the benefits that babies derive from being involved in the things that concern them?

Principle 2: Invest in Quality Time

The scene between Caitlin and her caregiver is a good example of one kind of quality time. The caregiver was fully present. That is, she was attending to what was going on; her thoughts were not somewhere else. How often caregiving tasks are done routinely, with neither caregiver nor infant present any way but physically!

Two Types of Quality Time   Magda Gerber calls the kind of quality time illustrated by the diapering scene **wants-something quality time.** The adult and child are involved in a task the caregiver has set up. Diapering, feeding, bathing, and dressing fit into this category of quality time. If the caregiver pays attention to the child and asks in return that the child pay attention, the amount of wants-something quality time mounts up. In child care programs this can provide the one-to-one interactions that may be difficult to attain in a group setting. Wants-something quality time is educational. Examples of this kind of quality time occur throughout the book.

Another kind of equally important quality time is what Magda Gerber calls **wants-nothing quality time.** This happens when caregivers make themselves available without directing the action—for instance, just sitting near babies, fully available and responsive but not in charge. Just being with toddlers while they play, responding rather than initiating, describes this type of quality time. (See Chapter 4 for examples of wants-nothing quality time.)

Floor time is a variation of wants-nothing quality time that the Child-Family Study Center at the University of California at Davis uses in their toddler program. Floor time is a concept they credit to Stanley Greenspan's work. When a toddler is exhibiting difficult behavior, instead of putting her in time-out and trying to ignore her, the caregivers do the opposite. They don't withdraw attention; they give more. The child is given a half hour of one-to-one time with an adult whose sole goal is to be *responsive* to that child and that child alone. The adult sits on the floor, available to the child. The environment is conducive to play, as there are interesting toys within reach. The adult has no plan or expectation but just waits to see what the child will do and then responds. This is the opposite of the common approach in programs where teachers and caregivers become even more directive rather than less in the face of difficult behavior.

The adults at the Child-Family Study Center are directive only when they remove the child from the classroom. They explain where they are going, but use no shame and no punishing overtones. Floor time may seem like being sent to the principal's office, but it's more like play therapy. However, the staff members

Reflect

Think about the benefits of quality time for an infant. Can you remember a time when someone was fully available to you without being directive? What was that like for you? Can you understand from your own experience how that might benefit an infant?

aren't therapists, and floor time isn't therapy. It's merely wants-nothing quality time. For a half hour the child is given total attention.

Does the child become "spoiled" with such lavish attention? No. According to reports, this approach works miracles. Its effectiveness seems to lie in the fact that it meets the child's needs.

Many psychotherapists attest to the benefits of being fully present to another person without being directive; yet most of us seldom get this kind of attention from the people in our lives. Think for a moment of the delight of having someone's whole attention at your command for more than a moment or so.

This kind of quality time is easy to give, but often not understood or valued. Caregivers just sitting on the floor where babies and toddlers are playing sometimes feel as though they are not doing their job. They want to play the role of teachers, which they interpret as "teaching something." It is very hard for most adults to be around small children and not be directive. Being receptive and responsive is a skill most adults need to learn; it doesn't seem to come naturally. Try it yourself. Choose a time when you will not initiate, but instead only respond. See how long you can keep in the receptive, responsive mode.

Another kind of quality time—perhaps the most commonly understood kind—is shared activity. The initiating mode moves back and forth between adult and child during playtimes as the two enjoy each other's company. These times are often rewarding for the caregiver in ways that the other two kinds of quality time are not.

The Right Amount of Quality Time   An interesting aspect of quality time is that a little goes a long way. No one wants (or can stand) intense interaction all the time—even when it is fun and games. Children (and adults) need to be private as well. Although privacy is not an issue with all families, for some it is a strong cultural value. In infant-toddler programs and in family day care, time alone is hard to attain. Some children manage to be alone only by sleeping. Others can focus inwardly and ignore what's going on around them. The adult can help young children gain private time by providing small spaces (see Chapter 12, "A Safe Environment").

When people never have time alone, they get it by drifting off, by not paying attention, by being elsewhere mentally if not physically. This attitude becomes a habit, so that when this person spends time with others, he or she is "only half there." "Half-there" time, even lots of it, never equals "all-there time."

Being able to "turn off" is an issue for both caregivers as well as infants and toddlers. No adult can be expected to be completely present and responsive to others all day every day. Both adults' and babies' needs must be provided for in programs if the adults are to be effective caregivers.

Of course every person's life is filled with time that is neither quality time nor private time. Children have to learn to live in a busy world of people. They are bound to be ignored, moved from place to place, or worked around sometimes. The point is that there is a difference between quality time and other kinds of time and that all children deserve and need some quality time in their lives.

Quality time is built in to the daily routine when diapering, dressing, and feeding become occasions for close one-to-one interactions. In group care, when a caregiver is responsible for several babies or a small group of toddlers, paying attention to just one child may be difficult unless caregivers free each other up by taking turns supervising the rest of the children. It is up to the director to ensure that each caregiver be freed at times from responsibility for children other than the one she is changing or feeding. That means that it must be permissible, and even encouraged, for a caregiver to focus on just one child.

In family child care where there is no other adult, the caregiver has no one else to turn to when she feeds or diapers a baby. But caregivers can still focus on just one child by setting up a safe environment and encouraging the rest of the children to play on their own. Of course the caregiver must still keep a watchful eye on the group—a skill that can be developed with practice. It's amazing to watch an experienced caregiver give full attention to one child but still manage to catch a dangerous or forbidden action going on in another part of the room.

Principle 3: Learn Each Child's Unique Ways of Communicating and Teach Yours

Notice how the communication between Caitlin and her caregiver worked. The caregiver talked directly to Caitlin about what she was going to do, using body movements that matched her words. Caitlin used her body, facial expressions, and voice to communicate her responses. The caregiver responded to her responses by interpreting, answering, and discussing. The caregiver did not carry on endless chatter. She said little, but what she said carried a lot of meaning, backed up by action. She is teaching Caitlin to listen, not tune out. She is teaching that talking is communication, not distraction. She is teaching words and language in context, by talking naturally, not repeating words over and over or using baby talk. She also communicated with her body and with sounds other than words, and she responded to Caitlin's communication (sounds, facial expressions, and body movements). The communication between Caitlin and her caregiver went way beyond words.

Think about someone you know very well. Can you remember some ways that person communicates with you without using words? Facial expressions are obvious ways, but each person has certain little gestures or actions that give hints about what he or she is feeling. If you make a list of the nonverbal means of communication that someone you know well uses, you'll see how each of us has a unique system. No one knows a baby's or toddler's system as well as those people to whom he or she is attached. For that reason (and others), programs for infants and toddlers should encourage attachment between the children and the caregivers.

It's also important to note here that each of us uses a system of body language that is particular to our culture and, within the culture, that is specific to gender and perhaps social class as well. Just one example is in the difference in how men and women in white, European-derived, North American culture cross their legs. Another example is the contrasting walk between the African-American

Reflect

Think about someone you know very well. Can you picture some ways that person communicates with you without using words?

VIDEO OBSERVATION 1

Baby Crying

See Video Observation 1: Baby Crying for an illustration of some of the principles in Chapter 1. You'll see a baby on a blanket crying. This is not a unique way of communicating, but it is communication. The caregiver comes around to pick the baby up. Notice how she comes from the front rather than approaching from the side or rear. That's a sign of respect, so she won't surprise the baby.

Questions

- How does the baby communicate that she needs something?
- How does the caregiver prepare the baby to be picked up?
- Notice that the baby is lying on her back. Do you know why? If not, you'll find out as you read further in the book.

To view this clip, go to www.mhhe.com/itc7e. Click on Student Edition, select Chapter 1, and click on Video Observation.

man and the African-American woman. These are unconscious positions and movements, but members of the culture know them well. Children learn the rudiments of culturally based nonverbal communication from adults in their lives, as well as creating their own specific body language.

Eventually babies come to depend more on words to express themselves in addition to other means of communication. They learn to express needs, wants, ideas, and feelings more and more clearly. They also learn to enjoy language for itself—to play with words, phrases, and sounds. Adult reactions and encouragement to use language facilitate their development. By late toddlerhood most children can express themselves in words, though, of course, they continue to use nonverbal communication throughout their lives.

It is important to recognize that some cultures value and depend on verbal exchanges more than others. European-Americans tend to use direct communication. Because babies can't talk (in fact the origin of the word *infant* can be traced back through Middle English to Old French, where it is a combination of "in" [not] and "fans" [speaking]), researchers at the University of California at Davis have discovered that they can introduce direct communication to babies by teaching a gesturing system.[2] Caregivers from highly verbal cultures need to be extra sensitive to children who use a good deal of nonverbal communication instead of words.[3]

Young children should see adults using words that match their nonverbal communication. If the face and body movements say one thing and the words say something else, children are receiving double messages, which get in the way of true communication. They not only have problems deciding which to believe, but they model after the adult and thus learn to give double messages themselves. Clear communication is important.

Principle 4: Invest Time and Energy to Build a Total Person

Recent brain research supports the goal of building a total person instead of concentrating on cognitive development alone. An article written by J. Ronald Lally for *Exchange* magazine, "Brain Research, Infant Learning, and Child Care Curriculum" (May 1998), explains the connections. Because some parents realize that the early years are important ones in intellectual growth, whether or not they have heard about the brain research, they may expect to see some evidence that caregivers are providing "cognitive activities." Their concept of cognitive activities may be based on what they know about preschool. They may expect caregivers to teach such concepts as colors, shapes, and even numbers and letters through an activity approach.

On the other side, caregivers, also concerned with intellectual development, may think that the way to promote it is through specialized equipment, exercises, or activities. Books and programs are readily available for a price to, as they say, "stimulate cognitive development." Catalogs and stores are full of toys, equipment, and gadgets advertised as making babies smarter. Of course providing a rich environment with interesting things to do is desirable. And, yes, it can promote cognitive development. But be careful about falling into the trap of thinking that you can stimulate cognitive development without working on physical, social, and emotional development at the same time. It isn't the clever little toys that you provide or the activities you do with the children that make a difference. It's the day-to-day living, the relationships, the experiences, the diaperings, the feedings, the toilet training, and the playing that contribute to intellectual development. And those same experiences help the child grow physically, socially, and emotionally as well.

Think of how rich the experience of diapering was for Caitlin. She was immersed in **sensory input**—visual, auditory, tactile, olfactory. How often are caregivers and parents told to hang a mobile over the changing table so that the diapering can be an "educational experience." How limited an experience a mobile provides compared with what Caitlin was enjoying.

Also consider that some cultures are not as concerned about cognitive development as others. Some have a different set of priorities; just keeping the baby healthy may be the primary concern. Those families spend little time worrying about how early experiences in infancy contribute to later academic success.

Principle 5: Respect Infants and Toddlers as Worthy People

Respect is not a word usually used with very young children. Magda Gerber introduced this concept in relation to infants and toddlers. Usually worries about respect go the other way, as adults demand (or wish for) children to respect them. There is no better way to gain respect for yourself than to model it for children.

What does it mean to respect a child? The diapering scene provides an example. Before the caregiver did anything to Caitlin, she explained what would happen. Just as a respectful nurse warns you before putting a cold instrument on your skin, so Caitlin's caregiver prepared her for what was to come. Until you realize the difference, the natural tendency is to pick up a child without saying anything. Babies are often carried around like objects, even when they are old enough to walk and talk. Adults often pick a child up and put him or her in a chair or stroller without a word. That kind of action is not respectful.

To clarify the concept of respecting an infant, try imagining how a nurse would move a fairly helpless patient from a bed to a wheelchair. Then just change the players and imagine one is a caregiver and one is an infant. Except for the size and weight involved, if the adult is treating the infant with respect, the scene should look much the same.

To better understand the concept of respecting a toddler, imagine you have just seen a man fall off a ladder. Think how you would respond. Even if you are strong enough, you would probably not rush over and set him back on his feet. You'd start talking first, asking if he was hurt or needed help. You'd probably extend a hand if he indicated he was all right and started getting up. You'd comfort him if that was called for. Most people have no trouble responding respectfully to an adult.

Why then do adults rush over and pick up a fallen toddler without a moment's pause? Why not see first what it is the toddler needs? Maybe all that is required is some reassurance—not physical help. Perhaps the child is angry or embarrassed and needs an adult who can accept those feelings and allow expression of them. Perhaps the toddler needs nothing and without adult interference will get up and go about his business on his own. More aspects of respect come out in the next scene.

Twelve-month-old Brian is sitting at a low table with several other children eating a piece of banana. He is obviously enjoying the experience in more ways than one. He has squashed the banana in his hand and crammed it in his mouth, and it is now oozing out between his teeth. He is relishing it. He reaches for his mouth with the very last piece and, plop, it falls on the ground. He stretches out a hand for it, but the caregiver is quicker. "I'm sorry, Brian, but the banana is dirty now. I can't let you eat it." Brian's eyes open wide, his mouth drops open, and a sorrowful wail comes forth. "That's all the banana we have," the caregiver adds as Brian reaches out to her for more. She sits back down at the table after having disposed of the dropped piece. She offers him a cracker, saying, "We're out of bananas, but you can have a cracker instead." Brian rejects the offered cracker. Aware now that he will get no more, he begins to scream.

"I see how unhappy you are," says the caregiver calmly but with genuine compassion. "I wish I had more banana to give you," she adds.

Brian's screams become more piercing, and he begins to kick his feet. The caregiver remains silent, looking at him as if she really cares about his feelings.

The other children at the table are having various reactions to this scene. The caregiver turns to them and explains, "Brian lost his banana, and he didn't like it." She turns back to Brian. He continues to cry. The caregiver waits. Sobbing, he gets off his chair, toddles over to her, and buries his head in her lap. She touches him on the back, stroking him soothingly. When he has quieted down, she says, "You need to wash your hands now." He doesn't move. She waits. Then gently she repeats, "You need to wash your hands, Brian. I'll come with you," she adds. Turning the table over to another caregiver, she gets up and walks slowly across the floor with Brian. Brian is licking globs of banana from his fingers. A last sob escapes from his lips as he reaches the sink.

The caregiver respected Brian's right to have feelings and to express them.[4] She offered support without gushing sympathy. Because she did not distract him with great amounts of warmth or entertainment, he was able to pay attention to what was going on inside himself. He was learning that it was all right to respond honestly to the situation.

Sometimes adult attention is so rewarding that children associate anger, frustration, or sorrow with attention. They use their feelings to manipulate. We would all be better off to ask directly for what we need than to use emotional displays to get hugs and touching. That's why the caregiver remained available but let Brian indicate what he needed. She did not pick him up but let him come to her. When he was ready for comfort, she was there to give it to him, but it didn't come so early that he was not able to express himself.

Following are some examples of less respectful ways to respond to Brian.

"Stop that screaming—that's nothing to get so upset about—you were almost finished anyway."

"Poor little Brian, let's go play with the doggie that you like so much—look, Brian—see him bark—bow-wow!"

Principle 6: Be Honest About Your Feelings

In the last scene the child was encouraged to recognize his feelings. He was angry, and he was not asked to pretend to be something else. What about adults? Is it all right for caregivers to express their anger to young children? Yes. Children in child care need to be around real people, not warm empty role-players.

Part of being a real person is getting angry, scared, upset, and nervous now and then. Here is a scene showing a caregiver expressing anger:

A caregiver has just separated two children who were coming to blows over a toy. "I can't let you hurt Amber," she says to Shawn, who is 18 months old. She has him firmly but gently by the arm when he turns to her and spits in her face. Her expression changes from calm to anger, and she takes his other arm as well. Looking him right in the eyes, she says clearly, but with emotion in her voice, "I don't like that, Shawn. I don't want you to spit at me." She lets go, stands up, turns her back, and walks away. When she is a few steps away, she gives a quick glance back to see what he is doing. He hasn't moved, so she walks to the sink and washes her face. She keeps an eye out to make sure he doesn't return to hitting Amber. By the time she comes back, she is calm. Shawn is climbing up the slide, and things have returned to normal.

This caregiver was saying honestly what effect Shawn's action had on her. Notice how she expressed her feelings. She didn't put on such a show that it encouraged him to do it again for his own entertainment—a problem that can occur when displays of adult anger are dramatic and lengthy. She didn't blame, accuse, judge, or belittle Shawn. She merely verbalized her feelings and connected them clearly to the situation. She let Shawn know what made her angry and stopped him from continuing the action. Having expressed herself, she left the scene. In short, she neither masked her feelings nor blew up.

And expressing her feelings seemed to have been enough to let Shawn know that this behavior was unacceptable. She didn't have to do anything further about it—this time, at least. If it occurs again, she may have to do something more than just tell Shawn how she feels.

Compare the reaction of this caregiver with the times you've seen people angry with a child, yet smiling and talking in a honeyed voice. Imagine the difficulty a child has in reconciling the two sets of messages at the same time.

Principle 7: Model the Behavior You Want to Teach

All the caregivers in the previous scenes have been modeling behavior that is acceptable for children as well as adults. You've seen examples of cooperation, respect, honest feelings, and communication. Take a look at how this principle works in a more difficult situation—when aggression is involved.

Shawn and Amber are struggling over a rag doll again. A caregiver starts to move near them. Before he reaches the pair, Shawn reaches out and gives Amber a slap on the arm. She lets out a wail. The caregiver kneels on the floor before the two children. His face is calm; his movements are slow and careful. He reaches out and touches Shawn, rubbing his arm on the same spot where he hit Amber. "Gently, Shawn, gently." At the same time he strokes Amber. Shawn remains silent. Amber continues to wail. The caregiver touches her again. "You got hit, didn't you, Amber? It hurt!" Amber stops crying and looks at him. All three are silent for a moment. The caregiver waits. Shawn clutches the doll and starts to walk away with it. Amber grabs it. The caregiver remains silent until Shawn raises his arm to hit again. "I can't let you hurt Amber," he says, catching the arm midair. He touches him softly. "Gently, gently." Amber suddenly jerks the doll and Shawn lets go unexpectedly. Taking the doll in triumph, she starts across the room. Shawn looks sad, but remains in the same spot. The caregiver stays near. "She has the doll," he observes. Amber sees a ball at her feet, drops the doll, and picks up the ball. She throws it and runs after it giggling. Shawn moves quickly over to the doll, picks it up, holds it tenderly, and coos to it. The scene ends with both children playing contentedly, and the caregiver is no longer needed.

Notice how this caregiver modeled gentleness—the behavior he wished to teach. A more common approach when an adult arrives on the scene of a dispute is to treat the children with even more aggression than they have been displaying themselves. "I'll teach you to play rough," growls the adult, jerking the child by the arm and shaking him. This approach models the very behavior the adult is trying to eliminate. (And shaking a young child is dangerous because the weight of the head whipping around on a young neck can cause damage.)

The caregiver in the Shawn-versus-Amber scene knew that both children needed assurance that control would be provided when needed. It is frightening to both aggressor and victim when there is no protecting adult around to stop the violent action. The aggressor needs to be dealt with gently and nonjudgmentally. The victim needs to be dealt with empathetically but not sympathetically (that is, acknowledging her distress without feeling sorry for her). Sympathy and a good deal of attention may reward victims. In that way they learn that being victimized pays off in adult love and attention. How sad that some children actually learn to become victims.

Principle 8: Recognize Problems as Learning Opportunities, and Let Infants and Toddlers Try to Solve Their Own

The same scene also illustrates this principle: Let children, even babies, handle their own problems to the extent that they can. The caregiver could have stepped in and taken care of this tugging situation by creating a solution for the conflict. He didn't, however. He let the toddlers make a decision themselves. (Though he did, of course, keep them from hurting each other further.) Very young children can solve more problems than many people give them credit for. The caregiver's role is to give them time and freedom to work on the problems. That means not responding to every frustration immediately. Sometimes a bit of facilitating will move a child forward when he or she gets stuck on a problem, but the facilitating should be the least help necessary, leaving the child free to work toward his own solution.

In a movie called *On Their Own with Our Help*, Magda Gerber illustrates this principle beautifully.[5] A baby crawls under a low table, then tries to sit up. When he discovers he can't, he starts crying. He doesn't know how to crawl out again, and he looks very fearful. Instead of rescuing him (it would have been easy to just

Reflect

Have you ever been rescued from a problem in a way that frustrated you? Have you ever seen an infant in the same situation? How did you feel? How do you think the infant felt?

lift the table up), Magda guides him out—reassuring and directing him with both her words and her hands.

Magda is using an approach called **scaffolding.** This term comes from Jerome Bruner and fits with the theory of Lev Vygotsky. To scaffold, adults keep a constant eye out for a child who is in a situation in which there is a potential for learning. The adult sensitively structures that situation so that problem solving is encouraged and supported. Sometimes scaffolding requires a little assist; sometimes the adult presence is all the scaffold an infant or toddler needs.[6]

Problems can be valuable learning opportunities. Another of Gerber's videos, *See How They Move,* illustrates this principle. The viewer is treated to scene after scene of children doing **gross motor** problem solving all by themselves. The adults stay back and let the children work without interference. The only scaffold provided is the adult presence, which is enough to allow the children to freely experience their own ways of moving and exploring.[7]

Principle 9: Build Security by Teaching Trust

For infants to learn to trust, they need dependable adults. They need to know that they will get their needs met in a reasonable amount of time. If it's food they need, food arrives in a timely manner. If it's comfort, a caregiver is there to provide it in the way that works best for the particular child. If it's rest, the caregiver is there to help her settle down in a place that's safe, peaceful, and quiet. If it's movement that is needed, the adult situates the baby so movement is possible. When infants discover that they can express a need and it will be satisfied, they develop trust in the adults who care for them. In this environment they learn that the world is a secure place for them.

The examples have shown dependable adults who met needs as well as offered strength and support. They didn't trick the children. One of the times adults are most tempted to deceive children is during good-bye times. When everyone knows that a child is going to suffer loudly with protests and wails when the parent leaves, some are willing to trick the child to avoid a scene. However, it is much better when the parent leaves a child by saying good-bye outright, and the caregiver accepts protests and wails. While providing security, support, and empathy, he or she can express acceptance of the baby's right to be unhappy. The baby learns that he can predict when his mother will go, rather than worrying constantly that she has sneaked away when he was occupied. He knows that as long as she hasn't said good-bye, she is still around. He comes to depend on his knowledge that the adults around him don't lie to him or trick him. Learning to predict what will happen is an important part of building trust. Always being happy isn't.

Principle 10: Be Concerned about the Quality of Development in Each Stage

We live in the period of the hurried child (a term coined by David Elkind in his book by the same title). The pressure starts at birth, as many parents anxiously await the time their child reaches each milestone, comparing his or her progress with that of other children or with developmental charts. The message is everywhere—"Fast is better." Books advertise "Teach your baby to read." Institutes promise miracles. Children are pushed, pushed, pushed. When adults have this hurry-up attitude, babies are propped up before they can sit on their own, walked around by the hand before they can even stand by themselves, taught to ride a tricycle when they can barely walk.

Caregivers feel the pressure from every side—from parents, sometimes even from directors, as they are urged to speed up development. Yet development cannot be hurried. Each child has a built-in timetable that dictates just when he or she will crawl, sit up, and start to walk. The way caregivers can help development is to encourage each baby to do thoroughly whatever it is that he or she is doing. Learning is what counts, not teaching. The important learnings come when the baby is ready, not when the adults decide it's time.

Some programs write objectives for each child. A hurry-up program will write objectives that focus solely on the next step. However, it is possible to write objectives that help broaden the child's experience in the stage where he or she is. Doing something very thoroughly is the best preparation for moving forward.

Take crawling as an example. Instead of standing the child up and continually encouraging him or her to walk, it is better to celebrate the crawling. The only time in his life that he'll ever be so conveniently close to things on the floor is the same time in his life when he is so very curious about everything that is within reach and just beyond it. Caregivers can provide experiences and opportunities for him to develop not only his crawling but also his curiosity.

If you are to help counteract the pushy approach, you need to sell parents on the idea that perfecting skills is more important than pushing children to develop new ones. The new ones will come when the child has thoroughly practiced the old ones. The age at which a child first walks in no way correlates with whether or not he or she will become an Olympic runner.

The ten principles for respectful adult-infant interactions carry with them regard for the individual. That means that differences are honored. Children are not all alike, and we want to emphasize that. Certainly the research done on ages and stages resulting in charts of milestones might lead us to believe the goal is for all children to be "normal." However, in this book we are anxious to set aside those ideas and regard each child as being on a unique path of development. Every child has strengths and challenges; we want to focus more on strengths than weaknesses and support the child in meeting the challenges. We also want to point out that the young child comes embedded in a cultural and family context. When we look at practice (which is what this book is about), we can't ignore that there are different ideas about what children need and how they grow. If a particular practice advocated in this book doesn't fit what a family believes is good for their children, their value system, or their goals, you can't ignore the difference. You and the family need to talk. One of our goals for caregivers is to honor diversity even when it doesn't fit what the caregiver believes or is in conflict with the program policies.

**NAEYC Program
Standard 2**
Curriculum

Exploring the Word *Curriculum* A word that is being used now more frequently in connection with infant-toddler care is **curriculum.** The term literally means "course"—as in a course of study. J. Ronald Lally uses the idea of courses of study to define curriculum for infants and toddlers by naming the classes that they take—for example, Physical Development 101, Social Relations 101, Intellectual Development 101.[8]

That's one way to help those unfamiliar with infants and toddlers to understand and see the legitimacy of their curriculum. Another way is to think of infant-toddler curriculum as the word *course* applies to a river. Like a course of study, it is a path from one point to another. But with a river there's a meandering flow. Using the principles on which this book is based means that the child not only gives input but is actually in charge of his or her own curriculum—in partnership with caregivers (who are partners with the family). So moving from point A to point B is not something that adults control except by the way they set up and adapt the environment according to each child's interests and changing needs. Besides being environmental planners, caregivers acting as curriculum designers also have roles as facilitators of learning, supporters of development, and assessors of both.

**NAEYC Program
Standard 4**
Assessment

Developmentally appropriate practice has three knowledge bases from which to determine appropriate practice. The guidelines for making decisions about developmentally appropriate practice tell early childhood professionals to consider the following:

1. Practice based on research and child development principles that relate to typical development. Developmentally appropriate practice (DAP) is both a general term and a specific term relating to this particular knowledge base.
2. Practice that fits what is known about individual differences. We're calling this knowledge base individually appropriate practice (IAP), and it relates to all kinds of differences, including variation from the norms guiding DAP and differences that may or may not be specifically related to disabilities or other kinds of mental, physical, or emotional challenges.
3. Culturally appropriate practice (CAP) includes practices that come from differences in perceptions, values, beliefs, priorities, and traditions outside the mainstream American culture.

It's important to realize that a practice may fit research and child development principles but may not fit some children and their families. In that case we can't call that practice appropriate in the larger sense. That's why we can't just go by research and child development principles. A practice can't be considered appropriate if it is culturally inappropriate. Bridging cultures is a concept that is carried throughout this book, and caregivers are continually challenged to look for ways to create culturally consistent environments and practices for infants, toddlers, and their families without giving up what they believe are best practices.

Instead of educating parents out of their culture, the goal is to create bridges across gaps that may lie between culturally diverse families and the culture of the program or the early childhood culture in general.

Developmentally Appropriate Practice

The 10 principles of respectful care correspond to the NAEYC document called *Developmentally Appropriate Practice.* In each chapter we will show you how the two sets of ideas parallel each other. We will also show you some dilemmas like the following one.

The Principles in Action

Principle 5 Respect infants and toddlers as worthy people. Don't treat them as objects or cute little empty-headed people to be manipulated.

The caregiver understands how important it is to respect even the youngest infant. She always talks to the babies to prepare them for what will happen; in fact, she never does anything to them without telling them first. She always thinks of them as people. That's why she talks to them all the time. In her culture, words are considered the ultimate way to communicate. A parent in the caregiver's class who is of a different culture never tells her baby what she's doing or why. In addition, she "wears" her baby in the baby-carrier of her culture and never puts the child down until she has to change her or when she leaves. The caregiver has explained principle 5 to the mother. The mother explained to the caregiver that in her culture, they think babies should have very close contact at all times. It makes them feel secure, she says. In her culture, adults don't talk to babies. Why should they? With all the body contact, communication is going on all the time. The ultimate is to communicate without words. That means you're very close to someone when you can do that. She admits that the caregiver has a different idea about what babies need. The caregiver wants to be culturally responsive, but she thinks she needs to understand more about what the term *respect* means to this mother.

1. Should the caregiver try to educate the parent about this child development principle? Why or why not?
2. Does one perspective make more sense to you than the other? If yes, which one and why?
3. Do you feel yourself taking sides in this situation?
4. What are the issues in this situation as you see them?
5. What does the idea of respecting babies mean to you?

Appropriate Practice

Overview of Development

According to the National Association for the Education of Young Children, quality care is about relationships. Relationships are part of every aspect of early development. Babies learn trust through daily interactions with dependable adults. They build a sense of security when they find they can communicate their needs and are rewarded with a sensitive response. They grow confident when they discover they can manage the challenges they meet. All this depends on relationships that grow through continuity of care and are developmentally, individually, and culturally appropriate.

Source: J. Ronald Lally, Abbey Griffin, Emily Fenichel, Marilyn Segal, Eleanor Szanton, and Bernice Weissbourd, "Development in the First Three Years of Life," in *Developmentally Appropriate Practice in Early Childhood Programs*, rev. ed. (Washington, D.C.: National Association for the Education of Young Children, 1997), pp. 55–69.

Developmentally Appropriate Practice

The following are samples of developmentally appropriate practices:

- Adults are especially attentive to infants during caregiving routines, such as diaper changing, feeding, and changing clothes. The caregiver explains what will happen, what is happening, and what will happen next, asking and waiting for the infant's cooperation and participation.
- Adults ensure that every infant receives nurturing, responsive care.
- Diaper changing, feeding, and other routines are viewed as vital learning experiences for both babies and caregivers.
- Adults express healthy, accepting attitudes about children's bodies and their functions.
- Caregivers ask parents what sounds and words their toddler uses so that the caregiver will understand what the child is saying when she uses beginning speech or a home language that the caregiver does not understand.
- Adults respond quickly to toddlers' cries or other signs of distress, recognizing that toddlers have limited language with which to communicate their needs.
- Adults recognize that routine tasks of living such as eating, toileting, and dressing are important opportunities to help children learn about their world, acquire skills, and regulate their own behavior. Meals and snacks include finger food or utensils that are easier for toddlers to use, such as bowls, spoons, and graduated versions of drinking containers from bottles to cups. Adults support and positively encourage children's attempts to dress themselves and put on shoes.

Source: S. Bredekamp and C. Copple, eds., *Developmentally Appropriate Practice in Early Childhood Programs*, rev. ed. (Washington, D.C.: National Association for the Education of Young Children, 1997).

Individually Appropriate Practice

The field of infant-toddler care is moving toward including more children of differing abilities and challenges into child care programs that have traditionally served only typically developing children. The need, then, is for caregivers to create inclusive environments, making sure that spatial organization, materials, and activities enable all children to participate actively. If every child is to receive nurturing responsive care, it must be individualized. The amount of adult intervention needed varies by individual child. Some need less and some need more. For many children it's enough to create a rich environment and let them experience it in an open-ended way. Adults can spend more time responding to what those children initiate than the reverse. Other children profit from selective and sensitive interventions. You will see examples throughout the book of diverse paths of development and adult responses to them.

Culturally Appropriate Practice

Caregivers honor cultural and family differences by listening to what parents want for their children and responding in culturally sensitive ways. Taking a partnership approach, caregivers discuss all decisions about how to best support children's development.

The principles explained in this chapter may not fit for everybody. Some families may find the caregiving practices shown in this chapter and elsewhere to be too standoffish. It may be uncomfortable for families in which the focus is more on teaching the child that he or she is a member of a group instead of an individual. Child-rearing practices reflect this focus, and some adults may downplay individuality. Instead of encouraging independence, families may instead focus on interdependence. The two are not mutually exclusive. Indeed, all families want their children to have relationships *and* grow up to be individuals who can stand on their own two feet. The perspective about what children need most to learn is what differs. We can't ignore the difference because the independence-interdependence dimension influences outcomes. We can't condone practices that are in opposition to what families want for their children. It may feel like a serious dilemma, but through building relationships of trust and understanding, caregivers and parents can figure out together what's best for this child in this family in this society.

Appropriate Practice in Action

Think about what you just read here and then go back and look at the Principles in Action on page 19. You will encounter dilemmas such as these throughout the book but will continually be asked to honor differences. It takes an open mind to do that. Would you be willing to try to understand *how* exactly to honor this parent's practice? You won't find the answer in this book. Each case is different; the outcome of the dilemma comes from interaction and communication between the people involved.

Summary

Relationships, Interactions, and the Three Rs

- Relationship is a key word in infant-toddler care, and relationships grow from interactions (another key word).
- The three Rs of infant-toddler care relate to the type of interactions that grow into relationships. The interactions are respectful, responsive, and reciprocal.
- Examples of the caregiver's respect for Caitlin in the first scene were:
  o Approaching her from the front so Caitlin could see the caregiver coming
  o Slowing her pace
  o Making contact by initiating a conversation before checking the diaper
  o Talking about what she was going to do before she did it, and giving Caitlin time to respond

Ten Principles Based on a Philosophy of Respect

- Key words or phrases for the 10 principles could be: (1) involvement, (2) quality time, (3) communication, (4) total person, (5) respect, (6) honest

Online Resources

Go to the Online Learning Center at **www.mhhe.com/itc7e** to access the student study guide that includes quizzes, practice with key terms, and a review of chapter content; links to websites related to the chapter; and additional resources.

feelings, (7) modeling behavior, (8) problems as opportunities, (9) security and trust, (10) quality of development.

Exploring the Word Curriculum

- The word curriculum, as it applies to infants and toddlers, can be defined as a course of study that is less like a class and more like a meandering river. Curriculum is also a framework for practice, or a plan for learning that is all inclusive and centers on connections and relationships.
- Adult roles in infant-toddler curriculum implementation are as partners, facilitators, supporters, and environmental planners.

Developmentally Appropriate Practice

- The guidelines for making decisions about developmentally appropriate practice tell early childhood professionals to consider three knowledge bases:
  - o Child development principles and research
  - o Individually appropriate practice, or what is known about individual differences
  - o Culturally appropriate practice, or what is known about particular group differences

Key Terms

curriculum 18	relationship 4	wants-nothing quality time 7
floor time 7	scaffolding 16	wants-something quality time 7
gross motor 16	sensory input 11	
interactions 4	three-R interaction 5	

Thought/Activity Questions

1. Explain two of the principles in the chapter.
2. What are some common themes that seem to run through all the principles?
3. Observe in an infant-toddler program and see if you can find evidence that it is using any of the 10 principles.
4. Visit an infant-toddler program and ask to see any written materials they have, such as a brochure, a parent booklet, registration materials. Compare and contrast what you read about the program with the information in this chapter.

For Further Reading

Alexandra Booke, "RIE: A Parent's Perspective," *Educaring* 22(2), Spring 2000, p. 2.
Perry M. Butterfield, "Child Care Is Rich in Routines," *Zero to Three* 22(4), February/March 2002, pp. 29–32.

Catherine Coughlan, "Using the RIE Approach in a Family Day Care Home," in *Authentic Relationships in Group Care for Infants and Toddlers: Resources for Infant Educarers (RIE) Principles into Practice*, edited by S. Petrie and S. Owen (London and Philadelphia: Jessica Kingsley Publishers, 2005), pp. 69–82.

Miriam David and Genevive Appell, *Lóczy: An Unusual Approach to Mothering*. Translated from *Lóczy Ou Le Maternage Insolite* by Jean Marie Clark; revised translation by Judit Falk (Budapest: Association Pikler-Loczy for Young Children, 2001).

Carolyn Pope Edwards and Helen Raikes, "Extending the Dance: Relationship-Based Approaches to Infant/Toddler Care and Education," *Young Children* 57(4), July 2002, pp. 10–17.

Polly Elam, "Creating Quality Infant Group Care Programs," in *Authentic Relationships in Group Care for Infants and Toddlers: Resources for Infant Educarers (RIE) Principles into Practice*, edited by S. Petrie and S. Owen (London and Philadelphia: Jessica Kingsley Publishers, 2005), pp. 83–92.

Magda Gerber, "RIE Principles and Practices," in *Authentic Relationships in Group Care for Infants and Toddlers: Resources for Infant Educarers (RIE) Principles into Practice*, edited by S. Petrie and S. Owen (London and Philadelphia: Jessica Kingsley Publishers, 2005), pp. 35–49.

Magda Gerber and Allison Johnson, *Your Self-Confident Baby* (New York: John Wiley & Sons, 1998), p. 23.

Janet Gonzalez-Mena, *Diversity in Early Care and Education* (New York: McGraw-Hill, 2004).

Janet Gonzalez-Mena, "What Can an Orphanage Teach Us? Lessons from Budapest," *Young Children*, September 2004, pp. 26–30.

Ruth Money, "The RIE Early Years 'Curriculum'," in *Authentic Relationships in Group Care for Infants and Toddlers: Resources for Infant Educarers (RIE) Principles into Practice*, edited by S. Petrie and S. Owen (London and Philadelphia: Jessica Kingsley Publishers, 2005), pp. 51–68.

Stephanie Petrie, "The Work of Emmi Pikler and Magda Gerber," in *Authentic Relationships in Group Care for Infants and Toddlers: Resources for Infant Educarers (RIE) Principles into Practice*, edited by S. Petrie and S. Owen (London and Philadelphia: Jessica Kingsley Publishers, 2005), pp. 17–34.

chapter 2

Infant-Toddler Education

Focus Questions

After reading this chapter you should be able to answer the following questions:

1 If you were describing the educational approach of this book to someone, what three words would you *not* include in the definition of infant-toddler education? Explain why those three words are not appropriate for infants and toddlers.

2 How can you describe what infant-toddler education is?

3 What does the word *curriculum* mean in relation to infant-toddler education?

4 What does it mean to take a problem-solving approach to infant-toddler education?

5 Name and explain four roles adults take to support problem solving in infants and toddlers.

What Do You See?

Emily is sitting on a soft rug when she sees a big, bright ball. She scoots on her bottom over to it, pushing with one leg and hand. She reaches out and touches the ball; it rolls away from her. She looks excited as she throws herself from sitting onto all fours and crawls quickly after the ball. She reaches it and tries to hold it, but it slips out of her arms and rolls away again. She follows it to where it has stopped by a small bed with a doll on it. She reaches for the doll, with one hand while balancing on the other and her two knees. She picks up the doll by one foot and drops it. She takes the blankets off the bed one by one, holding each to her cheek and comparing their textures. She picks up the last blanket by a corner of the binding and rubs it gently across her lips. Then she's off again crawling over the doll. As she does, she looks up and sees a picture on the wall at her eye level. It's a photo of the doll's face. She sits back on her bottom, staring at the picture. She then looks at the doll lying under her one leg.

"Yes, they are the same," says the adult nearby who has been sitting on the floor watching her. Emily turns, gives him a smile and then she's off again to see what else she can discover.

You just saw an example of infant education. If it didn't look like much to you, please read on. As you do, think back to this example. We will return to it later in the chapter.

Child care programs for infants and toddlers are necessarily educational, whether or not that is their primary purpose. There is no way to keep children for a number of hours every day without educating them. You can leave your car in a parking garage in the morning and expect to find it in the same condition that night when you pick it up again. But children aren't cars. Children are changed as the result of their child care experiences. How they are changed and what they learn can come without thought or planning, or the changes can be planned for in a systematic way. This chapter looks at a **philosophy of education** that is appropriate for infants and toddlers in child care. A philosophy of education means the set of theories or concepts related to development and the learning of knowledge and skills. Chapters 3 and 4 look at how you plan for that education.

What Infant-Toddler Education Is *Not*

Infant Stimulation

The word *stimulation* has become synonymous with the word *education* in the minds of many when talking about infants. **Infant stimulation** is defined as an educational approach designed to arouse or affect the five senses in order to provoke or increase development and learning. Although infant stimulation is more of a special education concept used for the infant with special needs or the at-risk infant, many group care programs feel pressure to incorporate it in their own approach. No one has ever proved that a program of carefully designed stimulation has a particularly beneficial effect on the development of a typically-developing child. It has been proved that if you shock rats, they run mazes better, which is some of the research on which the infant stimulation approach is based.

In this book the word *education* does not mean "stimulation." Of course the right amount of stimulation is important for all of us, but even more so for babies. But if you look at stimulation as something you do *to* babies, rather than something that happens because of a relationship and because of the way you meet a variety of needs, you may as well be training rats to run mazes.

If you are concerned primarily with stimulating—with doing something to the baby—you ignore a vital requirement for learning and development: babies need to discover that they can influence the people and things around them. Yes, they need stimulation, which they get from objects and, more important, from people. But they need to perceive their own involvement in these stimulating experiences. Their involvement comes when they are able to have some effect on—that is, interact with—the people and things that are part of the experiences. When stimulation is provided without regard to the baby's response, the baby is being treated as an object.

The attention on infant stimulation came partly in response to some crib-bound, institutionalized babies who failed to thrive. Being left alone, without much sensory input, but more important without attachment, they naturally failed to thrive. But adding mobiles, music boxes, or fish tanks to the crib isn't the answer. Getting somebody to meet the baby's needs is what is called for—not merely providing stimulation.

In group care for infants the problem is usually overstimulation rather than the opposite, as sights and sounds bombard the infants. So, in order to meet individual needs, infant education for some may involve cutting down the stimulation—the sensory input—rather than adding to what's already present in the environment.

Baby-sitting

The opposite view of infant stimulation as infant education is that all you have to do with babies is watch out for them and keep them safe; they'll develop fine on their own. In this view, babies are rosebuds that just need water, air, good soil, plant food, and sunshine to open up to their full potential. The idea of professionally trained caregivers seems superfluous. For someone who is an instinctively good caregiver and is caring for an easy baby, that may all seem true. It's when caregivers are faced with a baby whose needs are hard to determine—one who doesn't respond positively to attempts to get close, or one who lacks the kinds of behaviors that attract adults—that it becomes obvious that this view needs to be reexamined. Then put those caregivers into a situation where each has a number of babies to manage, and some of the babies are quite demanding. Without training, instincts alone may not work so well, and caregivers will have their hands full. Further, the easy-to-get-along-with babies in this situation may well be ignored, which means their development may be compromised. Infant education is a lot more than just baby-sitting.

Preschool

Education for infants and toddlers in child care is often built on the model of part-time preschools, where the children come in for a few hours in the morning and engage in a variety of activities set up especially for their learning. Infants are often left out of these activities until they can at least sit up, although including them in circle time with an adult holding them is a fairly common practice. So if the focus of education is on activities, preschool for infants means that circle time is the only so-called educational part. Toddlers, on the other hand, don't sit still for circle time and though they do engage in the activities set out for them, they explore the equipment, toys, and materials in ways that no one ever intended. They bang puzzle pieces, draw on themselves instead of on the paper, and put beans in their mouths instead of gluing them down into the puddles they've produced with glue bottles on paper. Unless they are watched closely, they are likely to lick the paint brushes; they experiment with scissors by cutting their clothes instead of paper. They look incompetent because they don't conform to the expectations of adults regarding either process or product.

Rather than find a more appropriate approach, some programs dedicated to this model seem to just wait for the toddlers to grow up and try to tolerate them in the meantime. But while they're waiting, they spend a lot of time restricting the children and teaching them to use the materials in certain ways, rather than letting them explore, which is what toddlers are designed to do! Inhibiting infants and toddlers exploratory urges is detrimental to their education.

What Infant-Toddler Education Is

Notice in the vignette at the beginning how Emily was exploring her environment and learning from her explorations. She was stimulating her senses on her own. Nobody was doing that to her. There was an adult nearby to appreciate what she was doing without interfering. He added a few words to support Emily's experience when she was comparing the picture to the doll. Without providing particular activities or setting predetermined outcomes, this scene was a perfect example of infant education. What we didn't see here, but will in chapters to come, was how the care component fits into the total picture. When infant-toddler education comes in a package with caregiving, everything that happens in the program can become educational if there is a philosophy and training to go with it so the adults are in tune with how infants and toddlers develop and learn.

NAEYC Program Standard 1
Relationships

Staff in programs that regard infants and toddlers as immature preschoolers and use an activity approach get frustrated with all the "noneducational" time spent in caregiving and transition times. In contrast, the Pikler Institute in Budapest, the residential nursery started by Emmi Pikler, sees care and education as a package and feels that learning goes on every minute of the day.[1] Resources for Infant Educarers (RIE), Magda Gerber's program in Los Angeles also refuses to separate care and education.[2] Both Pikler and Gerber and their respective programs are in tune with Nel Nodding's work at Stanford University on the ethics of care. Nodding, though not focused on the earliest years, nevertheless makes a strong case for care being a vital ingredient of education at all levels![3] All three of these theorists feel the primary focus of the first three years should be to establish a close and continuous relationship, which also fits with what brain research indicates.[4] Education then grows out of the relationship that results from caregiving. See Chapter 5 for more on this subject.

Curriculum as the Foundation of Infant-Toddler Education

NAEYC Program Standard 2
Curriculum

For a care program to be educational there must be a curriculum. We explored the word *curriculum* in Chapter 1. Here we will refine and expand on our definition. The appropriate curriculum should be a plan for learning and development that is all-inclusive and centers on connections and relationships with an infant or toddler in a center or home-based early care and education program. Trained caregivers who respond to and respect each child's needs in warm and sensitive ways that promote attachment focus on both education and care. Respectful and

VIDEO OBSERVATION 2

Toddler Playing with a Tube and a Ball

See Video Observation 2: Toddler Playing with a Tube and a Ball for an example of problem solving. This is another simple example of the kinds of educational experiences that children choose for themselves. This boy is older than Emily, who appears in the scene at the beginning of the chapter. He is exploring and experimenting too but is focused on just one problem.

Questions

- What problem is this boy trying to solve?
- What do you think about his persistence? Are you surprised that he has such a long attention span?
- What do you think made the boy pick this particular problem to solve?

To view this clip, go to www.mhhe.com/itc7e. Click on Student Edition, select Chapter 2, and click on Video Observation.

responsive curriculum is based on relationships that occur within planned and unplanned activities, experiences, and happenings.

A curriculum is not just a book of lesson plans or activities for a day, a month, or a year. It's not a package of posters, books, toys, and materials that go along with themes of the month. It's not a set of forms with blanks to fill in about what to do each day or season. A curriculum is much more complex than any of these things. It can be defined simply as a plan for learning, but to understand what that means in terms of infant-toddler programs takes a whole book. That's what this book is about. We'll get a start in this chapter and then focus on two aspects of curriculum—routines and play—in the next two chapters.

Think of the curriculum centering on relationships. In fact, the WestEd Program for Infant-Toddler Caregivers—the largest training effort in the United

**NAEYC Program
Standard 1**
Relationships

States that is related to the first three years—calls what it teaches a "responsive, relationship-based curriculum." This curriculum is explained in many volumes of guides, manuals, videotapes, and what are called video magazines. The training in this curriculum is extensive.

Although a curriculum does not have to be written out, labeled, or even talked about as such, somewhere there is a framework for decision making based on a philosophy that guides action. The framework and philosophy may only be in the heads of the founders of the program, but it must somehow be conveyed to everyone who works with the infants and toddlers in the program. It helps if that framework or curriculum is in writing, but the most effect way to teach the framework to the people working with the children is through training. To implement the curriculum, infant care teachers, caregivers, educarers, family child care providers, or whatever they are called need the skills to understand typical development, atypical development, and diversity. In addition they must have observation skills so they can be appropriately responsive minute by minute and over time. Here's where more writing comes in. In order to plan for each child and for the group, detailed record keeping is a must. Only then are caregivers able to effectively reflect on what they see, assess what each child needs, and plan environments and experiences for individuals and for the group that are a good fit. They also must be able to adapt the environments and experiences that work for typically developing children so they work for *all* children, no matter what kinds of physical, mental, or emotional challenges individuals bring to the program.

To carry out a curriculum, a caregiver must have goals or desired results, which are often unwritten and even unspoken but which most often are holistic and relate to the image of whole, healthy children who are able to reach their full unique potential as individuals and as group members. When expressed or written, the goals (sometimes called outcomes) are usually related to developmental domains—that is the child is divided into three separate parts that can be thought of as mind, body, and feelings. Feelings include the ability to relate to others. To use more sophisticated language, goals or outcomes are usually organized by the cognitive, physical, and social-emotional domains. Some programs also have separate spiritual and/or creative goals. Curricula at higher levels of education can focus on the mind alone, but that doesn't work for infants and toddlers. There is no way to separate intellectual needs and interests from other needs and interests at this beginning level.

Assessing the Effectiveness of the Curriculum: Observing and Recording

Any curriculum depends on caregivers determining what children need and are interested in, both as individuals and as a group, which is an assessment process. Two parts of the assessment process will be discussed here: observing and recording children's behavior.

Observation as an assessment process can't be overemphasized. Caregivers should develop and practice observation every day. Informal observation should become a daily habit, indeed a mode of being. Observations can be recorded in a number of ways, including as anecdotal records, formal written observations, or daily logs. **Anecdotal records** are descriptions of anything that captures your attention and are written as notes on the spot or, if written later, whatever sticks in your mind. By keeping anecdotal records you may notice that some children don't capture your attention very often or in the same way as others. You need to observe those children more carefully and keep written records of what you observe.

Formal written observations are called **running records** and involve carefully and objectively noting everything that happens as it happens. They can be recorded and transcribed later or written as notes and then rewritten later. Or video can be used with the observer commenting on what's being observed using objective, nonjudgmental terms. Still photographs, video without commentary, audio recordings of babies' vocalizations and toddlers' conversations are also recordkeeping devices, sometimes called **documentation,** that provide visual and auditory representations of learning and development. Carefully kept records and documentation of all sorts can provide important information that shows patterns used to assess individual developmental pathways.

Ongoing assessment tells how the child is doing; where the leading edge of learning, growth, and development lies; and what might be needed next. Lev Vygotsky, Russian researcher, called this leading edge the **zone of proximal development.** Appendix B, the Environmental Chart, can be used as a guide to the expected sequence of development and the kinds of behaviors that indicate progress. Part 2 of this book also can help you understand about developmental progressions and expectations.

When you keep good records, a developmental profile emerges that provides a picture of each child's development so caregivers can plan an individualized program. This picture should include the range of general and specific interests and needs for each child and the developmental tasks he or she is working on. It also should include the family's goals and expectations. Using developmental profiles, the caregiver can individualize the curriculum so that it meets each child's specific and special needs. This developmental picture also can help the caregiver notice any particular issues or concerns that may need to be discussed with the family and perhaps even with specialists. Some concerns call for professional observations, testing, and other kinds of evaluation. Certain kinds of interventions may be called for depending on what the assessment shows. Special training is needed to do these more sophisticated assessments, but caregivers do informal assessments on a daily basis as they work with children and learn what they know and can do. Magda Gerber used to say that caregivers should let the child be the teacher, and indeed, a good part of assessment is learning the child and what he or she has to teach you about his or her interests, skills, knowledge, capabilities, and needs. Of course, caregivers also learn from the family, not *just* from the child.

When building developmental profiles, it's tempting to compare a particular child to a chart or, worse, to another child. Using charts has nothing to do with what is right or wrong or good or bad; they should be used merely to understand the patterns of a particular child and how these patterns relate to norms. But remember that children have their own paths of development that may be very different from the typical one represented by the charts. Respect differences and remember that "normal" is not necessarily a goal! There is a wide range of typical development and each child is an individual. In Part 2, the feature called Diverse Developmental Pathways was created to drive this point home and help caregivers avoid making judgments. Please do *not* use assessment procedures to create developmental report cards or label children! Also avoid the notion that development is a race in which some children are ahead and others behind. Development isn't about winning and losing; it's about growing, learning, and unfolding to full potential. Children pick up early messages about their capabilities; negative messages can create self-fulfilling prophecies in which expectations influence outcomes.

Staff must also be able to relate to parents and other family members in ways that provide a good exchange of information so that what goes on outside the home matches, complements, or harmonizes with what goes on inside the home. One kind of record that has been mentioned only briefly so far is a daily log kept by the primary caregiver. The daily log has multiple uses. It can be a way for parents to receive a comprehensive and detailed report when they arrive to pick up their children. Some records have to do with the various caregiving activities and contain specific information that links to home. Diaper changes, elimination patterns, food offered and consumed, length of naptime, and any outstanding events are all interesting information that will help parents know what their babies might need or want after they take them home. This information is especially important in preverbal infants who can't make their needs or interests known. Some programs have a two-way journaling system where parents bring in a journal in which they've recorded what the caregiver might need to know about how the night and morning went. The caregiver uses that same journal to record the events and details of the day, and then the journal goes home again with the parent and child.

Because it is so hard to pin down curriculum or say exactly what infant-toddler education is (as stated earlier, this whole book is about infant-toddler education), the rest of this chapter will focus on one topic—infants and toddlers learning to solve problems and how adults can help them learn.

Education as Facilitating Problem Solving

One way to describe a focus of an infant-toddler curriculum is to pay attention to the development of problem-solving skills in children. That way of thinking about curriculum differs from both the stimulation and activity-centered points of view. A major aspect of the education in this book is based on a *problem-solving approach* in which babies and toddlers learn how to make things happen in their world. Sensory input, of course, is an important part of this approach, but it comes about mostly as a result of the children's actions. The children are in charge. The adults are facilitators rather than *stimulators.* Age-appropriate activities are also part of this approach, but they are only one small part, not the whole curriculum.

What kinds of problems do infants and toddlers face? Watch an infant or toddler for just one hour, and you will go a long way toward answering that question. You will note that infants and toddlers deal with a variety of kinds of problems, including physical ones, such as hunger or discomfort; manipulative ones, such as how to get a toy from one hand to the other or how to get one block to balance on top of another; and social and emotional problems, such as coping with separation from a parent or caregiver or trying to interact with a peer who is not interested in interacting. Some problems are specific to particular levels of development and will eventually be solved. Others are specific to the situation and may or may not be solved. Still others are ones the child will be dealing with, in one form or another, throughout his or her lifetime. Education for children under three lies in learning to deal with this enormous variety of problems, learning various ways to approach them, and learning when the problems can be solved and when to give up. As babies continually experience the problems that come from everyday living, the problems they encounter in play as well as in being fed, changed, dressed, bathed, and put to sleep, they eventually become toddlers who come to see themselves as problem solvers. If they come to see themselves as good problem solvers, and indeed they are, then they will have been, by the definition of this book, well educated.

The Principles in Action

Principle 8 Recognize problems as learning opportunities, and let infants and toddlers try to solve their own. Don't rescue them, constantly make life easy for them, or try to protect them from all problems.

Jasmine rides down the path in the play yard on a tot-sized tricycle, pushing with her feet on the ground instead of using the pedals. She runs off the edge of the concrete walk, and the bike tips over, spilling her into the sand. She lets out a lusty yell and lies on her back with the bike on its side next to her. A caregiver arrives in a hurry and crouches down next to Jasmine but doesn't touch her. She looks into her face and asks, "Are you okay?" Jasmine cries louder. The caregiver says, "You fell down." Jasmine stops crying and looks at her and nods. "You went right off the edge." Jasmine nods again. She starts to roll over on her side. Her caregiver offers a hand to help her. She refuses it and gets up, brushing herself off. The caregiver looks her over carefully and sees no scrapes or red marks, but says again, "Are you okay?" "Okay," Jasmine responds. She reaches for the bike handle. The caregiver gets out of her way. She struggles a little but persists until she rights the bike. The caregiver doesn't help. The caregiver says, "You did that all by yourself." Jasmine grins and pulls the bike back to the cement. She has a broad smile on her face as she rides off.

1. Do you see this as an example of infant education? Explain your view.
2. What if the parent had watched this and become uncomfortable that the caregiver was so standoffish? What might you have said to the parent if you had been the caregiver?
3. Why might the parent have been uncomfortable?

4. Do you have a different idea about how the caregiver should have handled this situation?
5. What would you have done and why?
6. Is this a problem you would try to prevent if you were the caregiver? If yes, how? If no, why not?

The Adult Role in Facilitating Problem Solving

**NAEYC Program
Standard 3**
Teaching

The primary function of the adult in infant-toddler education is to facilitate learning rather than to teach or train. Start by appreciating the problems the babies encounter. Allow them to work on solving those problems themselves. Also, as caregiver, you will present problems to the babies while you provide for their needs and set up the environment for their play. You facilitate infant education by the way you direct and respond to the problem-solving baby during wants-something and wants-nothing quality time.

The two kinds of quality time relate to two ways of being with an infant or a toddler in an educational way, which we'll call **caregiver presence.** To get an idea of these two ways of being, try this exercise. Find someone who is willing to be your mirror. Stand facing that person, and ask the person to copy each of your movements. Then, using your body, facial expressions, and hands, do something for the "mirror" to copy. You may want to move around. After you have experienced being the doer, try being the mirror. When you finish, discuss the experience with your partner. What role did you prefer—doing or mirroring (leading or following)? What was hard about each one? What are the advantages and disadvantages of each?

This mirroring exercise shows the kind of reciprocal interactions that constitute the responsive relationship first discussed in Chapter 1. It also illustrates the two kinds of caregiver presence—active and receptive. Perhaps you prefer the active mode—being a leader and directing what is going on. Or perhaps you prefer the receptive mode—following the child's lead and being responsive. To be a good infant-toddler educator, you need to develop both modes, no matter what your preference. Knowing which you prefer can help you concentrate on improving the other.

Notice in the following scene how the adult's being receptive or active works when the child has a problem to solve.

Jason toddles in crying loudly and holds his fingers out in front of him.

"Oh, Jason, something happened to you," says the caregiver.

Jason continues to cry and holds his fingers up for inspection. The caregiver touches his fingers gently. "It looks like you hurt your fingers," he says in a calm but understanding voice.

Jason pulls his fingers away and tugs at the caregiver's pants, indicating he wants to show him something.

"You want me to come," he verbalizes Jason's desire and follows him to an area behind a partition where another adult and several children are on the floor. Jason,

Figure 2.1 The Four Roles of the Adult in Infant-Toddler Education

1. **Determining optimum stress levels:** observing and deciding how much stress is too much, too little, and just right.

2. **Providing attention:** meeting children's needs for attention without manipulative motives.

3. **Providing feedback:** giving clear feedback so that infants and toddlers learn the consequences of their actions.

4. **Modeling:** setting a good example for infants and toddlers.

sobbing, leads him directly to a cupboard with the door standing ajar. His cries change slightly as he nears the scene of the accident.

"You pinched your fingers in the door?" guesses the caregiver.

Jason, angry now, picks up a wooden block and gets ready to throw it at the cupboard door.

"I see you're mad, but I won't let you throw the block. You might hurt something," says the caregiver firmly, holding Jason's arm.

Jason seems to reconsider. He puts down the block and goes to the cupboard. Still crying, he closes the door and opens it again. He is very careful in his actions.

"Yes, you can do it now without pinching." The caregiver puts Jason's actions into words.

Jason ignores the words and continues to open and close the door. The angry cries subside and pained whimpering takes their place. He sits down by the cupboard and remains there crying.

"Let's go put some cold water on your fingers," says the caregiver, bending over to him with his arms out.

This scene shows both active and receptive presence, with an emphasis on receptive. Only twice did the caregiver take the lead. Notice that the caregiver was calm and not overemotional, though he was able to empathize with Jason (to feel his hurt). Because he did not get drawn into the situation and could provide support to Jason in his pain, he facilitated Jason's problem-solving abilities. The scene might have been very different if the caregiver had given Jason advice or "taught him a lesson." The scene might also have been very different if the caregiver had offered sympathy. Imagine if he had picked up Jason and murmured phrases like "Oh, poor Jason, you got hurt, poor, poor little boy." But the caregiver gave neither advice nor sympathy. Instead, he gave his full calm attention, both receptive and active, thereby giving Jason the support, strength, and acceptance he needed to pursue the problem he had encountered. This scene shows infant-toddler education at work.

The adult role of directing and responding to infant-toddler problem solving is made up of four skills. The adult must be able to ascertain the optimum level of stress for the child faced with a problem, provide appropriately for the child's need for attention, give feedback, and model desired behavior. These roles are summarized in Figure 2.1.

Determining Optimum Stress Levels   One way the adult facilitates learning is by being sensitive to the stress levels of babies and toddlers. This sensitivity is important in scaffolding learning. When a young child faced with a problem is going beyond a tolerable frustration level, a little nudge from the adult can reduce the frustration enough so that the child can continue to work to solve the problem.

When a sensitive adult scaffolds as part of the infant-toddler education, he or she provides the smallest bit of help possible, not to get rid of frustration but to keep the child working on the problem. This type of help improves attention span and teaches children that they are capable problem solvers.

Most adults want to shield their charges from uncomfortable feelings. They don't realize that stress and frustration are an important part of infant-toddler education and come naturally with problem solving. In order to develop physically, emotionally, and intellectually, children occasionally need something to fight against, to pit their will and strength against. In this way they can discover that they are competent problem solvers. With no stress, no frustrations, and no problems, children have no way to try themselves against the world. Consequently, their education is severely limited. A young parent, thinking about stress as a part of infant education, wrote the following:

> I was watering my garden the other day and I found out more about stress and development. I'd been watering every day for some time and found that some of my seedlings weren't growing deep roots. As I thought about it—if a plant doesn't have some stress factors so that it has to look for food and water, its roots won't grow as deep, and therefore it won't be as stable in the world. Its foundation will be too shallow.[5]

Optimum stress is the right amount of stress—not too much and not too little. The right amount of stress means that it is enough to energize and motivate the child toward activity, including problem solving, but not so much that it hampers or inhibits the child's ability to act or solve a problem. Believe it or not, stress can promote learning and development, but it has to be the right amount. It's the caregiver's job to decide what is optimum stress for each child and then try to allow for it. Opportunities will arise naturally in daily life.

How can you decide what is enough stress? You can decide the optimum level of stress by watching the child's actions. Children under too much stress are not able to solve problems effectively; they may become greatly emotional, or they may withdraw.

You can also decide what is enough stress by being empathetic (imagining what a child is actually feeling) and by remaining calm and not being swayed by either the child's emotions or your own. Being calm gives a perspective that facilitates good decision making.

What should you do if children are either overstressed or understressed? Take a look at the problems each child faces. Perhaps there are too many of them, in which case some changes need to be made to cut down on the number. They may be too hard to solve, in which case the child may need more help.

NAEYC Program Standard 4
Assessment

If children are understressed, they may not be encountering enough problems in their lives—perhaps not enough is happening, the environment is lacking in variety or interest, or someone else is solving the children's problems.

Providing Attention   The way an adult responds to a child's actions is an important part of infant-toddler education. The adult response has a lot of power because infants and toddlers essentially live on attention from others, especially the others who are important to them. For each individual there is an optimum amount of attention—optimum again, not maximum. If the person gets enough attention, satisfaction results. An individual who doesn't get enough will seek it in a variety of ways.

Some typical ways to get attention that people learn early in life are:

- By being attractive to look at
- By being kind and sweet
- By being smart, skilled, capable, competent, or talented
- By misbehaving
- By being loud
- By talking a lot
- By talking little
- By being outgoing
- By being shy
- By being sick
- By being helpless

Are you aware that girls are more likely to be noticed for their looks than for their capabilities? How long do you think it takes for children to fall into patterns where they tend to get attention by taking on confining sex roles?

If babies find that smiling, cooing, and being peaceful are not enough, or toddlers find that playing and keeping a low profile does not bring them attention, they will try other behaviors. Children seriously in need of attention will find out how to "push the buttons" of the important people around them. Adults must recognize when children are trying to get attention by upsetting them and when children are directly communicating their real needs. It is not always easy to tell the difference. Take a look at the following scene:

A caregiver is sitting in a comfortable chair feeding a 6-month-old a bottle. A 17-month-old, Mike, at her feet, keeps tugging at her arm and trying to reach the bottle. Another adult removes Mike and tries to engage him in play while explaining that his caregiver is busy right now. When she turns her back to settle a dispute in another part of the room, Mike walks over to another child and grabs the toy he is playing with. Both caregivers admonish Mike, who glows with the attention. As soon as they turn back to their various occupations, Mike goes to the doorway separating the playroom from the kitchen. He hangs on the gate across the opening and fusses.

"You just ate!" responds his caregiver from her chair. "It's hard to believe that you're still hungry, but I'll get you a snack when I finish feeding Sierra," she tells

Reflect

Think of a time in your own life when stress was good for you. Can you relate your experience to that of an infant or toddler in group care? How good are you at telling the difference between optimum stress and too much stress in your own life? Does this ability relate to how you can tell when a child is having too much or too little stress?

Reflect

Think about how you satisfy your own needs for attention. How aware are you of the ways you get people to pay attention to you? List some ways you get attention from other people. Are you satisfied with the ways you get attention? Would you want infants and toddlers to get attention in the same ways?

him, then settles her gaze back on the baby she is feeding. Mike walks over immediately and pulls all the toys off the shelf and stamps on them. Both caregivers admonish him. Again he glows with the attention. But when both withdraw it, he starts throwing toys over the gate across the open kitchen door. Again he has two adults' full attention. The free adult helps him retrieve the toys and put them back on the shelf while his caregiver in the chair watches and comments from time to time. When order is restored, she puts her attention back to the feeding while the other caregiver starts to change a diaper. The scene ends as Mike walks over and slaps a child who has been playing quietly in the corner all this time.

In this scene Mike continually gets attention for undesirable behavior. It's easy to see that he knows how to get attention when he needs it, even when both caregivers are busy. There is no easy answer to this problem. However, if both caregivers are aware that he needs attention, they can concentrate on giving it to him when he is not misbehaving. Perhaps he'll have less need for adult attention when it's difficult to give it to him. The adults can also put into words what it is that he needs by saying things like "I know you need my attention right now, Mike."

If you are generous with your attention during caregiving times, most children can go on about their business during playtimes when you can't respond to them in playful ways. They won't hunger for adult attention. But if a child has learned that misbehavior is satisfying in terms of the reward it brings, you must change your approach.

Start by ignoring undesirable behavior that is designed to attract your attention (without disregarding needs or safety, of course). At the same time, pay lots of attention to behavior that is desirable. Be specific when you talk about the behavior—don't just throw out nonspecific global judgments like "good boy." Instead, say things like "I really like the way you're playing with that toy, Mike. You put the toy back when you're finished. Good for you, Mike. You're letting me feed Sierra without interrupting. You're doing a good job of waiting. You're being gentle with Jacob."

When behavior needs change, **positive reinforcement** can be quite effective. Positive reinforcement is defined as a response to a behavior that strengthens the likelihood of it being repeated—in other words, a reward. Rewards work, especially when you are changing learned behaviors—that is, those that have been inadvertently rewarded in the past, such as Mike's bids for attention.

But don't go overboard in using positive reinforcement. Attention and praise work and are powerful motivators. However, they can be addictive. Many activities are rewarding for their own sake. They lose that reward when adults add external rewards to the intrinsic ones. So, when a toddler is playing and an adult constantly interrupts to praise her, the message is that the activity itself is not that great, so the child needs motivation. Eventually the child gets the message and that comes to be the case. It's easy to spot a child who is used to a lot of praise while playing. She is the one who constantly looks to the adult after each little accomplishment while playing. She seems to constantly need someone to say "Wonderful! You stacked that block on the other one." The accomplishment itself is empty without the adult praise.

When children are overpraised, they may lose touch with their own feelings and motives. They look around after every act to see if they did it right. They seek approval for everything they do. Activities and accomplishments are pleasing only for the external rewards they bring. In short, these children cease to get pleasure and satisfaction from the activities themselves.

In *Toward a Psychology of Being*, Abraham Maslow states that when a child is faced with a conflict between inner delight at his own accomplishment and the rewards offered by others, he "must generally choose approval from others, and then handle his delight by repression or letting it die, or not noticing it or controlling it by will power. In general, along with this will develop a disapproval of the delight experience, or shame and embarrassment and secretiveness about it, with finally, the inability even to experience it."[6]

Maslow is giving a powerful message about the use of praise in infant-toddler education. His message is quite different from the common practice of many caregivers, who lavish praise on children so they will feel good about themselves. Children generally feel better about themselves when adults limit their praise and respond to successes with words like "You must feel good about finally getting that shoe off," thus acknowledging the child's own inner delight.

Providing Feedback   Closely related to the subject of praise and attention is feedback. Part of infant-toddler education depends on the child getting clear feedback, or responses. Feedback comes both from the environment and from people. Children need to learn what effect their actions have on the world and on others. If they drop a glass of milk, it spills. That's feedback about the qualities of liquids. The child needs no further feedback about milk. Now what's needed is a response about how to remedy the situation. "The milk spilled. You need a cloth to sop it up" is a good response.

Some things children do result in caregivers expressing pain or anger. That expression is also feedback. For example, a child who scratches a caregiver can be told, "It hurts when you scratch me. I don't like it." The message should be clear if the feedback is to be useful to the child. If the caregiver responds to a scratch in a honeyed voice, smiling all the while but holding the child tightly as if angry, the child gets a mixed message rather than clear feedback.

Adults also can help provide feedback about the environment and verbalizing the reaction they see in the child. In this way children learn to give themselves clear feedback. Here is an example of that principle:

Jamal is playing with several other toddlers when his caregiver comes in the door. As Jamal rushes over, he slams his elbow into a table. He approaches his caregiver crying.

His caregiver says, "Oh, Jamal, I saw that. You bumped your elbow on the table." Jamal confirms his caregiver's statement by holding his elbow up.

"Me!" he exclaims.

"Yes," replies his caregiver. "Right here is where you bumped it." He touches the spot gently.

Jamal goes back to the table that he bumped. "Table!" he explains.

"Yes," confirms his caregiver. "Right there—you bumped your elbow right there on the table." He knocks on the table. "It's hard."

Jamal touches the table. "It hurt when you hit your elbow on it," continues his caregiver.

"Hard," repeats Jamal. He cries less now. He concentrates on his elbow, then the table, then his elbow again.

Reflect

Think of a time in your own life when feedback was useful to you in a problem-solving situation. Can you apply your own experience to that of an infant or a toddler?

Jamal's caregiver helped him focus on what just happened, and Jamal learned something about cause and effect. Jamal was shown what hurt him and gained some understanding of the relationship of the pain to the source. His caregiver helped Jamal understand the full experience rather than letting him get lost in the pain, yet he didn't deny Jamal's pain or distract him from it.

Sometimes helping a child get feedback is just a matter of standing back and seeing if the child realizes what just happened and can figure out how to deal with it. Other times it helps to put words to the situation. The properties of objects are something infants and toddlers study intensely in their first three years. They want to know all about most every object they encounter. They learn through experience as they manipulate everything they can get their hands on. That's why it's important that they be in an environment set up for them with a variety of objects for them to explore. They gain feedback through their explorations. Talk to them about what they may be experiencing. "It's heavy, isn't it?" "You like the smooth feeling of that ball." In the first vignette in this chapter, the adult put words to the connection the child seemed to be making between the doll and the picture. Language gives them labels for their perceptions; helps them analyze, sort, and compare; and provides a means to store their perceptions of an object away for future reference. Be careful not to interrupt a child's concentration, though. Use language sensitively so that it adds to the experience rather than disturbs it. Use language to help out in problem solving if the child isn't reading the physical feedback. Saying, "That puzzle piece won't go in if you put it that way" will be more meaningful if the child is sitting there banging the piece rather than twisting and turning it to find a way to make it fit. Wait, though, until there are signs that the child is about to give up trying. That's the time to do some scaffolding. Give a little hint about what to do. For example, say, "Try turning it over." Adult feedback isn't useful just for helping children understand how objects work. It's also good for helping children understand the behavior of other children. "He didn't like it when you grabbed the book from him." Or "He ran away because you shouted at him." As you read through the many examples in this book, notice the number of times that adults give children feedback about their effects on others.

NAEYC Program Standard 3

Teaching

Modeling Practice, don't preach! **Model** the behavior you want from the child.[7] To model means to set an example by performing behaviors, actions, and interactive styles that the children observe and imitate. What you do speaks louder than what you say. For instance, if you want to teach the child to share, you need to *be* a sharing person yourself. You need to share your own possessions with others if that's what you expect a child to do. You can teach children to perform the actions of sharing by using rewards and punishments, or you can *make* them share by using your size and power. But neither of these approaches will make children become sharing people. They will become sharing people (with lots of modeling) only after they gain the concept of possession. Toddlers need to learn this concept (hence all the "Me!" and "Mine!" statements you hear when you work with children in this age group).

Children model after other qualities of their caregivers as well—qualities such as gentleness. Children who are treated gently are more likely to treat other children gently. Respect is another example. Children who are treated with respect are more likely to be respectful to others than children who are not.

Another example of modeling behavior is expression of anger. If you work all day, every day in an infant-toddler center, your own anger is bound to be an emotion you'll deal with at least occasionally. The children pick up on how you cope. If you smile and sing and deny that you're feeling furious, they learn to hide their feelings too. (And they learn to give the same mixed messages you are giving.) But if you use the energy to confront the source and problem solve, they learn that way of dealing with conflicts. Or, if confrontation is not appropriate, they can learn your coping mechanisms, such as working out the feelings through talking about them, through redirection into physical exercise or expression, or through soothing activities. (For some adults, washing dishes is as soothing as water play is to children.)

In short, modeling behavior is more effective than teaching it. Just think of the habits, mannerisms, attitudes, gestures, and expressions you use that came straight from your parent(s). We pick up behaviors and mannerisms without even being aware of doing so and without being taught. As a caregiver, you must be conscious of the behavior you model so that what you do and what you say are in accordance with one another.

Obviously, no one can be a model all the time. Everyone acts in ways they would rather not have children imitate. If you expect to be a perfect model, you set yourself up for disappointment. However, as you respond to your own weaknesses, your own imperfections, and your humanness, you are modeling. For example, when you make a mistake, you can show the children that mistakes can be forgiven by forgiving yourself. When you're feeling needy, you can tune in to your needs, modeling for the children that responding to needs is important. When you bring modeling to the conscious level of awareness, you can make decisions about it. Modeling is a powerful tool and can work either for you or against you. Because caregiving is already a difficult task, you may as well have all your tools working for you.

In summary, the adult role in infant-toddler education involves allowing for an appropriate degree of stress when a child is trying to solve a problem, responding appropriately to demands for attention, providing feedback, and modeling desirable behavior. The role of the infant-toddler educator can be carried out at any time—during caregiving tasks or when children are playing without direction.

The hardest part of infant-toddler education is trying to explain it to people who think learning comes only from school-like activities. A good task to prepare yourself to be an infant-toddler caregiver is to prepare an answer to the question "Do children learn anything in your program, or do they just play?" You're bound to be asked that question at some point in your career, or perhaps you may be asked, "Is your program educational or just baby-sitting?" A short convincing answer should be right at your fingertips.

Appropriate Practice

Overview of Development

According to the National Association for the Education of Young Children (NAEYC), quality care combines care and education. Some of the components of quality care include recognizing that ages zero to three covers a large span of developmental differences and must be broken down into three stages: young infants (ages birth to 9 months), mobile infants (ages 8 to 18 months), and toddlers (ages 16 to 36 months). Each age group needs particular environmental adaptations and sets of responses from caregivers. For a program to be educational, the caregiver must create a safe, interesting, developmentally appropriate, and orderly world. To do this requires individualized care in small groups with primary caregivers. Continuity of care is important too so that infants and toddlers are with the same caregiver for (ideally) three years. Care is educational when it's developmentally and culturally appropriate and when caregivers exhibit responsive interactions.

Source: J. Ronald Lally, Abbey Griffin, Emily Fenichel, Marilyn Segal, Eleanor Szanton, and Bernice Weissbourd, "Development in the First Three Years of Life," in *Developmentally Appropriate Practice in Early Childhood Programs*, rev. ed. (Washington, D.C.: National Association for the Education of Young Children, 1997).

Developmentally Appropriate Practice

The following are samples of developmentally appropriate practices that relate to infant-toddler education:

- There is sufficient continuity of care to ensure that every infant (and family) is able to form a relationship with a primary caregiver. As the caregiver comes to know a few infants very well, she is able to respond to the temperament, needs, and cues of each baby and to develop a mutually satisfying pattern of communication with each child and family.

- Adults engage in many one-to-one, face-to-face interactions with infants. Adults talk in a pleasant, calm voice, using simple language and frequent eye contact, while being responsive to the child's cues.
- Warm, responsive interactions with infants occur throughout the day. Observing the infant's cues, the adult is able to judge when the baby would like to be held, carried to a new place, or shifted to a new position. Adults often talk to babies, especially older infants, about what is going on.
- Children are acknowledged for their accomplishments and helped to feel increasingly competent and in control of themselves.

Source: S. Bredekamp and C. Copple, eds., *Developmentally Appropriate Practice in Early Childhood Programs*, rev. ed. (Washington, D.C.: National Association for the Education of Young Children, 1997).

Individually Appropriate Practice

Caregiving routines must be individualized so that they meet each child's specific needs. One infant may need special positioning on the diapering table in order to keep from becoming stiff, while another may need to be held on a pillow because skin-to-skin contact bothers her. Still another may need extra support to sit up so that he can feed himself finger food.

Culturally Appropriate Practice

One difference in view between caregivers and parents may be about children feeding themselves. In families where the tradition is to spoon-feed children for the first few years, the idea that they are left to feed themselves in the first two years may be upsetting. As one mother said, "I love to feed my baby. I don't want to stop just because he can feed himself. Feeding is a way I show him I love him." Remember that appropriate practice means that caregivers and parents confer in making decisions about how best to support children's development or handle problems or differences of opinion as they arise.

Appropriate Practice in Action

Look back on the Principles in Action scene on page 33 and reconsider your answers. After reading this chapter would you answer any of the questions differently? Now analyze that scene in terms of the information in the last bullet in the "Developmentally Appropriate Practice" section of the Appropriate Practice box.

- Did the caregiver acknowledge Jasmine's accomplishment? Do you think the caregiver helped Jasmine feel increasingly competent and in control of herself?

Now look at the "Culturally Appropriate Practice" section of the Appropriate Practice box.

- How might this scene have been different if Jasmine's culture saw the adult role as solving the problem for her instead of letting her solve the problem?
- What could you do if the caregiver's approach and the family's approach were different?

Summary

Infant-Toddler Education Is Not

- Infant-Stimulation, or doing things to babies with the aim of stimulating their senses, is not a focus of this book's approach to educating infants and toddlers.
- Baby-sitting, or just watching out for very young children to keep them safe, ignores the need for trained infant care teachers who understand how care and education go together.
- A preschool model, especially one where the educational focus of the day occurs only during circle time and when specific activities are available for the children.

Infant-Toddler Education Is

- Built on a foundation called curriculum, which is a plan for learning.
- The ways in which trained adults focus on and appreciate the problems that infants encounter in daily living in a rich and responsive environment.
- The means by which trained adults plan for, support, and occasionally facilitate problem solving, but only when infants show they need help.
- The roles that trained adults take in order to support problem solving in infants by determining optimum stress levels, providing appropriate attention, providing appropriate feedback, and modeling behaviors they wish to see in the children.

Online Resources

Go to the Online Learning Center at **www.mhhe.com/itc7e** to access the student study guide that includes quizzes, practice with key terms, and a review of chapter content; links to websites related to the chapter; and additional resources.

Key Terms

anecdotal records 31
caregiver presence 34
documentation 31
infant stimulation 26
model 40

optimum stress 36
philosophy of education 26
positive reinforcement 38
running records 31
zone of proximal development 31

Thought/Activity Questions

1. What makes an infant-stimulation program different from one that focuses on infant education?
2. What are four roles adults can play in infant-toddler education?
3. How would you define the term *curriculum* as it relates to an infant-toddler center-based program? Would the definition be different in a family child care home?
4. Think of an answer to give a parent when he or she asks, "Do children learn anything in your program, or do they just play?" How can you explain that your program is educational, not "just baby-sitting"?

For Further Reading

T. Berry Brazelton and Stanley Greenspan, *The Irreducible Needs of Children* (Cambridge, Mass.: Perseus, 2000).

Diane Carlebach and Beverly Tate, *Creating Caring Children: The First Three Years* (Miami: Peace Education Foundation, 2002).

Ruth E. Cook, Annette Tessier, and M. Diane Klein, *Adapting Early Childhood Curricula for Children in Inclusive Settings* (Columbus, Ohio: Merrill, 2000).

Miriam David and Genevive Appell, *Lóczy: An Unusual Approach to Mothering*. Translated from *Lóczy Ou Le Maternage Insolite* by Jean Marie Clark; revised translation by Judit Falk (Budapest: Association Pikler-Loczy for Young Children, 2001).

Lorraine DeJong and Barbara Hansen Cottrell, "Designing Infant Child Care Programs to Meet the Needs of Children Born to Teenage Parents," *Young Children* 54(1), January 1999, pp. 37–45.

Lella Gandini and Carolyn Pope Edwards, eds., *Bambini: The Italian Approach to Infant/Toddler Care* (New York: Teachers College Press, 2001).

Magda Gerber, *Dear Parent: Caring for Infants with Respect* (Los Angeles: Resources for Infant Educarers, 1998).

Janet Gonzalez-Mena, "What Can an Orphanage Teach Us? Lessons from Budapest," *Young Children*, September 2004, pp. 27–30.

Alfie Kohn, "Five Reasons to Stop Saying 'Good Job,'" *Young Children* 56(5), September 2001, pp. 24–28.

Sandy Petersen, Katherine Bair, and Anita Sullivan, "Emotional Well-being and Mental Health Services: Lessons Learned by Early Head Start Region VIII Programs," *Zero to Three* 24(6), 2004, pp. 47–53.

Frances Rofrano, "I Care for You: A Reflection of Caring as Infant Curriculum," *Young Children* 57(1), January 2002, pp. 49–51.

Marilyn Segal, Wendy Masi, and Roni Leiderman, *In Time and With Love: Caring for Infants and Toddlers with Special Needs* (New York: New Market Press, 2001).

chapter 3

Caregiving as Curriculum

Focus Questions

After reading this chapter you should be able to answer the following questions:

1 How does caregiving build the relationships on which curriculum depends?

2 Curriculum involves planning for learning, and learning is connected to attachment, so what are some ways that programs can plan for attachment?

3 How can caregivers assess the long-term and immediate needs and development of infants and toddlers?

4 What are caregiving routines? Name six of them.

What Do You See?

Four toddlers are seated at a low table intently watching a caregiver who has several plastic cups in his hand. He turns to the child on his right and holds out two cups. "Do you want the green one or the blue one, Aiesha?" he asks, holding out first one and then the other. Aisha reaches for the blue one. The caregiver puts the other cup on a table behind him and brings a pitcher around in front of him.

"Now everyone has a cup," he says, looking at the expectant children. "Here's the juice—it's apple," he says, pouring a small amount of juice in a tiny pitcher. He hands it to Xian, who grabs the pitcher and pours with great excitement, missing his cup. The caregiver hands him a cloth. "Here's a cloth for the spill," he says calmly. Xian quickly swipes at the spill, then looks carefully at the juice left in the pitcher. With precise movement, he pours the small amount into his cup. He abandons the pitcher and concentrates then on the cup, with a satisfied look on his face.

"Your turn, Nicole," says the caregiver, refilling the pitcher and passing it to her. She takes the pitcher, pours some juice, then shoves the pitcher toward the next child, who receives it gratefully. The child next to her bangs his cup, yelling, "Me!"

"You want your juice, Yei Hoon," says the caregiver.

"No!" says Yei Hoon, emphatically.

"Cereal?" says the caregiver, reaching for a bowl with dry cereal in it.

"No!" repeats Yei Hoon, pointing to a box of raisins.

"Oh, you want raisins," says the caregiver.

"Raisins!" repeats Yei Hoon carefully. He receives them with delight and with a careful pincer movement involving thumb and forefinger, he picks up two raisins and puts them into his mouth. He sits contentedly chewing and sucking on the raisins without removing his fingers.

Keep this scene in mind as you read this chapter and begin to think about caregiving as curriculum. Later we will revisit this scene.

Thinking Again About Infant-Toddler Curriculum

NAEYC Program Standard 2
Curriculum

As stated earlier, curriculum at higher levels of education can focus on the mind alone, but that doesn't work for infants and toddlers. There is no way to separate intellectual needs from other needs at this beginning level. In Chapter 2, curriculum was explained as having a problem-solving focus. When you put that light on it, this chapter and the next one on play provide multiple opportunities for infants to learn to solve all kinds of problems. Infants become good problem-solvers when they have a trusting relationship. This chapter focuses on how that kind of relationship starts and grows from the interactions between adults and infants or toddlers that occur during caregiving routines such as diapering and feeding.

Like other curriculum approaches, we are presenting an activity-based approach; however the activities we see as most important are *not* the ones adults set up specifically for children's learning but instead are those that occur throughout the day, *every day*—the essential activities of daily living, or caregiving routines. So unlike most other books, when the word *activity* occurs here, it usually refers to caregiving routines. We also want to make it clear that the word *curriculum* doesn't apply to just any old approach to diapering, dressing, grooming, washing, or feeding, but rather to a consciously considered approach. That's what this chapter is about—how to take the approaches that turn everyday routines into curriculum. We are basing this approach to curriculum on Emmi Pikler's work in Hungary and what Magda Gerber and her Resources for Infant Educarers (RIE) Associates teach in the United States.

Let's look at the aspects of caregiving activities that promote learning and development. As explained in Chapter 1 the interactions are respectful, responsive, and reciprocal. Part of the skills caregivers need include ongoing observation and assessment so that the interactions are individually effective and promote a close, warm, sensitive relationship between the child and adult.

NAEYC Program Standard 1
Relationships

Planning for Attachment

One important component of the curriculum as it occurs during caregiving activities is **attachment**—a tie to a special person. Through sensitive caregiving interactions, attachment grows, especially when there is consistency and, over time, children come to know the person who provides the care. Development, learning, and attachment are vitally related. From attachment come feelings of trust and security. Lifelong learning and attitudes can be initiated on the diapering table while babies are being washed, dressed, and groomed, and during feeding times. These essential activities of daily living provide multiple sensory experiences, much pleasure and satisfaction, and an opportunity to learn social and physical skills—all of which form the foundation of the intellect. Interactions with consistent caregivers actually build structures in the brain that have long-lasting cognitive effects, supporting our position that caregiving is curriculum.

Young children need attachment to someone who, in turn, gives them a feeling that they are important—that they matter. Although most infants and toddlers in child care are attached to their parent(s), if they are to spend long hours away from them, attachment to caregivers is additionally beneficial. Both caregivers and children benefit from attachment because communication is enhanced and needs are understood. The caregiver is rewarded by the child's feeling for him or her, and the child gains a feeling of importance. Through attachment the child knows that he or she is being cared *about* as well as *for*.

Policies that Support Curriculum as Caregiving

Three policies need to be in place to make caregiving curriculum.[1]

- A primary caregiving system
- Consistency
- Continuity of care

Let's examine each of these more closely. Attachment is promoted by assigning each caregiver to a small number of infants or young toddlers in what is called a **primary-caregiver system.** The idea behind this is that if caregivers see three or four children as their own special charges, they can promote a stronger attachment than might happen if attachment were left to chance or if all the caregivers relate to the whole group without differentiation. When some people hear about a primary-caregiver system, they worry that the children will become too attached to the primary caregiver and then suffer when that person goes on vacation or is sick. These are legitimate concerns. That's why it's important to create a system of teams so that there is always a familiar adult present even if the primary caregiver is absent. In a smoothly working primary-caregiver system, caregivers interact with children other than their special charges.

Consistency of care is important to aim for. When change is carefully thought out and minimized, infants and toddlers learn that they can predict what will happen. Their feelings of powerlessness are minimized and a sense of security grows. Magda Gerber was clear that things should be done in the same way that the child is used to so the child isn't always thrown off balance by trying to adjust to something new all the time. In the United States where novelty is highly valued, adults may have problems going along with the idea of consistency.

The Pikler Institute has firm policies about predictability.[2] Babies are picked up in the same way by every caregiver. Their routines are carried out the same way every day. Young babies are fed in the same order so they come to know when it is their turn. Observers at the Pikler Institute are impressed at the degree of predictability they see. Having the same person there to relate to in ways that are predictable is a part of consistency. Also, the caregivers are trained not to show extreme high and low moods so the children don't get confused by getting extra exuberant hugs and kisses one day and nothing the next. In fact, Pikler was clear that caregivers should never promise more than they can deliver so the relationship the caregiver builds with the children is a special one. The relationship should be close, but it should be distant enough that the child can leave the Institute and become part of a family without being devastated by separation from the caregiver.

Continuity of care—that is, staying with one caregiver for several years—is lacking in programs where children are "moved up" whenever they reach another developmental level, leaving behind their old room and teacher and sometimes even their companions, depending on the policy. Some programs that enroll babies in the first three months, move them a number of times before their first birthday. Other programs follow a school model moving the children every year to a new classroom and teacher. A program that values continuity of care finds ways to keep the group together with the same adults and either adapt the environment or move into a new room when they outgrow the old one.

Assessment

NAEYC Program Standard 4
Assessment

Any curriculum depends on caregivers determining what children need, both as individuals and as a group. Chapter 2 talked about assessment in terms of observation, recordkeeping, and developmental profiles. Here we are looking at assessment in terms of determining what a child needs at any given time, which is the first step in performing caregiving tasks. Infants and toddlers can't always let you know what they need, so you have to learn to read signs. Attachment helps here as you get to know children well enough to understand their unique ways of communicating, as stated in Principle 3.

Reflect
How do you determine your own needs and get them met? Can you remember a time when you needed something that you could not get by yourself? How did you communicate this need? Were you direct about it? Was your message received? Did you get the results you wanted?

When you do pick up signs that a child or the group has a need, put what you perceive into words. If you aren't sure what the signs mean, ask out loud—in words—even to very young infants. Look, listen, and feel for the answer. If you are beginning to learn the child's system of communication, you may get your answer directly from the child. By taking this approach, you're beginning to set up a two-way communication pattern that will serve the child well for the rest of his or her life. Children (even the youngest) who are encouraged to express their needs and interests can become quite skilled at doing just that. But also be aware that expressing needs directly is not appropriate in all cultures, so be sensitive to what the parents want for their child.

Adults sometimes develop a singular approach to responding to signs a child needs something. "Oh, he's tired; he needs a nap," may be one caregiver's standard response. Another caregiver may wish to feed all cranky children. Or a caregiver may tune in to his or her own need. The caregiver who thinks the heat is down too low may say, "He's cold," in spite of the fact that the child is plenty warm to the touch. Children who are given food when they aren't hungry or are bundled up when they aren't cold may lose the ability to determine what they need, or they may learn to substitute one need for another. Certainly comforting with a bottle often works even if the child doesn't need food. That's is how the bottle can become a substitute for cuddling or attention. How many adults reach automatically for food when they have some other kind of need? This behavior can be learned in the early years.

In infant-toddler care it sometimes happens that an adult's or the group's needs or interests conflict with an individual child's needs or interests. A child must be awakened from a nap because it is time to go home, or a child must be fed early for some reason or must wait to be fed. At the Pikler Institute the infants are fed in a particular sequence that the children come to know well. Although they may protest when they have to wait, the children know they will be fed. They learn to trust that their turn will come, and they learn to predict. If things change all the time children are confused. When consistency is present, they know what will happen and they feel more empowered than when they can neither predict nor control.

A word about crying: crying is communication. When adults regard it in that way, they feel different about it than when they perceive it as an annoyance that they just want to go away. The hungry baby who is crying needs to be acknowledged, even if you can't meet her needs right away. She is communicating.

Children can cope with their individual needs being put on hold. They are **resilient**—that is, they can adapt to hardship or recover from it. However, it can do permanent harm if very young continually have to wait and have no way to predict when their turn will come. When program or adult needs and interests always take precedence over infant and toddler needs and interests, or when meeting needs is done on a haphazard basis, children may experience negative long-term effects.

Caregiving Routines

As you read through the next pages, keep in mind the principles presented in Chapter 1. They are an integrating theme in this section. For caregiving routines to become curriculum, they can't be done mechanically. Each time a caregiver interacts in ways that focus fully on the individual child while performing one of those essential activities of daily living, the time spent furthers connections. When caregivers manipulate the child's body but put their attention elsewhere, they lose the opportunity to let the child experience an intimate human interaction. It's the accumulation of intimacy during these numerous interactions that turns ordinary tasks into a relationship-based curriculum.

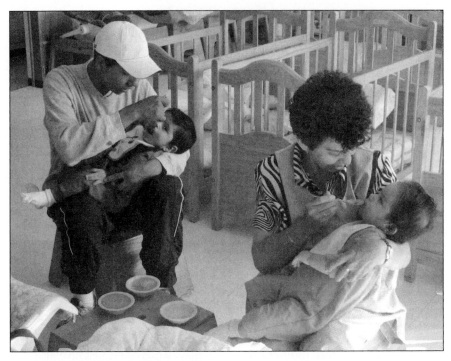

Feeding is a time that attachments are formed.

Feeding

Programs for infants and toddlers, in both centers and family child care, should make every provision possible for nursing mothers. Both mothers and infants benefit, even though it may be less convenient for caregivers. Help the mother feel welcome and provide a place for her and her infant to be quiet and comfortable.

Bottle-fed infants deserve the same kind of one-to-one attention and physical closeness that breast-fed infants receive. A well-organized center will find ways to release a caregiver to sit and feed an infant while holding him or her, without requiring that the caregiver jump up and down to take care of the needs of other children. In family child care this **release time** is harder to come by, but caregivers who make it a priority to hold each baby while feeding can find ways to work it out.

Imagine yourself as an infant with a bib around your neck.

Hear a familiar voice say to you, "Here's some applesauce for you." Look around and see a spoon, a hand, and beyond it a small dish of applesauce. Take time to really perceive all this. Feel the coziness as well as the anticipation. Hear the same voice say, "Are you ready?" See the spoon come up to your face. There is plenty of time for you to open your mouth for the bite. You feel the applesauce in your mouth. You taste it. You notice the texture and the temperature. You thoroughly explore this bite before you swallow. Some goes down your throat; some runs down your chin. You look up to find the familiar face. Seeing the face adds to your pleasure. You open your mouth again. You feel a gentle scraping on your chin and the next bite comes into your mouth. You explore it. You compare it to the first bite. You take your time and get the most out of this bite before you swallow it. When you swallow, you get an excited feeling in anticipation of the next bite. You look at the face again. You reach out, and your fingers touch something soft and smooth. All these feelings are present as you open your mouth for the next bite.

Compare your experience in the feeding scene with what Anne Morrow Lindbergh describes in her book *Gift from the Sea:*

> *A good relationship has a pattern like a dance and is built on some of the same rules. The partners do not need to hold on tightly, because they move confidently in the same pattern, intricate but gay and swift and free, like a country dance of Mozart's. To touch heavily would be to arrest the pattern and freeze the moment, to check the endlessly changing beauty of its unfolding . . . now arm in arm, now face to face, now back to back—it does not matter which. Because they know they are partners moving to the same rhythm, creating a pattern together visibly nourished by it.*
>
> *The joy of such a pattern is not only the joy of creating or the joy of participating, it is also the joy of living in the moment. Lightness of touch and living in the moment are intertwined. One can't dance well unless one is completely in time with the music, not leaning back to the last step or pressing forward to the next one, but poised directly on the present step as it comes.[3]*

Can you see how this quote relates to the feeding described previously? The key to effective caregiving is a good relationship.

Compare that first feeding to this one:

You feel yourself plopped into a high chair without a word. A strap is put around your middle, and you are left alone with an empty tray. You pound on the tray. It's cold and hard, as is the back of the chair. You feel impatient. It seems like forever that you are sitting there. You squirm and twist. Suddenly there is a spoon in between your lips forcing them open. You look toward the source of the spoon, at the same time tasting applesauce. You wiggle your tongue around, swallowing down the bite. The spoon again comes between your lips, and your teeth are forced open. You take another mouthful while looking into an expressionless face of a person who seems to have her mind somewhere else. You enjoy the taste and feeling of the applesauce as you push it around in your mouth and out between your teeth and down your chin. You feel metal scraping your chin harshly. More applesauce comes into your mouth. You are about to swallow this mouthful when the spoon arrives again. You take a second mouthful into the first, which you haven't swallowed yet. You work on swallowing while you feel scrape, scrape on your chin as the spoon gathers up what is running down. More applesauce arrives in your mouth. You swallow a little of the big load, and you get ready to swallow more. Before you can, the spoon finds its way in between your teeth again. Now your mouth is fuller than before. You sense a bit of urgency to get this down before the next load. You try to hurry, which only

Figure 3.1 Hints on Promoting Self-Help Skills at Meals

1. Use child-size utensils.

2. Provide finger food such as banana chunks (unless a family strongly disapproves).

3. Give only small amounts of food. It's better to let children ask for more than to discourage them with too large a portion. Also, it's easier to clean up a small amount.

4. Allow children to explore and experiment with the food (unless a family strongly disapproves), but be aware of your own limits. End the meal before you become uncomfortable. A tension-free setting promotes good digestion.

slows you down. More applesauce squishes out and runs down your chin. You feel the spoon—scrape, scrape, scrape—and more applesauce comes into your mouth. Hold on to that feeling now and stop imagining.

Feeding time should be quality time. One reason is that, during feeding, attachments are formed between caregivers and the children they feed. For this reason, the same caregiver should feed the same babies daily, if possible.

When infants begin to feed themselves, the mess level rises dramatically. Most caregivers are willing to put up with the mess because they value independence. They want children in their care to learn **self-help skills.** Accepted practice in this country is to let or even encourage children to take over their own feeding as soon as they are able. Usually when a baby grabs the spoon, he or she is given one and allowed to try getting it to the mouth.

Figure 3.1 gives some ideas on how to help children become self-feeders.

Eating is an emotional process. The adults bring to a feeding situation feelings, ideas, and traditions that have nothing to do with the immediate experience but that come from their own personal history and culture. People have strong feelings about what should or should not go on at the table. For some, the taboos about what cannot be done are deeply ingrained and very important. The way they eat seems to define who they are. For others, the resentment of the taboos is equally strong. The point is that eating is connected with strong feelings, and these feelings affect the way an adult approaches or reacts to children eating.

It is also important to recognize that not all cultures view early independence, self-feeding, and big messes in the same way. Although you may not wish to do it yourself, you should respect the fact that a parent may continue spoon-feeding a child long past the age you approve of.

Understanding each child's signals, giving some choices, defining limits clearly, reacting honestly, and interacting responsively are all keys to pleasant feeding experiences. Ending a meal for children when their hunger has been satisfied is important. Children cannot be expected to restrain from playing with their food if they are full and it is still in front of them.

Review the scene at the beginning of this chapter and reflect on how it illustrates the principles on which this book is based and the themes of this chapter. The caregiver was respectful, responsive, and reciprocal. The effect was a

NAEYC Program Standard 1
Relationships

NAEYC Program Standard 3
Teaching

VIDEO OBSERVATION 3

Children Feeding Themselves

See the Video Observation for Chapter 3 to view a mealtime and the interaction between an adult and a child.

Questions

- What about this scene makes eating "curriculum"?
- What is this child gaining from this experience besides food?
- What can you tell about the philosophy of this program from watching this scene?

To view this clip, go to www.mhhe.com/itc7e. Click on Student Edition, select Chapter 3, and click on Video Observation.

pleasant atmosphere at the table. The caregiver worked to understand each child's signals and responded by giving words to their wishes. He gave them some choices without setting out a whole smorgasbord. He set some limits.

Perhaps you have not seen toddlers eating at a low table instead of in high chairs. Seating them together provides a more social experience than seating them high up, side by side, in rows. They have more choice about leaving when finished. They don't have to wait for an adult to take them down. If independence is a value, this simple technique goes a long way toward promoting it.

Although the scene at the beginning was not from the Pikler Institute in Budapest, there are some similarities, because there toddlers eat together at low tables. What this scene did not show is what happens when a child isn't able to eat at the table within the limits at the Pikler Institute. There, they say the child simply isn't ready, so they take the child back to an earlier stage and spoon-feed him ahead of the others. It's not a punishment, but merely recognition that the child needs more adult help. At the Pikler Institute they never push or urge a child forward. Readiness is not a worry but a fact. The caregiver is there to meet the child's need for dependence during caregiving routines for as long as it lasts. You might think with this policy, children would remain helpless for a long time; however, children have strong urges for independence. That fact shows at the Pikler Institute as children learn to feed and dress themselves surprisingly well at a younger age than many children in the United States, where early independence is often emphasized.

Of course, there is more to feeding infants and toddlers than just making sure the food gets into their mouths. Care and attention need to go into insuring sanitation is part of the picture. Food preparation, feeding, food storage, and clean up should all be in accordance with local and national health standards. The procedures should be posted and monitored. Feeding and diapering should be kept entirely separate, and different sinks should be used for each. Some dangerous mistakes to avoid include:

- Heating bottles or jars of baby food in microwave ovens, because they can have hot spots that burn the baby's mouth.
- Keeping partially used bottles of breast milk or formula and serving them later, because they can be contaminated and unhealthy.
- Feeding commercial baby food out of the jar and putting the jar back in the refrigerator, because again, contamination can be a problem.

What about starting solid foods? Parents should be the guide about when to start solid foods and what foods to start with. Although for many years and in many cultures, some parents started solid food before four months, the standard recommendation now is to start solids no sooner than four to six months. Traditional starter foods are rice or barley cereals that are made especially for babies and mixed with formula or breast milk. Foods should be introduced one at a time with only a taste to begin with; the amount should be increased gradually. Foods to avoid in the first six months because they may produce allergic reactions are wheat cereals, white flour (including bread), eggs, citrus fruits. Nuts and peanut butter should be avoided for much longer, not only because of allergies but because they can be a choking hazard. Other foods to avoid up through the toddler years are hotdog rounds, marshmallows, popcorn, grapes, and anything else that might lodge in the throat.

Nutrition as it relates to obesity has become a problem as the numbers of obese children increase. According to the *Journal of the American Dietetic Association*, the rate of obese Americans has doubled since the mid-1980s.[4] The problem starts in infancy, and you'll know why when you see what else the research, called "Feeding Infants and Toddlers Study," reported in this journal says. Children between one and two years old take in 30 percent more calories than they need and many of these calories come from French fries, pizza, candy, and soda. Up to one-third of the children ate no fruit or vegetables, and of those who did eat a vegetable, it often was French fries. In fact 9 percent of the children studied who were between 9 and 11 months old ate French fries at least once a day, and 20 percent of those 19 months to 2 years old ate fries daily.

Diapering

Look at the following diapering scene. Notice how the adult is in perfect tune with the baby.

> The adult leans over the baby on the diapering counter. The two are face-to-face, and the adult has the baby's full attention as she talks to him about changing his diaper. The baby isn't lying sideways so he has to turn his head to see the adult's face; the counter is built so that he lies with his feet at her belly. The adult waits now for the tension to leave his muscles before she begins. She is gently directive as well as responsive. She tells him to do something and waits for a facial or body response before continuing. She talks to him each step of the way, always keeping him focused on the task itself and their interaction around it. The way she is doing the diapering is building the relationship between them. When she's finished, she holds out her arms and says, "I'm going to pick you up now." The baby responds with a slight forward thrusting of his head and body in anticipation and comes willingly into her arms with a little smile on his face.[5]

This diapering scene was based on an observation by one of the authors at the Pikler Institute in Budapest. Although this diapering went smoothly, they don't always, even at the Pikler Institute. Children go through periods of being uncooperative. It is important that they do so, even though it is hard on the care-givers. Resisting is a sign of growth; by resisting, children assert their individuality and independence. Even so, the principles are still the same—try to engage the baby and get him to cooperate. Don't give up trying to involve him in the task. Acknowledge his feelings and verbalize them for him. This is the time when many caregivers go for the distraction technique–they find something entertaining to keep the baby's mind off what is happening to him. Though it may be temping, we advise not going that route. One of the great dangers of the early years is teaching babies that they need to be entertained. Entertainment is addictive and once babies get into this habit, breaking it is difficult. Equally important is the warning that when diapering is done without the baby's full awareness and participation, it no longer is an intimate human experience that furthers relationships. It leaves the realm of curriculum.

Sanitation procedures are also important for diapering to prevent the spread of disease. These procedures should be in accordance with local regulations and health requirements, which should be posted in the diapering area for all to see. The diapering area must be away from food preparation and must be used specifically for diapering, not for other things as well. The following diapering procedure has been borrowed from WestEd's *Program for Infant-Toddler Caregivers Guide to Routines* (2nd ed.):

NAEYC Program Standard 5
Health

- Check to be sure the diapering area has been sanitized since the last diapering. If not, discard used paper, spray with a bleach solution, and put clean paper down.
- Remove the used diaper and dispose of it in a covered container.

- Wipe the child with a clean, moist cloth or baby wipe. Wipe girls from front to back to prevent urinary and vaginal infections. Dispose of the used cloth or the wipe in the container provided. If gloves are used, remove and discard them. To prevent the spread of germs, remove gloves after completing the soiled part of the diapering and before starting the clean part.
- Put a clean diaper and clean clothes on the child.
- Wash the child's hands under running water. Babies often touch their bottoms and the diaper-changing station, which are loaded with germs. Washing their hands after diapering helps prevent the spread of germs from the diapering procedure, and it begins to teach them the lifelong hygiene habit of washing their hands after going to the bathroom. Return the child to the play area.
- Clean and sanitize the diapering area by discarding used paper in the container provided, spraying the area with a bleach solution, wiping lightly with a paper towel to spread the bleach solution around, and discarding the paper towel. Put down a clean paper when the bleach disinfectant has air dried.
- Wash your hands thoroughly.

Although program policy or local regulations may require gloves, they are not necessary for every diapering. If the child has diarrhea or blood in the stool or if caregivers have open sores on their hands, then gloves are required.

Toilet Training and Toilet Learning

What used to be called **toilet training** is now called **toilet learning** by those who use a readiness approach and involve the child in the process. At the Pikler Institute it is called sphincter control—that is, control of the muscles specifically related to elimination. The ideas at the Pikler Institute relate more to toilet learning than to toilet training because they see it as a developmental process rather than a type of training. In any case, this way of looking at moving from diapers to toilet is regarded as a natural progress of the partnership involved in diapering. When children are around others in child care situations, they often start to use the toilet when they are old enough to want to imitate the other children they see who are out of diapers.

Here are some hints for making toilet learning easier.

1. Help children feel physically secure by providing potties (if licensing allows) or very low toilets, if possible. The easier it is for children to get on and off the toilet by themselves, the more independence is promoted.
2. If appropriate, ask parents to dress children in loose, simple clothing they can remove themselves (elastic waistbands rather than overalls, for example.)
3. Be gentle and understanding about accidents.
4. Avoid power struggles. You can't win them, and children can be left with long-lasting effects if toilet learning has been a highly emotional affair.

Most programs try to cooperate with the family when it comes to toileting. In many programs the policy is not to initiate toileting until the parent suggests it; then the staff is assured that the child will find consistency at home and in the program. Consistency may be more difficult if the parent is from a culture that believes in toilet training and sees it as a first-year task. Although staff may not be willing to try to "catch" children and put them on the potty at a young age, it is important to respect a different view. Those educated as caregivers in the United States and other Western countries may be concerned that toilet training is a harmful approach, especially when undertaken before the third year. It's important to understand that this is not a world-wide view. Around the world, and also in the United States, some families use the toilet training approach and their children do not show harmful effects. Toilet training is quite different from the toilet learning or sphincter control approach. We won't explain it here, but we want to acknowledge that differences exist. We urge caregivers to respect diversity in perceptions, timing, and styles of toileting.

Washing, Bathing, and Grooming

Most programs leave bathing up to parents except under very special circumstances. Some parents become insulted if their children are sent home cleaner than they arrived. Cleanliness can be a great point of conflict between parents and caregivers if they have different standards. Parents may be angry if a child with hard-to-wash hair comes home with a head full of sand. Cultural issues can give people different perspectives on the subject of cleanliness, so respect ideas that differ from your own.

Hand washing before meals is not as touchy an issue as bathing. Hand washing is popular with most children and can even be the highlight of the day for some toddlers. Short attention spans lengthen appreciably when toddlers are sent off to wash. Hand washing can be the most pleasant self-help skill to learn if low sinks are available and toddlers are allowed to use them at their leisure. In fact, hand washing can become a major activity because toddlers greatly enjoy the sensory properties of soap and water.

NAEYC Program Standard 4
Health

Grooming can be another touchy subject. How groomed children should look during the day and when the families arrive to pick them up is a matter of opinion. One family arrives to pick up their toddler whose hair is uncombed and whose clothes provide a record of everything she got into that day. The family is delighted to see that she had a busy day. The same family may be unhappy that their baby isn't clean and combed. They regard the baby in a different light. Another family whose daughter is in the same condition as the first toddler is horrified that she's not properly groomed. They are less upset about their son, whose clothes are even more filled with spots, spills, fingerpaint and dirt than the daughter's. Hair can be a big issue as mentioned previously. Most caregivers don't have the extensive knowledge needed to understand the care of all kinds of hair. Some caregivers don't care about hairdos, and some children care even less. Some of those caregivers are critical of parents who spend a good deal of time creating elaborate hairdos on their toddlers. When thinking about honoring diversity, include differing views on hair in your thinking!

⚐ Differing Needs and Perspectives

Children who come to the program with medical issues, disabilities, or other physical challenges must be accommodated during caregiving routines. Their needs may differ from those of the other children. Specialized instructions from parents or outside experts may be necessary. For example, asthma treatments may be required. Or the child may have a feeding tube that needs specialized care. Parents or specialists may have information about how to put children into positions that allow them the most freedom of movement. It's important that caregivers have that information. By experimenting, caregivers may discover what works best on their own, but that should be in addition to what the parents and specialists already know. For example, some infants are hypersensitive to touch and cry when picked up. That crying may be reduced if the baby is placed on a pillow and picked up that way. But, don't ever put babies down by themselves on a pillow, because it puts them at risk for suffocating.

It is beyond the scope of this book (or any book) to tell you everything you need to know about every child who might come into infant-toddler care with medical issues or disabilities. What you do need to know is that there are resources for finding out. Check out books in the library. They may help. The first resource is the child's family. They may well be connected to specialists who also can help you understand the condition and what is needed. And certainly, as with all children, you can look to the individual child to teach you about himself or herself. Careful observation will help you understand the messages the child gives. Look for signs of discomfort and notice what distresses the child. Find ways to make the child more comfortable and ease the distress. *Remember principle 3: Learn each child's unique ways of communicating (cries, words, movements, gestures, facial expression, body positions), and teach yours.* Even children with no words at all have ways to let you know what they need. You just have to learn to read their signals. Don't underestimate children's ability to communicate even though their verbal language skills may be nonexistent or minimal.

Paying close attention to the baby sometimes takes so much energy that caregivers don't notice the signals they receive from families. It's possible that the family's ideas about what should be happening with their child are different from the caregiver's or the program policies. Cultural practices related to caregiving routines may not be the same as what the caregivers are seeing. Take feeding, for example. What to feed and how are cultural matters. When to start solid foods may seem cut and dried, based on the latest research, but cultural and family traditions may not go by the research. Besides, research changes over time. Take sleeping, for example. Generation after generation of parents in this country were told by their pediatricians to put their babies to sleep on their stomachs. Since the 1990s, however, pediatricians have given the opposite advice—that

NAEYC Program Standard 4
Assessment

babies should sleep on their backs. The reason is to reduce the risk of sudden infant death syndrome (SIDS), or crib death. Times change.

One of the strong messages in this book is to encourage self-help skills. The reason for this message is the sometimes unspoken goal of creating an independent individual. Not all parents are as interested in their children becoming independent individuals as they are for them to feel strong, lasting family ties. Caregivers must respect what families want for their children and honor diversity. You'll see that as a continuing theme throughout this book. We can't tell you what to do when you run into a cultural bump except to talk it over. When caregivers and families are in close communication, they can work out their differences in ways that are good for children, families, and caregivers. Each situation has a unique solution, so we can't just list them here for you. Human relations are complex matters, and human relations are what we are talking about.

Dressing

Caregivers can promote autonomy by setting up tasks in such a way that the child makes maximum contributions.[6] You can easily see examples of this principle in dressing activities. For instance, when taking off the socks or booties of even a very young baby, you can pull them half off and ask the child to finish the job. It takes little coordination when the task is set up like this. Even young babies get real pleasure and satisfaction from helping out. The idea is to simplify the task just the right amount so that the child gets practice in the dressing and undressing process. At first it takes longer to work cooperatively, but as child and caregiver come to see themselves as a team, the earlier patience pays off. By toddlerhood, children who were encouraged to help dress and undress themselves have become proficient and need very little help except with such things as buttons and starting zippers.

Reflect

What do you know about cultural differences in caregiving routines? How does what you know differ from what's shown in this chapter? What would you do if you were told to "follow the book" and you didn't believe in it? What would you do if a parent's beliefs about carrying out a particular routine differed from yours?

The Principles in Action

Principle 1 Involve infants and toddlers in things that concern them. Don't work around them or distract them to get the job done faster.

The caregiver is trying to dress Nicky, who has cerebral palsy. Since this baby is new to this caregiver, the caregiver still has to learn not only about cerebral palsy, but also about Nicky as an individual. The caregiver always tries to involve Nicky in the dressing, but it's hard because muscle control is a challenge for him. Furthermore, the caregiver is trying to put a one-piece stretch pajama outfit on him and it's a little tight. She starts with a foot and the toes curl. It's hard to fit them into the foot of the pajamas. She wants to get Nicky to relax but doesn't know how to help him. When she finally gets one foot in, she picks up one leg; the other one comes too in a scissoring motion. And then his ankle goes into a spasm. She talks to Nicky but is getting more and more frustrated. She finally gives up and goes and gets a loose-fitting two-piece outfit that goes on much easier. She's happy that she was able to adapt to this situation and vows to talk to the mother about what she can do to make it easier on her and Nicky.

1. What would you have done if you were the caregiver?
2. Are there some other devices that would make dressing this baby easier?
3. Could the caregiver learn about some strategies to use in dressing this baby?
4. Did principle 1 work here, or is this a case in which it didn't work?

Notice in the Principles in Action scene how the caregiver tried to involve the baby but had a hard time because, although the baby might have been trying to cooperate, he couldn't control his muscles. Sometimes a caregiver needs more knowledge than he or she has. This scene is an example of that situation.

Here is a scene that shows how it would be if the caregiver did not aim for teamwork.

Imagine yourself a young toddler. You are about to be taken outside for a walk. Without anything being said to you, you feel your arm being grabbed. You're thrown off balance. Then you find yourself being hauled over to a coat rack. Your arm is held tight and then thrust into a sleeve. Your thumb gets stuck and stretches back as the sleeve comes up your arm. Then you feel yourself being swung around. You feel annoyed. When the other sleeve comes up your other arm, you stick your thumb out on purpose. Then you become all floppy. You feel a tighter grip on you, and some tension transfers from the hands holding you. You become even floppier. Finally a face comes down near yours, but the eyes look only at the zipper, which is resisting getting on the track. You feel the hands struggle with the piece of metal; then suddenly the zipper moves upward. It stops only when it touches your neck and feels cold, uncomfortable, and tight. The face disappears, and you're left standing alone while the child next to you is readied in the same impersonal way.

Not a very enjoyable experience, was it? This child was being treated more like an object than a person.

Reflect

Can you remember a time in your own life when you were treated as an object? If you can, then you know why it is important not to treat a child (of any age) that way.

Napping

It is important that infants be allowed to rest according to their individual needs rather than according to someone else's schedule. Infants' sleep patterns change—sometimes from day to day as well as over a period of time. No one napping schedule will fit all babies in a program, and each baby's personal schedule changes from time to time.

Not all babies express their need for rest in the same way. Experienced, sensitive caregivers learn to read each child's signals, which may range from slowing down and yawning to increased activity and low frustration threshold.

Parents are the best source of information about their baby's sleep patterns and needs. Experienced caregivers are aware how useful it is to know that the baby woke up extra early that morning or got less sleep than usual over the weekend. They understand fussy behavior in a different light if they know the reason for it.

Figure 3.2 Reducing the Risk of Sudden Infant Death Syndrome (SIDS)

- Always place the baby on its back to sleep, even for naps.

- Place the baby on a firm mattress, such as in a safety-approved crib.

- Remove soft, fluffy bedding and stuffed toys from the baby's sleep area.

- Make sure the baby's head and face remain uncovered during sleep.

- Do not allow smoking around the baby.

- Do not let the baby get too warm during sleep.

Source: The Back to Sleep Campaign, 31 Center Drive, Room 2A32, Bethesda MD 20892-2425. 1-800-505-CRIB

Babies should be put down for a nap in the way most familiar to them. However, it's also important that every caregiver know the results of recent research regarding the relationship between sleeping position and SIDS. SIDS is the label given to unexplained deaths, usually, but not always, occurring when a baby is sleeping. SIDS is not the same as smothering, choking, or dying from a disease. Infant deaths are labeled SIDS only when no cause can be found. For years, North American pediatricians have told parents and caregivers to put babies to sleep on their stomachs. Research now shows that *back sleeping* is associated with lower risk of SIDS. The evidence is compelling.[7] Figure 3.2 shows some concrete steps to take to reduce the risk of babies dying of SIDS.

Each baby should have a personal crib that is located in the same spot every day. That kind of consistency and security may help the baby feel at home faster. Decisions about when to put a baby in the crib and how long to leave him or her there depend on the adult's perception of the particular child's needs. Some children need to be confined for some time before they can fall asleep, even when they are very tired. They may play or cry before sleeping. Other children fall asleep immediately. The waking up period also takes some adult judgment. Does the child wake up energetic, active, and ready to play, or is there a long transition period between sleeping and waking during which the child may need to remain in the crib? Reading a young child's signals about rest needs is not always easy. Again, the parent is a good source of information. Find out what kind of self-calming behaviors a child has and encourage them. Some children stroke a blanket; others twist their hair. The most common self-calming behavior is thumb sucking. Ask how the child naps at home. Can you use some of the same devices or rituals the parent uses? Perhaps a favorite toy or blanket provides comfort.

Once again, cultural factors may enter into attitudes about sleeping. Some cultures see being alone in a dark room as the way to promote independence. Others feel that babies should not sleep alone. You may not agree with an attitude that is different from your own, but be sure to respect it. If you can't do what the parent wants, talk about it with him or her. Negotiate, discuss, and exchange viewpoints. Don't just ignore a parent's wishes and do what you think is best.

As children move through toddlerhood and nap only once a day, they can learn to rest according to a group schedule. However, individual needs are still important, and provision should be made for the toddler who needs a quiet time earlier in the day, if not an actual nap.

Toddlers who feel nervous, scared, or distrustful may have sleep problems that consistency would help alleviate. A favorite toy or blanket may also provide needed security. Sometimes a caregiver can do nothing at the moment to promote security but must acknowledge the child's insecure feelings and wait until he or she eventually learns that it's a safe place. In some programs, the children who need it have a back rub to help them go to sleep. Here are some further hints about how to help toddlers get to sleep.

1. Provide visual privacy for those children who need it. Some toddlers are too stimulated by being near another child to go to sleep.
2. Provide a quiet, peaceful atmosphere. Some programs use soft music to help. Start winding down before nap time.
3. Make sure all children get plenty of fresh air and exercise. Being tired is the best motivator for napping.
4. Don't let children get overtired. Some children have a hard time settling down to sleep when they are exhausted.

Caregiver Lynne sees the importance of creating a ritual around going to sleep. The toddlers she cares for are old enough to have an established group nap time. So after lunch she starts the ritual of first transforming the room so that it suggests sleeping instead of play. The toys are hidden away, lights are turned down, windows shaded, and there's a quiet story time for children who settle down that way. The atmosphere is subdued and hushed so that children feel the transition. As stimulation is lowered and the environment gives the message about what's expected, the children's activity level goes down and rest comes easier than when the transition is abrupt and children don't ease in to the nap time.

If adults regard caregiving tasks as vital learning experiences, they are more likely to approach them with patience and attention. In group care, even when the adult-child ratio is good, an infant's main opportunity to enjoy a long period of one-to-one interaction is during caregiving times like feeding, diapering, and dressing. If those times are used well, babies require far less adult attention during the other periods of their day. Babies can go about their play (interacting with the environment and with the other babies) with no more than general supervision from an adult who may be watching a number of babies.

As toddlers develop self-help skills, this built-in one-to-one time disappears. Therefore, caregivers must provide it in some other way, even to the oldest toddlers. The fact that required ratios of adults to children may change when the children are about two adds to the difficulty of giving the kind of individual attention each child needs. Some get it by being charming and appealing to adults. Others get it by exhibiting unacceptable behaviors. Some don't get it at all. One way to ensure that all children are getting individual attention, once the caregiving tasks are no longer such a focus during the child-care day, is to keep brief anecdotal records. If during nap time you write a single sentence about each child in your care that day, you'll soon see the patterns. You'll see that some children stand out because of their behaviors. Some children are practically invisible, and it's hard to think of anything to write about these youngsters. Once you see these patterns, you can make better conscious decisions about how to make sure that all children get individual attention each day.

When infants and toddlers are treated with respect and caregiving is done with a teamwork approach, relationships grow—relationships that help children learn about themselves and the world. They come to anticipate what will happen to them and realize the world has some predictability. They learn they have some power to influence the world and the people in it. They begin to make sense out of life. When used to their fullest, these times can become focuses in children's days— something they look forward to—their chance to "dance" with their partner!

Appropriate Practice

Overview of Development

According to the National Association for the Education of Young Children, the uniqueness of each young baby demands that caregivers learn babies' rhythms, when they eat, how they want to be held for feeding or comforting, and when they sleep. Caregivers' abilities to read babies' signals about needs and to respond appropriately help young babies develop a feeling of security. This same sensitivity is needed as young babies grow into mobile ones and become explorers. The exploration doesn't stop during caregiving routines, so it is up to caregivers to make the best of the child who is trying to touch everything while struggling to get off the diapering counter. Toddlers are concerned about who they are and who is in charge and continually test to find out. Independence and control are primary issues, and these can emerge during caregiving routines.

Source: J. Ronald Lally, Abbey Griffin, Emily Fenichel, Marilyn Segal, Eleanor Szanton, and Bernice Weissbourd, "Development in the First Three Years of Life," in *Developmentally Appropriate Practice in Early Childhood Programs*, rev. ed. (Washington, D.C.: National Association for the Education of Young Children, 1997), pp. 55–69.

Developmentally Appropriate Practice

The following are sample practices that link caregiving as curriculum to the statement above:

- Adults adjust to infants' individual feeding and sleeping schedules. Infants' food preferences and eating styles are respected.
- The infant sleeping area is separate from active play and eating areas. Babies have their own cribs and sheets brought from home. Family members bring special comforting objects to personalize their baby's crib. Infants' names are used to label every personal item.
- Infants have their own diapering supplies and extra clothes within reach of the changing table.
- Adults respect children's schedules with regard to eating and sleeping. Toddlers are provided snacks more frequently and in smaller portions than older children are. Liquids are provided frequently.
- Adults work cooperatively with families in encouraging children to learn to use the toilet. When toddlers reach an age when they feel confident and unafraid to sit on a toilet seat, caregivers invite them to use the toilet, help them as needed, provide manageable clothing, and positively reinforce them. The toilet, with a step stool, is in a well-lit, inviting, relatively private space. Children are taken to the toilet frequently and regularly in response to their own biological needs.
- Caregivers plan a transition into naptime with a predictable sequence of events. They choose a

(continued)

Appropriate Practice (continued)

quiet activity, such as reading a story. Toddlers get their own stuffed toys or blankets and go to their cots; soft music or a story tape may be played for toddlers who are still awake.

- Teachers work in partnership with parents, communicating daily to build mutual understanding and trust and to ensure the welfare and optimal development of the child. Caregivers listen carefully to what parents say about their children, seek to understand parents' goals and preferences, and are respectful of cultural and family differences.

Source: S. Bredekamp and C. Copple, eds., *Developmentally Appropriate Practice in Early Childhood Programs*, rev. ed. (Washington, D.C.: National Association for the Education of Young Children, 1997).

Individually Appropriate Practice

- Toilet training may vary greatly depending on children's physical and mental capabilities. Whenever it starts and how ever long it lasts, harshness should be avoided.
- Some children need more attention to feeding than others. Careful positioning for children old enough to feed themselves can make a big difference if those children are to use their hands capably. If they tend to slip in the chair, using nonskid cloth on the seat can help. Food texture can be an issue for some children with neurological involvement. Such procedures as massaging the throat to help swallowing or using a cloth or toothbrush to "wake up the mouth" can facilitate muscle control.

Culturally Appropriate Practice

Not all families value independence and individuality in the same way, and many have a different set of priorities for their children. Families whose goal is to downplay independence in order to help children see themselves first and foremost as members of the family or of the group in general may have a different approach to caregiving routines. Spoon-feeding children beyond toddlerhood is common practice among some cultures. Toilet training, on the other hand, may start in the first year of life. Both practices stress interdependence over independence. These practices may startle caregivers who have grown up in families where such things are frowned on. Remember that developmentally appropriate practice mandates that professionals work in partnership with parents to build mutual understanding and trust. The goal is to ensure the welfare and optimal development of the child. Chapter 13 looks at issues of identity development, which ties in to this issue of different ideas about caregiving practices.

Appropriate Practice in Action

Look back on the Principles in Action scene on page 61 and reconsider your answers. After reading this chapter would you answer any of the questions differently? Now analyze that scene in terms of the information in the last bullet in the "Developmentally Appropriate Practice" section of the Appropriate Practice box.

- What do you think was this caregiver's attitude about a partnership with the parents? Do you think she plans to learn something from them?
- What do you know about positioning a child with cerebral palsy so he has more control over his muscles? How could you learn more?

Now look at the "Culturally Appropriate Practice" section of the Appropriate Practice box.

- Was the caregiver stressing self-help skills?
- If this caregiver's major goal is to encourage self-help skills in Nicky, what if the mother has a different idea about what he needs? How would the caregiver find out? If the two have different goals, what should they do?
- What are your ideas and feelings about downplaying independence in children with the challenges Nicky has, even if encouraging independence is culturally inappropriate?

Summary

Infant-toddler curriculum means planning for learning, which includes:

- Planning for attachment
- Putting in place policies that support caregiving as curriculum
- Determining what children need

Caregiving routines are times when the caregiver pays close attention to each child and include such essential activities of daily living as:

- Feeding
- Diapering
- Toilet training and learning
- Washing, bathing, and grooming
- Dressing
- Napping

Online Resources

Go to the Online Learning Center at **www.mhhe.com/itc7e** to access the student study guide that includes quizzes, practice with key terms, and a review of chapter content; links to websites related to the chapter; and additional resources.

Key Terms

attachment 48
continuity of care 50
primary-caregiver system 49

release time 52
resilient 51
self-help skills 54

toilet learning 58
toilet training 58

Thought/Activity Questions

1. What does attachment have to do with caregiving as curriculum?
2. What are some ways that programs promote attachment?
3. Does attachment usually happen more easily in family child care homes? Why or why not?
4. What caregiving routines does a caregiver perform throughout the day, and what is an example of how to make them into curriculum?
5. What do you know about cultural differences in caregiving routines? How does what you know differ from what's shown in this chapter? What would you do if you were told to "follow the book" and you didn't believe in it? What would you do if a parent's beliefs about carrying out a particular routine differed from yours?

For Further Reading

Doris Bergen, R. Reid, and Louis Torelli, *Educating and Caring for Very Young Children: The Infant/Toddler Curriculum* (New York: Teachers College Press, 2001).
Jennifer Bernhardt, "A Primary Caregiving System for Infants and Toddlers: Best for Everyone Involved," *Young Children*, 55(2), March 2000, pp. 74–80.
Perry M. Butterfield, "Child Care Is Rich in Routines," *Zero to Three* 22(4), February/March 2002, pp. 29–32.

Ruth E. Cook, Annette Tessier, and M. Diane Klein, *Adapting Early Childhood Curricula for Children in Inclusive Settings*, 5th ed. (Columbus, Ohio: Merrill, 2000).

Miriam David and Genevive Appell, *Lóczy: An Unusual Approach To Mothering*. Translated from *Lóczy Ou Le Maternage Insolite* by Jean Marie Clark; revised translation by Judit Falk (Budapest: Association Pikler-Loczy for Young Children, 2001).

Magda Gerber, "RIE Principles and Practices," in *Authentic Relationships in Group Care for Infants and Toddlers: Resources for Infant Educarers (RIE) Principles into Practice*, edited by S. Petrie and S. Owen (London and Philadelphia: Jessica Kingsley Publishers, 2005), pp. 35–49.

Magda Gerber and Allison Johnson, *Your Self-Confident Baby* (New York: John Wiley & Sons, 1998).

Janet Gonzalez-Mena, *Diversity in Early Care and Education* (New York: McGraw-Hill, 2004).

Janet Gonzalez-Mena, *Infant-Toddler Caregiving: A Guide to Routines* (Sacramento, Calif.: Far West Laboratory and California Department of Education, 2000).

Janet Gonzalez-Mena and Navaz Bhavnagri, "Diversity and Infant/Toddler Caregiving," *Young Children* 55(5), September 2000, pp. 31–35.

Barbara Kaiser and Judy S. Rasminsky, "Opening the Culture Door," *Young Children* 58(4) July 2003, pp. 53–56.

Mary Martini, "How Mothers in Four American Cultural Groups Shape Infant Learning During Mealtimes," *Zero to Three* 22(4), February/March 2002, pp. 14–20.

Marion O'Brien, *Inclusive Child Care for Infants and Toddlers: Meeting Individual and Special Needs* (Baltimore: Brookes, 1997).

Stephanie Petrie, "The Work of Emmi Pikler and Magda Gerber," in *Authentic Relationships in Group Care for Infants and Toddlers: Resources for Infant Educarers (RIE) Principles into Practice*, edited by S. Petrie and S. Owen (London and Philadelphia: Jessica Kingsley Publishers, 2005), pp. 17–34.

Carol Brunson Phillips and Renatta M. Cooper, "Cultural Dimensions of Feeding Relationships," *Zero to Three* 7(5), June 1992, pp. 10–13.

Frances Rofrano, "A Reflection on Caring as Infant Curriculum," *Young Children* 57(1), January 2002, pp. 49–51.

Marilyn Segal, Wendy Masi, and Roni Leiderman, *In Time and With Love: Caring for Infants and Toddlers with Special Needs*, 2nd ed. (New York: New Market Press, 2001).

chapter 4

Play as Curriculum

Focus Questions

After reading this chapter you should be able to answer the following questions:

1 What are the four adult roles this chapter discusses as important for facilitating the play of infants and toddlers?

2 What is a primary consideration when setting up an environment for play and why is it important?

3 Why should you step back and observe after encouraging interactions?

4 What are five environmental factors that influence play in infant-toddler care and education program?

5 How is a *happening* different from an *activity*?

What Do You See?

Tyler is on the floor with a simple wooden puzzle on one side of him and plastic nesting cups on the other. Next to him is Kevin who reaches over and removes two of the puzzle pieces. Tyler picks up the puzzle board and drops it. The pieces clatter together when they hit the rug, which makes Tyler smile. Kevin looks at the puzzle and then at Tyler. Tyler takes the puzzle piece Kevin has in his hand. Kevin looks surprised. Then Tyler picks up another piece off the floor and bangs the two pieces together. He drops both pieces and Kevin picks them up. Tyler picks up the plastic nesting cups and walks over to a low platform, which he steps up on. He raises his arms in the air, then he quickly sits down and begins taking the nesting cups out. First he takes out the small one; he taps it on the wooden floor of the platform and cocks his head to listen to the noise. His fingers are working on the second one—feeling the shape, grasping the edge—and now it's out. He taps this one on the floor too before laying it down next to the first one. One by one he takes out the cups and taps each. When he gets to the last one, he lays it at the end of the row and looks satisfied. Then he puts them back together again as slowly and carefully as he took them out.

What you saw in the opening scene may not have looked like much to you. The way infants and toddlers play isn't the same as the way older children play. It takes an understanding of who toddlers are and what they are interested in to appreciate a scene like this one. It also takes good observation skills to notice the details. We'll go back to this scene later to discuss it.

NAEYC Program Standard 2
Curriculum

A main ingredient of any infant or toddler program should be play. Early childhood educators have long recognized play as vital to growth and learning. It is natural to young children and should be regarded as an *important* use of their time, not as something secondary or optional.

The benefits of play are enormous and go far beyond the kinds of things we talk about so easily, like developing skills and learning concepts. Play can be an avenue to early literacy skills, for one thing. According to one study, play is where many paths to literacy come together and "emerging understandings are integrated, practiced, and tested in a safe environment."[1] In fact, if you look carefully at play you can find all aspects of the kinds of skills children need for the foundations of reading and writing. Play offers children opportunities that come from nowhere else. Through play, children get involved in open-ended exploration. They are not confined by rules, procedures, or outcomes. Children at play have self-direction. They have power. Through total absorption during play, they make discoveries they might otherwise never make, they work on problems, they make choices, and they find out what interests them.

In the foreword to *Mindstorms*, Seymour Papert talks about a play theme that started when he was a toddler, continued throughout his childhood, and has been an important influence throughout his whole life.[2] He writes about how, as a toddler, he fell in love with car parts and wanted to know the names of all the parts. Eventually his interest focused mainly on gears, and he spent hours playing with circular objects, turning them as if they were gears. Much later this led to him turning gears in his head and making chains of cause and effect. Papert used gears as his model for learning mathematics and today is known for his work with computers, Piaget's theory, and artificial intelligence. Papert's story has two major points. One is that when children play with concrete objects the way Papert did with gears, they build models that transfer what they learn through their senses to their minds, which then allows them to mentally manipulate ideas for further understanding. The other point is that nobody made Papert learn about gears. In his own words, he "fell in love with gears." Obviously someone supported and encouraged him and provided materials. Papert was the one who made the choice to use them. Early play in Papert's life (as in all children's lives) provided an important foundation for later learning and understanding.

The way we respond to infants and toddlers at play by giving them freedom, by helping them pursue their special interests, and by providing resources may result in children gaining lifelong models such as Papert's gears (see Figure 4.1).

Elena Bodrova and Deborah Leong discuss how play influences development in their book *Tools of the Mind: The Vygotskian Approach to Early Childhood Education*.[3] They explain that Vygotsky had an integrated view of play when he wrote about its contribution to cognitive, emotional, and social development. He saw play as a tool of the mind with its roots in the manipulation and exploration of infancy and toddlerhood.

Free play is a theme of this chapter. By free play we mean undirected but monitored play when children have choices to pursue their special interests without continual adult control or expected outcomes. Letting free play remain free is difficult for some adults once they recognize how important play is for infants and

Reflect
What are the models from your own childhood that you carry in your head today? Can you relate your own experience to Papert's "gears"?

Figure 4.1 Three Ways Caregivers Create Curriculum Out of Play

Caregivers create curriculum out of play in these three ways:

1. By giving children freedom

2. By helping them pursue their special interests

3. By providing resources

toddlers. They want to set up activities with objectives and plan for and, control outcomes. This is especially true for programs with children from low-income families because of the urgency to prepare them for later schooling. We urge those adults who want to create activities and objectives—lessons—to appreciate what children gain from free play by observing them. You'll see that they create their own objectives and lessons, which are far more effective than those you set up.

Some visitors to an infant-toddler program arrived in the morning to see the children playing freely with a variety of toys. They were impressed with how involved and interested the children were. But then the director arrived breathless, apologized that things were late in starting that morning, and proceeded to organize groups, get out "activities," and herd toddlers into chairs around tables. Here they were drilled on names of objects in pictures, told to match shapes, and shown how to make circles and squares out of play dough. The teachers who had earlier been playing a background role, except when there was a call to be responsive, suddenly took charge of everything. The focus became very objective oriented. When the visitors later had a look at individual education plans, they discovered that cognitive objectives were defined very narrowly (for example, "shown pictures of a dog, a horse, and a cat, child will identify two out of three"). No wonder "playtime" was so objective oriented. It's not that adults don't have outcomes in mind (see Chapter 2). But instead of setting objectives for the way a child is to interact with materials, the adult should observe what the child is actually doing and appreciate what the child is getting out of it, even if it isn't immediately obvious. For example, if someone had watched Papert twirling round objects, he or she might well have missed that Papert was creating a model of gears in his head. How different his outcome might have been if he had been redirected continually to do some kind of activity with a particular objective that an adult had in mind.

One reason adults sometimes want to control toddler play is that they don't understand it. Go back and review that scene at the beginning of the chapter. Did you note that Tyler was exploring with his senses. He wasn't working the puzzle, he was enjoying the feel and the sound it of and of the nesting cups. He has no interest in using the materials "the right way." Tyler is figuring out his own way of discovering the properties of each material. Simple as this scene is, it is a good example of a young toddler playing. Preschool play is easier to understand because it can look involved and productive, and it fits into categories such as "dramatic play" or "art" or "block building." Toddler play may not look like much; toddlers seem to dabble at things. Sometimes they seem to just be wandering around,

Reflect

Recall an early play experience of your own. Relive it, if you can. Think about what you got out of this experience. How can you use your own experience to understand the importance of free play for infants and toddlers?

often carrying objects with them. But if you watch carefully, you see that they are neither uninvolved nor in transition. They are walking and carrying. They are making choices. In addition, perhaps they are enjoying the sensory changes as they move about. Sometimes they are keeping contact with the person they are most attached to (touching home base) when they explore the environment.

Toddlers are easy to satisfy as long as they have room to move and things to examine and manipulate. They may seem to have short attention spans because of their gross motor focus and the need to change location. However, they can also get very involved, especially in problem solving or a self-chosen sensory activity. Toddlers at a sink with soap, water, and paper towels can spend up to half an hour messing around. (That's not a short attention span.)

Adult Roles in Play

The caregiver takes many roles in supporting infants and toddlers in their play. Although we separate them for discussion, in reality they are all related to each other—with safety as one overarching theme and learning through interaction as another.

Setting Up Environments for Play

Safety is of primary importance and involves setting up a healthful environment free from hazards, then carefully monitoring what goes on in it. Without safety, there is no free play. Although some children are bigger risk takers than others, most children are comfortable only when they feel secure and know no one will let them get hurt. Thought must be put into the age and individual developmental level of each child and of the group as a whole. Health and safety hazards can be an individual as well as a group issue. Careful attention must be given to safety issues for children who may have physical or other challenges. Safety is the key to **exploration** for all children. By exploration we mean the act of discovering and examining what's around the child—the people and objects, as well as the properties of those objects—through touching, mouthing, smelling, seeing, and hearing. Only in a safe, developmentally appropriate and interesting environment can children have opportunities to make the kinds of discoveries that further their development and learning. When thinking about exploration, look again at the age and developmental level of each child. Also take children with challenges into consideration so that they have equal opportunity to safely interact with as much of the environment as possible. For example, consider how children gain eye–hand coordination from manipulating toys; then think about the child who is severely visually impaired. Make sure that child feels safe enough to get to the toy shelf, knows that toys are there, and is able to discover that those toys have features (such as making a noise) that could give the child experiences with ear–hand coordination. We'll cover this subject more in Chapter 12.

**NAEYC Program
Standard 9**
Physical Environment

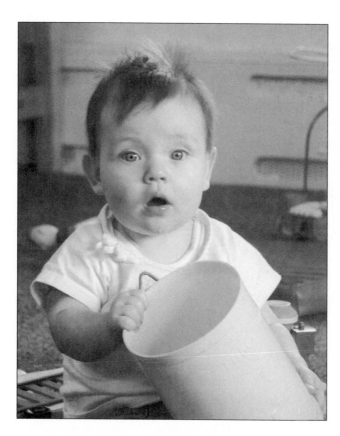

Children gain eye-hand coordination from manipulating toys.

Encouraging Interactions and Then Stepping Back

Children learn from other children. By interacting with their peers, infants and toddlers learn much about the world, their power in it, and their effect on others. Through the kinds of problem-solving situations that present themselves in child–child interactions, youngsters come to learn such valuable skills as how to resolve conflicts. The adult's role in these child–child interactions is to encourage them and then step back until needed. Sensitive caregivers know when to intervene. Timing is crucial. If you step in too soon, valuable learning is lost. But if you step in too late, children can hurt each other. Timing and **selective intervention** are important skills for caregivers to acquire in order to facilitate infant-toddler social play. What do we mean by selective intervention? Intervention means interfering or interrupting, and it is selective when it is limited to those times when the effect will be positive. Selective intervention should be used to protect (as in an unsafe situation) or to help facilitate learning when needed. Figuring out when to sensitively intervene appropriately is an adult skill that is important to facilitating play. But remember that encouraging children to solve their own problems is an important part of their education, so stepping back and not intervening is another adult skill that is equally important to practice. Adults

NAEYC Program Standard 3
Teaching

VIDEO OBSERVATION 4

Toddlers Playing Outside

See Video Observation 4: Toddlers Playing Outside for an illustration of toddlers playing pretend.

Questions

- How could you explain this scene to someone who says to you, "They aren't doing anything important—just messing around?"
- How is the play of these children the same as and different from the play of the two boys in the opening scene of this chapter?
- What makes this scene "curriculum?" What are the children gaining from it? Consider the developmental domains, mind, body, and feelings.

To view this clip, go to www.mhhe.com/itc7e. Click on Student Edition, select Chapter 4, and click on Video Observation.

should remain available while infants and toddlers are playing, giving wants-nothing quality time. They should refrain from interrupting the child who is really absorbed in play. Absorption is a quality we should value.

Reflect

Have you ever experienced a time when play was not playful? What happened? What was that like?

Adults can be part of the play, but they must remain in a playful mode, open to what happens, without setting goals or playing for particular results. Otherwise the play ceases to be play and becomes an adult-directed "activity." You'll see examples throughout this book of adults in a wants-nothing mode, playing with children.

Adults also engage in mutual play with children for their own enjoyment. But be careful about becoming a child's entertainment device. Some children get hooked on adults playing with them and are unable to play with other children or on their own when the adult steps back. In some programs, such as at the Pikler Institute, caregivers are trained to allow children to play uninterrupted.

They don't play with them. As a result, the quality of the play there is exceptional. Children need no adult entertainment and little intervention. This is the result of the emphasis put on adult-child interaction and cooperation during caregiving times, so that children have a close trusting relationship and feel secure enough to explore and play on their own and with each other.[4]

Supporting Problem Solving

Adults support problem solving. The caregiver must have sensitivity to recognize the intellectual value of the many problems that arise during free play. Maria can't get the ring on the stick; Blake's block stack keeps falling over; Jamal can't reach the toy just beyond his grasp. The frustrations from these kinds of problems seem to interrupt free play, and it's tempting just to solve the problem for the child. But rescuing a child takes away a potentially valuable learning experience.

NAEYC Program Standard 3
Teaching

Adults provide scaffolding for children's problem solving. It takes skill to know when to help. Often adults do too much and interfere with the child's ability to solve the problem. They deprive the child of discovering his or her own approach. The key to scaffolding effectively is to determine the point at which the child is about to give up. A small assist at just the right time will keep the child working on the problem. If it's too early or too late, the child loses interest. It's not that caregivers have to "motivate" children. Rather, the assist is the type of support that helps children stay with something long enough to finally gain a sense of satisfaction. Satisfaction is the kind of reward that lingers and is remembered the next time a problem arises. Figure 4.2 on the following page provides a quick look at eight adult roles in infant-toddler play. Magda Gerber gives some advice about scaffolding:

> *Allow children to learn on their own, without interference. If you wait, you will find out that many things get resolved on their own; even though you thought you had to help, the child didn't really need your help. We are child-loving people—too eager, so we think, "Oh, poor baby would like to get that toy but can't reach it," so we push it nearer. But the message we give is, "You need us. We are all-knowing giants and you are a helpless little creature." That's not the message I would like to give. I wait until the child really lets me know, "I cannot handle it any more."[5]*

Observing

The adults in a child care program that stresses free play sometimes look as though they aren't doing anything. Some people think that adults in a wants-nothing mode—available but not directive—look too passive. They may look passive, but they are busy observing. Observation is a key role if a caregiver is to understand what's going on and figure out how to promote learning. Keen observation skills are vital for all caregivers. Sitting still, focusing attention, and just taking in what's happening comes easily to some adults, but these skills must be

NAEYC Program Standard 4
Assessment

Figure 4.2 Adult Roles in Infant-Toddler Play

1. Encouraging interactions and then stepping back

2. Practicing selective intervention

3. Providing time, space, and materials

4. Remaining available but not interrupting

5. Providing safety

6. Supporting problem solving

7. Providing scaffolding

8. Observing

learned for those who don't naturally come by them. When adults are in an observer role, the pace of the children tends to slow down because the adult energy influences what's going on around them. A slow pace gives infants and toddlers a chance to focus their attention. *Remember principle 7: Model the behavior you want to teach.* While observing, you are modeling that mode of being, which benefits the children in more ways than one.

Read the following scene, which shows adults facilitating free play, and decide for yourself if the adults are too passive.

The play area is set up for older toddlers, who are busily exploring what has been put out for them. Two adults are sitting on the floor on opposite ends of the play area. In one end of the room four children are carrying around large plastic blocks. One seems to have a plan in mind; one is just carrying a block seemingly without regard to where she is going. A third child has built a four-block enclosure and is sitting in the middle of it. Another child is walking across the blocks that are lying flat on the rug. The first child lays down another block and joins the child who is walking on top of the blocks. The child who was wandering around comes over and takes the block that the child has just set down and a tussle starts. The teacher, who has been observing from a distance, comes to sit by the two children ready to intervene, but one child lets go and leaves and the other abandons the block he was fighting for, so the teacher goes back to her original position. At the other end of the room, a group of children is playing around a table set with plastic dishes. A child brings a "cup of coffee" from the table over to the adult on the floor. He pretends to drink it. The child takes the empty cup and goes over to the play sink to wash it, while another child who has just given a doll a bath gets the empty cup from the first child and gives the "baby" a drink out of it.

Contrast that scene to this one:

A group of toddlers sits on a rug with an adult directing a "circle time." She is singing a song that has a finger play to go with it. Some of the toddlers are trying to make their fingers perform, and others are just sitting watching her. None of them are singing. She finishes that song and starts another. Two children begin to squirm, but most are watching and listening. One child gets up and wanders off and second one follows. Another adult captures the two escapees and herds them back to the group saying, "Circle time isn't over yet." By the third song all but one of the children are squirming and making attempts to escape. The herding adult is having trouble keeping them all together. The other adult gets out a flannel board and begins to tell a story. She briefly captures most of the group's attention, but then one child comes up and tries to take the figures off the flannel board. The others can't see, so they get squirmy again and two start wrestling. As we leave this scene the two adults are getting chairs and firmly planting each child in one. It is clear that they *will* learn to sit still at circle time.

The adults in the second scene are *doing something*. It is more obvious what they are doing in this scene than in the first scene. They are being teachers. They are playing the role that most people expect them to play.

Which scene appealed most to you?

Did you notice that the toddlers in both scenes are making choices, as is appropriate in the play mode, but in the second scene choices weren't part of the plan? Did you notice how heavily taxed the adults were by being in charge?

Adults who are uninitiated to early childhood principles and practices can understand a program where children are engaged in adult-directed "learning activities" but may be critical of one where the adults just sit on the floor and respond. Parents may prefer that caregivers *teach* and look like they are in control of what is happening. They may not understand the role of facilitating learning through self-directed free play. Further, the caregivers themselves may feel like baby-sitters when in the wants-nothing mode during free play time. They may resist this role. All these factors work against a curriculum in which free play is a main ingredient. Caregivers need to find ways to articulate what they are doing so they can counteract the pressure that comes from all sides to *teach* infants and toddlers rather than let them play. What the adult does do that is more important than teaching is to structure the environment so that it is conducive to play.

Environmental Factors That Influence Play

You can't just put infants and toddlers into a room and expect great things to happen. Careful consideration needs to be given to the size of the space and how it fits the size of the group and the age span of the children in it. Then the adult needs to think about what is in the room and how appropriate it is for infants and toddlers. There are basic built-in features of the space and the furniture and equipment, plus what the adults bring as movable equipment, toys, and materials. What is to happen in the space is a factor in deciding how to set it up and what it needs. How much choice is to be encouraged is a consideration when setting up the environment. The degree of choice given to the children depends on the philosophy of the program and the age of the children; culture can have an influence too.

NAEYC Program Standard 9
Physical Environment

Group Size and Age Span

An important environmental factor is group size. Larger groups tend to be over-stimulating, and quieter children get ignored. It's much harder for children to truly get absorbed in play in a large group than in a small one, even when the adult-to-child ratio is good.

Mixture of ages is another environmental factor. Adult preferences in age mixtures in groups vary. Some programs work well with a variety of ages; others work equally well with most of the children about the same age.

If you do mix ages, be aware of protecting the youngest children. In the case of infants mixed with toddlers, you must protect those who can't move around from those who can. One way to do this, if they are in the same room, is to fence off a portion of the room for the immobile children. Don't just keep

Figure 4.3 Setting Up the Environment to Support Play

- Keep play space separate from caregiving areas.

- Make sure everything in the play space is touchable.

- Provide for both fine and gross motor activity.

- Provide both soft and hard materials and play surfaces.

- Let children find unique ways to combine toys and materials.

- Put out the right number of toys.

- Provide the right number of choices.

them in playpens and cribs. They need floor space and room to stretch and move, as well as interactions that come from several infants and adults sharing floor space.

Sometimes the mixture is toddlers with preschoolers. In that case the toddlers need to be protected from equipment they aren't mature enough to use, as well as from conflicts they can't win. You can't just stand back and let the children solve their own problems if one is two and the other almost five. The two-year-old will probably need some help to hold his or her own.

Setting Up the Environment to Support Play

Caregivers aren't providing structure by directing the play itself, but they structure the play environment. You can do away with most rules by setting up the environment so that a good deal of undesirable behavior is eliminated. For example, if the children aren't allowed to play in the kitchen, put a gate across the access. For a summary of what's involved in setting up the environment to support play, see Figure 4.3.

Make sure that everything in the environment is touchable and even **mouthable.** Mouthable, of course, means that an object is clean and safe for infants to put into their mouths. You can expect older children not to put things in their mouths, but infants and toddlers learn through mouthing. Sanitize toys periodically rather than restricting children from their natural inclinations.

Provide for **gross motor activity** inside as well as outside. Gross motor activity is an activity using the large muscles of the arms, legs, and trunk, such as climbing, rolling, sliding, and running. Toddlers run, climb, roll, jump all the time—not just when invited to. You should think of your toddler play area as a gym more than a classroom and set it up for active play.

Provide plenty of softness, both for the active play and for the quiet times. Cushions, pads, mattresses, and foam rubber blocks on the floor invite children to bounce, roll, flop down, as well as cuddle and snuggle with books or stuffed animals.

NAEYC Program Standard 9
Physical Environment

Reflect

Where was your favorite place to play as a child? How can you use your own experience to design a play environment for infants and toddlers?

Provide hard surfaces as well. A vinyl floor provides a contrast to carpeting and is interesting to crawlers as well as beginning walkers. Hard surfaces also make cleanup easier when you set up such activities as cooking or perhaps water play. (A thick bath mat under a plastic dishpan gives toddlers a chance to play in water without making too big a mess.)

Make available toys that can be used in many ways rather than toys meant to be used in only one way. Large foam blocks are an example. They can be hauled around, stacked, put together to make a structure, or sat upon. There is much more to do with large foam blocks than, say, a battery-operated or wind-up toy that puts the child in the role of a spectator.

Let children combine toys and materials as much as possible. If they want to haul stuffed animals into a block structure they have built, let them. If they take pots and pans out of the play stove to put the play dough in, let them.

Of course you can't let everything be combined. Play dough in the water play table makes a mess nobody wants to have to clean up and wrecks the play dough besides. If you don't want something combined, make a clear **environmental limit.** An environmental limit is a physical barrier that keeps a child or material out of or inside of a given space and is often accompanied by a verbal limit. Fencing off stairs provides an environmental limit. Keeping the play dough inside when the water table is set up outside is another form of an environmental limit. Another example is leaving the play dough in the cupboard when water play is available inside. Without an environmental limit or in addition to one, verbal limits become important. "Water stays in the water table," is a clear and positive statement of a limitation.

Determine the right amount of toys to make available. Don't put out more than you can stand to pick up. Watch out for **overstimulation** or too much sensory input. Excited toddlers who have too many choices are more apt to make themselves and everyone else unhappy than those who have just enough to do. On the other hand, bored toddlers in a nearly empty room create as many behavior problems as those in a room overstuffed with toys and people. Be aware of the optimum number of things to do. You can judge the right number by the children's behavior. The optimum number changes with the day, the group, and even the time of year.

Happenings

We avoid the term *activities* when we focus on play because we want to move away from a preschool model for infants and toddlers. Instead, we use the term **happenings,** which broadens the idea of what infants and toddlers engage in and learn from. The use of the term *happenings* is intended to encompass the simplest event as well as more prolonged and complicated experiences. We borrowed the term from James Hymes, a pioneer in early childhood care and education and a longtime leader in our field. We've been asked over the years to include ideas for activities in this book, and we have resisted. Instead, we offer numerous examples throughout the book in the various scenarios. We do not point out that they are happenings. We leave it up to the reader to notice. We also avoid creating learning goals and objectives for happenings, because once an adult has a specific outcome in mind, the happening leaves the realm of free play and becomes something else.

Happenings can be very simple and still be deeply satisfying. When we use the word *happenings*, we don't mean they always occur by happenstance. Some things do come up by chance, and when they arise, it's the adult's job to take advantage of them. The first fall day after a big wind, a happening can be raking leaves in the play yard.

Other happenings are planned for by bringing them into the environment purposely. A favorite at one center is an ongoing collage. A large piece of contact paper put up on the wall (sticky side out) invites the children to stick various items on. The continual rearrangement of the elements of this collage shows clearly how much more important the process is than the product at this age. This particular happening lasted for weeks. We often think of infants' and toddlers' attention span as quite short, but the nature of this happening and the caregivers' ability to support and encourage the children showed otherwise. When older children's interest in a particular theme or subject lasts for a long period, it is often called a project. The sticky collage wasn't exactly a project. We like to think of it as an extended happening.

Some happenings that toddlers enjoy are modified versions of preschool activities. For example, easel painting can be done with plain water on chalk boards or thick soapsuds (colored with food coloring) on plexiglass easels. Sponge painting can become squeezing sponges in trays with a little water covering the bottom.

One clever caregiver who knew how much infants and toddlers enjoy pulling tissues out of their box made a toy consisting of a tissue box filled with scarves tied together. Another simple happening the very young enjoy is crumpling tissue paper. (Use white so that if it gets wet, you don't have dye all over everything.)

Simple food preparation tasks (mashing bananas or peeling hard-boiled eggs) can delight toddlers. Even snapping spaghetti can be involving and satisfying for toddlers.

Free Choice

The environment should be set up to provide choices. Free choice is an important ingredient of play. Here is a scene that shows a playroom set up to encourage free play with numerous choices.

> One end of the room is fenced off. In it three infants are lying on their backs, waving their arms, and looking around. An adult sits near them, rearranging brightly colored scarves to be within the reach of each child. A floppy beach ball is also available. One of the infants grabs it, waves it in the air, and lets it go. It lands near another of the infants, who regards it briefly, then turns back to gaze at the red scarf standing puffed up near his face.

Beyond the small fenced-in area is a larger space where nine young toddlers are playing. Two are busily engaged in crawling in and out of the rungs of the ladder that is lying flat on the floor. One leaves to sit in an empty laundry basket nearby. He climbs out, turns it over, then crawls under it. He lifts it up to look out at two children who are trying on hats from a collection they have found in a box near a shelf of toys. One of these children puts three hats on his head, then picks up two in his hands and runs over to the fence and throws the hats, one by one, into the area where the infants are lying. He giggles delightedly at the reaction he gets from the surprised infants. The other hat player in the meantime has loaded several into the back of a small toddler trike and is riding around the room. He stops at a low table where several children are squeezing plastic zip top bags full of different substances. He looks at the caregiver sitting there when she says to one of the squeezers, "You really like the soft one, don't you?" He briefly pokes one of the bags. Finding it interesting, he abandons the hats and the trike and sits down at the table to explore the other bags.

In another area of the room, a girl is hauling large plastic-covered foam blocks from one corner and piling them on the couch, which is pulled out a few feet from the wall. Then she climbs up on the couch and proceeds to throw the cushions over the back until she has nearly filled the space. She gets down, walks around, and jumps on the pile she has made.

In another part of the room, a child is sitting with an adult on a large mattress (which actually is two sheets sewed together and filled with foam rubber scraps). The two are "reading" a book together. They are joined by one of the bag squeezers, who plops down on the adult's lap and takes the book away. It is quickly replaced by the other child, who has a stack of books next to her on the mattress.

In this scene the children have a number of choices. Free choice is an important ingredient of play as well as an important prerequisite to learning.

The Problem of the Match

J. McVicker Hunt talks about the relationship of learning to choice in terms of what he calls the "problem of the match." He says that learning occurs when the environment provides experiences just familiar enough that children can understand them with the mental ability they have already attained, but just new enough to offer interesting challenges.[6]

Learning occurs when there is optimum incongruity between what is already known and a new situation. If the situation is too new and different, children withdraw, become frightened, ignore it, or react in some way other than learning. If it is not novel enough, children ignore it. They won't pay attention to what has already become so much a part of them that it no longer registers.

McVicker Hunt relates to Jean Piaget's theory on assimilation and accommodation. Thinking evolves through adaptation as children seek to make sense of the environment by modifying it to fit personal needs as well as modifying the way they think in response to something new in the environment. Piaget saw adaptation as a two-part process—he called one part assimilation and the other accommodation. Assimilation means that new elements of experience are incorporated into existing structures of thought, which creates a tension when they don't fit. That's where accommodation comes in—new mental patterns are created or old ones are transformed in order to include the new information and make it fit.[7] This is another way of explaining McVicker Hunt's problem of the match.

The question is, how can you set up an environment so that it has elements of optimum incongruity? How does anyone know exactly what a match is for each child in his or her care? The answer is to have some knowledge of ages and stages (see the environmental chart in Appendix B). The developmental information in Part 2 should help, too.

The other answer is by *observation*. When you watch the children, you have a good idea what kinds of things to put into the environment for your particular group. By providing a number of choices of appropriate toys, objects, and occurrences and letting the children play, you give them the opportunity to move to novel situations and novel uses of materials. No one is more creative than infants and toddlers when it comes to inventive uses of materials and objects. They have a need to learn, a desire to understand. Caregivers can capitalize on this need by letting them determine their own use of the environment (within reason of course). By directing children with either praise or pressure, we distract them from the inner delights mentioned by Abraham Maslow in Chapter 2. Children get these inner delights from struggling with a problem that matches their learning level.

Sooner or later children in an interesting, challenging environment are bound to find a problem that they want to solve but can't. They "get stuck." If they can't figure out the next move, the adult can intervene by providing a tiny bit of help. Sometimes it's hard for adults to wait when they can solve a problem so easily. But if they wait, they provide children the best learning opportunities. Don't rescue children from problems; help them problem solve.

And don't push children. Here's another view of "getting stuck." Sometimes children get stuck by becoming satiated with something. They have had enough of some activity. *Adults* decide that children are bored, and they want to do something about it—quickly! Many adults have a great fear of boredom for infants as well as for themselves. This fear has perhaps been heightened by the trend for infant stimulation and pressures for academics before kindergarten. Yet boredom is educational and can be considered part of the curriculum or learning plan of any program. As Maslow says,

> *The single holistic principle that binds together the multiplicity of human motives is the tendency for a new and higher need to emerge as the lower need fulfills itself by being sufficiently gratified. The child who is fortunate enough to grow normally and well gets satiated and bored with the delights that he has savored sufficiently, and eagerly (without pushing) goes on to higher, more complex, delights as they become available to him without*

danger or threat. . . . He doesn't have to be "kicked upstairs," or forced on to maturity as it is so often implied. He chooses to grow on to higher delights, to become bored with older ones.[8]

Children cannot push themselves on until they have done very thoroughly what it is they need to do. Until they have reached the state of boredom, they are still motivated by unfinished business and can't move on. Boredom, when they finally attain it, provides the push to move on—but the push comes from within, not from without. They can then leave behind the old level, the old needs, and deal with the new ones, giving them their full attention. When the push to move on comes from without—from the adult or the environment—children never quite satisfy themselves. They may move on to the next stage, task, or activity with leftover feelings from the previous one, perhaps unable to give full attention to the new one.

This idea of children deciding for themselves when to move on is the basis of the original play yard design of Jerry Ferguson, who is an architect as well as an early childhood educator.[9] Ferguson designs environments uniquely suited to allowing infants and young toddlers to decide when and whether they are old enough to leave each developmental area. For example, she designed a play yard for the Pacific Oaks Infant-Toddler Program in Pasadena, California, in which the very youngest infants were in a low-stimulation area in the middle yard but cut off from the rest by a variety of barriers. In this area was a grassy place, completely safe for tiny babies. Beyond the grass was a sandy place with a tunnel at the end connecting the sand to a still more challenging play yard. Between the grass and the sand there was also a low wooden walkway designed to present a sufficient barrier to infants who were not yet ready to cross it. Children who were just beginning to move around had to conquer the raised walkway before they would get to the sand. They could test the sand from the safety of the walk before deciding to go into it, and they did this, sometimes for a week at a time, before they were ready. By the time they chose to go into the sand, they were able to handle the risks it presented, and the sand then became a safe environment for them. The tunnel at the other end, though obviously open, presented a formidable barricade, and few children chose to go through it until they were nearly ready to walk.

Thus, by the time the infants were able to leave the safe inner yard (by their own choice), they were developmentally ready for the bigger challenges of the yard beyond. This yard was designed for the beginning walker and good crawler and was interesting and safe, yet challenging (that is, optimally risky). Beyond was the most challenging yard, with climbing equipment and wheel toys for the toddlers. Although all the children who left the inner yard could return to it, few did so except for occasional visits. They chose to play where the environment had more to offer them.

Jerry Ferguson stresses that her approach works only because the infants have learned to take some responsibility for their own well-being. They come to depend on their ability to make choices, which means they have had the opportunity to gain experience in making decisions.

Appropriate Practice

Overview of Development

According to the National Association for the Education of Young Children, infants and toddlers love challenges and are interested in everything. When they are free to explore because warm adults encourage and take pleasure in their interests and skills, they grow, develop, and learn. Young infants play when they feel secure in a relationship. They play with people and objects using all their senses. They enjoy practicing a new skill and exploring objects and people by grasping, kicking, reaching, pulling. A responsive and stimulating environment with plenty of time to fully experience the people and things in it provides young infants with the simple joys of relating. Mobile infants with their increased skills expand their playfulness by exploring space as well as objects and people. They develop their muscles through these explorations. They also develop cognitively as they experience and learn about what's around them. A sense of security allows infants and toddlers to make use of their capabilities to continually make discoveries and learn through playing.

Source: J. Ronald Lally, Abbey Griffin, Emily Fenichel, Marilyn Segal, Eleanor Szanton, and Bernice Weissbourd, "Development in the First Three Years of Life," in *Developmentally Appropriate Practice in Early Childhood Programs,* rev. ed. (Washington, D.C.: National Association for the Education of Young Children, 1997), pp. 55–69.

Developmentally Appropriate Practice

The following are sample practices that link play as curriculum to the statement above:

- Playful interactions with babies are done in ways that are sensitive to the child's interests and level of tolerance for physical movement, loud sounds, or other changes.
- Adults show their respect for an infant's play by observing the child's activity, commenting on it

verbally, and providing a safe environment. The quietly supportive adult encourages the child's active engagement.
- Adults frequently observe the infant at play. Appropriate games, such as peek-a-boo, are played with interested infants, the adult being careful not to intrude on how the infant wants to play.
- Adults engage in reciprocal play with toddlers, modeling for children how to play imaginatively—for example, playing "tea party." Caregivers also support toddlers' play so that children stay interested in an object or activity for longer periods of time and their play becomes more complex, moving from simple awareness and exploration of objects to more complicated play like pretending.
- Children have daily opportunities for exploratory activity, such as water and sand play, painting, and clay or play dough manipulatives.

Source: S. Bredekamp and C. Copple, eds., *Developmentally Appropriate Practice in Early Childhood Programs,* rev. ed. (Washington, D.C.: National Association for the Education of Young Children, 1997).

Individually Appropriate Practice

Older infants and toddlers who are not mobile on their own need a more hands-on approach from caregivers than the typically developing mobile infant and toddlers. They can use what exploratory skills they have when caregivers move them around, find ways for them to move themselves, and make environmental adaptations that make it easier for these children to participate and play.

Culturally Appropriate Practice

Some families may not value play in the way others do. Some may not have an environment at home that allows for safe play and exploration. Others may not have a tradition of free play for children.

(continued)

Appropriate Practice (continued)

It is important for caregivers to honor differences and seek to understand them.

Appropriate Practice in Action

Look again at the Principles in Action feature on page 80.

- Can you see the connection between the quality time in principle 2 that Mike is giving the

children in his care and the points made in the "Developmentally Appropriately Practice" section of this Appropriate Practice box?
- Consider culturally appropriate practice. What might Mike or Fiona do if the families in the program did not have a safe environment for play at home and/or did not have a cultural tradition of free play for children?

Summary

Online Resources

Go to the Online Learning Center at **www.mhhe.com/itc7e** to access the student study guide that includes quizzes, practice with key terms, and a review of chapter content; links to websites related to the chapter; and additional resources.

- The four adult roles important for facilitating the play of infants and toddlers are:
  o Setting up environments for play and making safety the primary consideration so that children are free to explore and discover.
  o Encouraging interactions and then stepping back so children aren't interrupted.
  o Supporting problem solving so that children come to see themselves as capable.
  o Observing as a way of understanding each child and in each situation to promote learning.
- The five factors to consider when setting up environments for play are:
  o Group size and age span so that children get the attention they need and can become absorbed in play.
  o How the set up of the environment supports play.
  o Moving from activities to happenings, which broadens the idea of how infants and toddlers learn—includes both planned and unplanned occurrences.
  o The amount of free choice available.
  o The problem of the match, which allows children to choose happenings that match their interest level of learning.

Key Terms

environmental limit 82
exploration 74
free play 72

gross motor activity 81
happenings 82
mouthable 81

overstimulation 82
selective intervention 75

Thought/Activity Questions

1. How is the term *model* used in this chapter?
2. If play is so important, should adults let children play freely? Why or why not?
3. Most books on infant-toddler care and education use the term *activity*. Why don't we?
4. What is scaffolding and what does it have to do with play?
5. What is the problem of the match and how does it related to Piaget's theory on assimilation and accommodation?
6. What are some advantages of the caregiver being in an observation mode?

For Further Reading

Doris Bergen, Rebecca Reid, and Louis Torelli, *Educating and Caring for Very Young Children: The Infant-Toddler Curriculum* (New York: Teachers College Press, 2001).

David Elkind, "Thanks for the Memory: The Lasting Value of True Play," in *Spotlight on Young Children and Play*, edited by D. Koralek (Washington D.C.: National Association for the Education of Young Children, 2004), pp. 36–41.

B. Hatcher and K. Petty, "Visible Thought in Dramatic Play," *Young Children*, November 2004, pp. 79–82.

J. Isenberg, and M. Jalong, *Creative Expression and Play in Early Childhood*, 3rd ed. (Columbus, OH: Merrill-Prentice Hall, 2001).

Ruth Money, "The RIE Early Years "Curriculum," in S. Petrie, and S. Owen, *Authentic Relationships in Group Care for Infants and Toddlers: Resources for Infant Educarers (RIE) Principles into Practice*. (London: Jessica Kingsley, 2005), pp. 51–68.

Sharon Rosenkoetter and Joanne Knapp-Philo, Eds. *Learning to Read the World: Language and Literacy in the First Three Years* (Washington D.C.: Zero to Three, 2005).

S. R. Sandall, "Play Modifications for Children with Disabilities," in *Spotlight on Young Children and Play*, edited by D. Koralek (Washington D.C.: National Association for the Education of Young Children, 2004), pp. 44.

part two

Focus on the Child

chapter 5

Attachment

Focus Questions

After reading this chapter you should be able to answer the following questions:

1 Define *attachment*. What factors influence its development?

2 How is brain development influenced by attachment?

3 Why is it important to know about *Attachment Milestones*?

4 What are some circumstances in which Ainsworth's patterns might be questionable when it comes to understanding and labeling the degree or kind of attachment?

5 What can adults do to foster attachment in young children? Include any unique issues related to children with special needs.

What Do You See?

A small baby, lying on the floor on a blanket in the family room of the home where he is being cared for, is crying. A reassuring voice comes from the other room. "I know you are hungry! I'm coming!" The cries cease at the sound of the voice, but then begin again when no one immediately appears. The family childcare provider hustles into the room carrying a warm bottle. "I'm sorry you had to wait." The crying continues. "I know, I know. I'm going to pick you up now so that you can eat." She bends over with her arms outstretched and gently lifts the baby. The crying slows down; the caregiver walks across the room to sit down in a soft chair.

As he is picked up, the baby's whole body shows his anticipation of what is to come. He stiffens and his arms wave in excitement. He looks intensely into his caregiver's face. Once settled into the chair, he begins to squirm frantically, his mouth searching for the nipple. As it comes into his mouth, he closes his eyes, clenches his fists, and sucks furiously. "There you are. That's better, isn't it?" coos the caregiver. He begins to relax after a few minutes, and both adult and child settle back, moving around until comfortable. "You were really hungry, weren't you?" The baby continues to suck without stopping; after a few moments, he begins to ease up a little. His fists unclench, and one hand reaches out, groping. The caregiver touches his hand with her finger; he wraps his fingers around her finger and holds on tight. The caregiver snuggles him a little closer and kisses the top of his head. He opens his eyes and looks up at her. She looks back, a warm smile on her face. He stops sucking and lets go of the nipple. With his gaze fixed on his caregiver's face, his mouth breaks into a big grin. Then he snuggles in even closer and continues to suck contentedly, his little fist wrapped around her finger, his eyes looking into hers.

This is what **attachment** looks like! It is a complex, ongoing process. Its definitions may vary, but in essence it involves a *closeness* and a *responsiveness* to an infant. This chapter discusses this important and special two-way relationship between an infant and an adult, and describes how brain development is influenced by early quality care experiences. It examines behavioral milestones related to attachment, the measurement of secure and insecure attachment patterns, and related contemporary issues. It also discusses what can happen if a child cannot make an attachment and the special needs that result from such a breakdown. Continuity of care and the importance of responsive relationships are discussed throughout the chapter as key to the development of early healthy attachments.

Brain Research

More has been learned in the last 10 years about the human brain than in the last 100 years! See Table 5.1 for a summary of how our understanding of brain development has changed. Today technologies in neuroscience that are noninvasive (they don't interfere with natural brain function) are making detailed exploration of the brain possible. Amazing tools exist for mapping the brain and for understanding brain chemistry, as well as for appreciating the effect of

Table 5.1 Rethinking the Brain

Old Thinking	New Thinking
How a brain develops depends on the *genes* you are born with.	How a brain develops hinges on a complex *interplay* between the *genes* you're born with and the *experiences* you have.
The *experiences* you have before age three have a *limited impact* on later development.	Early *experiences* have a *decisive* impact on the architecture of the brain and on the nature and extent of adult capacities.
A *secure relationship* with a primary caregiver creates a favorable *context* for early development and learning.	*Early interactions* don't just create a context; they *directly affect* the way the brain is "*wired*."
Brain development is *linear:* the brain's capacity to learn and change grows steadily as an infant progresses toward adulthood.	Brain development is *nonlinear:* there are prime times for acquiring different kinds of knowledge and skills.
A toddler's brain is much *less active* than the brain of a college student.	By the time children reach age three, their brains are *twice as active* as those of adults. Activity levels drop during adolescence.

Source: Rima Shore, *Rethinking the Brain: New Insights into Early Development.* Copyright © 1997, Families and Work Institute, 330 Seventh Avenue, New York, New York 10001. 212-465-2044. Website: *http://www.familiesandwork.org.* All rights reserved.

environmental factors. This information has taught us many valuable lessons about how infants learn and why early experience is so vital to development. Looking at a brief overview of how the brain functions may help to foster an appreciation of just why particularly responsive, positive experiences are so important to an infant's early development.

The basic building blocks of the brain are specialized nerve cells called **neurons.** Each neuron has an **axon,** or output fiber, that sends energy, or impulses, to other neurons. Neurons also have many **dendrites,** which are input fibers that receive the impulses from other neurons. The dendrites grow and branch out forming "dendrite trees" that receive signals from other neurons. These connections, or **synapses,** are formed as an infant experiences the world. The connections used regularly in everyday life become reinforced, or protected, and become part of the brain's permanent "circuitry." The human brain at birth is still very immature, so these early experiences can have a dramatic effect over time on an infant's growth and learning.[1]

In the early years, young brains produce almost twice as many synapses as they will need. The dendrite trees grow and become very dense. By age two, the number of synapses a toddler has is similar to that of an adult. By three the child has twice as many synapses as an adult. This large number is stable throughout the first 10 years, but by adolescence about half of these synapses have been discarded or "pruned." The brain prunes, or selectively eliminates, unnecessary synapses.

The key question is how does the brain *know* which synapses, or connections, to keep and which ones to prune, or discard? Early experience seems to be much more critical than first realized. Experiences activate neural pathways, and information in the form of chemical signals gets stored along the pathways. Repeated experiences strengthen specific pathways. A particular pathway takes on a "protected" status; it is not pruned because it has been repeatedly used. These protected, strong pathways remain into adulthood. The "use it or lose it" saying applies to early brain development.

This text has emphasized numerous times the importance of quality experiences and responsive care for very young children. Now the brain development research indicates that these early experiences, if repeated, actually form stable neural pathways. The way we think and learn has everything to do with the extent and nature of these pathways. When a very young child experiences something new, or a problem, brain activity increases. If neural pathways are strong, signals travel quickly and the child can solve problems easily.

Pause for a moment and think about a 10-month-old child whose mom is taking him to his child care provider as she goes off to work. He may experience a certain amount of stress (this is called "stranger anxiety" and will be discussed in more detail later in the chapter). However, when his caregiver is familiar with and can be responsive to his stress signals, he comes to *know* that he will be okay (the caregiver is a familiar friend and today his blanket is of particular comfort to cuddle and smell). His mother will return. In his brain, connections have been formed that allow him to separate with relatively little effort. Through his

**NAEYC Program
Standard 1**
Relationships

experiences he has already developed efficient neural pathways. Responsive, positive experiences stabilize connections in his brain. These very early connections in the brain are related to attachment experiences. *Remember principle 2: Invest in quality time, when you are totally available to individual infants and toddlers.* Don't settle for supervising groups without focusing (more than just briefly) on individual children.

Through attachment, two individuals come together and stay together. John Kennell defines attachment as "an affectionate bond between two individuals that endures through space and time and serves to join them emotionally."[2] The mother is usually the first and primary attachment the baby makes, but babies are becoming more and more strongly attached to their fathers, especially as issues involving working moms expand. When infants experience child care at a young age, these secondary attachments (people other than their parents) become very important.

Attachment to caregivers differs from that to parents in many ways. One obvious way is in duration. The long-term, even lifetime attachment a parent has is a much shorter period for caregivers. From day one, caregivers know that the children will leave their charge long before they grow up. The departure may come without warning because parents' lives and need for child care sometimes change suddenly. There is a big difference in this expectation of permanence of the adult-child relationship between parents and caregivers.

Parental attachment, this feeling of closeness, starts right at birth for some. In the ideal situation, where parents and an alert newborn are allowed time together to get acquainted, what is called "bonding" may occur as they fall in love in a very short time. It might even be called "love at first sight." This love at first sight can occur between caregivers and children too, as an adult and a child are drawn to each other at first meeting. More commonly, attachment grows slowly over time as individuals get to know each other and learn each other's special ways of communicating. These special ways grow and change as children reach developmental milestones. The brain research now available to parents and caregivers validates that warm, positive interactions stabilize connections in the brain. High-quality, responsive care must be provided in order for this critical process called *attachment* to thrive.

The Principles in Action

Principle 9 Build security by teaching trust. Don't teach distrust by being undependable or often inconsistent.

"Look at this dolly, Cameron," says her mother as she tries to get 12-month-old Cameron involved in the dress-up area. The two have just arrived, and this is the mother's first day to leave her daughter. The caregiver approaches, says hello, and then gets down at Cameron's level. The baby looks at her. Cameron has visited the center several times and recognizes the caregiver, but she's never stayed without her mother. She smiles happily and holds out a doll to show the caregiver. When the caregiver stands up to talk to the mother, she discovers the mother is gone. She had said earlier that she can't stand to see her daughter cry, so apparently she just decided to sneak out. Cameron continues holding the doll, but then she looks around and can't find her mother. She looks puzzled, and then she begins to cry. She ends up wracked in sobs, and the caregiver has a hard time comforting her. The caregiver decides to speak to the mother at the end of the day and tell her about the importance of saying good-bye so that her daughter can predict when she is going to leave. In her experience, children who have no good-bye ritual can't relax because they never know when people come and go in their lives. She knows that trust is an important issue for Cameron, and she knows it will take time. The first step is to get the mother to say good-bye. Imagine that you are this caregiver.

1. How do you feel about the mother's behavior?
2. How do you feel about Cameron?
3. How do you feel about the situation?
4. Do you agree that the caregiver should talk to the mother? Why or why not?
5. Could the mother's behavior come from a cultural difference?
6. What else might you do to help Cameron establish trust?

Milestones of Attachment

Important milestones of attachment influence mental, social, and emotional development. A baby's crying, pulling away from strangers, and trying to follow a departing parent indicate how attachment changes. Looking at these behaviors in more detail clarifies how competent an infant is.

Babies are designed to promote their own attachment. Think for a moment about the variety of behaviors that attract adults to babies. A newborn's cry elicits feelings in the people who hear it. It is hard to ignore. Crying becomes one of the infant's strongest signals to the people responsible for his or her care.

Another strong attachment behavior most babies have at birth is the ability to establish eye contact. When a newborn looks right into their eyes, most adults melt. And if you touch the little fingers, they are likely to curl around your big one. If you talk to alert newborns, they are likely to turn toward the sound of your voice. And if you move away from them slightly, their eyes will follow your face. All these behaviors promote attachment.

Studies indicate that babies react differently to the people they are attached to right from the beginning. Later this preferential response becomes obvious as babies cry when the object of attachment leaves the room. This is an important indication that **trust** is developing. They follow the person with whom they have the attachment, first with gaze alone, then, when they are mobile, by crawling after them.

Pause and review the scene at the beginning of this chapter involving the feeding experience and the interaction between the baby and caregiver. This is a special relationship. These two are a unit. Both feel that this is an intimate moment of a close relationship. This special form of communication—**interactional synchrony**—is like an "emotional dance." The caregiver and the baby send each other important signals. Both partners share emotions, especially positive ones.[3] The infant has the capacity to elicit delight from another; this in turn gives him pleasure. The example of the feeding experience illustrates some of the repertoire of behaviors involved in attachment. Through these mutually responsive behaviors, which include touching, fondling, and eye contact, as well as feeding, infants and adults form an extremely close relationship. Remember, too, that the new information on the brain indicates that these early behaviors begin to form pathways in the brain. These pathways form the *physical foundation* of trust. Positive experiences stabilize the brain connections. Infants need this relationship because they cannot physically attach themselves to people in order to get nourished and cared for. They are dependent. Attachment is nature's way of ensuring that someone will care (in the emotional sense) and provide care (in the physical sense). *Remember principle 1: Involve infants and toddlers in things that concern them.* Don't work around them or distract them to get the job done faster.

Once babies can distinguish their mother or caregiver from other people, two new worries begin. First, at about 8 to 10 months of age, they begin to fear strangers. Second, now that they know who mother is, they worry about losing her. This latter fear usually appears by about 10 to 12 months. Both of these fears indicate the infant's ability to discriminate and recognize difference and therefore are obvious signs of mental growth. Corresponding to this second developmental fear is the baby's inability to understand that objects gone from sight still exist. Jean Piaget called this "object permanence"; it will be discussed further in Chapter 8. Infants' worry about losing their mother is understandable. They cannot foresee that a separation is only temporary. Knowing this, caregivers find it easier to understand a baby's desperate protest when he or she is left behind as a parent walks out the door.

It may be helpful to emphasize the interplay between dependency, mental development, and trust in this process of attachment. When an 18-month-old child is clinging to his mother and crying for her not to go (obvious dependent behavior), he is also saying "I *know* I need you" (a mental function). As his mental capacity grows, and his experiences teach him that he can trust his mother to return, from attachment comes trust as he learns that the world is basically a friendly place where he can get his needs met. From attachment also comes **autonomy,** or independence, as babies grow and begin to take over their caregiving by learning self-help skills. They also find it easier and easier to let go because they know that their parent will be back. This ability to trust a relationship is the foundation for independence—a focus of the toddler period.

This worry about leaving the parent or primary caregiver is called "separation anxiety." It is usually at its peak as the baby nears the end of the first year of life. If the child enters child care just at this time, the beginning can be very difficult. Children do better if they enter before or after the peak of separation anxiety.

Reflect

Remember Cameron in the Principles in Action box on page 96? What would you try to tell her mother about the developmental milestones of attachment? How can you help this mother better understand her child's crying?

Babies explore by using their caregiver as a base and checking in periodically.

In a quality infant-toddler child-care program (center or home-based), children gain courage to explore and participate (fostering mental and social skills) by using their parent or known caregiver as a home or trust base. Checking in periodically provides renewed energy to move out and continue exploration. It is important when the parent leaves that he or she not sneak away. By saying good-bye, the parent helps the child appreciate that the departure is predictable. Gradually a child learns that coming back is also part of saying good-bye. A sensitive caregiver can put into words what she perceives a potentially upset child to be feeling. Acceptance of these feelings, and not distraction from them, provides a young child with a secure base for emotional development.

The following suggestions may assist caregivers in helping parents with toddler's suffering from separation anxiety:

1. Help the parent understand that once the good-byes are said, the departure should be immediate. Some parents have as much or more trouble than their toddlers separating. Help the parent know that you understand it is hard to leave, but that it is easier on the child if departure is quick once the good-byes are said.

2. Allow the child his or her feelings, but don't get involved in them yourself. Separation feelings are hard for some adults because they trigger issues they may want to forget. One way caregivers respond to this situation is by trying to get rid of the child's feelings, through distraction or

VIDEO OBSERVATION 5

Toddler "Checking in" While Playing with Chairs

See Video Observation 5: Toddler "Checking in" While Playing with Chairs for an illustration of how toddlers "touch home base" during free play. You'll see a child interrupt his play by going over to the caregiver, almost as if to recharge his batteries. This behavior is a sign of attachment.

Questions

1. If you were trying to explain behaviors that show the child is feeling attached to a caregiver, how would you describe this scene?
2. Have you ever seen a toddler "checking in" like this toddler did? If yes, think about how that scene was the same as or different from this one. If no, think about how it *might be* different. For example, sometimes the child just looks over at the adult instead of making physical contact.

To view this clip, go to www.mhhe.com/itc7e. Click on Student Edition, select Chapter 5, and click on Video Observation.

by minimizing them. ("Come on now—it's not that bad. She'll be back before you know it.")
3. Have an interesting, even enticing environment that calls out to children so that when they are ready, they can easily get involved in something.

Attachment is vital to infants' and toddlers' development and should be promoted in child care programs. At the same time, caregivers should realize that parents may fear their children may gain secondary attachments outside the home at the expense of their primary ones with parents. Caregivers can help ease parents' fears by letting them know they are unfounded. The secondary attachments are in addition to the primary ones, not replacements for them. Separation anxiety and all the feelings that go with being left in child care are also of

DEVELOPMENTAL PATHWAYS

Attachment

Preattachment: Indiscriminate Reactions (birth to approximately 12 weeks)

Early behaviors—crying, gazing, grasping—are designed to bring adults close to infants and to provide nurturance and comfort. The infant is not yet *attached*, since this care can be provided by any adult.

Making the Attachment: Focusing on Familiar People (10 weeks to 6–8 months)

Infants now begin to respond differently to different people. Social responses—cooing, smiling, babbling—are readily displayed with familiar caregivers. A stranger may receive a long stare and cause fear or distress. This stage is when trust begins to develop.

Clear Attachment: Active Closeness Is Sought (8 months to 18–24 months)

Now attachment to familiar people is clear. Young children show separation anxiety, becoming distressed when familiar people they trust leave them. Now young children *know they need* someone (a cognitive function) and send deliberate social signals, like clinging and resisting separation, to keep familiar people near them. The child is using her caregiver as a *secure base* from which to gradually explore a new environment and then return for emotional support.

A Reciprocal Relationship: Partnership Behavior (24 months on)

Young children now begin to understand an adult's coming and going. They are more able to let go and can be more flexible. Language helps them to process the separation experience (for example, "I'll be back after your nap").

concern to both parents and caregivers, who have to help children cope until they feel comfortable. It may comfort parents to know that these feelings are a sign that attachment is strong and that it will hold. Children will learn to cope with separation, and this skill will serve them for a lifetime. The various attachment behaviors and coping skills that develop in children indicate they are establishing trust in others and, at the same time, becoming self-reliant.

Measuring Attachment

What happens to the child who cannot get nurturing responses from people in her environment? And what about the child who seems indifferent or rejecting of the people around her? Developmental psychologist Mary Ainsworth created the **Strange Situation,** a sequence of staged situations, to answer such questions and to measure attachment strength between a mother and child. In this experiment the mother and infant enter a new environment and the baby is free to play.

Then a stranger enters, and the mother leaves, and finally the stranger leaves and the mother returns. During this series of departures and reunions the reactions of infants can vary a great deal and are used to indicate a *pattern* of attachment behavior.

Securely attached infants and toddlers seem comfortable in the new setting and explore independently as long as the parent is present. Their degree of distress may vary when the parent leaves, but they immediately go to the mother when she returns and seek contact and comfort. Young children with an insecure avoidant attachment pattern do not seek closeness to the mother and do not seem distressed when the parent departs. They also seem to avoid the mother when she returns—they seem indifferent to the to mother's behavior. Finally, young children with an insecure ambivalent (resistant) attachment pattern show positive and negative reactions to their parent. Initially, they seem very anxious, are reluctant to separate, and are in such close contact to their mother they hardly explore the new setting. They show great distress when their mother leaves and show ambivalent reactions when their mother returns (seeking closeness, but also hitting and kicking the mother in anger and remaining resistant to comforting). Secure attachment patterns were related to mothers who responded rapidly and positively to their babies. In contrast, insecurely attached infants were ignored or rejected, or were responded to inconsistently by their mothers.[4]

Some expansion of Ainsworth's research (especially work with abused and neglected children) indicates a fourth pattern called disorganized-disoriented. Young children with this attachment pattern show contradictory behavior by approaching the parent/caregiver but also looking away. They also show signs of fear, confusion, and disorientation, and they may be the least securely attached children of all.[5]

Most of the early research on attachment (especially that of John Bowlby, 1951 and Mary Ainsworth, 1978) focused on mothers and attachment. Things have changed since that research was done. Now there is more focus on men's roles in nurturance, sensitivity, and support, which leads to the attachment that used to be considered only mothers' territory. Fathers are not necessarily just the *other* parent; in some cases they are the *only* parent. Child care has made a difference in attachment patterns, as has the growing awareness of cultural diversity. Some children live in extended families or kinship networks and may have multiple attachments rather than a single strong one to just the mother. The mother, or even the father, may not be the primary person to whom the child is attached. Many more children from all kinds of backgrounds now are in early care and education settings starting from a few weeks old.

Reflect

Have you observed a child in a new situation who did not react in the ways Ainsworth described? What might account for these different reactions?

Imagine a child who is almost three years old and barely looks up from the sandbox when his mother arrives to pick him up. Is this indifference to the parent really a sign of insecure attachment? Could it be that he feels at home in the child care setting where he has been for most of his life? Maybe he is engaged in something interesting at the moment of her arrival. If he gets tested in the Ainsworth Strange Situation maybe he is so used to *separating* from his mother and going to other people that he just takes advantage of the toys in the room. He doesn't respond like Ainsworth's "securely attached" child when his mother leaves or when she comes back. We have to be careful about generalizing from research that was done in a certain time period, in different circumstances, and on different populations from the ones in child care today. Judging the degree or kind of attachment without understanding the bigger picture—including diversity, cultural awareness and varied family lifestyles—can be harmful!

Attachment Issues

Not all babies enjoy an ideal relationship that fosters a secure attachment. The infant and caregiver may not respond to each other in ways that bring mutual delight and the quality care necessary for the infant.

Sometimes infants are born without a strong set of attachment behaviors. They may not be responsive or attractive. Adults may find it neither rewarding nor satisfying to interact with such babies or to meet their needs. Not only may these infants lack a set of pleasing behaviors, they may even reject any advances. They may constantly stiffen when cuddled or cry when touched. Some babies are just not responsive. They may be too active to attend, or too passive. In these cases, it is up to adults to promote attachment.

Caregivers can promote a secure attachment by being supportive, persistent, and not being put off by the baby. Sensitive caregivers find ways that cause less discomfort to hold the babies who reject them. They continue to touch and talk to these babies despite rejection. They use caregiving times to interact and pay attention to the child at other times as well. Sometimes just observing such babies regularly and in depth will help caregivers develop more positive and respectful feelings for them.

Caregivers also find ways to help too active and too passive babies attend. They discover ways to reduce stimulation or increase sensory input, depending on what is needed.

Center-based programs can provide for attachment needs through a primary-caregiver system in which babies are assigned to a particular caregiver. Group size is important if babies are to be responded to consistently and sensitively in order to promote attachment. More than about 12 babies works against such attachment.

Sometimes the attachment issues lie with the parents. The infant may be fully equipped with attachment behaviors, but the parent may fail to respond. Indifference, for whatever reason, can be devastating to an infant. The infant doesn't give up for a long time and may develop a set of behaviors that elicits a negative response from the adult, which is better than no response at all.

If the baby has no attachment or negative attachment, that is cause for alarm. Outside help is required. Child care workers may perceive the problem and refer the families, but it is beyond their realm of responsibility to solve it.

You may suspect this problem when a baby in your care does not thrive in the same way the other babies do. He or she may not be gaining weight or reaching milestones within a reasonable time. This attachment problem and failure to thrive may be related to a variety of other causes. You may see that the baby is unresponsive and resistant to everybody. Or perhaps you see him or her responding exactly the same to everyone—parent, caregiver, and stranger.

What happens if there is no attachment? A significant answer came from Harry Harlow, who learned something about attachment without even setting out to study it. He was interested in isolating rhesus monkeys so that they could live in a disease-free environment and not infect one another. He raised 56 newborn monkeys in separate cages, away from one another and their mothers. He was surprised to find that they grew to be very different adults from the rest of their species. They were more unsocial, indifferent, and aggressive than other rhesus monkeys, which are normally social and cooperative. None of the monkeys raised in isolation mated.[6]

Let's examine the implications for child rearing. Although virtually no one attempts to raise a child in total isolation, children are too frequently raised without enough human contact, without opportunities for interaction, and without consistent treatment. In such a situation, the problems are multiple. Though the infants have contact with adults who feed and change them, the adults may vary from day to day. The infants may be unable to distinguish one from the other or may find that their attachment behavior brings no consistent caregiving response. They find no one to call their own—no one whom they can influence. Eventually, such children give up and no longer try to influence anyone. Lacking not only attachment but also adequate physical contact, these infants are deprived of the variety of sensory input that comes with a healthy relationship. They become passive and noncomplaining, their development slows, and they may fail to thrive. Researchers believe it is important for babies to establish a consistent attachment to at least one person before four to six months of age.[7] *Remember principle 9: Build security by teaching trust.* Don't teach distrust by being undependable or often inconsistent.

Caregivers and home-based care providers who have some understanding of the attachment process can do a great deal to help parents recognize their importance and their impact on their infant. Offering labels for facial expressions and baby sounds and encouraging parents to slow down and observe their child's growing competence can go a long way to foster the vital, secure attachment relationship between an infant and parent.

This consistent and sensitive care is emphasized in the brain development research mentioned earlier in this chapter. When infants experience these secure attachments, hormones called **neurotransmitters** are secreted, and they induce a sense of well-being. Positive, nurturing experiences seem to reinforce certain pathways in the brain. There is a dynamic relationship between the *care* an infant receives and his or her brain *growth*. Healthy attachment develops when caregivers are consistent and responsive; relationships are primary to development.[8]

Studies of children in institutions have kept many people from considering group care for infants. But infants in child care are different from infants in orphanages. They have parents (at least one). Most of them arrive in child care attached, and they remain attached. But we have learned from those sad orphanages of yesterday. We know now how vital attachment needs are. We know, too, that infants need ongoing, reciprocal, responsive interactions when they are outside their own home for significant periods during the day. We know that infants in child care retain their attachments to their parents.

Knowledge about caring relationships is transforming caregivers' work with very young children. Building and maintaining positive relationships that will continue over time, sometimes over several years, is a critical principle in "attachment-based" programs. This continuity of care begins with the creation of small groups of infants, each with its own qualified caregiver. Caregivers plan for each child, creating individualized portfolios for them. They plan for parents, too, encouraging them to observe the program and visit often. The caregiver-child relationship becomes an extension of the parent-child relationship. The environment is even organized with relationship continuity and secure attachments in mind; each group has its own room or space, and it is used exclusively by that group.[9] Research shows that infant care is not detrimental to development and to secure attachments if the *quality* of care is exemplary. Relationship-based programs appreciate that quality care is vital. Infants not only deserve but *must have* fine care, not just care that is good enough.

 ## Children with Special Needs: Infants Affected by Drugs and Alcohol

Some infants today have severe attachment problems because their mothers took drugs during pregnancy. (The drugs vary, but cocaine or crack are among the most common.) These babies usually have medical and behavioral problems. The following scene shows a typical profile of an infant exposed to substance abuse and suggests ways to care for such a baby. Special thanks to David Kaplan, pediatrician, for this information, for his specialized work with crack-addicted infants, and for his ongoing support to foster parents.[10]

Jenny is six months old. She is being undressed for her usual weekly medical exam in the doctor's office by Kathy, her foster mother. Jenny's mom took crack cocaine during her pregnancy with Jenny, and although she contacts Kathy regularly, she has seen Jenny only three times and remains unable emotionally and physically to care for her baby. Jenny was born full-term but weighed only four and a half pounds. No other prenatal information was available to Kathy.

Kathy undresses Jenny slowly and speaks quietly to her. She tries to avoid unnecessary stimulation because Jenny is still prone to high-pitched, frantic crying. When the doctor comes in, he checks Jenny's color, reflexes, and weight. During the examination, Jenny does *not* make eye contact with the doctor. He, too, moves with gentle firmness in an effort to avoid overstimulating Jenny. His remaining assessment is done through conversation with Kathy. Jenny is placed on a soft flannel blanket in Kathy's lap in a sitting position with her shoulders and arms forward.

Doctor: Kathy, I see that Jenny has gained a little weight this week, although she remains below normal for her age. Has her feeding situation improved?

Reflect

Think about what you have read concerning attachment and maybe anything that you have had the opportunity to observe. What can caregivers do to demonstrate their sensitivity to young children? What do infants and toddlers do to demonstrate their needs to caregivers?

KATHY: Yes, I think so. I always try to feed her in a quiet place, and swaddling is no longer necessary. I think her sucking is stronger, and there is less spitting up. She still does not like to look at me, but generally she is more calm than a month ago.

DOCTOR: That's a very good sign. Remember, to help prevent the spitting up, feed her in a sitting or semireclining position. Feed slowly, burp frequently, and avoid overfeeding. After feeding, keep Jenny vertical for a few minutes. You seem to be more able than anyone else to calm her.

KATHY: Yes, I think so, too. Rocking her gently in a vertical position has really helped. When she is stiff, the warm bath and gentle massage you suggested have also helped.

DOCTOR: Good, glad to hear that. Just keep alert to her warning signs of overstimulation—yawning, frowns, eye aversion, flailing limbs, whimpering. I know once she starts crying, she is difficult to stop, and prolonged crying may complicate her respiratory problems.

Jenny's movement on Kathy's lap has been gradually increasing during this brief conversation between Kathy and the doctor. She is beginning to stretch her legs forward and her shoulders back. Kathy notes her restlessness and shifts her slightly forward in her lap to avoid back arching and potential muscle cramping.

KATHY: I think we are getting ready to leave now. (Both doctor and foster mom pause to observe Jenny.)

DOCTOR: Yes, I'd agree. Jenny is fortunate to be with someone who reads her signals so quickly. I think she is doing well. Kathy, you know that I can't make long-term projections for her, but we will stay in close contact. Play is important for Jenny. Avoid any assistive devices—walkers or jumpers. I'll see you in about 10 days; keep up the good work!

KATHY: Thanks! We'll see you then.

Kathy begins to dress Jenny. Jenny's muscle tone has remained relaxed. She makes no attempt, however, to cuddle or hold on to Kathy. And although she is making gurgling sounds, crying does not develop.

It is obvious, even in this brief scene, that with an infant exposed to drug abuse, attachment behaviors are lacking, and handling needs to be slower and more deliberate. Responsiveness and observing infant cues remain *very* important. Few specialists and doctors are willing to make long-term assessments of such babies because each child and situation are unique. Learn each child's unique ways of communicating (cries, words, movements, gestures, facial expressions, body positions), and teach yours. Don't underestimate children's ability to communicate even though their verbal language skills may be nonexistent or minimal.

It is important to acknowledge that mothers who drink large amounts of alcohol during pregnancy may have infants with some of the same behaviors discussed above. These infants may also have slower physical growth and specific facial abnormalities (widely spaced eyes, a thin upper lip, a small head). The brain may not have fully developed, and there is often mental retardation. Brain testing often reveals that there is structural damage and abnormalities in brain functioning (especially in transferring messages from one part of the brain to another).[11] It is hard to determine the dividing line between safe and dangerous drinking levels during pregnancy. It is no doubt best for pregnant women to avoid alcohol entirely.

Remember that the attachment process is influenced by the responsiveness of the caregiver *and* the characteristics of the child. This is of particular significance to children with disabilities or those who are considered "at risk." For instance, deaf or blind children may be slower to develop secure attachments to their parents and caregivers. If they can't hear special caregiving sounds, or gaze at and make clear eye contact with their key people, they may not respond in ways that promote sensitive interactions. Also low birth weight preterm (or at risk) babies may seem insecurely attached because they may be more difficult to soothe and less socially responsive. At risk and disabled infants can and do form healthy attachments, but their behaviors may not encourage parent and caregiver responsiveness to the same extent that other babies do.

Don't hesitate to get more information and program support if you have questions concerning any child in your care. The key point concerning infants with special needs, as with all infants, is that they must have the opportunity to form a secure attachment. Responsive caregivers who foster the attachment process can buffer some of the negative effects of a child's environment and even some of a child's own predisposing (less than ideal) characteristics.

NAEYC Program Standard 4
Assessment

DEVELOPMENTAL PATHWAYS

Attachment Behaviors

Attachment Behaviors

Young Infants (up to 8 months)	• Show they recognize their primary caregivers by sight, sound, and smell within the first two weeks of life • Respond with more animation and pleasure to the primary caregiver than to others • React to strangers with soberness or anxiety around the second half of the first year
Mobile infants (up to 18 months)	• May exhibit anxious behavior around unfamiliar adults • Actively show affection for a familiar person • May show anxiety at separation from the primary caregiver • Show intense feelings for parents
Toddlers (up to 3 years)	• May exhibit the same attachment behaviors as mobile infants but become increasingly aware of their own feelings and those of others • Express emotions with increasing control • May verbalize feelings once they start talking

Source: S. Bredekamp and C. Copple, *Developmentally Appropriate Practice in Early Childhood Programs* (Washington, D.C.: National Association for the Education of Young Children, 1997).

(continued)

DEVELOPMENTAL PATHWAYS

Attachment Behaviors *(continued)*

Diverse Developmental Pathways

What you see	Opal, 14 months old, has been in child care for 7 months. She still enters the infant/toddler program looking very anxious and clinging tightly to her mom, Joyce. Opal does not really *play* with any of the toys and expresses few emotions other than fear. Joyce does not seem able to comfort Opal; they rarely look directly at each other.
What you might think	This seems like insecure attachment, but Opal may just be slow to warm up to people. Her mom seems very remote and uncomfortable.
What you might not know	Joyce, Opal's mom, experienced four different foster homes before she was five years old. She was finally placed in the permanent care of her maternal grandmother when she was six. Joyce knows she has a hard time reading Opal's signals for care and nurturance, and it seems that she often feels overwhelmed by the parenting experience.
What you might do	Encourage Joyce to visit the program and, when you can, create a quiet, simple area where the three of you can play together. Watch Opal's facial expressions and try to label them for Joyce (especially the positive ones!). Joyce needs to develop trust in you and the program as much as Opal does.

Cultural Diversity and Developmental Pathways

What you see	Most mornings 22-month-old Kyoko is still carried into the child care setting by her mother (even though she is quite able to walk alone). She clings to her mother while her mom puts her jacket and various toys in her cubby. She often cries for a long period after her mother (reluctantly) leaves her, and she has little contact with the other children.
What you might think	Kyoko seems passive and too dependent on her mother. She should be doing more things for herself. She's been in the program for almost 8 months. Why is separation still so hard?
What you might not know	It has been very difficult for Kyoko's mom to leave her in child care. She was raised to value close physical contact and intimacy between infants and mothers; in her culture this is important for close-knit family relations. Kyoko's father believes this program will help her become more independent, and since moving to this county four years ago he has been looking for ways to make sure that his children become "successful."
What you might do	Even though you've chatted with Kyoko's mother, try to make more contact with her. Try to find out more about her expectations for the program and share yours with her. Listen carefully before you make judgments about attachment and dependency.

Summary

Attachment is an ongoing interactive process influenced by the responsiveness of the caregiver and the characteristics of the infant or toddler.

Brain Research

- Current technology has provided insight into how the brain functions and the importance of early quality caregiving.
- Secure attachment relationships directly affect the way the brain gets "wired," and positive, warm interactions stabilize brain connections.
- Strong neural pathways support all areas of growth, especially cognitive and social development.

Milestones of Attachment

- Behaviors that promote the attachment experience—including crying, eye contact, and grasping—are present in an infant at birth.
- In the second half of the first year infants usually indicate fear of strangers (8 to 10 months) and separation anxiety (10 to 12 months).
- Sensitive caregivers can assist toddlers and their parents/families in the process of establishing trust. This supportive care fosters self-reliance and exploration into a larger world.

Measuring Attachment

- The research of developmental psychologist Mary Ainsworth stands as a hallmark for the measurement of attachment strength between a parent and an infant or toddler.
- Secure infants respond with stress to a parent leaving them in a strange setting, but they seek closeness and are comforted when the parent returns. Insecure infants may or may not respond to a parent's exit, and they can respond in avoidant or ambivalent ways when the reunion takes place.
- Remember that fathers, as well as mothers, who provide sensitive, responsive care to their infants can create the secure base needed for healthy attachment. It is also important to appreciate cultural values and listen carefully before making judgments about attachment and dependency.

Attachment Issues and Children with Special Needs

- Sometimes children are born without a strong set of attachment behaviors and caregivers may have to *promote* secure attachment and trust in especially supportive and persistent ways.
- If an attachment problem persists, or no attachment seems evident, outside assistance should be sought.

Online Resources

Go to the Online Learning Center at **www.mhhe.com/itc7e** to access the student study guide that includes quizzes, practice with key terms, and a review of chapter content; links to websites related to the chapter; and additional resources.

- Children with special needs who have obstacles to the attachment process are in particular need of knowledgeable, sensitive caregivers to help them form the healthy attachments so vital to their ongoing development.

Key Terms

attachment 94
autonomy 98
axon 95
dendrites 95

interactional synchrony 98
neurons 95
neurotransmitters 104
Strange Situation 101

synapses 95
trust 97

Thought/Activity Questions

1. Imagine a dialogue with a new parent concerning the topic of attachment. What would you like to share about this process? How would your comments change with the parent of a two-year-old?
2. Review Table 5.1, "Rethinking the Brain," on page 94. What points are the most important? Why? How might you share this information with a parent?
3. What happens to development if little or no attachment is made? Consider specifically emotional, social, and mental/cognitive growth.
4. Observe an infant-toddler program when the parent of a toddler is about to leave. What attachment behaviors do you see in the child? How does the parent respond? Consider what changes or additions you might like to see.
5. Describe the kinds of interactions that build a secure attachment. What obstacles might contribute to attachment concerns?

For Further Reading

Beginnings Workshop: "Working with Parents of Children with Differing Abilities," *Child Care Information Exchange* 88, November 1992.

B. Cunningham and B. Dorsey, "Out of Sight but Not Out of Mind: The Harmful Absence of Men," *Child Care Information Exchange* 156, March/April 2004, pp. 42–43.

A. Gopnik, A. Metzoff, and P. Kuhl, *The Scientist in the Crib: What Early Learning Tells Us About the Mind* (New York: HarperCollins, 1999).

H. Gray, "You Go Away and You Come Back—Supporting Separations and Reunions in an Infant/Toddler Classroom," *Young Children* 59(5), September 2004, pp. 100–107.

M. Hartzell, "Emotional Attachment and Healthy Development," *Child Care Information Exchange*, May/June 2004, pp. 80–83.

A. S. Honig, *Secure Relationships: Nurturing Infant/Toddler Attachment in Early Child Care Settings* (Washington, D.C.: National Association for the Education of Young Children, 2002).

J. Szamreta, "Peekaboo Power—To Ease Separation and Build Secure Relationships," *Young Children* 55(3), January 2003, pp. 88–94.

M. Watson, "Attachment Theory and Challenging Behaviors: Reconstructing the Nature of Relationships," *Young Children* 58(4), July 2003, pp. 12–20.

P. Wesley, "Early Intervention Consultants in the Classroom," *Young Children* 57(4), July 2002, pp. 30–36.

chapter 6

Perception

Focus Questions

After reading this chapter you should be able to answer the following questions:

1 What is perceptual development? How is it influenced by brain development?

2 What capabilities do newborns have in the areas of hearing, taste, smell, touch, and sight?

3 What can caregivers do to foster young children's perceptual development?

4 What adaptations can a caregiver make in the environment for a child with a sensory impairment? What does a caregiver need to know to do this appropriately?

What Do You See?

Bea is exploring some beads. She looks at them, perhaps noting the different colors. She looks at the caregiver while touching the beads, exploring the shape and texture. She puts them in her mouth and then smiles at the caregiver when she hears, "You really seem to like those beads, Bea. How do they taste?" She keeps looking at the caregiver but then turns to the center of the room when she hears another caregiver comment about getting ready for snack. She sniffs slightly and seems to be noting the smell of the cornbread baking—the smell that has been filling the room for the last 10 minutes. She drops the beads and crawls over to the area of the room being set up for snack.

Did you notice how many different senses Bea was using to explore the beads? She also seemed to use the caregiver's words, the smells from the kitchen, and the setting up of the snack area to anticipate that food would be arriving soon.

Very young children are immediately involved in the process of gathering information and using it. Sensation is the stimulation of the sense organs (for example, eyes, ears, and taste buds), and **perception** is the ability to take in and organize this sensory information. It is an innate tendency to search for order and stability in the world, and it becomes increasingly fine-tuned as we age.[1] Sensory information provides an important link to all other areas of development. Learning in this area can be considered a *dynamic system*—"dynamic" in that it is an ever-changing process as we grow and mature and "system" because it constantly influences other growth areas. Think about Bea in the opening scene of this chapter; she was obviously able to coordinate a great deal of sensory information! As infants and toddlers repeat experiences, they begin to make meaningful connections about the people and objects in their world. **Neural pathways,** or the dendrite connections between brain cells, are strengthened as they gather, apply, and benefit from their sensory encounters. This chapter reviews these perceptual, or sensory, abilities. It also includes some early warning signs for determining if a child might have a sensory impairment and potential interventions or adaptations to make.

Sensory Integration

The increasing public awareness of early brain development has validated what many parents and caregivers have known for a long time—learning for infants and toddlers is interrelated, and growth in one area influences growth in another. **Sensory integration** is the process of combining and integrating information across the senses and it is critical to the development of perception. As infants become aware of their sensory experience, they can discriminate between people and make attachments. They learn to move their bodies in specific ways to accommodate new sensory information. They begin to relate what they have learned about an object or person through one sense (for example, sight) to what they have learned through another sense (maybe touch). This interrelatedness between sensory experience and motor experience is strong, and it provides the base for cognitive development. Young children need sensory experiences with opportunities for lots of repetition if they are to build healthy learning pathways in the brain. *Remember principle 4: Invest time to build a total person.*

To become more aware of your own perceptions so that you can better understand those of an infant, try the following exercise:

Choose something you like the taste and smell of (a sprig of mint, a piece of apple), and take it to a place where you can be undisturbed.

Block out all your senses except smell and taste. Then pay attention to what you have brought along to smell and taste. Concentrate first on your sense of smell only, then on your sense of taste. When you have fully explored these, put the substance away. Notice how the sensation fades. When the flavor is gone, move on.

Become aware of your body. Sense the places on your body where your clothes touch, where you feel pressure. Pay attention to these sensations. Alter your position and note the changes you feel.

Be aware of your body in relation to the space it occupies. Feel the space around you. "Sense," without touching, where your body ends and the space begins. Explore the relationship between your body and this space. Try expanding and contracting your body; alter the space it takes up.

Now move your attention from your whole body to your hands. Explore around you with your hands, noticing the textures and forms your fingers encounter. Pay attention only to what your fingertips feel.

Move your focus from your hands to your ears. Pay attention to everything that is coming in through your ears. Now pick out the noise closest to you and listen to it carefully. Next shift your attention to the noise that is furthest from you. Now see if you can concentrate on sounds coming from inside you. Finally, turn on all the noises at once and take them in without sorting them out.

Now move your attention to your eyes. Open your eyes. Look around. Focus on an object near you. See if you can make the object disappear by looking only at the spaces around it and between its parts. Concentrate on these negative spaces for a minute or so. Then take in more objects. Look at them carefully. Then concentrate on the space around and between them. Shift your focus from the space back to the objects and back to the space again. Try concentrating only on background, then on foreground, then on a single object. Let your eyes go out of focus.

Come back to your normal perceptive state.

Now reflect on the order in which you experienced your senses. If you did the exercise the way it was set up, you went from perceiving through very localized physical contact (your taste buds) to generalized physical contact (your skin). Then you went on to perceive with two senses that extend beyond physical contact—hearing and seeing. With these you took in events or objects at a distance.

Infants learn to use their senses in much the same order. They first depend most on perceptions that are direct and physical, especially those that come in through their mouths. An infant's mouth is his or her main learning tool in the first months of life. As infants grow, they learn to "extend" themselves by tuning in to the senses that bring information from a distance. See Figure 6.1 on the next page for a summary of how and where the senses develop in the brain.

This ability to tune in to experience and concentrate on certain aspects of it allows an organizational process to develop. This process is neurological—it cannot be seen. But we can see infants adjust to their experiences. Even though all the senses are operating, infants initially do not realize that the information they receive from these senses has continuity. They cannot yet perceive the repetitiveness of events or interpret them. In a short time, however, connections between separate events are clarified. For example, crying infants will calm down as they realize that hearing a particular voice or seeing a particular face means that food or care is about to be given.

This book talks about only **five senses** (hearing, taste, smell, touch, and vision) but it is interesting to speculate about possible other senses and whether

Reflect

Think about Bea, the infant that you met at the beginning of this chapter. How is she demonstrating **sensory integration?** How can her caregivers help her coordinate her sensory exploration?

Figure 6.1 Making Sense of the World. *Source:* Adapted from "World of Senses" by Joan Raymond, *Newsweek Special Issue,* Fall/Winter 2000, p. 18.

Infants come into the world wired to perceive it, and their early experiences complete their brain circuitry.

Touch: The primary sensory cortex is responsible for touch. This critical area of the brain can process tactile sensations by the fourth month in utero. By week 10, skin nerves appear.

Vision: Some simple signals in the visual cortex can be received from the fetus' eye at seven months in utero. But this is the slowest sense to develop, and the neurons in the vision pathway remain immature for several months after birth.

Taste: As early as 7 weeks after conception, 10,000 taste buds on the tongue and soft palate begin to appear. The specific tastes that the fetus is exposed to before birth (what mom eats) can shape later likes and dislikes in infancy.

Hearing: Prenatal exposure to sounds can have a lasting effect. By 28 weeks gestation, the auditory cortex can perceive loud noises. A newborn can usually recognize his or her mother's voice and prefers it to all others.

Smell: At birth, infants can distinguish their mother's smell. Even in utero, infants can detect the smell of amniotic fluid. The sense of smell seems closely linked to emotions and memories.

infants may have many more sensory abilities than we retain as adults. Examine the following passage from *The Metaphoric Mind,* a book that argues that we have not 5 or 6 but 20 or more senses.

> *Some human beings clearly detect minute changes in gravitational and magnetic fields. Others can detect the energy created by a flow of material in pipes, movement through soil, or electrostatic currents in the air. As adults these people are considered unique, mystical, or deviant in some other way. It may well be that these people have simply retained an awareness of senses they possessed as children.*[2]

Hearing

Newborns can hear at birth (and even before). They can sense the direction sound comes from as well as its frequency and duration. Researchers have found that sounds of 5 to 15 seconds seem to have the most effect on the infant's level of activity and heart rate (the two measures most frequently used to reflect an infant's awareness of a change in an event). If the sound lasts more than several

VIDEO OBSERVATION 6

Boy Exploring Toy Car Using Touch and Sound

See Video Observation 6: Boy Exploring Toy Car Using Touch and Sound for an illustration of learning to coordinate sensory information. You see a boy who is being helped to use hearing and touch to learn about a toy car that he can't see.

Questions

- Why do you think the man chose to give the boy this particular toy?
- Are you aware of how many senses you use at once to explore a new object? What do you think is your strongest, most useful sense?
- In this example the adult is in more of a teaching role than in most other examples. Why do you think this is, and how do you feel about it? Would you feel differently if you knew this child became blind not long before the video was taken?

To view this clip, go to www.mhhe.com/itc7e. Click on Student Edition, select Chapter 6, and click on Video Observation.

minutes, the infant becomes less responsive. In other words, an infant is more attentive if you speak and then are quiet than if you make long speeches.[3]

Newborns recognize the sound of their mother's voice. Experiments have shown that infants only 20 weeks old can discriminate between the syllables "baw" and "gah." Listening to people's voices and noting differences seems to be an early skill. Young babies are especially responsive to a high-pitched, expressive voice, using a rising tone at the end of phrases. This describes a speech pattern now referred to as "parentese" (replacement for "baby talk"). Infants' early responsiveness to such sounds and patterns seems to encourage parents and caregivers to talk to them. This interaction strengthens both the emotional tie between them and the infants' readiness for the complex task of language development.[4] The way infants react to sounds or any other sensory stimulation, however, depends a great deal on the situation in which they experience them. A loud or strange noise may be frightening, but the presence of a familiar, comforting caregiver transmits a sense of security and allows the infant to remain calm and open to learning. Young infants are also able to hear certain sounds that distinguish one language from another. By four and a half months, they are able to discriminate their own names from similar sounding words. By five months, they can distinguish the difference between English and Spanish passages.[5]

Infants need the opportunity to experience a variety of sounds, and they need quiet times in order to appreciate the differences in sounds. If the noise level in the environment is too high, the infant spends a lot of energy tuning out and focusing. The optimum noise level varies with each child. Sensitive caregivers can determine what is more or less right for the individual after they get to know the child. Part of this awareness comes from knowing your own optimum noise level.

Some adults like background music, and others don't. However, a point to consider is this: if you want an infant to focus on a sound, that sound should be isolated and have a beginning and an end. For example, if a music box or CD player is constantly playing, the infant eventually stops listening because the sound is no longer interesting. Caregivers should be sure that mechanical toys and other noisemakers do not become substitutes for the human voice. Infants can determine a great deal from the inflection of a person's voice, and attending to the human voice and its inflections is the beginning of language development.

Toddlers have a greater ability to tolerate higher noise levels, so they can be in slightly larger groups than infants can. However, toddlers too vary individually, and some children are greatly overstimulated by multiple sounds. These children may be unable to focus when surrounded by noise. One way to help solve this problem is to have quiet spaces where one or two overstimulated children may retreat when they choose. We've seen pillow-lined closets, tents, and even large wooden boxes available for this purpose.

Toddlers, as well as infants, benefit when the sounds they hear most are live, human voices directed to them personally. Other appropriate sounds in the environment include voices of all sorts (children and adults), music (both live and recorded), and the sounds that naturally go along with free play in a rich environment. Helping children tune in to the sounds of nature, a worthy activity, is often accomplished on short walks, depending, of course, on the environment in which the center or family child care home is located.

NAEYC Program Standard 3
Teaching

Be aware of talking to one sex more than the other. Boys and girls need equal treatment if they are to grow up feeling like equals.

Smell and Taste

Researchers know that smell and taste are present at birth, and they develop rapidly in the first few weeks. Newborns can distinguish the smell of their own mothers from that of other women who have just given birth, so smell obviously plays a role in attachment. (Mothers also often report that the smells of their babies are pleasing to them.)

Newborns respond to unpleasant strong odors such as ammonia or acetic acid by turning away, but they seem insensitive to less interesting odors that are fainter. They respond positively to the odor of banana, somewhat negatively to fishy odors, and with disgust to rotten eggs.[6] An increase in breathing rate and activity level can be noted when odors are present in the air, and the greater the saturation of the odors, the greater the heart rate and activity level.

An environment rich in smells adds to a toddler program. They can be part of the daily program, such as food cooking, or they can be introduced by caregivers in such ways as "smell bottles." Be careful of making things that aren't edible smell delicious—such as chocolate shaving cream or peppermint flavoring in play dough—unless the toddlers are well conditioned to the idea that play dough and shaving cream are not for eating.

Some taste reactions are clearly developed at birth. Infants show disgust over bitter tastes and seem to have an innate sweet tooth.[7] Since breast milk is quite sweet, taste is another sense that may contribute to attachment. Salt taste is recognized soon after and will be accepted if the infant is hungry. A 10-day-old infant can show surprise if water is substituted for the expected milk, but there seems to be a correlation with whether the baby has been well fed; infants whose diets have been inadequate do not seem to notice taste differences rapidly.

Be careful not to condition infants to the taste of salt and other additives. There is no reason to spice food for the very young; they appreciate and enjoy the natural flavors if not covered. Most of us have learned that food in its plain state "needs something," and we are suffering for that acquired taste as people's blood pressures soar and many are on salt-restricted diets.

Tasting can be an important part of the toddlers' day as they are exposed to a variety of foods at meals and snack times. Of course, care should be taken to choose foods that don't present a choking hazard. We'll present more about this subject in Chapter 12.

Reflect

How do you feel about infants and toddlers playing with their food? What might be the benefits? What possible cultural, and even gender, issues need to be acknowledged?

Touch

Sensitivity, or responsiveness to discomfort and pain, increases rapidly after birth. Some parts of the body are more sensitive than others. The head, for example, is more sensitive than the arms and legs. Individual babies vary in their sensitivity to touch, and for some, touch is unwelcome. Caregivers need to learn to handle those "touch-defensive" babies in ways that cause minimal discomfort. One way is to lift such young infants on a pillow instead of picking them up as you would other babies. Some babies and toddlers respond better to strong touch than light touch, which seems to pain them.

Where and how we touch is related to culture. It is a good idea to find out what is forbidden or disrespectful in cultures different from your own if children from other cultures are in your program. For example, in some cultures children are never touched on the head, and to do so upsets parents. Consider the message mainstream America gives when one person touches or pats another on the head. How would you feel if your boss patted you on the head? Pats on the head are reserved for the very young or dogs, never for an equal or a superior. Though it seems very natural to most adults, perhaps it would be more respectful to restrain from patting babies and young children on the head.

Be aware if you are differentiating between boys and girls in the way you touch the children in your care. Sometimes people unconsciously touch one sex more than the other. Try to be equal in your treatment of both sexes.

Tactile perception (touch) relates to motor abilities (movement skills). As babies increase in their ability to move around, touch gives them more and more information about the world. And they seek this information almost emphatically. All environments for infants and toddlers should be touchable and mouthable (the mouth also gives the very young a good deal of information). While you are filling the environment with plastic toys (that are both touchable and mouthable), don't forget to provide some natural substances that the children can explore such as wood or wool. (One educational approach, Waldorf Education, believes that young children should experience only objects [toys] made from natural substances because artificial ones—things that look like something else—fool the senses.)

Give toddlers words for what they are feeling—soft, warm, fuzzy, rough, smooth. Be sure they have plenty of soft objects in their environment. Some programs occur in predominantly hard environments because hard surfaces and objects last longer and are more sanitary. Reducing softness is not a way to increase cost-effectiveness because a hard environment changes the whole program. Behavior tends to improve when an environment is softened.

Provide a variety of tactile (touching) experiences for toddlers. Even though they are up and around, they haven't outgrown their need to explore the world with their skin. Here are some ideas for offering toddlers tactile experiences that involve the entire body:

1. A dress-up area filled with silky, slinky, furry, and other textured clothes
2. A sensory tub filled with such things as plastic balls or yarn balls (securely fastened so children don't get tangled in loose ends) to climb into
3. Swimming in plastic pools in the summer
4. Sit-in sandboxes
5. Mud baths (Nothing more is needed than a warm day, a hose, some dirt, and the willingness to clean up afterward. The toddlers themselves know what to do with the mud.)

If you're willing to let children wallow about getting whole body tactile experiences, be careful you don't tread on cultural values. Some cultures have strong prohibitions against children getting dirty or messy.

Other kinds of tactile experiences are designed mainly for the hands (or hands and arms). Some simple, one-step cooking allows children to have a tactile experience. Other possibilities include water play, sand play, play dough, and finger painting (which has several variations, such as shaving cream [not for the youngest toddlers], cornstarch and water, and chocolate pudding [not if food is frowned on as a play medium]). Be sure you emphasize the process and not the product. The point of finger painting is to feel the paint and squish it around, not to make a pretty picture to take home.

Be careful not to exclude girls from these tactile activities because they might get messy. (Some people tolerate messy boys more easily than they do messy girls.) And be aware that some toddlers do not want to get messy. Don't blame parents for this. It may be that the parent has discouraged messiness (for personal or cultural reasons). But sometimes the reluctance comes from the child's personality or stage of development. Many toddlers go through a period of refusing to get their hands messy.

Not all tactile experiences have to be messy. Many excellent programs for toddlers have very limited messy experiences. No one expects you to encourage children to muck around in mud or Jell-O unless you really want to set up that kind of experience. Some simpler but also valuable experiences include a pan of cornmeal with spoons and sifters; a pan of birdseed (just to feel) or birdseed with pitchers, spoons, and cups; and a tray of salt to feel (and perhaps some little cars to run around in it). Just letting children go barefoot provides them with a variety of experiences as they encounter different textures underfoot.

NAEYC Program Standard 2
Curriculum

The Principles in Action

Principle 7 Model the behavior you want to teach. Don't preach.

Tyler is sitting up on the rug looking at his caregiver, who is close to him. She smiles. He smiles back. He gets up on all fours and takes off, stopping for a moment when he notices that he has left the soft thick rug. He crawls back and sits back down. He looks at his caregiver, who is idly poking her fingers into the rug. He also pokes his fingers into the rug. "Soft," she says, and he cocks his head to listen to her. Then Tyler gets up on all fours again, headed for a shelf of toys. Along the way he encounters an infant smaller than himself lying on her back on a blanket. He stops to investigate, and as he leans over to get a closer look, he notices a caregiver has come to sit beside him. He reaches for the baby's face, touching the smooth skin and patting the hair. He puts his lips on baby's head and looks up at the caregiver and smiles. She smiles back. He gets more vigorous in his investigations, and a hand comes down over his, touching him lightly. "Gently, gently," the caregiver says. He goes back to the original soft stroking.

1. Are these educational interactions?
2. What is the caregiver doing to encourage the child to touch and explore?
3. What relation does all that touching have to developing perception?
4. Can you tell how old this child is? What clues are you using?
5. Can you tell if this is a typically developing child? What clues are you using?
6. If the child hadn't responded to the caregiver's modeling of gentleness and had reached over to grab the baby's hair, what could the caregiver have done next?

Sight

We know more about sight than about the other senses, probably because most people depend so heavily on it. Infants can distinguish light and dark at birth. The pupillary reflex (the automatic narrowing of the pupil in bright light and widening in dim light) can be seen at birth, even in premature infants. Within a few hours infants are capable of visual pursuit. Their fixed focus seems to be about eight inches away. In other words, infants are equipped to see the mother's face while breast-feeding.

Within a few weeks, infants can discriminate among colors and prefer warm ones (red, orange, yellow) to cool ones (blue, green). Eye movements are somewhat erratic at first, but they rapidly become more refined. By the end of the second month, infants can focus both eyes to produce a single, though probably blurred, image. By the fourth month, they can see objects with clarity, and by six months, the average infant's vision is nearly 20/20.[8] Their ability to see is now comparable to that of an adult, though they have to learn to perceive and interpret what they are seeing.

Most newborns find all people and objects placed in front of them interesting—though some are more so than others. The human face is the most interesting of all (because newborns' visual abilities are clearly designed to promote attachment).

Infants of all ages need to be able to see interesting things. However, in the first weeks, eating and diaper changing provide sufficient visual input. As infants get older, a variety of visual material becomes more appropriate because it encourages them to move around in their world. Something interesting to see becomes something to reach for and eventually to move toward. Too much visual stimulation, however, can lead to a "circus effect." Infants become entertained observers rather than active participants and grow into passive toddlers who demand entertainment instead of inventing their own. Children used to outside entertainment are drawn toward television—the ultimate entertaining visual experience.

An entertained observer is quite different from a scientific observer. Entertained observers get hooked on a constant flow of novel visual stimulation. They get bored quickly and demand constant visual change. They may become television addicts. Because they experience such a strong assault on one sense (the visual), they ignore the fact that they are not actually involved physically or socially with the world around them. This eventual habit of observation and lack of involvement is detrimental to the development of a wide range of abilities.

Take cues from the infants themselves when setting up an environment that develops visual skills. Otherwise, it's hard to know how much sensory input is too much and when interesting new visual experiences will be welcome. If infants cry at certain things, too much may be going on, or they may not yet be ready to leave what they were paying attention to. If they are very quiet, they may be concentrating on something in particular or may be turned off by too many events. When infants find their world interesting and are allowed to explore it at their own pace, they learn to entertain themselves in the process of discovery. *Remember principle 7: Model the behavior you want to teach.*

Toddlers' visual worlds are larger, as they move around more. They also have a better understanding of what they are seeing. To get an idea of what toddlers' visual environments are like, get down at their level and look around. Things look very different from down there.

To cut down on visual stimulation for toddlers, put up low barricades to block areas of the room. Adults can see over the barriers in order to supervise, but children experience a visually calming room. (Barriers also can muffle sound to some extent.) Some rooms invite children to really focus on what's available; in others, toddlers get overexcited and have a hard time focusing.

Pictures add visual interest to a toddler's environment (though of course pictures also belong in an infant environment). Hang them low enough for the toddlers to see at their own eye level. Change them periodically, but not constantly, because toddlers appreciate seeing the familiar on a regular basis. Choose pictures that clearly depict familiar objects or other children in action. Be sure to represent different races in your picture display. Also be aware of the sex of the children in the pictures you hang. Don't show pictures that are predominantly little girls looking pretty and doing nothing and little boys involved in engaging activities. We've all been brought up on books that had that particular bias. Let's not pass it on to the children in our care.

One way to hang pictures is with clear contact paper that covers the picture and extends out beyond to stick to the wall. This way the picture is sealed in with no loose corners to pick at and tear and no tacks to swallow.

Aesthetics, or that which is judged beautiful, is a worthy, but often unconsidered, goal when designing a visual environment for infants and toddlers. Children are more likely to grow up with an eye for beauty if the adults around them demonstrate that they value aesthetics.

Children with Special Needs: Sensory Impairments

It is clear that infants and toddlers learn a great deal through their senses and that sensory information (perception) provides an important link between all other areas of development. If a young child has a known sensory problem or impairment, there are several helpful things to remember. First, ask about the child's **individualized family service plan (IFSP).** A young child who has already seen a doctor or specialist will have this, and it will give you information about the degree of impairment, age of onset, cause, and some curriculum ideas. (See the Glossary for a full definition of IFSP.) Always help a child make the most of the abilities he or she already has, and don't focus on the disability. Remember, too, that even if a child has a sensory impairment, there is usually still some residual ability in that area. For example, most babies with visual impairments see some things, and it is very rare for an infant with a hearing impairment to hear nothing at all.

Table 6.1 Early Warning Signs of Sensory Impairment

Remember, any child may demonstrate some of these behaviors and *not* be having difficulty. Certain behaviors may be part of a particular child's personality or temperament and should be looked at in the light of *the whole child*.

- Frequently rubs eyes or complains that eyes hurt

- Avoids eye contact

- Easily distracted by visual or auditory stimuli

- Often bumps into things or falls frequently

- By six months does not turn toward source of sounds

- Talks/communicates in a very loud or very soft voice

- Shies away from touch

- Uses one side of the body more than the other

- Usually turns the same ear toward a sound to hear

- Reacts strongly to the feel of certain substances or textures

Source: Information adapted from the California Department of Education, the California Child Care Health Program, and the Portage Project TEACH, Region 5 Regional Access Project, 1999.

NAEYC Program Standard 7
Families

Parents can be your most helpful resources. Caregivers and parents working together provide a critical component for the special-needs infant or toddler. You will have valuable information to share with each other. If you suspect that a young child has a sensory impairment, discuss your specific observations with the parent as soon as possible. (See Table 6.1 for early warning signs.) Early intervention and awareness will be mentioned often in this text. The longer children experience deprivation, or the nonrecognition of a disability, the more effect it will have on their development.

Also try to be aware of your own misconceptions and possible myths. A blind baby is not necessarily mentally retarded; a deaf toddler is not necessarily socially withdrawn. Children quickly learn to use compensating skills. But it would be inaccurate to assume that a blind infant has more acute hearing than a sighted child or that a deaf baby will have sharper eyesight than an infant with normal hearing. Sometimes individuals want to "make up for" what they think a child is lacking. Don't feel sorry for children with special needs. Provide a safe environment for them, plan for their specific play needs, and encourage (don't push) their unique strategies or adaptations to help them acquire necessary skills. *Remember principle 10: Be concerned about the quality of development in each stage.*

The following guides offer more information. They focus primarily on young children with either visual or hearing impairments or both. This list is not meant to be complete, but it may be helpful to caregivers who have children with special needs in their program.

1. Be aware of signals that may indicate sensory impairments. For example, an infant with a hearing impairment may be "surprised" by your appearance (did not hear your approach), or he may start babbling (around four months), then stop. An infant with a visual impairment may not reach for interesting toys (cannot clearly see them), or may be slow to creep. Developmental signals depend on a caregiver's knowledge of the usual sequence of growth.

2. Familiarize yourself with any special devices a young child may be using. Hearing aids do little good if they are inserted incorrectly. Glasses worn at an inappropriate angle may cause additional fatigue for a visually impaired toddler.

3. Be sure when communicating with a child with sensory impairments that you get his or her attention first. This is appropriate to do with any child, but you may have to be more deliberate with a child who has special needs. For example, make sure a child with a hearing impairment can see you before you begin speaking. For a visually impaired child it may be helpful to speak the child's name clearly, then pause (allowing the child to orient toward the sound), and then continue speaking. These focusing techniques help alert sensory-impaired children to the importance of speech and language as a means of gathering and clarifying information.

4. Guides to foster speech and language for a child with sensory impairments depend on the unique strengths and disabilities of that child. Some guides should be available to you in the child's IFSP. Remember that language development is a complex task (more details on this in Chapter 9). When a child's sensory abilities are not intact, that child is at risk for incomplete or delayed concept formation. It is difficult for a visually impaired child to understand fully the "label" of an object he may never have seen. A child with auditory problems may be confused by gestures and facial expressions made in the effort to communicate language he cannot clearly hear. It is important not to overdramatize information you are sharing and to repeat it frequently so that the child has time to organize important details in his own way.

5. Young children with sensory impairments may tire more quickly than their peers. Watch for stress signals and provide frequent rest periods. A blanket and pillow close by may be all the cues necessary to encourage a busy toddler to pause for a rest. A rested child is more ready to pursue and repeat experiences from which she will learn.

6. Provide for appropriate play. Support and encourage all areas of sensory learning. Don't limit a child's experience because you think he will not see or hear something. A visually impaired child may be fascinated by the contours of a particular toy he is seeing. A child who is hard of hearing may thoroughly enjoy the song of a music box, no matter how muffled the sound.

Reflect

Where would you go in your community to gather resource information related to sensory impaired children? How would you organize it?—Topic folders? A notebook? A file box? How would you share this information with your staff? What guides would you give them when assessing children in your care?

Most of the activities presented in this chapter are perfectly appropriate for children with sensory impairments. Consult further with parents and program specialists if you feel an activity needs to be adapted to foster a particular child's abilities.

Caregivers need to be sensitive to each infant's sensory needs and provide for the development of all the child's senses. The infant's task is to learn to interpret the sensations that come in through the senses. Children don't just take in information; they learn to perceive and organize it. They learn to hear and eventually to listen. They learn to discriminate the feelings on their skin, the various tastes in their mouths, the smells around them, the sights they take in. They learn to make sense of sensory information. Responses or reactions to this information from the senses depend on muscles, or motor skills, the topic of Chapter 7.

DEVELOPMENTAL PATHWAYS

Behaviors Showing Development of Perception

Young infants (up to 8 months)	• Show they recognize their primary caregivers by sight, sound, and smell within the first two weeks of life • Look to the place on their body where they are being touched • Begin to distinguish friends from strangers • Hit or kick an object to make a pleasing sight or sound continue
Mobile infants (up to 18 months)	• Push their foot into a shoe and their arm into a sleeve • Actively show affection for a familiar person by hugging, smiling, running toward that person • Understand more words than they can say • Show heightened awareness of opportunities to make things happen
Toddlers (up to 3 years)	• Identify self with children of same age or sex • Classify, label, and sort objects by group (hard versus soft, large versus small) • Identify a familiar object by touch when it is placed in a bag with two other objects • When playing with a ring-stacking toy, ignore any forms that have no hole. Stack only rings or other objects with holes

Source: S. Bredekamp and C. Copple, *Developmentally Appropriate Practice in Early Childhood Programs* (Washington, D.C.: National Association for the Education of Young Children, 1997).

Diverse Developmental Pathways

What you see	Zyana is a crawler; she does more sitting than crawling around. She's quiet and immobile much of the time, but it doesn't take much to entertain her: a sunbeam on the floor, a scrap of paper on the floor, the breeze from an open window. She seems to be able to float above the chaos that sometimes occurs in the infant room. She rarely demands attention.
What you might think	She needs to be more active. Some of the other children her age are ten times more active than she is. Maybe she is depressed.
What you might not know	Zyana is very perceptive and she enjoys what she perceives. She is aware of her senses and finds them infinitely entertaining. Her temperament is such that she makes few demands. She's easygoing and able to concentrate on what's close to her without being disturbed by what else is going on in the room.
What you might do	Appreciate her as an individual. Be sure she gets enough attention. Just because she is easy to get along with doesn't mean that she should be ignored. Find out from her family what she is like at home and if they appreciate her or find her lacking in some way.
What you see	Seth, a toddler, cries a good deal. A lot of things bother him. For example, he fusses when you dress him and also when you undress him. He shies away when you touch him.
What you might think	This is simply his temperament. Or maybe they "spoil" him at home. Or maybe he doesn't like you. Or maybe he misses his mother.
What you might not know	Seth is hypersensitive. He is easily overstimulated and he is tactile-defensive. The textures of some clothing bother him, and he doesn't like the feeling of air on his arms and legs. The labels on clothing irritate his skin. Even your touch disturbs him.
What you might do	Find out what you can from his family about how to keep him comfortable. Observe carefully to see if you can figure out what bothers him and what doesn't. Cut the labels out of clothes or put them on wrong side out. Reduce excess stimulation. Don't quit touching him, but figure out what kind of touch is most acceptable. Try different things and watch for the effects.

Summary

Perception is the ability to take in and organize sensory experience.

Sensory Integration

- Sensory experiences are combined and integrated and influence other major growth areas.

Go to the Online Learning Center at **www.mhhe.com/itc7e** to access the student study guide that includes quizzes, practice with key terms, and a review of chapter content; links to websites related to the chapter; and additional resources.

- Specific sensory organs are located in particular areas of the brain and, as the brain matures, there is a constant interchange of action and reaction.

Hearing

- Newborns can hear at birth and are especially responsive to high-pitched, familiar voices and sounds.
- Caregivers need to be aware of the unique preferences of young children; the optimum noise level varies with each child.

Smell and Taste

- Newborns can distinguish numerous smells and tastes and prefer pleasant smells and sweet tastes.
- An environment rich in smells adds to an infant/toddler program; be careful of making things that are not edible smell delicious.

Touch

- Newborns have a well-developed sense of touch; sensitivity to discomfort and pain increases rapidly after birth.
- Caregivers should be alert to potential cultural and gender issues related to touch.

Sight

- Newborns' vision is blurry (compared to adults); they can distinguish light and dark areas, and within a few weeks they can distinguish colors.
- Take cues from infants themselves when planning an environment to foster visual skills. Avoid the "circus effect"—more is not necessarily better.

Children with Special Needs: Sensory Impairments

- Help a child make the most of the sensory abilities she or he already has; don't focus on the disability. Provide for the development of all senses.
- Early warning signs may indicate that a child needs further assessment. Seek professional assistance immediately if you suspect a child in your care may have special needs.

Key Terms

aesthetics 123
five senses 115
individualized family service plan (IFSP) 123
neural pathways 114

perception 114
sensitivity 119
sensory integration 114
tactile perception 120

Thought/Activity Questions

1. Look around an infant-toddler environment. List the experiences that you feel foster perceptual development. How can you determine when there is perhaps "too much of a good thing"?
2. Focus on one aspect of perceptual development (one of the senses). Create a toy to foster this area of growth. What do you need to consider?
3. Observe a child with a sensory impairment. What adaptations can you see the child making? How is the environment supporting his or her efforts?
4. After reading this chapter, imagine that you are planning a parent meeting for your infant-toddler program. The topic is perceptual development. What key points about each sense would you want to share?
5. Think about your personal orientation to perceptual development—your sensitivity to your own senses. Which sense do you use the most? The least? Which one triggers the most memories? Are there any implications for your interactions with very young children?

For Further Reading

C. F. Abbott and S. Gold, "Conferring with Parents When You're Concerned That Their Child Needs Special Services," *Young Children* 46(4), May 1991, pp. 10–15.

Sue Bakley, "Through the Lens of Sensory Integration: A Different Way of Analyzing Challenging Behavior," *Young Children*, November 2001, pp. 70–76.

M. Buchanan and M. Cooney, "Play at Home, Play in the Classroom," *Young Exceptional Children* 3(4), 2000, pp. 9–15.

M. Davis, J. Kilgo, and M. Gamel-McCormick, *Young Children with Special Needs: A Developmentally Appropriate Approach* (Boston: Allyn & Bacon, 1998).

L. Flynn and J. Kieff, "Including Everyone in Outdoor Play," *Young Children* 57(3), May 2002, pp. 20–26.

Pam Schiller, "Bright Beginnings for Babies," *Child Care Information Exchange*, March 2003, pp. 8–12.

chapter 7

Motor Skills

Focus Questions

After reading this chapter you should be able to answer the following questions:

1 How does the developing brain influence the growth of motor skills?

2 What is the function of reflex behaviors and why do they *change* during the early months?

3 Describe the growth patterns related to large motor skills and small motor skills during the first two years?

4 What can caregivers do to support the growth of children with developmental delays?

What Do You See?

Anthony stands in the sandbox looking around the play yard. He bends over and picks up a sieve and spoon that are lying at his feet. He plops down, legs out straight, and starts spooning sand into the sieve and watching it pour out onto his knees. After several minutes he notices a tot bike that is sitting at the edge of the sandbox. He gets up and toddles toward the bike. When he reaches the edge of the sandbox he concentrates his effort on getting his feet, first one, then the other, over the board that rims the sandbox. Once he gets to the bike, Anthony begins to move it away from the sandbox area. He alternates between standing and walking the bike, and sitting on it and scooting it with his feet (there are no pedals on the bike). He keeps on the walk which is bumpy asphalt and slightly uphill. He allows the bike to coast down the slight incline and ends up near the gate. He starts to climb the gate, but an adult nearby walks over and gently redirects him to a climbing structure several yards away. As she moves toward a group of children washing dolls in dishpans on a low table, Anthony follows her. He grabs a sponge lying on the table and squeezes it, watching the soapy water drip out. He puts the sponge into the pan, holds it up dripping, and squeezes it again on the tabletop. He scrubs the tabletop briefly, then puts the sponge back into the water. He takes a doll out of another tub and puts it on top of the sponge in the tub in front of him. Another child reaches over and takes the doll back, and there is a slight tussle as Anthony tries to keep the doll. He lets go when he hears a call for snack time. He gives the sponge in the tub a pat, which splashes water onto his face. He smiles, pats it again, then races tripping across the yard to the snack table, where he is just in time to pour his own juice from a small, half-filled pitcher.

Movement is the natural, healthy experience of childhood. Most infants and toddlers move a lot. Anthony certainly demonstrated a great deal of movement! It is through movement, muscular coordination, and the organization of perceptions that young children find out about and make sense of their world. Infants' motor skills may seem limited, but sensitive observation reveals competent abilities. Within a year and a half, most infants have learned many of the basic motor skills—arm/hand coordination, walking—that they will need throughout their lifetime. Their sensory experience has given them important feedback. They spend the next years perfecting, expanding, and refining the original postures and movements that they learned early on.

This chapter provides an overview of the progression of motor development. It includes major growth patterns, examines how the brain develops, and looks at how reflexive, large and small motor abilities all change and refine themselves in the first two and a half years. It includes guides for fostering motor development as well as some information concerning children with motor delays.

Physical Growth and Motor Skills

The average newborn weighs just over 7 pounds and is about 20 inches long. She is helpless and could not survive on her own. But growth occurs rapidly in a healthy, caring environment. By five months of age the infant's birth weight has doubled, and by her first birthday it has tripled. Even though the pace of weight gain slows during the second year, it has nearly quadrupled since birth.[1] Length also increases, and by the end of the second year, most children are about three feet tall. Physical growth is generally predictable. Numerous growth charts exist in books and doctors' offices, but each child is unique, and it is not unusual for growth during this time to occur in "spurts." The appearance of specific motor skills during this time can vary widely.

As a young child's overall size increases, parts of the body grow at different rates. At birth the head accounts for one-fourth of the newborn's entire body size, and the legs are only about one-third. By age two, the infant's head is only one-fifth of her body length, and her legs are almost one-half of her body length. This rapid growth provides a challenge; very young children must learn to coordinate the movements of bodies that are constantly changing. Watching infants learn to coordinate their bodies and refine their movements reflects amazingly well-organized growth patterns.

Stability of motor development can be explained by two major growth principles. The first is the **cephalocaudal** principle, which in Latin means "head to tail." This principle states that growth follows a pattern that begins with the head and moves down the rest of the body. For example, children generally lift their heads, before they sit up and before they stand. The second principle is the **proximodistal** principle, which is also from Latin and means "near to far." It indicates that development moves from the center of the body outward. For example, young children generally use large sweeping movements of their arms before they use their hands and fingers. Overall you can see young children use their heads (and their sensory skills, like vision) before they walk. And you can see them move their arms in circling patterns before they have the ability to pick up that pot potato bug hiding in the corner of the sandbox (pincher grasp)!

Growth is not just a process of getting bigger; although as discussed above, that certainly happens. The brain matures and growth within it moves from the brain stem at the base of the neck to the cortex in the frontal area. Movement becomes less reflexive and more voluntary. Growth is also the process in which motor skills, both large and small, are refined. As motor skills grow and expand, young children are better able to clarify their needs and explore the world.

Brain Growth and Motor Development

Motor development is largely observable; we can see infants make voluntary movements and refine their physical skills. Now, thanks to neuroscience technology, we can also see how the brain changes and grows as young children develop. At birth the brain weighs only about 25 percent of its eventual mature adult weight of three and a half pounds. It reaches nearly 90 percent of that weight by age three. By age six the brain is almost adult size, although specific skills continue to develop into adulthood.[2] Everyday behaviors that are observable also give us insight into brain growth. The development of reflexes are a good example (see Table 7.1).

It is important first to acknowledge that the number of neurons (brain cells) a child is born with does not increase throughout life. What changes is the number of connections between the brain cells. What also happens is something called **myelinization,** a process by which brain fat (myelin) coats and insulates the neural fibers. It accounts for the rapid gain in overall brain size after birth. These neural fibers, or axons, are then better able to transmit electrical impulses (synapses) and make more stable "learning connections."[3] Brain growth in the first year is primarily a process of insulating neural fibers and expanding, or growing, "dendrite trees." In addition, the neurons in the brain move around and become arranged by function. Some move into the upper layer of the brain—the **cerebral cortex**—and others move below this area to subcortical levels. The subcortical levels are fully developed at birth and regulate most of the reflexes and such fundamental activities as breathing and heart rate. As growth continues, cells in the cerebral cortex become more mature and interconnected. These cells will become responsible for complex motor skills and higher-order processes such as cognition and language.

This activity can be measured by an EEG, or electroencephalogram, which detects and measures brain wave activity, and growth in the first year can be seen as surges in brain activity. For example, there is a surge in activity at 3 to 4 months, when infants are doing voluntary reaching, at 8 months, when they crawl and search for objects, and also at 12 months, when they are walking.[4] Surges are related to the massive production of synaptic connections; the brain is busy making sense of experience. There seems to be clear evidence now that what forms the brain circuitry early in life is *experience.*

The brain research also has clearly indicated that there are *sensitive periods* for development (this will be discussed more in Chapter 8, on cognition, and Chapter 9, on language). But there is also tremendous **brain plasticity**—that is the brain's tendency to remain somewhat flexible. Plasticity is greatest before age two when the new synapses are still expanding and have not yet been pruned. The brain is amazingly adaptable. In some cases of early trauma, regions of the brain will take over the function of a damaged area of the brain. While we are still in the process of appreciating more about the vital "windows of opportunity" for learning, don't forget that it is never too late to provide quality experiences for a young child.

Reflexes

Newborns can make few voluntary movements beyond gross random arm and leg movements. Most of the first movements are **reflexes,** which are unlearned, organized, involuntary responses that occur in the presence of different kinds of stimuli. The muscles seem to react automatically.

Reflexes serve several functions. Some, like blinking, swallowing, and clearing the face for breathing, are protective. Others, such as kicking the legs alternately (reciprocal kicking), are precursors of later skills—in this case, walking. Pediatricians and other infant specialists pay attention to reflexes because they indicate brain growth. As the growth of the brain shifts from the brain stem to the cortex, reflexes change or disappear. Healthy babies have the same breathing reflex that adults have, as well as a cough and gag reflex that keeps the breathing passage clear. Their eyes blink and squint, and their pupils narrow just like those of adults. They coordinate sucking and swallowing, and they pull away from painful stimuli. These are all common reflexes that are present at birth and remain throughout a person's lifetime.

Some reflexes are specific to newborns and change or disappear as the child grows. Other reflexes make their appearance during the first few months. As the new reflexes appear, some of the ones present at birth begin to disappear. Some of the most visually obvious reflexes—and those most often assessed by physicians—are summarized in Table 7.1 (p. 136) and shown in Figure 7.1. The reflexes are grouped into those present at birth, and those that appear after birth.

Not only is it interesting to see how reflexes serve as the basis for later movement, it is useful for caregivers to know what reflexes indicate about infants' behavior and development. It is sometimes useful to know that babies have not chosen to move in a certain way (for example, rooting before starting to suck), but that they have to do so.

The appearance of certain reflexes, the lingering of reflexes, and the absence of others can indicate differences in development. This aspect of development is complex. When parents or caregivers notice that a baby is showing what seems to be inappropriate reflexive behavior, they may want to discuss what they have noticed with a developmental expert or a doctor.

Reflect

Do you think infancy might be an ideal time to teach swimming? Why or why not? Why might some people think it would be an ideal time? What are some reasons *not* to teach infants to swim?

Figure 7.1 Reflexes at and after Birth.

AT BIRTH

Moro reflex
(Startle reflex)

Palmar grasp reflex

Tonic neck reflex

Rooting reflex

AFTER BIRTH

Landau reflex

Reciprocal kicking

Parachute reflex

Table 7.1 Some Basic Reflexes in Infants	
Reflexes at Birth	
Rooting	Head turns toward things that touch the cheek
Sucking	Tendency to suck things that touch the lips
Stepping	Legs move when held upright with feet touching floor
Palmar Grasp	Hands curl around object placed in them
Babinski	Toes fan out if sole of the foot is stroked
Moro	If head support released, arms fling out and seem to grasp
Startle	Arms fling out in response to sudden noise
Tonic Neck (fencing)	Head turns to one side and arm extends, while other arm flexes
Swimming	Swimming movements occur when placed in water
Reflexes after Birth	
Reciprocal Kicking	If held outward, kick legs alternate (bicycling)
Neck Righting	If head turns, the body follows
Parachute	If falling, arms go forward.
Landau	If placed on stomach, arms and legs extend in "U" position

The Principles in Action

Principle 10 Be concerned about the *quality* of development in each stage. Don't rush infants and toddlers to reach developmental milestones.

An infant-toddler center treats all children as individuals. It never pushes development but instead watches its babies reach developmental milestones each on his or her own schedule. One child in the program was born prematurely, and another one has been determined to be developmentally delayed, so the idea of each on his or her own schedule has even more meaning in this program. The child with the development delays is being carefully monitored by an infant interventionist and has an individualized family service plan (IFSP) that has been carefully thought out. All the children see pediatricians regularly. Recently this program received a notice that its continued funding will depend on its ability to get all children in the program to developmental milestones on time, except for any children officially identified with special needs. The staff has been mandated to take training on a diagnosis and prescription method of using activities and exercises to bring all children closer in their abilities to reach the milestones. The staff and director are horrified. Their motto (which they got from Magda Gerber's work) is "*in* time; not *on* time."

1. What is your reaction to this situation?
2. Is there value in allowing children to develop at their own pace? Explain your answer.
3. Are there disadvantages to allowing children to develop at their own pace? If yes, what are they?
4. Do you think the activities and exercises make a difference? Explain your answer.
5. Do you have experience with being pushed to achieve? If yes, does your experience relate to infants and toddlers? If it does, how?

Large Motor Skills and Locomotion

Eventually infants make movements that are voluntary instead of reflexive. These movements are generally divided into two broad types: large or gross motor skills, which have to do with large muscles and big movements, and small or fine motor skills, which have to do with small muscles and more delicate movements.

The brain, the body, and the environment all contribute to move an infant toward increased strength and **locomotion,** or the ability to move from one place to another. Various developmental areas work together to advance a child to more complex and refined levels of growth.

Large muscles contribute to an infant's ability to move in two directions: up (to an upright position) and around (on a horizontal plane). The two are intertwined because the child needs to get up to move around and needs to move around to get up. Little by little, babies gain control over these muscles. The first muscles to develop are those that control head movements. As babies perfect the skills involved in turning the head from side to side and lifting it up, they strengthen the shoulder muscles. As they begin to move around and squirm, lifting their arms and legs, they develop the trunk muscles. All this preparation is for turning over, just as turning over is preparation for (that is, strengthens the muscles necessary for) sitting up. A child will learn to come to a sitting position without ever having been propped up. The ability to sit comes from developing the muscles prerequisite to the upright position. Infants get ready to sit by learning to move the head and by turning over. The building of the muscle systems is vital; practice at sitting is not.

According to Emmi Pikler's research and experience at the Pikler Institute in Budapest, if no one interferes by praising or otherwise motivating children, they will develop movement skills in a predictably sequential manner. If children are put on their backs from the beginning of life and no one manipulates them by putting them into positions they can't get into by themselves, they will learn to

VIDEO OBSERVATION 7

Children Climbing Stairs

See Video Observation 7: Children Climbing Stairs for examples of children using gross motor skills by practicing stair climbing. Notice how each child goes about it in a little different way.

Questions

- How many different ways did these children use to get on and off this low platform? Describe each way.
- What other environmental features might give children an opportunity to practice stepping up and down safely?
- What does this scene tell you about the program's philosophy?

To view this clip, go to www.mhhe.com/itc7e. Click on Student Edition, select Chapter 7, and click on Video Observation.

turn over, roll, creep, crawl, sit, stand, and walk on their own. They accomplish all this by playing with each movement over and over and becoming absorbed in each little detail. They are scientists studying movement and patiently experimenting. Infants are born ready to learn. Through their fascination with their bodies and strong motivation to develop movement, they prove to be highly competent, independent learners. Their persistence to increase movement skills sets a theme for later learning. In contrast to Pikler's approach of keeping a child unrestricted so that they can move freely, many adults place babies in an infant seat a good part of their waking hours. Additionally, instead of allowing the baby to focus on his own body and inner motivation, they put him in front of a television or use other entertainment devices because they think babies get bored. Those babies who are both restricted and entertained are thus deprived of important motor play. Instead of finding their own bodies enormously interesting, they learn to look for entertainment outside of themselves. That kind of early experience can set a theme that lasts a lifetime.

A general principle involved in motor development is that *stability is the means to mobility.* Infants cannot move until they gain a good solid base from which to move—whether the movement is vertical, as in sitting and standing, or horizontal, as in crawling and walking. This same principle operates on another level as well. Chapter 5 pointed out that exploration (mobility) is related to psychological stability (trust in attachment).

The plan for developing muscular stability is a part of the infant's makeup—as is the plan for mobility. Nobody has to "teach" either sitting or walking. When normal babies have gone through the necessary muscle development, they will be able to sit and walk without any lessons or practice.

Early motor experiences can be described from the dynamic systems approach mentioned in Chapter 6 on perception. Each action is made up of bits and pieces of experience, and motor skills change each time they are used.[5] As infants' muscles grow, they achieve strength and balance, their brains mature, and they put together the necessary skills that lead to mature movement and walking. Each skill is necessary and they work together to produce effective ways to explore the environment. Figure 7.2 shows the major milestones of gross motor development and locomotion. Use it with caution. Such charts are based on averages, and no individual baby is average. The sequence of motor development is mostly standard, but within it lies a good deal of room for individual variation in timing and style. Remember principle 10: *Be concerned about the quality of development in each stage. Don't rush infants and toddlers to reach developmental milestones.*

Reflect

What experience do you have with developmental charts? Do you have any feelings about them?

Small Motor Skills and Manipulation

The small muscles that an infant gradually begins to control include those of the eyes, mouth, speech organs, bladder, rectum, feet, toes, hands, and fingers. This section focuses on the development of the hands and fingers, known as **manipulation.** The achievements within this area are not isolated skills; they are organized and combine themselves in an increasingly refined manner.

The sequence in which infants learn to manipulate objects shows how complex this ability is. Figure 7.3 illustrates the developmental sequence. At first, newborns generally hold their hands in tight fists (although the clenched fist is more relaxed in those babies who were treated to gentle birth procedures). They hold on to any object put into their hands, gripping so tightly that they can, if held up, support their own weight. But they have no control over their grasp and cannot let go, no matter how much they want to. At some time before six months (usually at a little over two and a half months), the tight fists remain relaxed most of the time, and the hands are open.

During the first three months, more of the hand and arm movements become voluntary. Infants begin to reach for objects, first with their eyes, then with open

Figure 7.2 Gross motor development milestones: birth to 30 months

Source: Some items in this chart were taken from the *Bayley Scales of Infant Development*. Copyright © 1969 by the Psychological Corporation, a Harcourt Assessment Company. Reproduced by permission. All rights reserved.

Raises self by
arms in prone position
2.1 months
(range 0.7–5 months)

Prewalking progression
7.1 months
(range 5–11 months)

Pulls to sit
7.3 months
(range 6–8 months)

Pulls up on furniture
8.6 months
(range 6–12 months)

Stands alone
11 months
(range 9–16 months)

Walks alone
11.7 months
(range 9–17 months)

Walks backward
14.6 months
(range 11–20 months)

Jumps on floor
23.4 months
(range 17–30 months)

Figure 7.3 Fine motor development: manipulative skills, birth to 21 months
Source: Some items in this chart were taken from the *Bayley Scales of Infant Development.*
Copyright © 1969 by The Psychological Corporation, a Harcourt Assessment Company.

Grasps and holds ring
.8 month
(range .3–3 months)

Hands predominantly
open and relaxed
2.7 months
(range .7–6 months)

Reaches for dangling ring
3.1 months
(range 1–5 months)

Closes on dangling ring
3.8 months
(range 2–6 months)

Fingers hand in play
3.2 months
(range 1–6 months)

Palmar grasp
3.7 months
(range 2–7 months)

Neat pincer grasp
8.9 months
(range 7–12 months)

Pattycake (Midline skills
9.7 months
(range 7–15 months)

Scribbles spontaneously
14 months
(range 10–21 months)

Much fine motor development comes from encouraging children in self-help tasks.

hands. By around three and a half months, they can often close on an object within reach. They may also begin to play with their own hands at about this time. The way they grasp at first is distinctive: They use all the fingers together as if they had a mitten on, drawing objects into the palm of the hand. This motion is called the palmar grasp. Although at this stage the palmar grasp is a voluntary movement, it comes from the earlier palmar grasp reflex present at birth. After learning to pick up objects with one hand, infants soon begin to pass them back and forth between the two hands. By the sixth month, they have begun trying to use thumb and forefinger in what is called a "pincer grasp." They can then manipulate objects with more skill and a variety of motions.

By about the ninth month, infants have perfected the pincer grasp and can pick up small objects with great adeptness. Playing with the hands—picking up and dropping objects for a helpful adult to retrieve and playing pattycake—provides pleasure. The dropping game shows infants' joy in and awareness of now being able to let go. By the ninth month, infants may also be using their forefingers alone—poking, hooking, and probing. Eventually, they can differentiate the use of the hands and can then do two different activities at once (for example, holding something with one hand and maneuvering with the other).

By 11 months, infants can hold crayons and mark on available surfaces, and they can probably get a spoon to their mouths. By a year, the variety of movements has come a long way from the compulsive grasping that was present at birth. Infants can take covers off objects, undress themselves to some degree, take one thing out of another, and take things apart and move them around. They continue to expand their manipulative skills, refining and perfecting their movements. From here on, individual children vary greatly.

Much fine motor development in toddlers comes from encouraging them in self-help tasks. As they get more adept at eating with utensils, pouring their own milk, taking off their own shoes, and zipping up their jackets (with a start from an adult), their ability to use their hands and fingers grows.

Toys and materials add to their chances to practice as they play with what you provide them (such as dress-up clothes, dolls and doll clothes, play dough, button and zipper boards, latch boards, stringing beads, nesting toys, simple shape sorters, snap-together blocks, telephones, paint and paintbrushes or water and paintbrushes, crayons, felt pens, scissors, simple paper puzzles, blocks, small figures, cars, and trucks). The tactile experiences mentioned in the "Touch" section in Chapter 6 also promote fine motor development. See Appendix B for age-appropriate fine motor toys, materials, and activities. Be sure that you encourage boys and girls to engage equally in fine motor activities.

Remember Anthony at the beginning of the chapter. He was encountering many chances to build his skills in walking, running, climbing, and balancing just by being in an environment with equipment and choices. He was also building fine motor skills as he practiced grasping, holding, scooping, pouring, and squeezing with the toys and materials available to him. These experiences not only helped him develop his perceptual skills, but also contributed to cognitive development. Remember principle 8: *Recognize problems as learning opportunities, and let*

infants and toddlers try to solve their own. Don't rescue them, constantly make life easy for
them, or try to protect them from all problems.

Fostering Motor Development

Caregivers can do several things to foster motor development in infants. Try to
keep children in the position in which they are freest and least helpless during their
waking hours. Emmi Pikler's research shows that even the youngest babies change
position an average of once a minute.[6] So, if they are strapped into an infant seat
or a swing, they are not able to do what they would do naturally if free. Avoid con-
traptions that confine infants. (Car seats are, of course, a necessary exception.)

Don't "teach" motor skills. Encourage infants to practice what they know
how to do. Babies get ready for the next stage by doing thoroughly whatever it is
they are doing in the present stage. Trying to teach babies to roll over or walk
keeps them from fully exploring and perfecting the skills they already have. They
reach each milestone just when they are ready, and their own inner timetable
dictates when that will be.

Large muscle activity
cannot be saved for
outdoor times, but must
be allowed and
encouraged indoors.

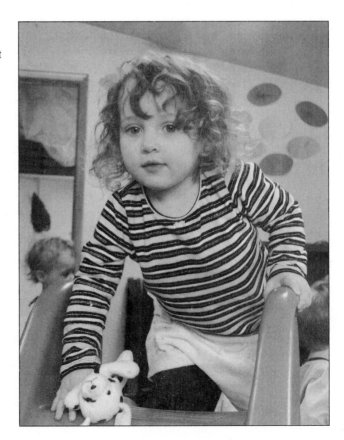

Don't put babies into positions they cannot get into by themselves. The process of *getting into* a position is more important than *being in* the position—the process promotes development. Babies get ready for standing by sitting and crawling, not by being stood up.

Don't shield babies from all physical stress. The body needs a certain amount of stress to grow. Don't *rescue* babies when they get in an uncomfortable position, but wait and see if they can get out of it on their own. Obviously, you don't leave babies in great distress alone and unsupported, but you don't want to always make everything easy for them either. Reasonable, or optimum, stress stimulates growth, increases motivation, and strengthens the body as well as the psyche.

Above all, *facilitate* development in all motor areas, don't *push* it. Because we live in a "hurry-up" culture, some people are most anxious for babies to reach milestones "on time" or even early. "In time" is a better guide for milestones. Each baby has his or her own timetable. There is no reason to impose someone else's. The question to ask is not "Is this baby progressing rapidly in development?" Note how well babies use the skills they have and whether they are progressing in their use of those skills. With these two concepts in mind, you will not have to be so concerned about where they fit on the chart. Remember principle 2: *Invest in quality time, when you are totally available to individual infants and toddlers. Don't settle for supervising groups without focusing (more than just briefly) on individual children.*

Promoting motor development in toddlers follows the same principles as that of infants. Toddlers need freedom to move and experience a variety of ways of using the skills they possess. Large-muscle activity cannot be saved for outdoor time but must be both allowed and encouraged inside. A soft environment—pillows, mattresses, foam blocks, and thick rugs (indoors) and grass, sand, pads, and mats (outdoors)—helps toddlers roll, tumble, and bounce around. Various kinds of scaled-down climbing and sliding equipment (both indoors and out) allow the toddler to experience a variety of skills. Wheel toys (these can be saved for outdoors for the older toddler) give a whole different kind of experience as toddlers learn first to walk them and later to pedal them. Large lightweight blocks encourage building skills as toddlers carry them around, form them into walks, houses, and abstract structures, and then practice gross motor skills on them.

Wandering, carrying, and dumping are gross motor skills that toddlers practice a great deal. Rather than seeing these as negative, caregivers can provide for them in the curriculum. Some programs have things available to dump (and put back). One center even suspends from the ceiling a bucket of objects whose sole purpose is dumping (and refilling). Wandering usually involves picking up objects, carrying them to another location, and putting them down. Sometimes they are actively discarded, and sometimes just dropped—abandoned as if forgotten. The map in Figure 7.4 shows the path of a two-year-old over a period of 20 minutes. The black dots represent each time the child picked up or put down an object. Notice the territory he covered and the number of times he

NAEYC Program Standard 2
Curriculum

Figure 7.4 Map tracing the movements of a two-year-old

picked up and put down objects. This is not unusual two-year-old behavior. Typically, as children get older, they are able to spend more and more time with specific activities. The closer they get to three, the less likely toddlers are to spend good parts of the day moving from one place to another. But early in toddlerhood this constant movement is part of gross motor development, and the environment, both indoors and out, should be set up to accommodate that need.

A word of caution concerning the new brain development information: Be alert to any marketing that uses brain research to sell toys and materials. Natural everyday experience and interactions are the best ways to foster significant neural connections. Interpretation of research must be done with care and sensitivity, and the uniqueness of each child should always be preserved.

Notice whether you are encouraging gross motor movement more in boys than in girls. Girls need strong, skillful bodies as much as boys do. Both sexes in toddlerhood enjoy running-and-chasing games. The freedom to roll around on the floor, jump onto pillow piles, wrestle, and somersault is just as appropriate for girls as for boys. Music and movement, dance, and circle games encourage all young children to move and have fun. Here is a wonderful place for multicultural ideas, too. Take walks and examine interesting things along the way. Just remember to give children a choice and keep group size small.

Reflect

How do you think environment influences motor development (don't forget to include nutrition and practice)?

👫 Children with Special Needs: Developmental Delays

The rate and sequence of motor development for the child with special needs or developmental delays may be slower and more divergent. Reflexes were reviewed in this chapter. They remain an important guide for parents and caregivers because they indicate brain growth and possible brain damage. It is particularly important that their progression be noted carefully during a child's first year.

Motor development may be influenced by a number of disabling conditions. An infant with visual impairments may be slower in his rate of motor growth because limited visual information may reduce his exploration of the world. An infant with cerebral palsy may show poor or limited muscular control because of related brain damage. Infants with atypical motor development show a consistent progression or sequence of motor abilities but at a much slower rate.

Often it is not totally understood why a child experiences a motor delay. Prenatal care, premature birth, or trauma during or after birth may influence motor development. Early intervention remains the key way to help a child with special needs reach his or her full developmental ability. Caregivers and parents may find the following symptoms, observable signs, or complaints helpful as a guide for further discussion with a specialist. (*Note:* The presence of one or two symptoms does not mean a child has a problem.) Seek assistance if a child:

- Has stiff arms or legs or the opposite and has floppy or limp body posture
- Has poor coordination or moves in a clumsy manner compared with other children of the same age
- Uses one side of the body more than the other
- Shows signs of pain during exercise
- At approximately three months still has difficulty holding the head up
- By age one, has difficulty sitting without help, standing up, reaching for objects, or picking up objects
- By age two, has difficulty walking without help, kicking a large ball, or building a tower with two or three blocks
- By age three, does not walk up or down stairs, run without falling frequently, or turn pages of a book.[7]

Early intervention is based on an understanding of what (developmentally) tends to happen when. An attitude that encourages infants with delays to experience and explore the world in a way appropriate for them remains critically important.

Caregivers and parents should remember to:

- Provide for basic play experiences that emphasize use of the senses.
- Provide young children with typically developing role models as playmates.
- Give children some direct instruction or prompting to complete an activity.
- Reduce prompting as the child gains skills through experience.
- Provide nurturance and support for effort.[8]

Consider these guidelines while reading about Peter, a developmentally delayed toddler. He is 18 months old. He is still crawling and has made no attempt to stand. For unknown reasons, Peter experienced anoxia (reduced oxygen) at birth. Three mornings a week he attends an early intervention infant-toddler program.

Peter is sitting on the floor watching two other toddlers and an adult roll a ball to each other. He has been interested in the ball game for several minutes. His eyes carefully follow the ball as it rolls from one person to another, and if the ball leaves the circle, he turns his head to watch one of the toddlers run to retrieve it. He makes no other indication of involvement.

"Peter, would you like to join our ball game?" the caregiver asks. He does not look at her but continues to watch the ball.

"We can move closer to you so that you can play, too." The adult slowly rolls the ball toward Peter. It stops at the edge of his foot. He makes no movement toward the ball but has visually followed it constantly.

"The ball touched you, didn't it, Peter? Would you like to touch it?" the adult says encouragingly. He slowly looks up at her and then to the ball. Peter points at the ball with one finger and "pokes" at it. It moves slightly, and he smiles with pleasure.

Suddenly the toddler sitting next to Peter reaches across his lap and gives the ball a swipe. It rolls back to the adult.

"David must want us to continue our ball game. He has rolled the ball back to me," the teacher comments. "Marissa, open your hand a little more this time when the ball comes to you." The teacher demonstrates with her palm up and her fingers curled. "Peter, watch Marissa push the ball away." Marissa rolls the ball toward Peter. This time it stops near his knee. Peter looks at the ball. This time he does not poke at it but attempts to swing at it with his palm up. Even though his movement is slow and deliberate, he misses hitting the ball.

"Good try, Peter. Do it again," says the caregiver. After two more swings, Peter connects with the ball, and it rolls out of the circle. He follows it with his eyes but makes no attempt to crawl after it.

David jumps up to get the ball. On his way back he notices a bug on the floor nearby and drops the ball. Marissa by this time has wandered toward the block area. The adult reaches for the ball. "Peter, would you like me to roll the ball to you?" Peter, who was watching David and the bug, looks back to her and opens and closes and opens his hands.

"You look ready. Here it comes." The ball rolls to Peter. He stops it and holds on to it tightly. He does not lift it or attempt to roll it back to the teacher. Gradually, he moves the ball in a back and forth motion between his hands. After several minutes he lets the ball roll away and turns to watch David, who has joined Marissa in the block area. "Would you like to continue playing with David and Marissa? You can move into the block area." Peter looks at the teacher. Then he slowly gets into his crawling position and proceeds toward the block section.

Peter will no doubt have plenty of opportunities to play with the ball—and with David and Marissa. The adult is providing him encouragement and some demonstration, but she does not push him. Like other children, children with special needs need time and opportunity to practice activities.

NAEYC Program Standard 4
Assessment

It may be helpful at this point to combine some of our information about fine and gross motor coordination with a brief "stage/age" view of physical growth. This is meant to be a supportive guide to all caregivers (whether or not children with special needs are in your program).

Magda Gerber refers to motor skills as an infant's growing **"body wisdom."** From birth to about eight months, a child has to have basic needs met (food and nurturance) in order to develop in a healthy way. *Trust and security* are growing as a child reaches out to the world. Implications for attachment are clear. Between 8 and 14 months, motor skills have expanded so that *exploration* almost seems to drive the young child. Giving choices, providing safety, and allowing for play are the primary tasks for caregivers and parents at this age. Motor development and problem solving combine for the young explorers, and limit setting and childproofing become issues for the adults. By the time children reach 18 to 30 months, they may feel they own the world and can do anything. Obviously, their judgment is limited, and parents and caregivers need a lot of energy to keep up with the toddlers! Freedom with guidance is the motto.

DEVELOPMENTAL PATHWAYS

Behaviors Showing Development of Motor Skills

Young infants (up to 8 months)	• Use many complex reflexes: search for something to suck; hold on when falling; turn head to avoid obstruction of breathing; avoid brightness, strong smells, and pain • Reach, grasp • Lift head, hold head up, roll over, transfer and manipulate objects
Mobile infants (up to 18 months)	• Sit up • Crawl and pull up to stand • Walk, stoop, trot, walk backward • Throw objects • Use marker on paper
Toddlers (up to 3 years)	• Walk up and down stairs, can jump off one step • Kick a ball, stand on one foot • Thread beads, scribble with marker, handle scissors • Draw a circle

Source: S. Bredekamp and C. Copple, *Developmentally Appropriate Practice in Early Childhood Programs* (Washington, D.C.: National Association for the Education of Young Children, 1997).

Diverse Developmental Pathways

What you see	Morgan hasn't been walking very long, but she is all over the place. She not only walks but climbs everything in sight. This child is never still for a minute unless she is sleeping, and she does sleep well. No wonder. She uses a lot of energy with all the moving she does.
What you might think	This is a hyperactive child. She's the kind they give medication to when they get in school.
What you might not know	Morgan is a lot like her father. They both have a good deal of energy. Her father is an athlete, and he has a job that is physically demanding, so he's glad he has all that energy. He's glad his daughter does too. He isn't worried that she is hyperactive, because he has seen hyperactive children and they are different from Morgan. For one thing, they don't seem to sleep much, and Morgan sleeps very well.
What you might do	Give her room to move and make sure she is safe. Arrange the environment so she can't climb up things that aren't safe. Make sure she spends enough time outdoors to get the fresh air and the feeling of space that keeps her able to use her energy in positive ways. Help her appreciate quiet activities as well. Even though she is not drawn to the book area, you can probably find some ways to get her over there.

What you see	Vincent arrives all dressed up and is obviously inhibited by his clothes. His shoes have slippery leather soles, making him afraid to run. He never climbs outdoors. Indoors he is inhibited too, because he avoids all the sensory experiences (like water, sand, play dough, and even using felt pens) that might dirty his clothes.
What you might think	This family puts their child's appearance before his developmental needs. They are limiting his ability to develop physically and obviously don't understand the importance of freedom of movement and sensory experiences.
What you might not know	This family is from another country where going to school is an important privilege, and they consider your program to be school. They have strong ideas about children being properly dressed, and they wonder why the other children are dressed in jeans and old clothes. They feel that Vincent's appearance is a reflection of their family's caring for him.
What you might do	Get to know this family and what their perceptions are. Establish a relationship that is based on trust. Don't push them to change, but help Vincent develop his physical skills within the confines of the situation. Eventually you may be able to figure out together with the parent(s) how the child can gain more freedom to get involved physically and still be a positive reflection of his family.

Summary

The progression of physical growth and motor skills follows a generally stable pattern of development.

Physical Growth and Motor Skills

- Infants learn to coordinate the movements of their bodies as they are constantly changing; numerous factors influence the *rate* of motor development.
- Stability of motor development is fostered by the cephalocaudal and proximodistal principles.

Brain Growth and Motor Development

- Myelinization and expanding dendrite connections account for brain growth after birth.
- Motor development is influenced by neurons moving into the cerebral cortex and surrounding area of the brain.

Online
Resources

Go to the Online
Learning Center at
www.mhhe.com/itc7e
to access the student
study guide that in-
cludes quizzes, practice
with key terms, and a
review of chapter con-
tent; links to websites
related to the chapter;
and additional
resources.

Reflexes

- Reflexes are unlearned, involuntary responses to different stimuli; some are present at birth, some appear several weeks or months later.
- Reflexes change and/or disappear as brain growth occurs.

Large Motor Skills and Locomotion

- Large, gross motor skills progress as an infant practices generalized movement.
- Milestones for large motor development exist but should be used with caution; each child is unique and growth rates may vary.

Small Motor Skills and Manipulation

- Small, fine motor skills related to hand and finger movements advance rapidly during the first 18 months.
- Self-help tasks are some of the best activities to foster small motor skills.

Fostering Motor Development

- Encourage infants and toddlers to practice what they know how to do; avoid "teaching" motor skills.
- Everyday experiences and interactions are the best ways to foster brain growth and neural connections, and thus impact motor development.

Children with Special Needs: Developmental Delays

- Early intervention concerning a developmental delay is based on an understanding of healthy child development.
- Providing basic play experiences and more *practice time* with a nurturing adult can be the most helpful way to support children with motor delays.

Key Terms

body wisdom 149	cerebral cortex 133	myelinization 133
brain plasticity 134	locomotion 137	proximodistal 132
cephalocaudal 132	manipulation 139	reflexes 134

Thought/Activity Questions

1. Review Figure 7.2. Suppose the mother of a child in your care found this chart, or one similar to it, in a popular magazine. She wants to discuss its meaning with you. Consider the following and what you would say:
   A. Her child is healthy and motor growth seems very normal. What would you say?
   B. You have some concerns about some lags in motor development and have been waiting for such an opportunity. What would you say?
   C. The father brings you this chart instead of the mother. What would you say?

2. Invent a toy to foster motor development in infants. Think about and discuss how this toy promotes physical growth.
3. Pretend that you are going to conduct a parent meeting. Outline the details of a discussion regarding how to set up an environment to promote gross motor development. Consider the following:
   A. Promoting safety
   B. Fostering development, *not* pushing it
   C. Teaching parents about developmentally appropriate environments
4. Discuss how you might adapt an infant-toddler environment to meet the needs of a developmentally delayed infant. What would you want to consider?

For Further Reading

P. A. Chandler, *A Place for Me: Including Children with Special Needs in Early Care and Education Settings* (Washington, D.C.: National Association for the Education of Young Children, 1994).

M. L. Dichtelmiller, "New Insights into Infant/Toddler Assessment," *Young Children*, 59 (1), January 2004, pp. 30–33.

D. Koralek, ed., *Young Children at Play* (Washington, D.C.: National Association for the Education of Young Children, 2004).

Mary Benson McMullen, "Achieving Best Practices in Infant and Toddler Care," *Young Children* 54(4), July 1999, pp. 69–76.

Nina Sazer O'Donnell, "Using Early Childhood Brain Development Research," *Child Care Information Exchange* 126, March 1999, pp. 58–62.

Emmi Pikler, "Data on Gross Motor Development," *Early Childhood Development and Care* 1, 1972, pp. 297–310.

S. W. Sanders, *Active for Life: Developmentally Appropriate Movement Programs for Young Children* (Washington, D.C.: National Association for the Education of Young Children, 2002).

Anna Tardos, "The Pikler/Loczy Philosophy," *Educaring* 7(2), Spring 1986, pp. 1–7.

Phyllis S. Weikart, "Facing the Challenge of Motor Development," *Child Care Information Exchange* 121, May 1998, pp. 60–62.

chapter 8

Cognition

Focus Questions

After reading this chapter you should be able to answer the following questions:

1 Describe what is meant by "the cognitive experience." How does it change from infancy to toddlerhood?

2 How would you compare and contrast the theories of Piaget and Vygotsky?

3 What are appropriate guidelines for adults to foster cognitive development in young children?

4 How do brain-based learning principles support infant-toddler cognition?

5 What are some effective ways to assist young children with cognitive delays?

What Do You See?

Nick stands holding an empty pitcher in his hand. He goes over to a box of toys; reaches in; and brings out a small plastic bowl, an egg carton, and the lid to a peanut butter jar. He sets these in a row on a low table and pretends to pour something in them from his pitcher. He is careful in his actions and methodically fills each container, including each compartment of the egg carton. Then, seemingly satisfied that the task is done, he tosses the pitcher aside with a joyous shout. He starts across the room in another direction when he notices a plant standing on a table. He immediately runs back to where he left the pitcher and rummages through the pile of dolls and blankets hiding it from his view. He finds it, carries it over to the plant, and carefully pours pretend water into the pot. He abandons the pitcher again and picks up a doll. He scolds the doll, bangs it on the floor several times, wraps it in a blanket, and then lovingly puts it to bed in a box of toys. As he bends over the box, he spies a picture book with fire engines on the cover. He looks at the pictures for a moment, puts the book on his head, and races around the room screaming in what seems to be an imitation of a siren. As he passes by a toy shelf, he sees a wooden fire truck. He pulls it out and proceeds to push it around on the floor. He stops and looks at the holes on the truck where the little firefighters are suppose to sit. No little firefighters are in sight. He pauses for a moment, looks around, and goes to the pitcher once more. Nick carefully fills each hole in the fire truck with whatever pretend liquid the pitcher contains.

Knowing and understanding the world come from active involvement with people and things. Infants and toddlers are naturally active and interactive. Nick is a good example of a young child who is actively involved in his world. His previous experiences are clearly reflected in his ability to combine known things in new ways. He seeks experiences that are interesting to him, and he shows that he can make adaptations that lead to problem solving. These skills and others related to cognition, or mental development, are the focus of this chapter. Some of the work of Jean Piaget, the leading Swiss cognitive psychologist, and Lev Vygotsky, the Russian developmental psychologist, will be discussed. The information on early brain development is confirming how young children learn, and implications of that understanding will be included. The chapter concludes with guidelines for fostering cognitive growth in children, including those with special needs.

The Cognitive Experience

The process of gathering information, organizing it, and finally using it to adapt to the world is the essence of the **cognitive experience.** Whenever a topic such as cognition or mental growth is discussed, it is easy to also include such terms as *intellect, learning,* and maybe eventually *academics* as related concepts. Most people think of the cognitive process as it relates to IQ scores and school-type experiences (including grades!). A quality infant-toddler program will promote cognitive and intellectual growth in young children, but it will not look the same as a traditional classroom setting. Understanding *how* children grow and learn is basic to planning a developmentally appropriate setting that will foster cognitive development.

How do infants develop knowing and understanding? Initially, they perceive experiences directly with the senses. For infants to acquire the ability to comprehend this sensory information, they must be able to distinguish between the familiar and the unknown; later they will begin to consider, to formulate, and eventually to form mental images in this process of experiencing and clarifying the environment.

This process is primarily unseen; therefore certain assumptions concerning cognition must be inferred by observing obvious physical movements. Infants begin by exploring the world with their bodies. They internalize what they take in through their senses and display it in their physical movements. Infants gather vital information through such simple acts as mouthing, grasping, and reaching. You can see infants practicing these acts, repeating them over and over, and they refine them rather quickly. For example, when newborns first bring the mouth toward a nipple, the mouth opens wide and ready. With only a few trials, they learn just what size opening the nipple requires and adjust the mouth accordingly in anticipation of what will go into it. They have refined a simple action. Soon they will judge how far to reach and what shape the fingers must take to pick up a cup or a toy. Much later, as adults, they may refine their actions further in order to reach without looking and strike a particular chord on the piano or input data on a computer keyboard. All these muscular refinements had their beginnings in that tiny mouth adjusting itself to the appropriate size for the nipple. In this example, cognition has been tied to fine motor development. You can think of other examples in which cognition is tied to gross motor development, social development, and emotional development. Learning and thinking support all areas of development.

The knowing process—cognition—also involves language abilities. As young children use their senses to experience the world, they need labels to categorize and remember these experiences. By creating these labels, children increase their ability to communicate and begin to control their own behavior. These expanded abilities give young children additional opportunities to understand the world.

Sensorimotor Experience: Piaget

The theorist who has contributed the most to our understanding of cognitive development in infants and toddlers is Jean Piaget. He was most interested in how children come to know about their world. He was not so much interested in how much a child knows (that is, quantity, or IQ), but rather in the quality of a child's understanding and how the child can eventually justify or explain it. He named the first stage—birth to two years of age—the **sensorimotor stage.** This name, which means the coordination of sense perception and muscle movements, is appropriate because that coordination is the beginning of thinking. Table 8.1 lists the components of the sensorimotor stage.

Gradually, infants come to know that they can control the interaction between themselves and objects. They like this new piece of knowledge, and they keep

Table 8.1 The Sensorimotor Stage		
Age	**Sensorimotor Behaviors**	**Examples**
Birth–1 month	Reflexes, simple inborn behaviors	Crying, sucking, grasping
1–4 months	Refines simple behaviors, repeats and combines them	Reaching, grasping, sucking on hands/fingers
4–8 months	Repeats activity using objects, begins limited imitation	Accidentally makes a mobile in the crib move, notices it, tries to make it happen again
8–12 months	Intentionality: Plans a movement to make something happen	Pulls a string to bring a toy closer
12–18 months	Experiments with objects to create new events	If a ball rolled from the table will bounce, what will a book do?
18–24 months	Imagines events and solves problems, invents through mental combination, begins to use words	Pretends to throw a ball, calls to a caregiver or parent, "Here ball"

testing it. This process of taking in new information and processing it (or *playing* with it), is what Piaget called **assimilation.** This process allows infants to make information their own and to incorporate new experience into previously developed mental concepts or categories. Piaget uses the term **accommodation** to describe what happens when this new information refines or expands previous mental categories. Initially the senses assimilate everything, but then they begin to accommodate to particular sights and sounds (focusing on a face for example and ignoring the bright light). It is through the ongoing dynamic system of assimilation (taking in experience) and accommodation (adjusting to it) that young children adapt to the world, and it is a life long process.

When babies are practicing and combining these first actions, they are in love with their own bodies—fascinated by what they are feeling and doing. Eventually that fascination moves from their own bodies to the effects their actions have on the environment. They get interested in what happens when they shove their arm out and hit a toy. A new understanding develops with this shift of focus from self to environment, from action to consequence. Babies begin to realize that they and the objects in the world are separate.

You can see this same progression of development a bit later in toddlers having art experiences. At first, children are most interested in what it feels like when they scribble or scrub with a paintbrush on paper. Later they start looking at the product of their action—the drawing or painting. Some children don't focus on the product until after three years of age.

Knowing they are in a world full of objects and part of it, but not the whole of it, is a great step forward in understanding for infants. Nevertheless, their ideas of objects differ greatly from those of adults. Infants acknowledge the existence only of things they can see, touch, or otherwise know with their senses. When you hide her favorite toy, the infant does not look for it, because she believes it no longer exists. The very young infant thinks, "Out of sight, out of mind." If you bring the toy out of hiding, it has been re-created for her. This understanding of the world makes a game of peek-a-boo extremely exciting: What power—to create and uncreate a person in an instant. No wonder peek-a-boo has universal fascination. What the young infant lacks is what Piaget called **object permanence,** or the ability to remember an object or person even though they cannot be seen, touched, or heard. Eventually, infants become aware that objects continue to exist even when they can't see them. But gaining this awareness is a gradual process.

At about one year of age, children begin to think in a more sophisticated way and to use tools. Give them a stick and they will use it to gain an out-of-reach toy. Give them a string with something they want at the end and they know just what to do. Novelty becomes an end in itself. Children will deliberately manipulate the environment to find out what happens.

With all this experimenting, children develop some new abilities: the ability to anticipate where an object will be when they drop it, the ability to remember an action after a short interruption, and the ability to predict. Watch an 18-month-old child who has had experience with a ball. He may roll the ball off a

Table 8.2 Piaget's Stages of Cognitive Development	
Stage	**General Description**
Sensorimotor Stage (0–2 years)	Child progresses from reflexive action to symbolic activities; has ability to separate self from objects; has limited awareness of cause and effect.
Preoperational Stage (2–7 years)	Child is able to use symbols, such as words; has better reasoning skills but is still *perceptually* bound in the here and now.
Concrete Operational Stage (7–11 years)	Child has logical thought, but only in regard to concrete objects; has ability to order things by number, size, or class; also has ability to relate time and space.
Formal Operational Stage (11 years and older)	Child has abstract, logical thought; has ability to consider alternatives in problem solving.

table and turn his head to the place where it will land. Or if the ball rolls under a chair, he may look for a way to get it out again. Or if he rolls a ball toward a hole, he will run to the hole to watch the ball drop into it.

The next step in the development of understanding comes when infants can find solutions mentally. After enough experience using their sense perceptions and muscles, they can begin to think of ways of acting and try them out in their head before doing them. They can think of past and future events. You can see they are using mental images and connecting thoughts to experiences and objects that are not present. They can throw an imaginary ball or contemplate the solution to a problem before they begin to tackle it.

Table 8.2 provides a brief overview of all four of Piaget's stages of cognitive development. The focus of this chapter is stage one—sensorimotor—and a small part of stage two—preoperational.

Sociocultural Influences: Vygotsky and Piaget

The beginning of language and the ability to pretend signal the end of the sensorimotor stage and the beginning of what Piaget calls the **preoperational stage.** Piaget was not alone in his appreciation of thought and language and their impact on how children come to understand their world. Recently, numerous developmentalists have looked more closely at infant-toddler cognitive growth. The work by Lev Vygotsky gives another perspective on the importance of language and how young children acquire problem-solving skills.

The findings by Piaget and Vygotsky suggest that infants and toddlers are competent in problem solving and that their cognitive skills develop rapidly. A comparison of Piaget and Vygotsky can help caregivers and parents understand cognitive growth and developmentally appropriate practices, especially as to how they pertain to a child's sociocultural world. By highlighting the skills of preoperational children and by reviewing the ideas of Piaget and Vygotsky, we

Reflect

What problem-solving skills have you observed in infants? How do those skills expand in toddlerhood?

can better understand how young children become independent, self-regulating learners.

Preoperational children can use mental images for their thinking processes. Thinking, though still tied to the concrete, is not limited to sense perceptions and body movements. Although toddlers don't practice this very much, they *can* think while standing or even sitting still. (However, they still need to be gathering a great number of concrete experiences *to think about*, so don't let anyone pressure you into sitting toddlers down in order to educate them.)

Because of their increased ability to hold and store mental images, toddlers entering the preoperational stage have increased **memory,** or recall, of past events. Although the word *yesterday* may not yet be in their vocabulary, they *can* remember yesterday—and the day before.

Their sense of the future also increases as their **ability to predict** grows with their experience in the world. They continue to use trial and error to strengthen this skill, not only in the concrete world ("I wonder what will happen if I pour sand in the sink.") but also in the social one ("I wonder what will happen if I pour sand in Jamie's hair."). Sometimes these experiments are both social and physical and are thought out on the conscious level ("If I pinch the baby, will he cry?"). Sometimes children don't make such clear decisions, but they are still problem solving in a trial-and-error way ("I wonder if hitting Erin will get an adult over here to pay attention to me." or "If I break enough limits, can I get my caregiver and mother to quit talking to each other so we can go home?"). What appears to be naughty behavior may in reality be this scientific testing.

Step back for a moment (mentally) and review some of Piaget's major points. Piaget believed knowledge is *functional*—it leads to something. The purpose of information (gained from experience) is to help an individual adapt in the world. The most significant knowledge is that which can be used in behavior to accomplish something. (This is particularly important when considering children's *play* experience.) Piaget's view of the young child's cognitive growth contains four major assumptions.

First, interaction with people and the environment is essential. As young children grow and mature, they use experience to build, or **construct new knowledge.** The child's action on objects (sucking, pulling, pushing) is the central force for cognitive development.

Second, Piaget viewed the growth of the young child as gradual and continuous. The concept that objects are permanent grows slowly from the first few days of a child's life. As the "quality" of that concept matures, it provides the memory base, and the language, from which the toddler can create "pretend" play experiences.

Piaget believed that there is a connection between successive periods of development. This third assumption indicates the importance of the *quality* of development in *each* stage of a child's life. A skill or ability later in life depends on the maturing and improving of earlier achievements. In other words, don't push infants and toddlers to be "smarter." The "growth of mental structures," according to Piaget, will foster natural (appropriate) learning.

A fourth basic point Piaget made involves the young child's *ability to construct a plan*. He believes that this is one of the major competencies to develop during the first two years, and he refers to this as **intentionality.** Intentionality gradually emerges as a child selects objects, plays with them, repeats actions on them, and creates a plan. This experience often involves a great deal of absorption; the young child may appear to be "lost in thought."[1]

Take a moment to think about the complexity of creating and using mental images and the ability to construct a plan for thinking. Thinking is not limited to sense perceptions and body movements. It is also a social experience. While infants and toddlers actively explore things in their world, they are often also interacting with other people.

Vygotsky believed that cognitive activities have their origins in these social interactions. His work emphasizes the importance of social interaction and adds a significant piece to Piaget's view that mental development occurs only in stages (the child is capable only because biological growth has occurred). By comparing the perspectives of Piaget and Vygotsky, one can better understand how infant-toddler thinking emerges (see Table 8.3).

Table 8.3 A Comparison of Piaget and Vygotsky

Similarities

- Both believed that young children *construct* their knowledge—they build their information base from experience.

- Both believed that young children acquire abilities when they are *ready*—previous skills serve as a base for new learning.

- Both believed that *play* provides an important opportunity to learn and practice life skills.

- Both believed that language is significant for cognitive development to advance.

- Both believed that cognition was fostered by "nature and nurture."

Differences

Piaget believed that knowledge is primarily *self-constructed* and discovery-oriented.	Vygotsky placed emphasis on the importance of *co-constructed* knowledge and assisted discovery.
Piaget believed that *maturation* (moving through stages) allows for cognition to advance; development leads to learning.	Vygotsky believed that learning can be "advanced" (not pushed) with the *assistance of an expert* (adult or peer); learning can lead to development.
Piaget believed that hands-on, *sensory-rich play* provides valuable practice for later adultlike behavior.	Vygotsky was more specific and emphasized *pretend play* that allows children to distinguish between objects and their meaning and to experiment with new cause-and-effect relationships.
Piaget believed that language provides labels for many previous experiences (egocentric speech), and that it is the primary means through which children interact.	Vygotsky believed that language is absolutely essential for mental growth; *self-talk* is eventually internalized into higher levels of mental development and self-directive behavior.
Piaget's stages are universal and apply to children around the world; the nature of thinking is largely independent of cultural context.	Vygotsky stressed the importance of culture and society for fostering mental growth; cultures influence the course of cognitive development (reasoning skills may not appear at the same age in different cultures).

Vygotsky, like Piaget, believed that children *construct* their understanding of the world. Infants and toddlers gather and practice important learning constantly. Vygotsky would agree with Piaget that knowledge is functional in that it helps individuals adapt to the world. However, Vygotsky would emphasize that this learning is *co-constructed*. Young children acquire important skills (especially those skills unique to people, such as specific memory and symbolic thought) with the help of another, more experienced learner. This help is certainly not always in the form of a lesson. Caregivers who work with infants and toddlers often provide appropriate prompts to help children think about their own experiences. In Part 1, particularly in Chapters 1 and 4, you read numerous examples of adults supporting children's learning experiences. As mentioned there, timing is crucial. If caregivers step in too early or too late, valuable learning may be lost. Vygotsky's views on **assisted learning,** and how learning can lead to development, differ from Piaget's. Vygotsky's focus is that social interaction is a prerequisite for children to develop problem-solving skills and that early language experience is critical to this process. Vygotsky believes that children, through assisted learning are constantly learning from others and then they make that learning their own, through play. For Piaget, children *discover* learning through their play experiences, and then take that learning into their social interactions with others. Piaget believed that development precedes learning ("that mental structures" mature and foster learning). The **"zone of proximal development" (ZPD)** is the phrase used by Vygotsky to describe how adults can appropriately assist children's learning. ZPD is the difference between what children can do on their own (independent performance) and what they can do with further guidance (assisted performance).

Consider an infant who, after crawling under a very low table, tries to sit up. There's no room. He continues to try to lift his head until he realizes that he is stuck. He starts screaming. His caregiver peers under the table, lending her quiet presence. While maneuvering the infant's head, the caregiver talks to him so that he stays low and in a crawling position. She uses verbal and physical cues to guide him out from under the table.

Vygotsky would label the head bumping and squirming the child experienced as the child's "level of independent performance." The way the child got out from under the table was what Vygotsky would call the "level of assisted performance." You might ask yourself, why go to all the trouble? Why not just lift the table off? According to Vygotsky, if caregivers appropriately assist children in problem solving, children stay with the situation longer and learn more. (Note: The Reggio Emilia schools are proving what Magda Gerber has been saying for years about problem solving. Problem solving and learning work best when in a positive, responsive environment that encourages interactions. The adult, taking cues from the child, assists the child only until he or she can work independently. If the child doesn't need or want help, the adult backs off.)

Appropriate is a key word for understanding the concept of helping and guiding children. Appropriate help has to do with being respectful and sensitively responsive and always takes into consideration what is best for the child. The approach of this book, which follows Vygotsky's theory, never pushes learning. *Remember principle 8: Recognize problems as learning opportunities, and let infants and toddlers try to solve their own. Don't rescue them, constantly make life easy for them, or try to protect them from all problems.*

A "guided," or socially shared, cognition is at the root of Vygotsky's theory regarding the mental development of children. When caregivers and parents interact with children in collaborative ways, they provide the tools for mental growth that are important to language development. Language, according to Vygotsky, plays a central role in cognition. Language is the first type of communication between infants and adults. Caregiving experiences provide the opportunity for infants and adults to experience these communication opportunities. Gradually, during infancy and toddlerhood, all the gestures, words, and symbols of social interaction that a young child experiences become internalized. It is this eventual communication with self (internalized language) that Vygotsky believed was so important to cognition. Although language development will be discussed more thoroughly in Chapter 9, it is important to note here its link to mental growth. Vygotsky's theory acknowledges that cognition and language develop separately, but that they begin to merge within a social communication context. The language of others helps a young child organize her own behavior verbally.[2] How many times have you heard a young child repeat (maybe in abbreviated form) what she has just heard or been told? Vygotsky stressed the importance of this private speech (and, later, make-believe play) to cognitive development more than did Piaget.

Today much thought is being given to the importance of a child's cultural background and how these early social interactions contribute to mental development. In his sociocultural theory, Vygotsky focused on how social interaction helps children acquire the important skills and ways of behaving native to their culture. He believed that the sharing of cultural activities (e.g., cooking) between child and adult contributes significantly to the child's understanding of his or her world. Although some of Vygotsky's ideas may seem obvious to most parents and caregivers, misinterpretations do occur. Some people force children to learn things inappropriate for their age, for example, math flash cards at three years of age! and use the work of Vygotsky to justify it. After reviewing some of Vygotsky's concepts, we can't help but appreciate how much he valued the uniqueness of each child and that child's cultural history.

NAEYC Program Standard 7
Families

Piaget and Vygotsky have both contributed to our knowledge of the mental growth of young children. Piaget focused on the biological changes that contribute to cognition. Vygotsky stressed how social interaction might transform a child's thinking and problem-solving abilities. Today neither theory by itself would be enough to completely explain cognitive development. As they grow and mature, children need the support of sensitive adults.

Look now at the behavior and play of three children and see how they relate to the biological and social perspectives of Piaget and Vygotsky. Try to determine what might be going on for each child and how the environment might be influencing them. By being able to discuss the ideas of Piaget and

Vygotsky, we can resist the pressure to apply inappropriate schoollike academic experiences to the education of infants and toddlers. Remember, both Piaget and Vygotsky believed that play is extremely important to the child's learning and that pushing a child does not foster real understanding of the world.

The first child is lying on his back on a rug surrounded by a few toys. He turns slightly toward a ball lying near his arm. He stretches, and the movement causes him to accidentally touch the ball. It moves, making a sound. He startles at the sound and looks toward the ball. He lies still again; his gaze wanders. Then he moves his arms again—a big, sweeping gesture—and the ball moves again, making the same jingling sound. He again startles, and a look of surprise comes on his face. You can almost hear his question, "Who did that?" He looks at the ball, looks around, and looks at the ball again. Then he lies still. A few moments later his arms come up and out again, this time tentatively waving. He misses the ball. Nothing happens. He lies still again. He repeats the action, again tentatively. This time his hand passes in front of his eyes, and a spark of interest comes over his face. He looks intently at his hand, and you can almost hear him saying, "What's that thing? Where did it come from?" He moves his fingers, and delight comes into his eyes. "Hey, it works!" he seems to say. His arms continue to wave, taking the fascinating fingers out of his line of vision. He breezes by the ball again, causing it to make just a whisper of sound. His eyes search for the source of the sound.

The second child is sitting on a rug near the first, but they are separated by a low fence. She has a rubber toy in her hand and is banging it up and down on the floor, giggling at the squeaks issuing forth. The toy bounces across the rug as she lets go, and she crawls happily after it. She stops to explore a string with a large bead on the end, but glances to see where the other end is. The string disappears into a pile of toys on the lowest shelf at the edge of the rug. She expectantly pulls the string and laughs delightedly. Then she catches sight of a bright red ball that has rolled out from the pile of toys that fell off the shelf. She crawls over to it and begins to smack it with her hand, making noises while doing so. She seems to expect the ball to move. When it doesn't, she tries again with more force. The ball moves slightly, and she moves after it. She is getting more and more excited, and as she approaches the ball, one hand accidentally swipes it so that it rolls some distance and disappears under a couch in the corner of the room. She watches it roll, starts after it, but stops when it disappears. Looking puzzled, she crawls over to the edge of the couch but does not lift up the ruffle at the bottom to check underneath. She looks a little disappointed, but then she crawls back to the rug and the squeaky rubber toy. As the scene closes, she is once again banging the toy against the floor and laughing at the noise it makes.

The third child is sitting at a table putting puzzle pieces in a three-piece puzzle. When she gets stuck, she looks to a nearby adult, who gives her verbal hints about how to turn the pieces. When she completes the puzzle, she turns it upside down and smiles at the clatter of wooden pieces hitting the tabletop. She works the puzzle again, faster this time, with no help from the adult. When she finishes the puzzle, she puts it back on a low shelf and moves to another table where several other children are poking and squeezing play dough. She asks for a piece, and when none is forthcoming, an adult intervenes, helping each child give her a bit off the hunks they are playing with. She sits contentedly poking and prodding her play dough, periodically conversing with the other children about what she is doing. Her monologue is not in direct response to anything they are saying. There is little interaction at the table, though there is lots of talking. The child we are focusing on rolls her play dough into a ball, then sits looking at it for a minute. Then she begins to pat and shape it, obviously with purpose in her actions. When she has produced a lopsided lump, she sits back, satisfied, and announces to no one in particular that she is finished. She gets up and walks away. As she leaves the table, another child grabs her piece and incorporates it into his own. This act goes unnoticed. The girl, seeing a cart of food being wheeled into the room, runs to the corner to a row of sinks and begins to wash her hands. We leave her thoroughly soaping her hands and arms and obviously enjoying the experience.

It is essential to recognize the importance of play to a young child and how it contributes to his or her cognitive development. When observing children, it is difficult to infer from their physical behaviors and play what they are thinking. By using Piaget's and Vygotsky's ideas of early cognitive development, we can attempt to guess what these children are thinking and how they are being influenced by their environment. We can begin to see the transition from unintentional, even accidental, behavior to purposeful behavior that manifests through problem solving, mental images, representational thought, and pretend play. We can also see how appropriate adult support can help children learn how to foster cooperation among themselves. Chapter 4 examined the importance of play and provided valuable guides to help plan play sessions. Let's use this cognitive development perspective to reexamine the importance of play.

By the second year, children can think about their world even when they are not directly experiencing it. They also begin to represent things by the use of symbols. Engaging in **pretend play** marks an important step in a child's thinking, and it usually is joined by the beginning of language. Pretend play is when children can represent things through symbols and have the ability to think of their world when not directly experiencing it.

Take the time to observe a two-year-old and a three-year-old involved in pretend play. You may be able to see three different changes or trends that have come about as a result of cognitive growth.

The younger a child is, the more apt he is to be the center of his own pretend play. As he gets older, he gradually acquires the ability to remove himself from center stage. He is then ready to take the role of other imaginary characters. Notice a one-year-old pretending to feed himself. When he gets a little older, he will pretend to feed his doll rather than himself. His doll, however, remains very quiet. By about two years, the child has the ability to make the doll "wake up." Now he can make his doll feed itself. The child can now assume the role of others in his play. He can stand back and consider the other's feelings and one role in relation to another (Is the doll hungry? How much "food" should he supply for his doll?). As he gets older, this becomes more complex and involves other

NAEYC Program Standard 2
Curriculum

people (for example, several four-year-olds "grocery shopping" in a dramatic play area).

Another change in pretend play can be appreciated when a child begins to substitute one object for another. A very young child needs a real object, or realistic replica, for pretend play. If she is feeding herself, she needs a real cup or real spoon (or plastic replica). As a child gets older (closer to about 22 months), she acquires the ability to substitute one object for another. Now perhaps a stick can be used as a spoon, especially when feeding a doll.

At first this substitution is quite limited. Objects need to look like the real thing, and the child may not be able to substitute too many things at one time. Young children need to have available objects to enhance their play. It is important to appreciate that as children get older (closer to four years), it may be difficult for them to substitute a well-known object for something else. A plastic golf club is too much like a real golf club to become a fishing pole. This finding indicates how important it is to have "raw" materials on hand such as tubes, blocks, and an assortment of paper. A paper tube or rolled up newspaper more easily becomes a fishing pole for the young preschooler.[3]

As pretend play continues to develop, a child can invent several actions and combine them. These combinations expand and become more complex as the child gets older. A young child may initially just pretend to feed himself. As he combines actions and integrates them into other experiences, he may eventually pretend to "open a restaurant" and feed several dolls (and no doubt any people who will cooperate).

A toddler's cognitive growth is visible in numerous areas. Pretend play, however, is one of the most dramatic abilities to be observed in a young child. The development of purposeful behavior needs to be planned for and respected by adults.

The Principles in Action

Principle 8 Recognize problems as learning opportunities, and let infants and toddlers try to solve their own. Don't rescue them, constantly make life easy for them, or try to protect them from all problems.

Caitlin and Ian are two 18-month-olds in your family child-care home; they have been with you since they were six months old. Caitlin is spirited and alive with activity; Ian is not as active and tends to observe Caitlin a lot or follow her lead. This morning Caitlin is busy dropping shapes through holes in a plastic box. When a shape does not fit readily into a hole, she pounds it vigorously with her hand to make it fit and then quickly turns the box to find another hole. She giggles with delight at the sound of each shape dropping into the box. Ian is watching her from a slight distance holding his stuffed dog; he seems interested but makes no attempt to approach Caitlin and her activity. Caitlin is suddenly finished with the plastic box. She moves over to the block area where you have arranged a few blocks on the floor and added a new small red car. She immediately notices the new car and says, "Car!" This attracts Ian's attention, and he moves over to the block area, too. Caitlin gives the new car a push, and it rolls (faster than she realized) under a nearby bookshelf and is out of sight. Caitlin rushes over to the bookshelf intent on retrieving the car even though it has probably rolled too far under the shelving for her to reach it. Ian looks over to you with an expression that seems to say, "Now what?"

1. How would you describe each child's approach to exploration and problem solving?
2. How would you interact with each one to foster their individual learning opportunities?
3. Are you at all concerned with Ian's approach to problem solving? Or with Caitlin's approach? Why or why not?
4. What would you do about helping the children retrieve the red car?
5. What would you try to provide in an environment to foster problem solving in young children?

Supporting Cognitive Development

The prerequisite for promoting cognitive development is security and attachment. Through the attachment process, infants develop skills such as differentiation as they distinguish the person(s) they are attached to from others in their world. Attachment also shows intentionality as infants and toddlers use all their behaviors to bring the attached person(s) close and keep them there. Clinging, crying infants or toddlers are exhibiting strong intentionality (a mark of early cognitive behavior) as they try to get the parent to remain. This may be annoying, and it is not usually recognized as cognitive behavior; yet in truth it is very purposeful and intelligent.

Responding to other needs is also one of the prerequisites for promoting cognitive development. Children with unmet needs put their energies into trying to get someone to meet them, which focuses their cognitive development in a narrow way. Children whose needs are met consistently will feel trusting and comfortable. Children who feel comfortable will *explore the environment*. From continual exploration comes cognitive development.

You promote cognitive development by inviting and encouraging exploration in an environment rich in sensory experience. When given the opportunity to play with objects in any way they wish, children encounter problems. As mentioned earlier, problem solving is the basis of infant-toddler education as it is outlined in this book. Allowing infants and toddlers to solve the kinds of problems they run into during the course of a day promotes their cognitive development. Free choice ensures that children find problems that are meaningful to them. Solving someone else's problem is not nearly as interesting to most of us as solving the ones that are related to something that really matters to us.

It helps problem solving if adults do such things as adding words (labeling sensory input—"That rabbit feels soft and warm." or "That was a loud noise." or "That sponge is soaking wet."). In addition, adults can help by asking questions, pointing out relationships, reflecting feelings, and generally supporting the child.

Encourage children to interact with one another during problem solving. The input infants and toddlers get from their peers can be both useful and can offer more than one way to a solution. Remember, both Piaget and Vygotsky believe that interaction—with objects and with other people, especially peers—promotes cognitive development. Include dramatic play props for toddlers. Through pretend, they build the mental images that are so important for the thought process.

Resist pressure to teach or to introduce academic kinds of experiences. Children will learn the names of colors and shapes in the course of normal conversations if you use them naturally ("Please bring me the red pillow." or "Do you want a round cracker or a square one?"). A better use of your time than teaching colors and shapes is to help children learn a variety of approaches to meeting their needs (both physical and social) and making things happen in the world. The concepts will then be embedded in real life experience and therefore have meaning, rather than ending up as an academic exercise.

Number concepts can be learned in a natural context. "More" and "less" have real meaning when things are being handed out—such as apple slices. Mathematical concepts come as toddlers play with blocks and sand, compare the size and weight of objects, make other comparisons, and figure out relationships.

You will teach reading in your job, but at a toddler level—that is, in a developmentally appropriate way. Your job as a reading teacher of infants and toddlers is not to teach the alphabet but to promote whole language development as well as to provide plenty of emergent literacy experiences from which to build concepts so that later, when they see a written word such as *bean*, they'll have had many associations with it. It won't be empty of experience and therefore feeling. Children who can recall planting, watering, debugging, picking, snapping, washing, and eating beans really understand what the word means. The word *bean* has meaning as well as rich associations (called connotations). Later, when the children are ready to decode written words, they have real life experience with the words they're reading about. You can help give children an appreciation of reading and an idea of what it is all about by reading book after book to them. The idea and the joy of reading are important prerequisites to reading itself.

Infants and toddlers are naturally creative. If you don't hinder them with restrictive limits and an impoverished environment, they will give you lessons in how to use toys and materials in ways you never thought of. Curiosity is part of this push for creativity and needs to be valued and nurtured. Infants and toddlers are newcomers to the world, and they want to know how everything works. They

Reflect

Have you seen caregivers do too much for young children? What effect do you think this has over time?

NAEYC Program Standard 3
Teaching

don't want to be told; they want to find out on their own. They are scientists. They don't take anything for granted but rather must prove each hypothesis. Nurture this quality in them! *Remember principle 4: Invest time and energy to build the total person (concentrate on the "whole child"). Don't focus on cognitive development alone or look at it as separate from total development.*

Infants and toddlers are in the process of creating knowledge (according to Piaget and Vygotsky). They don't just take in information and ideas and manipulate toys and materials. They are not empty vessels to be filled. Instead, they are builders of their own understandings. They use a creative construction process to structure their experiences. And they need caregivers who understand how to appropriately support and co-construct such experiences.

In this active process of creating knowledge, young children learn to combine known things in their world in new ways. Think about the development of pretend play. As a result of exploring and manipulating things, toddlers experiment with new combinations and recombining known elements in new ways. This is the essence of creativity—the process of combining known things in new ways.

The appreciation of creativity as part of cognitive development emphasizes the importance of planning for it and of not pushing it. When a young child has opportunity to explore and experiment, understanding is fostered. Once children understand how something works (usually as a result of playing with it), they seem naturally to start using it creatively. Exploration is not the same as creativity. Exploration is the beginning point. When promoting cognitive development, try to follow some of the suggestions given in this section. Then step back and watch for the creative, problem-solving process.

Brain-Based Learning

The research on early brain development that has gotten so much attention nationwide may confirm what many parents and caregivers already know about how young children learn. It may also cause many misinterpretations about development and may fuel marketing strategies for "smart toys" and "super-stimulating" environments. This is an important time to think about young children and to care about how they learn and grow. Consider for a moment your understanding of how young children learn; compare your ideas with Piaget's and Vygotsky's. Pause and review the 10 principles of caregiving in Chapter 1. Review Table 5.1, "Rethinking the Brain" (page 94), in Chapter 5. No doubt in the next few years many questions about brain development and learning will be answered. Right now, however, some significant things do seem clear about how the brain learns.

Attachments are primary to development, and learning takes place best in trusting, responsive relationships. The brain functions as an integrated whole; all of the developmental areas are involved. Infants are active learners, and the brain becomes more active when adults respond to infants' cues and signals for attention. Environments are powerful; learning context is as important as learning

Reflect

Have you noticed "smart toys" in stores or shopping areas? What are their claims? What do you think of such marketing?
(Hint: "Smart Toys" are usually those props advertised as making your child smarter or raising his or her IQ.)

d

Father Diapering Toddler

See Video Observation 8: Father Diapering Toddler for an example of an activity that relates to cognitive development.

Questions

- Why do you think we picked a diapering scene instead of one that showed a child in a more obviously intellectual pursuit of some sort?
- Do you see evidence that the child and man have a relationship? What part do relationships play in cognitive development?
- Can you explain how the child was showing that potty training is more than a physical issue and has cognitive connections?
- Explain how this scene illustrates a child learning language in context.

To view this clip, go to www.mhhe.com/itc7e. Click on Student Edition, select Chapter 8, and click on Video Observation.

content. Routines need to be sensitive to relationships (be aware of group size, ratio, and time spent caring for an infant). Meaningfulness of an experience increases the possibility that it will be remembered. Repetition strengthens neural pathways in the brain's circuitry, but don't confuse drill with repetition. Repetition is child-sensitive and comes from the child; drill is adult-directed and adult needs (not the child's) are being addressed.[4]

It is brain density (or neural connections) and myelinization rather than brain size that contributes most to learning. The brain circuits that have been reinforced and refined translate experience into learning. These branching dendrites in the cortex allow for specific measurement thanks to today's advanced technology. Growth spurts, reflected by increased brain activity, in the first two years actually align themselves with the sensorimotor experiences of Piaget's theory.[5]

More and more we realize that no one theory completely explains how children learn. The theories of Piaget and Vygotsky can be combined to help appreciate cognitive development in the early years. Brain-based learning principles—hands-on, discovery-oriented, collaborative, open-ended experiences—very similar to Piaget's and Vygotsky's ideas and developmentally appropriate practice, also help us appreciate the essential interconnectedness of young children's learning.[6]

Go back and take another look at the three children playing (pages 164–165). Try to be sensitive to what might be happening in their brains. Can you see neural circuitry being strengthened? Can you see the "magic trees of the mind" (title of Marion Diamond's book on brain growth) growing more dense? Allow yourself to imagine, to wonder. We will certainly be learning more about the brain in the future, but we have much to appreciate today. *Remember principle 5: Respect infants and toddlers as worthy people. Don't treat them as objects or cute little empty-headed people to be manipulated.*

 ## Children with Special Needs: Cognitive Delay

The focus of the chapter has been on how children begin to understand and learn about their world. The most obvious characteristic of cognitive delay is a reduced ability to learn. We have already noted that because learning and thinking are internal processes, we must infer what is going on for young children by observing them. The most obvious aspect of development to observe is physical movement. This was discussed to some extent in Chapter 7 when we reviewed developmentally delayed children.

Before we go any further, we need to mention "labels." We believe that each child is unique and that labels tend to categorize and create generalizations about individuals. In the area of special needs, however, labels can be very important in recognizing children's abilities and limitations. If used appropriately, labels can be guides to caregivers when helping infants and toddlers achieve their greatest potential. Labels, used as identification criteria, also allow programs to seek additional funding resources and community support. We hope labels will always be used in a context that is developmentally appropriate by caregivers who are nurturing and respectful of each child.

The terms *cognitive delay* and *developmentally delayed* are sometimes used interchangeably. Cognitive delay goes beyond motor assessment and involves more of the cognitive areas of development. For example, specific areas of concern may relate to attention skills, memory, language, and problem-solving abilities. Think about how these four areas link together for a young child. A child who has a limited ability to attend to an experience—become absorbed or deeply involved—may never gather important details to remember. Memory is critical to acquiring labels for these experiences and thus developing language. Language allows for more logical and organized thinking. There is, we might say, a "cognitive" domino effect for the young child with cognitive delays.

These abilities, which may be limited, depressed, or nonexistent, also relate to a child's "adaptive" behavior. How well a young child adapts to or copes with the world is, of course, age- and situation-specific. If an eight-month-old who was very recently enrolled in an infant program cried for the majority of the morning (even though comfort was offered), her behavior could be considered developmentally appropriate. However, if a three-year-old who had been attending a child-care program for several months did the same thing and could not be comforted and establish trust, additional questions would need to be asked. **Adaptive behaviors** can be considered cognitive. They allow a child to predict and therefore generalize trust. They also allow a child to change or adjust to new experiences and apply familiar skills to better fit a situation. These behaviors are significant, and when they are slow to develop, children may experience frustration. Young children with cognitive delays tend to have a difficult time adapting to changes. They need more time and the support of a sensitive caregiver.

Trying to assess an infant's or toddler's intellectual functioning (IQ score) is very difficult. Few really reliable tests exist. It is generally believed that the younger a child is when tested, the less predictive the results will be. The definition of cognitive delay usually involves some degree of assessment in this area. Today observations and descriptive evaluations are considered the most helpful. It is difficult in the first three years to determine a "mild" cognitive handicap or a concern that may eventually be related to a learning disability. These milder concerns or processing problems may not be identified until a child reaches school age and is faced with the challenges of reading, writing, and math. More moderate, severe, or multiple concerns will, it is hoped, be identified early (before school age), and intervention will be available.

Causes for cognitive delay may be varied or difficult to determine. They may range from genetic (for example, Down's syndrome) to brain damage as a result of infectious diseases (for example, meningitis or rubella). Prenatal environmental hazards such as poisons (for example, cocaine and alcohol used by the pregnant mother) may also result in delay. The importance of prenatal care cannot be stressed enough.

Promoting the cognitive growth of a young child with cognitive delays follows the general guidelines previously given. You may need to be more deliberate (not exaggerated) with your involvement, and you may need to provide for more "practice" time for the infant or toddler. The infant stimulation programs developed in the late 1960s provided experiences to promote perceptual (motor, language, and social) development. Emphasis was on language and concept formation. Some people became very uncomfortable with such programming because it often involved a great deal of drill. Some felt that things were "done to" infants rather than involving them in appropriate play activities. Our sensitivity has expanded considerably today, and appropriate developmental programming (involving families) is more widespread.

Examine the following guides for preparing environments for and working with young children with cognitive delays. Compare them to the 10 principles on which this text is based (review Chapter 1).

- Provide multisensory experiences.
- Divide learning experiences into small segments or steps.
- Carefully sequence these steps from simple to the most difficult.
- Use concrete examples to teach concepts.
- Provide much practice.
- Give consistent, supportive feedback.[7]

Caregivers of infants and toddlers with cognitive delays may need to adapt some aspects of their programs. As with all children, the key is a sensitivity to quality time in which the "whole child's" unique abilities are appreciated. Learning is facilitated when children trust the people around them. Appreciating the quality of his or her accomplishment may be even more significant for a child with cognitive delays.

DEVELOPMENTAL PATHWAYS

Behaviors Showing Development of Cognition

Young infants (up to 8 months)	• Respond to human voices, gaze at faces • Look for dropped toy • Try to cause things to happen • Identify objects from various viewpoints and find a toy hidden under a blanket when placed there while watching
Mobile infants (up to 18 months)	• Try to build with blocks • Persist in a search for a desired toy when toy is hidden under other objects (e.g., a blanket or pillows) • Use a stick as a tool to obtain a toy • Push away someone or something not wanted
Toddlers (up to 3 years)	• Help dress and undress themselves • Define use of many household items • Use names of self and others • Begin to realize others have rights and privileges

Source: S. Bredekamp and C. Copple, *Developmentally Appropriate Practice in Early Childhood Programs* (Washington, D.C.: National Association for the Education of Young Children, 1997).

(continued)

Behaviors Showing Development of Cognition *(continued)*

Diverse Developmental Pathways

What you see	Madison often asserts her independence (lots of "Me do it!" in her vocabulary). At two-and-a-half years old, she enjoys sorting objects, and you've heard her "teaching" the other children specific labels like "hard," "soft," and even names of colors. She loves to listen to stories and often comments about the characters she knows. She prefers indoor activities and *working* alone. She often has a problem cooperating with the other children.
What you might think	Madison is one smart little girl! She is not at all empathic with her peers, and she often seems bored with them. She should play outside more in group activities. How long will it be before she is bored with the whole program?
What you might not know	Madison is the only child of a professional couple. They spend a lot of time with her—usually reading stories and playing language games. They'd like to see her have more friends (the reason they are sending her to your program), but future academics will be much more important.
What you might do	Continue to support Madison's love of stories. When she's with a small group of children at story time, let her hold the book and even tell part of the story. Use "feeling" words (*happy, sad, surprised*) related to the story and to the other children. When you can, read stories outside and plan "extension" activities in the play yard supporting her interactions with others. Encourage Madison's parents to observe the program. Try to find out more about their goals for her development.
What you see	Devon is a gentle little boy; he doesn't protest about anything! He usually just watches the other children and makes no effort to interact. When you *give* him a toy to play with, he simply looks at it, then drops it. At almost three, he uses very little language and seems content to have you do all his talking. When his mother drops him off, she usually leaves quickly.
What you might think	You are worried because Devon should be *doing* more things. His mother is avoiding something. What is going on?
What you might not know	Devon's mom had a long and difficult delivery with him; there was some concern of mild oxygen deprivation to the brain, but no specifics were provided. She is worried about Devon's lack of responsiveness, too. She has talked with Devon's pediatrician and is doing some simple games at home with Devon. She really wants to talk to you—she's feeling guilty about the situation—but she just doesn't know where to start.
What you might do	Continue to interact with Devon without overwhelming him. Offer him sensory-rich experiences—lots of sand and water play—and *demonstrate* the steps of an activity ("Here is the soap, put it in your hand. Now reach for the water."). Plan to be really available to Devon's mom at arrival and departure times. As soon as possible, make a time to talk with her.

Summary

Cognition refers to thinking and mental skills, and it includes the ability to receive, process, and use information.

Cognitive Experience

- Knowing and understanding come from active involvement with people and things.
- The ability to adapt to the larger world begins with processing sensory information and matures to include language abilities and problem-solving skills.

Sensorimotor Experience: Piaget

- The beginning of cognition, as described by Piaget, is the coordination of sense perception and muscle movements.
- The six substages of the sensorimotor period gradually move from simple reflexes at birth to inventing mental images and beginning to use language by age two.

Sociocultural Influence: Vygotsky and Piaget

- Both Vygotsky and Piaget believed that young children use experience to construct or build new knowledge, but for Vygotsky this was primarily a co-constructed experience—the assistance of another person was significant.
- Vygotsky emphasized the importance of a child's social and cultural world, and that cognition grew rapidly after the second year because of language and the advent of pretend play.

Supporting Cognitive Development

- Cognitive growth is best supported by inviting and encouraging infant-toddler exploration in an environment that is rich in sensory experience.
- Mathematical concepts, emergent literacy, and creativity are all fostered when young children have the opportunity to explore, experiment, and problem solve in a safe, appropriate environment.

Brain-Based Learning

- Learning for young children is holistic and it takes place best within trusting, responsive relationships.
- Brain-based learning principles are very similar to the ideas of Piaget and Vygotsky concerning cognitive development; the principles also align with developmentally appropriate practice.

Online Resources

Go to the Online Learning Center at **www.mhhe.com/itc7e** to access the student study guide that includes quizzes, practice with key terms, and a review of chapter content; links to websites related to the chapter; and additional resources.

Children with Special Needs: Cognitive Delay

- The most obvious characteristic of cognitive delay is reduced or delayed ability to learn, but each child is unique and labels always need to be in a context that is respectful of every child.
- Promoting the cognitive growth of a cognitively delayed young child generally involves providing more practice time; use of multisensory experience segmented into small steps; and consistent, supportive feedback.

Key Terms

ability to predict 160	cognitive experience 156	preoperational stage 159
accommodation 158	constructing new knowledge 160	pretend play 165
adaptive behaviors 172	intentionality 161	sensorimotor stage 157
assimilation 158	memory 160	zone of proximal
assisted learning 162	object permanence 158	development 162

Thought/Activity Questions

1. What behaviors indicate that a child is developing cognition? Describe at least three of them.
2. Discuss Piaget's and Vygotsky's major views about the mental development of children. What guides would you share with parents and caregivers concerning each approach?
3. Design a toy for an infant or a toddler that would foster cognitive growth. Include reasons why the toy would be good for this.
4. You are the guest speaker at a parent meeting for an infant-toddler program. The topic is cognitive development. What main points do you want to share?
5. What are possible drawbacks to pushing early learning ("academiclike" activities) for toddlers?

For Further Reading

D. Bergin, R. Reid and L. Torelli, *Educating and Caring for Very Young Children: The Infant/Toddler Curriculum* (New York: Teachers College Press, 2001).

Division of Research to Practice, Office of Special Education Programs, *Synthesis on the Use of Assistive Technology with Infants and Toddlers* (Washington, D.C.: U.S. Department of Education, 2001).

L. Berk, "Vygotsky's Theory: The Importance of Make-Believe Play," *Young Children* 50(1), November 1994, pp. 30–39.

Marion Diamond, *Magic Trees of the Mind* (New York: Penguin Books, 1999).

J. H. Flavell and B. H. Hartman, "What Children Know about Mental Experiences," *Young Children* 59(2), March 2004, pp. 102–109.

J. Gowen, "The Early Development of Symbolic Play," *Young Children* 50(3), March 1995, pp. 75–84.

H. Gray, "Initiation into Documentation: A Fishing Trip with Toddlers," *Young Children* 56(6), November 2001, pp. 84–91.

S. Greenspan, *The Growth of the Mind* (Menlo Park, Calif.: Addison Wesley, 1997).

The National Academics, *From Neurons to Neighborhoods: The Science of Early Childhood Development* (Washington, D.C.: National Research Council Institute of Medicine, January 2000).

J. L. Phillips Jr., *The Origins of Intellect: Piaget's Theory* (San Francisco: W. H. Freeman, 1969).

M. L. Rump, "Involving Fathers of Young Children with Special Needs," *Young Children* 57(6), November 2002, pp. 18–22.

J. K. Sawyers and C. S. Rogers, "NAEYC Resources in Focus: Helping Babies Play," *Young Children* 58(3), May 2003, pp. 52–53.

L. Segatti, J. Brown-DuPaul, and T. L. Keys, "Using Everyday Materials to Promote Problem Solving in Toddlers," *Young Children* 58(5), September 2003, pp. 12–20.

J. Shreeve, "Beyond the Brain," *National Geographic Magazine* 207(3), March 2005, pp. 2–32.

C. T. Tamsey, *Right from Birth: Building Your Child's Foundation for Life* (New York: Goodard Press, 1999).

M. Vaught, "Another Look at Brain Research," *Young Children* 56(4), July 2001, p. 33.

chapter 9

Language

What Do You See?

A caregiver is seated at a low table with a baby; they are sharing a snack. "Do you want a drink of milk, Alex?" he asks.

The child answers, "Mmmmmmm mmm, ooo, milk!" and reaches for the cup.

Mike pours a small amount of milk into the cup for Alex. The child lifts it to his lips and takes a sip. Then he says, "Mimimim-imi, burrrr, burr" into the cup, delighted with the effect of the movement of his lips on the milk. Milk splashes on his face. Mike reaches for a wet washcloth. Alex sets the cup down, and it tips over making a puddle on the table. "Oooooo milk . . . ," he says, pointing to the puddle.

Mike reaches for a sponge with one hand and puts it on the puddle; with the other hand he begins wiping Alex's face with the washcloth. "Eeeeeeee." Squeals of protest accompany the face cleaning. When all is in order again, Mike reaches for the milk carton, holds it out, and asks, "Do you want more milk?"

Alex answers, "Uhuh, milk!" emphatically, with a vigorous shake of his head while shoving the cup toward his caregiver.

In this brief scene Alex conveyed a variety of meanings through a few sounds and a single word. In a short time, this same scene might include a verbal sequence that could look something like:

"Me milk." (meaning, "Yes, please, I'd like some milk.")

"Milk spill." (meaning "Hey, somebody spilled the milk!")

"Me, no." (meaning, "No, thank you, I don't want any more milk.")

And by the time Alex is a toddler, he will be saying this same thing using longer phrases, such as:

"Give me milk." (perhaps with a "please")

"Oh, oh, Mike, me spill milk."

"Me no want more."

Without ever being corrected, Alex will eventually say:

"I want some milk (please)."

"Oh, oh, Mike. I spilled my milk."

"I don't want any more, thank you."

This exchange between Alex and his caregiver represents the early ability to learn to talk and use language, and it is an amazingly complex process. Very early in life infants begin to coordinate their gestures and make meaningful sounds. They begin to organize their experiences to make themselves understood—to communicate. This ability to develop language involves all the other areas of growth discussed so far in this book (attachment, perception, motor skills, and cognition) and is influenced by emotional and social development (Chapters 10 and 11). Through language young children learn to coordinate their experiences (just as Alex did in the scene above), and give and receive feedback on them.

This chapter examines the foundations of language growth and what a person needs in order for language to develop. We will review what language allows an individual to do, how the environment may influence language, brain growth, and early literacy. Guides for fostering language development, bilingualism, and some communication disorders will also be discussed.

The Progression of Language Development

Language represents experiences and events through abstract symbols or words. Although there are rules for combining words, young children begin putting them together in creative and unique ways. We define **language** as the systematic arrangement of arbitrary symbols that has generalized meaning. It allows us to communicate about things that are not visible, and those that are past or future. It is important to remember that these sounds, symbols, and interactions that we begin to experience early in life are tied to the way we think about and understand the world.

Infants are born with communication intent; they are not born with language. It is not clearly understood how children acquire the ability to use language. Usually language development is discussed in terms of *what* tends to happen *when* (see Table 9.1). No one theory or approach completely explains the development of

Table 9.1 Language Development: What Happens When

Age	Hearing/Understanding	Talking
Birth–3 months	• Child will awaken at loud sounds, startle, or cry.	• Child will make pleasure sounds.
	• Child will listen to speech, turn to you when you speak.	• Child will repeat same sounds a lot (cooing, gooing).
	• Child will smile when spoken to.	• Child will cry differently for different needs.
	• Child will recognize your voice and quiet down if crying.	• Child will smile when he or she sees you.
4–6 months	• Child will respond to tone of voice (loud or soft).	• Child will make gurgling sounds when alone.
	• Child will look around for sound (e.g., phone ringing, dog barking).	• Child will tell you (by sound or gesture) to repeat something. May be a form of play.
	• Child will notice noise or sound from toys.	• Child will use speech or noncrying sounds to get and keep your attention.
7–12 months	• Child enjoys games like peek-a-boo and pat-a-cake.	• Child will use speech or noncrying sounds to get and keep your attention.
	• Child will listen when spoken to.	• Child will imitate different speech sounds.
	• Child will recognize words for common items like "juice," "cup," "doll."	• Child's babbling will have both long and short groups of sounds such as "tata, upup, bibibibi."
		• Child will have 1 or 2 words (bye-bye, no, dada), although they may not be clear.
12–24 months	• Child will follow simple commands and understand simple questions ("Roll the ball," "Where is the doll?").	• Child can use many different consonant sounds at the beginning of words.
	• Child will point to a few body parts when asked.	• Child can put two words together ("no juice," "more milk").
	• Child will point to pictures in a book when they are named.	• Child can use one- to two-word question ("Where kitty?," "Go bye-bye?").
24–36 months	• Child can follow two requests ("Get the ball and put it on the table").	• Child will ask for or direct your attention to objects by naming them.
	• Child will continue to notice sounds (telephone ringing, TV sound, knocking at the door).	• Child's speech is understood most of the time.
	• Child will understand differences in meaning ("go–stop," "in–on," "big–little," "up–down").	• Child uses two- to three-word "sentences" to talk about and ask for things.
		• Child has words for almost everything.

Adapted from *How Does Your Child Hear and Talk?* American Speech-Language-Hearing Association (10801 Rockville Pike, Rockville, MD 20852), 1988. Reprinted with permission.

this ability. It may be more helpful to combine several approaches in an effort to appreciate how language develops. We have already discussed the importance of attachment for infants. Within this responsive relationship, infants learn about **social interaction**—the back and forth imitative and caring exchange between a caregiver and an infant. This is a critical component of language growth. When they are cared for and find pleasure in this caring, infants **imitate** their caregivers, and their caregivers, in turn, continue to respond to them. This back and forth behavior seems almost to **reinforce** itself.

Infants all over the world begin to develop language in very similar ways. The *ability* to acquire language seems to be inborn, or *innate*. Certain mental and physical skills have to be present for language to progress. As infants grow, *maturation* contributes to the ability to develop words (or labels) and understand symbols. Piaget noted that object permanence sets the stage for language development. Young children have to be able to make sense of, or interpret, their world before using their first words. Vygotsky stressed the sociocultural context of language development. Social interaction helps young children understand the relationship between experiences and appropriate labels for them.[1]

In essence, several important things seem to happen at the same time when children acquire language. Thinking of them as the "three I's" may help. *I*nnate abilities have to be present; a child has to have certain cognitive skills and mental structures to develop language. A child also needs the opportunity to *I*nteract with others in a responsive way in order to *I*mitate them. This process of imitation, involving interaction, based on innate abilities, should be viewed in a bit more detail. Looking at two developmental levels of language—receptive (birth to one year) and expressive (end of first year to beginning first words)—gives more insight into the progression of language.

Receptive Language

Infants share their pleasure in making sounds with their parent or caregiver. They come to associate language with a social occasion. As they coo and babble, they find that they are responded to, which in turn encourages them to respond to and imitate their partner. They become aware of rhythms, pitches, and sounds of words. Language can become a way to excite or to soothe a baby.

Eventually, babies begin to make connections between sounds or sound patterns and events or objects. They notice, for example, that when they are handed a particular object (such as a teddy bear), the same sound pattern occurs time after time. Their storybooks have the same sounds with the same pictures. They notice that whenever their diapers are changed, they hear one of the same sounds and patterns. What the infant takes in and understands is called "receptive language."

From the beginning, of course, infants react to being spoken to, but it is the voice—pitch and tone—rather than the meaning of the words that they respond to. Later, when they begin to respond to the meaning behind the words, this response is true receptive language. Caregivers are sometimes surprised to discover that receptive language is so advanced. When children are spoken to in meaningful ways, they understand what is being said to them much earlier than might be expected.

Expressive Language

As their early cries and vocalizations are responded to, infants learn to refine them, eventually sending more specialized vocal signals. The more they know that their signals or messages are received, the more skilled they become in sending them. From their partnership with a caregiver or two, they learn to convey a variety of feelings—hunger, discomfort, anger, and pleasure. The key to infants' beginning to connect sounds with meaning is the adult's responsiveness. If no one responded to their initial cries and vocalizations, infants would have no reason to strive to make signals.

The actual moment a child utters her first word may be quite a surprise to the person who is present to hear it. One day a little girl may see a banana on a counter and reach for it, saying "nana." She may be surprised by the reaction—a flutter and flurry of smiles, hugs, and pats, followed by a piece of banana being placed in her hand. She will probably smile back and say her new word two or three more times. Later on she may be asked to repeat her performance when the late shift of caregivers arrives. Perhaps the caregivers, so pleased with this new accomplishment, will report it to the parent. Or maybe they'll keep their pleasure to themselves and let the parent discover this special event and be the one to report the first word when he or she hears it.

Most young children acquire these first words, and their meanings, amazingly quickly. Certainly the words they hear most frequently from their parents and caregivers influence their vocabularies. But young children, sometimes by about 18 months, use a process called **fast mapping** to acquire language rapidly. Fast mapping is a process in which a young child uses context cues to make a quick and reasonably accurate guess about the meaning of an unfamiliar word. This partial understanding of a word can happen after hearing it only one time.[2] For example, a young child can quickly learn new animal names because the brain has already "mapped" known (or familiar) animal names. *Dog* is easy if you already know *cat* (and have made some assumptions about fur, four legs and a tail). This mental charting of new words occurs relatively quickly because the young child does not stop to figure out the exact definition. She uses familiar contexts and repetition to *generalize* the meaning of the new word. Sometimes, of course, errors do occur and a child's understanding of words may be limited. Joint attention with caregivers, or the time in which the adult and the child focus on the same experience, helps toddlers learn word meaning appropriately. "Dogs" and "cats" get sorted out quickly, and we're on to "birds" and "airplanes"!

Children refine their language and develop grammatical rules on their own. They don't need corrections or language lessons. They learn by being part of real conversations—ones that move forward. Sometimes conversations just go around in circles when the adult tries to teach by repeating everything the child

**NAEYC Program
Standard 3**
Teaching

says in a more correct form. If nothing the adult says adds to the content, these merry-go-round conversations are meaningless. It is more important for adults to realize that as children begin to use longer phrases to communicate, they are also using language as an important tool for thinking.

What Language Allows a Child to Do: The Cognitive Link

There is an obvious increase in the ability to communicate as a child moves into and through toddlerhood. This ability to clarify needs and gather information is expanded as a young child acquires language. In addition to facilitating communication, language has a dramatic impact on thought and cognition.

Infants and toddlers can "think" before they acquire language, but when children really begin to use language, their cognitive abilities take a major step forward. The ability to label experiences, indicating object permanence, allows children to enter into a symbolic realm. As noted in the definition of *language*, experiences do not have to be "in the moment"; they can be remembered, and a *word* can stand for an object. As children gather labels for experiences, their memories also grow. This memory bank will soon have categories within it. And the categories will eventually allow for a complex classification system. The experience of seeing a cat and learning that label gradually moves into a child's understanding that there are many breeds of cat and that this particular four-legged creature also belongs to a larger category of "animals." Information can be generalized from this understanding, but it all began with the label "cat."

Reasoning and the ability to order experiences are developed as a result of language. Watch (and listen) to a toddler as she plays. You may often overhear her actually telling herself what to do ("Now I'm going to the sandbox. Then I'm going to make a road."). This "verbal instruction" allows a child to plan her own behavior and to move her learning experiences from one situation to another. This ability to organize information eventually allows for abstraction and more formal cognitive thinking. Language increases our adaptation and coping skills. It provides us with the skills to be more clearly understood by others and to more concretely understand events around us. In a world with ever-increasing demands, appreciating how children cope effectively would be a good goal for parents and caregivers.

The Brain and Early Language Development

What is happening in the brain while a young child is trying to acquire language? Some of the brain research in this area is the most fascinating, and the most specific. Several key findings should be noted and reviewed. Genes and experiences (nature and nurture) work together for healthy brain growth. As already noted in this chapter, an infant may be physically capable of producing sound, but without nurturing interactions a language delay is likely. These early

VIDEO OBSERVATION 9

Children Eating at Table with Caregiver

See Video Observation 9: Children Eating at Table with Caregiver for an example of how children gain meaning from context.

Questions

- What was the adult doing that helped the children expand their language skills?
- Do you think that special "language lessons" would be more effective than what you saw here?
- If someone asked you to explain how feeding is curriculum, could you use this scene to illustrate your answer?

To view this clip, go to www.mhhe.com/itc7e. Click on Student Edition, select Chapter 9, and click on Video Observation.

interactions actually influence the circuitry, or wiring, in the brain. Language development is dependent on the early neural connections (synapses) that are stimulated through responsive interactions with others. And these early experiences seem to be linked to prime times, or optimal periods, for particular aspects of language learning to occur.

During the first few months, a child's brain is **neuroplastic,** or very flexible and responsive. This is no doubt why young infants initially respond to all the sounds of all languages. But this plasticity lessens with age. Early in brain growth neurons seem to cluster around particular sound patterns called "phonemes" (the smallest units of sound in a language). When these patterns (for example, "pa" or "ma") are repeated, "auditory maps" are formed; neural pathways are reinforced, and brain circuitry is made more permanent.[3] This allows an infant to organize patterns of sounds within her native language. By the end of the first year, if certain sound patterns are not heard with regularity, it is very difficult for a child to construct new pathways. (Remember the "pruning process" mentioned in Chapter 5.) This is why it is so difficult to learn another language after we get older. Those pathways will never be as easily formed as they are in the first 12 months.

As young children acquire language, their brains become increasingly specialized for this complex task. Increased electrical activity tends to be concentrated in the left hemisphere of the cortex. Increased brain activity and increased language competency are linked in the second half of the first year. It is at about 7 to 12 months that infants join phonemes to syllables and syllables to words.[4] Look back at Table 9.1 and at Alex and his caregiver at the beginning of the chapter. Try to imagine brain dendrites, those "magic trees of the mind," expanding rapidly as a young child makes sense of sounds as a result of experience. The first word, usually at the end of the first year, is just the beginning of the language explosion.

Experience also relates to vocabulary. A toddler's vocabulary is strongly correlated to how much interaction she experiences. Infants need to hear words! And these words need to be linked to real events. These are the kinds of experiences that create permanent neural connections. Meaning fosters connecting! Television doesn't do it; TV is just noise to a very young child. The emotional context of language seems to influence neural circuitry, too. Connecting words to pleasant experiences (or negative ones) affects memory. A young child is more apt to remember the label for her special toy or favorite food!

Some debate exists about prime times, or optimal periods, particularly as they relate to language development. Do those "windows of opportunity" slam shut? Probably not. But more is said in the brain research about the specific timing of language than about any other developmental area. Two particular events that are critical to brain development happen in the first two years. The sensorimotor systems are strengthened through myelinization (referred to in Chapter 7), and attachment relationships are established. These events dramatically influence brain functioning and growth, and since brain growth is holistic, they must also play a dramatic role in early language acquisition. These two events (myelinization and attachment) may be most significant to our understanding of critical periods of brain growth. Many questions will be answered by researchers in the next few years. In the meantime, appreciating the complexity of language development and its relationship to what we know about neural circuitry can help us provide nurturing, appropriate experiences for infants and toddlers.

The following section lists guidelines for fostering language development in young children. As you read it, review what you know about brain growth. How are these guidelines related to what is happening in a child's brain?

Fostering Language Development

Caregivers and parents can foster language development in infants by using language with them from the start. *Talk* to them long before they can talk to you. Use real, adult talk. Include them in conversations with other people. Also *play* with them using sounds. Interact with them—create dialogues. Listen to infants, and encourage them to listen, too. Make sure that you have an infant's attention when you are talking together, and be sure to give him or her yours. Even very young infants are very responsive to language. The rhythm of their body movements corresponds with the rhythm of language when engaged in one of these early dialogues. Consider these guidelines for fostering language development in infants and toddlers:

1. Engage in dialogue from day one, during caregiving times and during play time (when appropriate). With younger infants, exchange sounds. This is a natural activity most adults engage in without being told. They imitate the baby's sounds as well as initiating their own sounds. This kind of dialogue sets the stage for later, when the dialogue on both sides will contain words.

2. Create monologues. Discuss the present. Describe what is happening as it occurs. Your running commentary will contain the labels children need to learn—labels for people, feelings, actions, objects, and events. When the infant responds, turn the monologue into a dialogue. (It's best always to talk *with* a baby, not *at* him or her.)

3. Discuss the past—remark about what happened just now to infants; with toddlers, you can talk about earlier in the day, yesterday, and last week. The older the child, the further back you can go.

4. Discuss the future. Knowing what's about to happen helps infants predict events and begin to understand labels for things, actions, events, and people. Toddlers can be involved in discussions about the future, including what will happen this afternoon, tomorrow, and next week. The older the child, the further into the future you can go.

5. Tell stories, sing songs, and recite or create rhymes and poems. Make room in your telling, singing, or reciting for the children's participation or responses. Don't just entertain them; interact with them. They learn language from using it, from being involved, not just from listening.

6. Play games with sounds and words. If you're not good at this yourself, take lessons from the children. Many young children have an outstanding ability to create playfully with sounds and words. This starts early with those first cooings and babblings and continues, if valued and encouraged, until children are creating their own nonsense rhymes and sound games.

7. Be sure older toddlers have plenty of experiences to talk about. The infants will find enough subject matter in the day-to-day play and caregiving routines, but as they grow, their world needs to expand a bit. It's up to you to be sure that expansion occurs. Create "happenings" inside and outside. Bring in visitors. If possible, go on short field trips. A walk around the block can provide conversation material for some time.

8. Read books aloud to children from infancy on. Read to children individually or to small groups at any appropriate time when there is an interest. Don't make a daily circle time with required attendance for the whole

group. Make it a frequent, short, spontaneous activity accompanied by lots of cuddling and snuggles. Stop when interest wanes and don't require each child to stay and listen to the whole book. Make this an interactive activity rather than an entertainment. Allow children to "read" to you or to other children. Story or book time for infants and toddlers should resemble what parents do at home more than what preschool teachers do at circle time. The purpose is to familiarize infants and toddlers with books and to create a number of pleasurable associations with books, and eventually with reading. The language goals, though important, are secondary.

9. Bring in pictures, novel objects, and bits of science and nature, and carry on extemporaneous discussions when a child's interest is sparked. Again, these should be dialogues, not lectures.

10. Ask questions that require a choice. Do you want the square cracker or the round one? Do you want to go for a walk before snack or after snack? Ask questions that have no right answer (called open questions). How does the bunny feel to you? Tell me about Grandma's visit. What did you see on your walk? Closed questions (those with one right answer) are fine, too, as long as the child enjoys them and doesn't feel interrogated. (They are often overused in an attempt to teach language.)

11. Encourage children to ask questions. A favorite game of beginning talkers is "What's that?" They like to ask the question as well as answer it, and in doing so, they practice and collect labels for objects.

12. Encourage children to clarify what they don't understand. Some people try to teach children through questioning them. If pressured for correct answers, children can learn to act as if they understand things they don't. If you encourage an inquiry attitude, they'll ask about words they don't know and then practice them on their own without being taught or pushed.

13. Put language into gross motor activities. Don't regard your language curriculum as something that happens during sedentary times. Children learn about spatial relations and the prepositions that go with them by experiencing these concepts with their own bodies. When adults add a label, they help the child classify, store, and remember the concept. "Mario is *under* the box. See him hiding?" "Who's going to sit *beside* you at the table? Oh, Emily's going to." "I see you're *on top* of the steps, Jason. Are you going to stay *up* there, or are you going *down*?"

14. Really listen when toddlers talk to you. Resist the temptation to rush children or interrupt them. Give them time to say what they want to say.

15. Help children listen to each other. Talk for them or interpret when necessary, but keep the focus *off* yourself and *on* the two children who are trying to communicate with each other. "She's trying to tell you she doesn't like you to push her." "Ask her what she wants." "Tell him you want some play dough too."

16. Recognize and respect the parents' ability to understand their own child. Get them to explain or interpret. As you get to know each child's unique method of communicating, you'll no doubt need less interpretation.

The Principles in Action

Principle 3 Learn each child's unique ways of communicating (cries, words, movements, gestures, facial expressions, body positions) and teach yours. Don't underestimate children's ability to communicate even though their verbal language skills may be nonexistent or minimal.

You have just been hired as a child care provider in a new infant-toddler program. The director suggests that you spend your first few days gradually getting to know the children. On your first morning you observe the following interactions. A volunteer mom is happily playing peek-a-boo with her 14-month-old daughter. The little girl is obviously delighting in the turn-taking pattern of conversation; there are lots of giggles from both of them. One of the caregivers is changing a child; she is talking to him about the clean diaper she is going to put on him. He is looking at her intently and reaches for the diaper while she is talking. Another child is crying softly near the entrance; her mom has just left. A caregiver is sitting beside her offering comforting words ("I can see you are feeling sad." "Your mommy will be back after lunch"). The sobbing toddler is leaning against the caregiver but does not seem to want to sit on her lap. Over in the far corner of the room you can see two toddlers playing with small blocks; a caregiver is sitting near them. One child is using a few Spanish words; the other is using only English. You can hear the caregiver repeating some of each of the toddlers' words, easily using both Spanish and English.

1. Describe the language and communication patterns you see.
2. How are the children's unique ways of communicating being acknowledged by the adults?
3. Clarify how each child is being shown respect.
4. Would you do anything differently than any of the adults you were observing?
5. What do you find most challenging when trying to communicate with young children?

Early Literacy

Young children learn literacy skills much the same way they learn language skills, and the rapid brain growth that is going on to facilitate language is also setting the stage for literacy. The attachment relationships that are being established, the perceptual-motor experiences that are being organized, and the cognitive events that are being processed all contribute to emerging literacy during infancy and toddlerhood.

Literacy—the ability to listen and speak, and eventually to read and write—has its beginnings in a variety of early, everyday experiences. Becoming literate is a process that starts in the context of the family. Infants and toddlers listen to the voices around them, and they engage in vocal interactions with their caregivers. They observe the facial expressions of the people near them, and they look at the detail on objects that interest them. They enjoy rhymes and songs and hearing spoken language with rich intonations. Once they start using words themselves, they gradually realize that those words can be written down and read back to them. Young children develop an awareness of oral and written language in an interrelated and holistic way rather than in a series of stages. Meaningful experiences and interactions with others are key to the development of literacy.

This *meaningfulness of interactions* has been documented further by Professor Amy Wetherby at Florida State University. Her First Words Project examined what early literacy looks like. The project found that predictors of emergent literacy skills in preschoolers could be traced back to early interactions between infants and toddlers and their caregivers. Early sharing behaviors, such as sharing attention, sharing feelings, and sharing intentions, were significant to the development of language and later literacy. Infants who had a wide range of gestures and sounds and began understanding and using words early, became preschoolers who showed clear and stable emergent literacy skills. Toddlers who enjoyed the use of a variety of objects in their play and who demonstrated book knowledge (for example, how to hold a book, how to turn pages) became preschoolers who enjoyed and displayed preliteracy skills.[5] All these early interactions with infants and toddlers emphasized a caring and responsive environment with adults who enjoyed sharing language and literacy activities.

Fostering the growth of literacy is a big topic today. Many people are very interested in making sure that all children know how to read (at least by third grade). That in and of itself is a relevant goal. But *how we do what we do* is critical—especially when dealing with very young children. Early literacy, or emergent literacy, is different from reading readiness, which focuses more on teaching shapes and colors and using writing tools. New approaches involve making sure young children have appropriate books and relevant experiences related to listening, speaking, reading, and writing. Children learn by their third birthday that people read books for pleasure and to obtain information. It is significant to remind ourselves that general good health and proper nutrition are essential to optimal brain development and learning. An interesting, sensory-rich environment supports motor exploration, and stimulating, responsive social interactions directly influence language acquisition.

Remember that development cannot be hurried. Take your cues from the young child. Overstimulating environments and adult expectations that exceed infant-toddler capabilities get in the way of healthy growth. In confusing and overwhelming settings, young children become stressed and even depressed. Oral language is fundamental to literacy, so have frequent one-to-one conversations with infants and toddlers and maintain eye contact. Repeat early baby sounds ("ba, ba" and "da, da") back to infants. When coos and babbled sounds give way to words, repeat and elaborate those words back to the toddler. Much of the literacy research that exists today is focused on the importance of early interactions that are responsive and interactive.

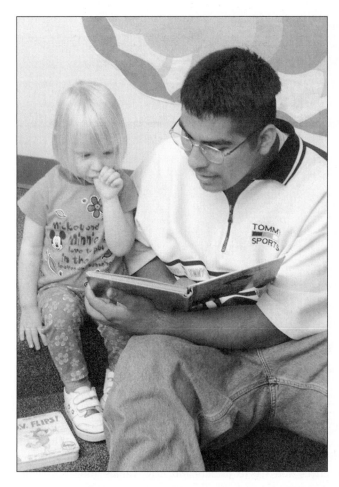

Helping children enjoy books is an approach to early literacy. Notice how print is part of this picture—not only in the book, but also on the clothes of both the caregiver and child. Being aware of print is a skill that will eventually help children learn to read.

Principle 7, *Model the behavior you want to teach*, deserves specific emphasis when considering early literacy. Allow very young children to see you engaged with language and print. Let them see you reading and enjoying books and using print for everyday experiences (adding an item to your grocery list, writing yourself a reminder note). Several more guides are listed in Figure 9.1. As you read them, think about how you are fostering literacy in very young children and how you are ensuring their future enjoyment of their own literacy skills.

Cultural Differences and Bilingualism

All these guidelines are culturally bound (as is everything else in this book). Some cultures view language practices and the language socialization process differently from the way we have presented it here. They may have different goals

Figure 9.1 Guidelines for Fostering Literacy in Infants and Toddlers

1. Provide a sensory-rich environment, including vocal and verbal interactions, singing, shared baby books, cheerful surroundings, and simple pictures on the wall.

2. Provide an enriched social environment that allows opportunities for infants and toddlers to watch and interact with others.

3. Periodically change the scenery: move furniture; change pictures or the carpet in the play area.

4. Explore the environment with a young child, look out the window, gaze into the mirror, play with water in the sink.

5. Take infants and toddlers on outings. Talk about where you are going and what you are doing, and name objects you see along the way.

6. Have fun with infants and toddlers when they initiate playfulness, and express your interest and enthusiasm with their new accomplishments.

7. Respect linguistic, sociocultural, and economic differences among young children and their families.

8. Remind yourself that each child is unique in her or his literacy development (just as in any other area of growth).

9. Provide an interesting variety of materials to allow talking, listening, drawing, and reading.

10. Demonstrate your own interest in and curiosity about the world.

for their children regarding language and literacy. They may also use different methods from the beginning. You may or may not approve of the cultural approach to language that some of the parents in your program use, but you must respect cultural differences and try to understand how values and approaches other than your own may serve the individual in the particular culture.

An example of a cultural difference in language is provided by S. B. Heath, who describes a culture in which babies are made a part of everything that is going on by being held continually but are rarely talked to during the first year. They pick up language by being immersed in it, not by having it directed at them. This shows later in their use of language. They have a holistic view of objects in context. They have difficulty talking about an object out of context, such as sorting out the attributes of that object and comparing them with those of another object out of context. When shown flash card pictures of a red ball and a blue ball and asked, "Is the red ball or the blue ball bigger?" children from this culture would have difficulty sorting out the attributes of color and size, though in a real-life situation they could determine the larger ball and throw it when asked to do so. Rather than teaching the concepts accepted as important by the mainstream Canadian and U.S. culture (such as color, shape, and size), this culture values the creative use of language, including metaphors. These children show great skill at creative verbal play and use of imagery.[6]

Children in child care are influenced by the caregiver's culture. Children who grow up in two cultures and incorporate both are said to be bicultural. Whether or not those two cultures conflict and cause the child to feel torn between them depends on the child, the parents, the caregiver, and the cultures themselves. Sometimes children seem to get caught *between* two cultures and experience a lot of pain in their upbringing. A child can be bicultural and still be English-speaking, as are many children in this country and other parts of the world. Many bicultural people, however, speak more than one language.

Infants can learn two languages from day one, and by the time they are toddlers, they can be very skilled at switching back and forth between them to different people and in different contexts. **Bilingualism** is a skill to be valued and nurtured. Child care can provide excellent opportunities for this skill to develop as children of one language background come into contact with caregivers of another. Take advantage of any chance you have to help children become bilingual (with the parents' permission, of course). You can do this by talking to children in your own language (if their family speaks a different one) or another language (if you are bilingual yourself).

Keep in mind the "language relationship." The language relationship is established without fanfare when two people meet for the first time. For two monolingual English-speaking people, there is no option; the language of their relationship is English, and they never even think about it. But when two bilingual persons meet, the situation is different. There is a choice, and once the choice is made, the two feel most comfortable when they speak the language of their relationship to each other, though both may be fully capable of speaking the second language.

NAEYC Program Standard 1
Relationships

When a bilingual caregiver meets a young infant, the choice of language is present to some extent because the baby is not yet a full-fledged member of a language community. If bilingualism is a goal, establishing a relationship in the target language from the beginning is quite simple.

Establishing this relationship is a little more difficult with a child who is already partway along in his or her language development, because of the difficulty in communicating until the child learns the second language. The strength of the bilingual goal and the extent to which children feel secure and are able to get their needs met should determine whether to establish a language relationship in a language other than the child's own with the primary caregiver. When both caregiver and child are skilled at nonverbal communication, the choice isn't so difficult. Once the language relationship is established, there is a motivation to learn the second language, and it isn't long before verbal communication is established. It is important, however, to remember that, although some children seem to "pick up" language fast, language acquisition doesn't happen overnight. Communication is necessarily weak at the beginning and often for a long time afterward. It's very hard on some older babies and toddlers to be put into situations where they can't understand what is said to them. Just imagine how you would feel being totally dependent on someone who didn't speak your language.

When bilingualism is a strong goal and the child is liable to suffer from the initial lack of communication, it is best to have two caregivers to relate to the child. One can then establish a relationship in the second language while another is present to establish a language relationship in the child's own language. Thus the child can become bilingual in a secure situation. This way of ensuring bilingualism is common practice in many families in different parts of the world.

Be careful that you don't ask bilingual or limited-English-speaking parents to speak English to their children when their inclination is otherwise. If you do, you are disregarding the language relationship. And you may be impairing the communication between parent and child. Magda Gerber, a bilingual person herself, says that it is natural for parents to speak to their children in the language they themselves were spoken to in infancy and toddlerhood. Even parents who have become proficient in English may find that the words of caring come more easily in the language of their own beginnings. Be careful not to hinder parents' ability to communicate caring and tenderness to their children.

Be concerned about the quality of verbal communication in your environment or program if bilingualism is a goal. Unless you are proficient in the language you are using to communicate with the child, the goal of bilingualism may get in the way of communication. If your ability to express yourself in the target language is limited, you should weigh communication and the child's language development against the goal of bilingualism.

As already mentioned, a solution to this problem, if there is more than one adult and bilingualism is a goal, is for one adult to establish relationships in one language and the other to establish them in the second language. In this way, children establish a relationship with someone who is proficient in one language and are assured of good communication while they progress in a second language. Without someone to communicate with who is proficient, the child misses out. With one proficient speaker and one less-than-proficient one, the child can gain some added benefits without losing out on first language development. This scene shows how bilingualism can work in a family child-care home.

It's late in the afternoon, and a woman is heating tortillas on the stove. A three-year-old watches her from the kitchen table. He tells her that he is hungry—in Spanish. She smiles and answers him in Spanish, at the same time handing him a warm, soft, rolled-up tortilla. Another three-year-old appears at the doorway, requesting a tortilla in English. She obliges with a second tortilla and again answers in Spanish. Both children stand by the table chewing their tortillas, obviously relishing the flavor.

A man enters the kitchen. "Ummm, something smells good," he comments.

"Yes," replies the woman. "Guess what?"

"Tortilla. It's yummy," says the first child, holding his out to show the man.

"Want a bite?" asks the second child.

"Here's one for you," says the woman, handing the man his own fresh, hot tortilla.

All three chew contentedly. Then the man says, "How about Grandma? Go ask her if she wants a tortilla."

The first child runs from the room, calling, "Abuelita, Abuelita, quieres tortilla?"

This child, only three years old, is managing to learn two languages and, further, is learning when to use each one. The other child is getting exposure to a second language and developing his receptive language skills. Depending on the circumstances, he may begin to use it himself one day. In the meantime, he's in a situation where he can use and be understood in his own language while learning another one.

The skill of using language appropriate to the situation is not limited to children using two languages. All speakers learn early to distinguish between language styles. Listen carefully to the difference between the way two three-year-olds talk to each other and the way they talk to adults. Listen, for example, to the way children "play house." The one playing the mother talks the way she perceives adults talk; the one playing the baby speaks in a different way altogether. Clearly, they have learned that there is one style for talking to peers and another for talking to adults. Children also distinguish among the adults they speak to. The way they talk to mother may be different from the way they talk to father, caregiver, or a stranger on the streets.

Language is culturally bound and influences our lives immeasurably. Infants and toddlers learn to use language in natural settings when they are spoken to, responded to, and listened to. Language influences how they perceive the world, organize their experience, and communicate with others.

Reflect

Why is bilingualism and bilingual education such an important topic today? What are the implications for programs for infants and toddlers?

✦✦ Children with Special Needs: Communication Disorders

The process of acquiring language is clearly complex. Numerous factors affect its development. Communication disorders, therefore, are particularly complex. Many aspects of a child's environment may contribute to a communication problem. It is important that parents and caregivers have an overview of healthy language development (as presented in Table 9.1). If they suspect a problem, they should quickly consult a speech-language therapist. Early intervention is vital if a young child experiences communication difficulties.

Communication disorders tend to occur in two major areas: language production and speech patterns. Language is a code, or symbol system, that we learn in order to share ideas. It allows us to send and receive information. Speaking and gesturing (and eventually reading and writing) are forms of language. Speech

Figure 9.2 Milestones and Warnings Signs

Young Infants (birth to 8 months): Young infants communicate initially to get their needs met and then expand their communication to include playful exchanges, learning the rhythms of interacting with their caregivers. Warning signs for the young infant include the following:

- A general lack of interest in social contact (infant avoids eye contact, holds body rigidly)
- Lack of response to the human voice or other sounds

Mobile Infants (6 to 18 months): Mobile infants playfully experiment with language and communicate with purpose. At this stage, infants often speak their first words. Mobile infants will practice newly acquired words over and over and try to use them whenever they can. Warning signs for the mobile infant include the following:

- At 8 to 9 months, the child stops babbling (infants who are deaf babble at first and then stop).
- The child does not show interest in interacting with objects and caregivers in familiar environments.
- At 9 to 10 months, the child does not follow direction of point.
- At 11 to 12 months, the child does not give, show, or point at objects.
- At 11 to 12 months, the child does not play games such as pat-a-cake or peek-a-boo.

Older Infants (16 to 36 months): There is typically a language explosion at the beginning of the older infant stage. The number of words that toddlers know increases rapidly, and they start to use simple grammar. Warning signs for the older infant include the following:

By 24 months, the child

- Uses 25 or fewer words

By 36 months, the child

- Has a limited vocabulary
- Uses only short, simple sentences
- Makes many more grammatical errors than other children at the same age
- Has difficulty talking about the future
- Misunderstands questions most of the time
- Is often misunderstood by others
- Displays fewer forms of social play than other children at the same age
- Has difficulty carrying on a conversation

From "Early Messages," Child Care Video Magazine. Reprinted by permission of J. Ronald Lally, Far West Laboratory for Educational Research and Development and California Department of Education.

is the spoken aspect of language. It is the forming and sequencing of sound. Language disorders are generally more serious for a child. For example, a young child may have no problem producing speech—his voice is appropriate and the muscles around his mouth and lips are coordinated. But this same child may not be able to make sense when talking or may not understand the meaning of what he hears. A delay in language or speech generally means that words or sounds are not understood or made correctly at the expected age. Each child is unique in learning language, but all children should follow (within several months) developmental guides for language growth. Delays may happen for a variety of reasons. A child may have a physical impairment. The lack of muscle coordination (especially the small muscles in the face, mouth, and throat) will cause a delay in speech production. Brain damage or mental retardation will impair cognitive abilities, which will in turn affect language. Hearing loss (a sensory problem) will result in some language concerns. Emotional and social deprivation can also cause a communication disorder. All areas of growth support children in their efforts to acquire language, and a problem or concern in any one of these areas may result in a language delay.

A parent or caregiver may wonder at what point to be concerned about a child's language development. Some of the guidelines in Figure 9.2 may help. Use caution when applying any measure of development to a child. Individual differences or special circumstances need to be accounted for.

Normal speech in a young child that has some "interruption" in speech flow is often referred to as "stuttering." Be careful about calling normal disfluency—repeating or stumbling on words—stuttering. It is not unusual for young children (under four years old) to pause frequently when trying to think of how to say something. Labeling this behavior incorrectly may cause unnecessary frustration to the child. And it may result in inappropriate behavior from the adult. Only about 1 percent of children and adults are considered stutterers.[7]

The treatment of a communication disorder obviously depends on the child. If there is a structural problem (a cleft lip or cleft palate), it needs to be corrected. Ear infections need to be treated promptly. Early intervention programs (especially for children under three years old) usually involve helping parents and caregivers create responsive play experiences with appropriate verbalizations. It means talking to a child about objects and experiences in the way most mothers talk to their babies. In general, the more severely disabled the young child, the more responsive and repetitive the practices of the caregiver must become.

Communication is intertwined with all areas of a child's development. Intervention plans or treatment strategies must be a part of a child's everyday world. The guidelines for fostering language development mentioned in this chapter certainly are relevant for most children with a communication disorder. Interactions that are part of a child's daily routines, and appreciative of individual effort, seem to be the most effective.

Reflect

Imagine that you have a child with a communication disorder in your program. What would you need to consider? List several appropriate language activities.

Behaviors Showing Development of Language

Young infants (up to 8 months)	• Use vocal and nonvocal communication to express interest and exert influence (cry to signal distress, smile to initiate social contact) • Babble using all types of sounds • Combine babbles; understand names of familiar people and objects • Listen to conversations
Mobile infants (up to 18 months)	• Create long, babbled sentences • Look at picture books with interest, point to objects • Begin to use *me, you,* and *I* • Shake head no, say two or three clear words • Demonstrate intense attention to adult language
Toddlers (up to 3 years)	• Combine words • Listen to stories for a short while • Have a speaking vocabulary that may reach 200 words • Develop fantasy in language, begin to play pretend games • Use *tomorrow* and *yesterday*

Source: S. Bredekamp and C. Copple, *Developmentally Appropriate Practice in Early Childhood Programs* (Washington, D.C.: National Association for the Education of Young Children, 1997).

Diverse Developmental Pathways

What you see	Jai always lets everyone know when he has arrived! He runs into the room, leaving his mom to put his things in his cubby, and immediately begins to order the children about in a loud voice. His language is clear and most always *command-oriented* ("Get car," "Come now"). He likes vigorous toddler play but always seems to need to be boss and gets frustrated quickly if he is *not* the boss. He still expresses most of his feelings in actions (hitting and grabbing) and not words.
What you might think	Jai is an aggressive little boy. He doesn't have much language to express his feelings. He's beginning to be a *problem*!
What you might not know	Jai is the youngest of three boys. His two older brothers boss him around a lot and often tease him. They enjoy television and include him in some of their games based on television, often using a lot of pretend hitting and fighting (which sometimes gets out of control).
What you might do	Give Jai some space and time to vent when he arrives; let him get some of his apparent frustrations out. Providing some water and sand play, before any specific activities, is a good idea. Let him know that he is safe with you and that you will help him (by modeling with words) to get what he needs—he doesn't always have to be boss. Encourage his friends to use their words, too, especially if you can see that they don't want to follow Jai's *orders*. You have observed that sometimes in the afternoons he

	does enjoy listening to books. Make the most of this time by using books about feelings and his interests (cars!). You might want to send some of these books home with his mom. Ask her if the children watch much television at their house, and be ready to provide some alternative activities for young children.
What you see	Hema is a very quiet little girl; English is her second language. When she arrives with her mother, her mother does all the talking. She says that her daughter talks a lot at home, and she thinks that she should be reading books by now (Hema is not yet three). Hema usually plays by herself in the doll area and in the quiet (book) area. She doesn't avoid other children, but she does nothing to initiate contact.
What you might think	Hema's parents are very demanding. They are creating too much stress for her, and this is causing her to withdraw from social contact with the other children.
What you might not know	In Hema's culture, a child is considered a special gift to a family. Everything is done for her; she has little opportunity to express her needs. Conversations with children are not valued, but academics and school achievements are very important. It is assumed by Hema's parents that she will be successful in school.
What you might do	Get to know Hema's parents more and appreciate what they value. Encourage them to come and visit your program. Let them see you interacting and having conversations with children. Encourage Hema to use the words she knows and gradually involve other children in her play (maybe just one at a time). Let the family know that you value literacy, too, but share more information with them about its *emergent* qualities.

Summary

Language is a symbol system that has generalized meaning.

The Progression of Language Development

- Social interaction is critical to *what* happens *when* concerning language development.
- Interactions, the opportunity to imitate, and the maturation of innate abilities, combine to move language forward.
- **Receptive Language** (0 to one year) is the time in which infants *take in*, organize, and understand experience.
- **Expressive Language** (end of the first year to beginning of first words) is the time in which young children refine and *send* more specialized sounds and words.

Online
Resources

Go to the Online
Learning Center at
www.mhhe.com/itc7e
to access the student
study guide that in-
cludes quizzes, practice
with key terms, and a
review of chapter con-
tent; links to websites
related to the chapter;
and additional
resources.

What Language Allows a Child to Do: The Cognitive Link

• Label experiences, indicate object permanence, enter into a *symbolic* realm.
• Reason and develop the ability to order experiences, expand adaptation and coping skills.

The Brain and Early Language Development

• Language development is dependent on early neural connections (synapses), which become more permanent pathways as frequently heard sounds are "mapped" in the brain.
• Two events that are critical to brain development (and to language develop-ment) happen in the first two years—myelinization and attachment.

Fostering Language Development

• Guidelines for language growth focus on interactions *with* young children, not *at* them.
• Interesting, relevant experiences give young children a variety of things to listen to and talk about.

Early Literacy

• Young children learn early literacy skills much the same way they acquire language skills—all developmental areas work together in a meaningful, relationship-oriented context.
• Guides related to early literacy revolve around sensory-rich experience in which young children see adults engaged with and sharing language and print.

Cultural Differences and Bilingualism

• Bilingualism exists when a child has been exposed to and has learned two languages right from birth.
• Establishing a "language relationship" requires sensitivity, understanding, and respect; *quality* verbal communication in caregiving is the goal.

Children with Special Needs: Communication Disorders

• Communication disorders tend to occur in two major areas—language production and speech patterns.
• Early intervention programs usually involve helping adults create play experiences for young children with lots of opportunities for appropriate verbalizations and vocal practice.

Key Terms

bilingualism 193	language 180	reinforcement 182
fast mapping 183	literacy 189	social interaction 182
imitation 182	neuroplasticity 185	

Thought/Activity Questions

1. Review Table 9.1. A parent asks you about her eight-month-old child's language growth. How might the information in this chart help you? How might it be used inappropriately?
2. Visit the library in your area and review the children's section. Select at least five books that you think are appropriate for toddlers. Justify your choices.
3. Observe a child under three years of age. What language behaviors do you see? How does this child get his or her needs met? What does language allow him or her to do?
4. Compare the guides for language development with the guides for literacy development contained in this chapter. What similarities and differences do you see? How are the two areas of development linked?
5. What do you know about how literacy is fostered in other cultures? Compare your experience with that of a friend or colleague. Do you remember being read to? Or learning to read?
6. Imagine that you have a young child in your program who speaks another language. What would you do to communicate with this child and facilitate her interactions with the other children?
7. Imagine that you have a child with a communication disorder in your program. What would you need to consider? List several appropriate language activities.

For Further Reading

B. S. Bardige and M. M. Segal, *Building Literacy with Love: A Guide for Teachers and Caregivers of Children from Birth through Age 5.* (Washington D.C.: Zero to Three Press, 2005).

N. K. Duke, "Reading to Learn from the Very Beginning: Information Books in Early Childhood," *Young Children*, 58 (2), March 2003, pp. 14–20.

L. M. Espinosa, "The Connections Between Social-Emotional Development and Early Literacy," in *Set for Success: Building a Strong Foundation for School Readiness Based on the Social-Emotional Development of Young Children* (Kansas City, MO: The Ewing Marion Kauffman Foundation, 2002), pp. 30–34.

L. W. Fillmore, "Loss of Family Languages: Should Educators be Concerned?," *Theory into Practice* 39(4), 2002, pp. 203–210.

Magda Gerber, "Babies Understanding Words," *Educaring* 3(4), Fall 1982, pp. 5–6.

Gonzalez-Mena, J. "Caregiving Routines and Literacy," in *Learning to Read the World: Language and Literacy in the First Three Years*, edited by S. E. Rosenkoetter and J. Knapp-Philo (Washington, D.C.: Zero To Three Press, in press).

J. Ronald Lally, Peter L. Mangione, and Carol Lou Young-Holt, eds., *Infant/Toddler Caregiving: A Guide to Language Development and Communication* (Sacramento, Calif.: Far West Laboratory for Educational Development and California Department of Education, 1992).

Joan Lombardi, "Promoting Language, Literacy, and a Love of Learning Makes a Difference," *Child Care Information Exchange*, no. 129, September/October 1999, pp. 48–52.

National Research Council, *Starting Out Right: A Guide to Promoting Children's Reading Success* (Washington, D.C.: National Academy Press, 2002).

Gretchen Owocki, *Make Way for Literacy! Teaching the Way Young Children Learn* (Washington, D.C.: National Association for the Education of Young Children, 2001).

R. Parlakian, *Before the ABC's: Promoting School Readiness in Infants and Toddlers,* Washington, D.C.: Zero to Three Press, 2003).

L. Robinson, "Technology as a Scaffold for Emergent Literacy: Interactive Storybooks for Toddlers," *Young Children,* 62 (4), November 2003, pp. 42–48.

I. Schon, "Books in Spanish for the Very Young: From! Buenos Dias! To Mama Ganza," *Young Children,* 59(2), March 2004, pp. 110–111.

L. Vygotsky, *Tools of the Mind* (Englewood Cliffs, N.J.: Prentice-Hall, 1996).

chapter 10

Emotions

Focus Questions

After reading this chapter you should be able to answer the following questions:

1 Describe emotional development in very young children. How does it change from the first year (infancy) to the second year (toddlerhood)?

2 How would you define *temperament* and *resiliency*? How is research related to these two developmental concepts helpful to caregivers of very young children?

3 Compare fear and anger in young children. What caregiving strategies can adults use with very young children to help them cope with these two strong emotions?

4 How can adults support a child's sense of self-direction? How might such adult behavior also support early brain development?

5 Why is it difficult for adults to clarify and describe *emotional disorders* in very young children? What guides are most effective when trying to do this?

What Do You See?

The scene is a family child care home. Tara, a two-year-old, is taking the toys off a low shelf and putting them in a cardboard box. She wanders off from this activity and stops briefly to look out the window, touching her tongue to the cold glass. Then she meanders over to a three-month-old who is lying on a blanket beside a caregiver. Dropping down heavily, she reaches for the baby's head. The caregiver reaches out and touches the toddler's head softly, saying, "Gently, gently, Tara. You may touch, but you have to be gentle." Her abrupt motion turns into a light touch, and she strokes the infant for a minute the way she has just been stroked. But then she gets more energetic, and her stroking becomes a heavy pat. The caregiver holds her hand back and once more says, "Gently, gently," as she strokes her head again and holds her hand. But this time Tara's response is different, and she lifts her free hand to hit the infant, an expression of determination crossing her face. The caregiver stops her, firmly grasping her hand. Thwarted in her attempt, Tara turns on the adult, eyes flashing, and begins to struggle. At the same time, she starts to make protesting noises. The scene ends with a very angry little girl being removed from the vicinity of the helpless infant. The last thing you hear is the caregiver's calm voice saying, "I know you're angry, Tara, but I can't let you hurt little Trung."

Tara will learn over time to manage her emotions, and the adults in her life are helping her by accepting her strong feelings and respecting her right to have them. They are also, of course, *not* allowing her to hurt others or herself. She will learn that strong feelings can be expressed in socially acceptable ways and that coping skills will help her manage her very real, everyday frustrations.

Emotions and feelings are linked early in a child's development. What they are and where they come from can be of special interest to caregivers and parents. The word *emotion* comes from a Latin word meaning to move away and to disturb or excite. Emotions are the affective response to an event, and they come from within an individual, though they may be triggered by an external event. A **feeling** refers to a physical sense of, or an awareness of, an emotional state. It also involves the capacity to respond to that emotional state.

The point is that emotions and feelings are real. They may be triggered from the outside (for example, by someone else), but the feelings themselves belong to the person experiencing them. You should never discount another's feelings. A young child may be in distress over something you consider very minor. But his or her feeling is real and should be acknowledged and accepted. From this acceptance base, young children can learn to value their own emotions and feelings, to calm themselves, and to act in ways that are considered socially acceptable. When caregivers and parents help infants and toddlers recognize their own feelings and cope with them, they are contributing to children's inner sense of self-direction and competence.

This chapter focuses on emotional development and how feelings in the very young change over time. It discusses factors that influence this development, the importance of appreciating individual temperament, and how to foster resiliency. Specific attention is given to helping infants and toddlers (like Tara in the opening scenario) cope with fear and anger. It covers the fact that strong (stress-related) emotions can affect the neurochemistry of the brain and provides caregiving guidelines for children with special needs and emotional concerns are also included.

The Development of Emotions and Feelings

Feelings and emotions develop and change over time. Newborns' emotions are related to immediate experiences and sensations. Newborns' emotional responses are not very defined but are rather a general stirred-up or calmed-down response. Refined responses depend on development that occurs after birth. Memory and the ability to understand and anticipate are examples of how emotional expression evolves through the cognitive development that occurs gradually during the first two years.

Gentle-birth advocates, such as Frederick Leboyer, the French obstetrician, share a concern that infants do have emotions from the first moments of life. Until Leboyer advertised his gentle-birth techniques, it was widely believed that babies did not feel much at birth. If they had sensations, the possibility that they had emotional responses was discounted. Research now shows that infants do have the use of their senses at birth. Consequently, researchers and caregivers are not questioning the emotional aspects of what infants feel. Although infants cannot talk about what they experience emotionally at birth, their physical reactions can be observed. Evidence exists that they react to harsh stimulation with tenseness. We once thought that the panicky birth cry and the tightly clenched fists were normal and even necessary. Now that Leboyer and others have demonstrated what happens when you reduce such harsh stimuli as bright lights, loud noises, and abrupt changes in temperature, we know that a newborn can be relaxed and peaceful. Some babies born under Leboyer's method even smile right after birth.[1]

In the first weeks of life, infants' emotional responses are not very refined. Either very young infants are in a stirred-up state or they are not. They may cry with great intensity, but it is hard to put any labels on what they are feeling. As they mature, however, the stirred-up states begin to differentiate into familiar adultlike emotions such as pleasure, fear, and anger. By the second year, you can see most of the finer variations of these basic emotions. Toddlers express pride, embarrassment, shame, and empathy.

Sometimes people want to divide feelings into two categories: good and bad. However, all feelings are good; they carry energy, have purpose, and provide us with messages that are important to our sense of self-direction. A better way to divide them is into "yes!" feelings and "no!" feelings.

Some examples of "yes!" feelings are joy, pleasure, delight, contentment, satisfaction, and power. Infants and toddlers should experience plenty of these kinds of feelings. Power is a feeling you might not expect to find in a list of "yes!" feelings in infants and toddlers, yet it is vital to very young children. Power comes as they discover they can make things happen in their world—they can influence the objects and, most especially, the people around them. Attachment, and the sense of trust that comes with it, is one means of ensuring a sense of power in infants. Child care programs should be very aware of whether each child is feeling powerful and take steps to remedy the situation if some are not.

The "no!" feelings, especially fear and anger, are the ones that command the most attention, and we will discuss them here at length. It is important for caregivers to understand how to support children in their efforts to learn to use coping techniques. Equally important is knowing about temperament and how to foster resiliency. The healthy establishment and understanding of these two developmental concepts—temperament and resiliency—directly relates to a child's positive sense of self-direction and self-esteem.

Temperament and Resiliency

Temperament is an individual's behavioral style and unique way of responding to the world. It involves a set of personality characteristics that are influenced by nature (genetics) and by nurture (interactions). These unique patterns of emotional and motor reactions begin with numerous genetic instructions that

Figure 10.1 Nine Characteristics of Temperament

1. **Activity Level:** Some infants and toddlers move around a lot and seem to be constantly doing something; others tend to stay in one place and move very little.

2. **Rhythmicity:** Some infants and toddlers eat, eliminate, and sleep on a schedule almost from birth; others do not and are unpredictable.

3. **Approach-Withdrawal:** Some infants and toddlers enjoy everything new and approach easily; others withdraw from almost every new experience.

4. **Adaptability:** Some infants and toddlers adjust quickly and easily to new experiences; others do not.

5. **Attention Span:** Some infants and toddlers play happily with one object for a long time; others wander from one thing to another.

6. **Intensity of Reaction:** Some infants and toddlers laugh loudly and howl when they cry; others simply smile or whimper.

7. **Threshold of Responsiveness:** Some infants and toddlers sense every light, sound, and touch and react to it, usually with distress; others seem not to notice changes.

8. **Distractibility:** Some infants and toddlers can be distracted easily from an interesting (or perhaps dangerous) experience; others cannot be sidetracked.

9. **Quality of Mood:** Some infants and toddlers seem to be always smiling and in a pleasant mood; others are often irritable.

Adapted from S. Chess, A. Thomas, and H. Birsch, "The Origins of Personality," *Scientific American* 223, 1970, pp. 102–109

guide brain development and then are affected by the prenatal and postnatal environment. As an individual infant continues to develop, the specific experiences she has and the social context of her life influence the nature and expression of her temperament.

Trying to assess temperament and measure how individual traits are shaped has proven to be a challenge. The longest and most comprehensive study of young children's temperament began almost four decades ago with the work of Alexander Thomas and Stella Chess. Their research inspired a growing body of information related to temperament, including its stability, its biological roots, and how it can *change* based on childrearing and caregiver interactions. The nine temperament traits described by Thomas and Chess are summarized in Figure 10.1. They are often measured along a continuum of "low" to "high," depending on the individual trait.

The traits discussed by Thomas and Chess were grouped into three temperamental types. The easy, flexible baby (about 40 percent of the population) is adaptable, approachable, and positive in mood. The slow-to-warm baby (about 15 percent) is at first negative in new situations, but with time and patience, eventually adapts. The feisty, spirited, difficult baby (about 10 percent) is often in a negative mood, is unpredictable (especially related to eating and sleeping), and has intense and irritable reactions related to new settings and people.[2] Notice that about 35 percent of the young children did not fit any specific category, but instead they displayed unique *blends* of temperamental characteristics.

Understanding temperament can help parents and caregivers a great deal in their efforts to foster positive interactions with young children—even when the children's dispositions are quite different. The Goodness of Fit model (again the work of Thomas and Chess) clarifies how to do this by creating caregiving environments that acknowledge each child's temperament while encouraging more *adaptive* interaction. (*Note:* The goal of the Goodness of Fit model is a positive, respectful interaction—the same goal that links all the principles in this book!) Caregivers of slow-to-warm children are encouraged to give them time to adapt and draw them in slowly to new situations. Allow independence to unfold. Caregivers of happy, curious children need to make sure that they are safe while exploring and set aside special time to interact with them. Sensitive attention is always appreciated, even by easy, flexible children who do not demand it. Caregivers of feisty, intense, and moody children need to be flexible, prepare them ahead of time for change, and provide for vigorous play. Patiently guide them and build positive interactions.[3]

NAEYC Program Standard 3
Teaching

Recognizing and appreciating individual differences can help adults respond to the challenges of young children's temperaments in caring, supportive ways. Caregivers need to be aware and cautious, however, when *applying* categories and labels. Self-fulfilling prophecies can occur if adult expectations begin to inappropriately shape the way children behave. If "difficult" children (you notice how many other words are substituted for that word) are treated as such, the behavior may be set regardless of the child's *real* temperament.

So, how real is an infant's temperament? Is temperament stable at birth or not? Some behaviors do seem to have what researchers call "long-term stability." Infants and toddlers who scored low or high on irritability, sociability, or shyness, for example, are likely to respond similarly when assessed years later. Thomas and Chess believed that temperament was well established by three months of age. Much of our information today states, however, that there is more stability in temperament after two years of age than before. Temperament itself may develop with age—early behaviors change and reorganize themselves into new, more complex reactions.[4] The *predisposition* a young child has to behave a certain way gets molded and modified by experience. Cultural diversity, as noted numerous times in this book, plays a tremendous role in how children are responded to and socialized. Each family is unique.

What contributes to the stability of certain temperament patterns has led numerous developmental specialists to examine the trait of **resiliency** and how it contributes to healthy emotional growth. Resiliency is the ability to overcome adversity in an adaptive manner. Much of the research in this area has been done with troubled youth, especially young adolescents. These youths were also often identified as *already* in problem situations, the most obvious being poverty. Some of the current information on resiliency shifts the approach from a "bounce-back from adversity" focus to a focus on competency and inner strength. The idea of

Figure 10.2 Caregiving Strategies to Promote Resiliency

1. Know the children in your care (developmentally, individually, and culturally) and build a positive, caring relationship with each child.

2. Build a sense of community in your program where each child experiences a sense of belonging while appreciating the rights and needs of others.

3. Build strong relationships with families that foster trust and mutual respect.

4. Create a clear and consistent program structure so that children can predict routines and feel safe.

5. Make learning meaningful and relevant so that each child can see connections and experience his own competence.

6. Use authentic assessment procedures, like portfolios, so that families can appreciate and take pride in their child's unique development.

Adapted from Bonnie Bernard, *Turning the Corner: From Risk to Resiliency,* (Portland, Oreg.: Western Regional Center for Drug Free Schools and Communities, Far West Laboratory, 1993).

fostering inner strength and competency early in development (and, it is hoped, preventing problems) is a primary focus of this book. As you read about the "protective factors" related to caregiving and promoting resiliency, review the 10 principles in Chapter 1. What similarities do you see? Fostering resiliency in a person and showing respect are approaches that share the same goal of healthy emotional development.

Resiliency is the ability some people seem to have to *thrive* despite adverse environmental conditions. Today it is viewed as a dynamic process and not as a stable trait. Children may not be resilient in all situations, but they can learn to cope with problems and comfort themselves. It is impossible to shield a child from all stress (and the research on resiliency usually examines multiple stressors—poverty, high-risk conditions, absent parents), but fostering resiliency can bolster a positive adaptation to some stress, resulting in new strengths.[5] We will apply this later in the chapter in the discussion on fear and anger.

Resilient children have several specific characteristics. They have an *active approach* to life's challenges; they look for resolutions to problems. They also seem to understand cause and effect; things usually happen for a reason. Resilient children are able to gain positive attention; they are appealing and sociable, with an easygoing disposition. Finally, they see the world as a positive place, and they believe in a meaningful life.

Research on resiliency tells us that there are protective factors that can enhance its development. Caregivers of young children can incorporate these protective factors when they plan curriculum and design environments. Very young children can learn early in their lives that they are competent people and that the world is an interesting place. Such early learning promotes emotional stability and health and fosters lifelong coping skills. Examine the list of strategies presented in Figure 10.2. What strategies that foster resiliency can you add?

Helping Infants and Toddlers Cope with Fears

The scene that follows shows a child who is afraid.

A baby is sitting on the floor playing with a soft rubber ball. She stops playing for a moment and looks around the room, searching. She finds her mother close by, a look of relief passes over her face, she gives a big smile, and she continues to play. She hears a door open and sounds coming from the other room. Two people enter. The baby freezes. One of the persons approaches her enthusiastically—holding out her arms, talking warmly and excitedly. The baby stiffens. As the individual moves nearer, the baby's whole body attitude is one of moving back, away. She remains in suspended animation until the moment the person's face arrives close to hers. She then lets out an enormous howl. She continues to scream and stiffen even though the person talks soothingly and moves away slightly. She stops only when the caregiver moves away and her mother comes in close to soothe and comfort her. She clings to her mother, swallowing her last sobs while keeping a suspicious eye on the stranger.

"I'm sorry I scared you," says the caregiver, gently keeping her distance. "I see that you are really afraid of me." She continues to talk in a quiet, calm, reassuring voice.

This child is obviously attached and experiencing strong feelings of fear that result from her cognitive ability to distinguish her mother from strangers. Stranger anxiety is a common and perfectly normal fear. The caregiver in this scene found it effective to back off from the infant. Next time she will probably approach more cautiously and slowly, allowing the child time to "warm up to her." She will discover what it takes for this particular child to accept her. Some children will allow a direct approach; others do better when the stranger ignores them but remains near enough so that the child can decide to approach when he or she is ready to do so.

The causes of fear change as infants grow into toddlers. After the first year or two, the fears of noise, strange objects, unfamiliar people, pain, falling, and sudden movements decrease. However, new sources of fear take their place (for instance, imaginary creatures, the dark, animals, and the threat of physical harm). Notice that the movement is from immediate events and sensations to more internal events, imagined, remembered, or predicted. This change is related to the child's growing ability to think and consequently understand potential dangers. Consider the caregiver's response in this scene.

The toddler room is full of activity. A jack-o-lantern on the shelf gives a clue to the time of year. Three children are on a low loft in a dramatic play area putting on hats and shawls and other dress-up clothes. A child enters the room, holding on to his father's hand. He is wearing a mask. He sees the three children in the loft and immediately comes up to join them. Two children go about their business, but the third one takes one look at the mask and begins to cry quietly. He backs off and tries to hide behind the box of dress-up clothes. He keeps his eyes on the masked face. A caregiver, seeing his distress, approaches quickly.

She speaks matter-of-factly to the masked child. "Kevin, Josh doesn't like your mask. He needs to see your face." She takes the mask off Kevin and holds it out toward Josh. "See, Josh, it's Kevin. He had a mask on. That's what scared you." Josh still looks nervous as he glances from the mask in the caregiver's hand to Kevin's face and back to the mask. "Here, do you want to see it?" She offers to hand it to him. Kevin protests, grabs the mask, and puts it back on. Josh looks terrified again. The teacher firmly removes the mask. "I won't let you wear that, Kevin, because Josh is scared." She hands the mask to another caregiver and asks him to put it away. Kevin protests mildly and then gets occupied trying on a furry hat and admiring himself in the mirror. Josh then crawls out from behind the box, watches the mask disappear across the room, and looks at Kevin's face. Then he picks a hard hat out of the box, puts it on, and goes to stand by Kevin to look in the mirror. The caregiver, seeing the situation is over, leaves to mop up a spill at the drinking fountain.

This caregiver, like the first one, understood and accepted the child's fear. Acceptance is vital if children are to come eventually to recognize, identify, and accept their own feelings.

Compare the following two responses to a crying, fearful infant:

"I know you're afraid right now. I will be here if you need me to help you."

"Oh, poor baby . . . don't be afraid . . . I'll make everything all right. . . ."

By saying "Don't be afraid," the caregiver in the second example is telling the young child that his feelings are not all right or appropriate. Instead of offering security and helping the infant find his own ways of coping, the caregiver in the second instance is "saving" the baby, teaching him that he cannot manage on his own. Comforting should be done in a way that leads children to learn to comfort themselves and to know when to ask for help.

Sometimes it helps if an infant can "relearn" a situation that was once frightening. This relearning is called **conditioning.** For example, a particular object or activity that provokes fear can be proved harmless if it is presented along with something that is pleasant or if a loved person is present to explain the situation. It may take several introductions. Stop if the child seems highly anxious and try again in a few months.

Here is a summary of guidelines to help infants and toddlers cope with their fears:

1. Accept all fears as real and valid. Do not minimize the child's feeling, even though the incident that provoked it may seem insignificant to you. Acknowledge the fear.
2. Give the child support and show confidence that he or she can find ways to cope.
3. Use foresight to prevent fearful situations when possible. The caregiver in the first scene could have approached more carefully. The caregiver in the last scene could have met Kevin at the door and taken the mask. (In a toddler program there is sure to be at least one child who is afraid of masks.)
4. Prepare toddlers for potentially frightening situations. Tell them what to expect.
5. Break frightening situations into manageable parts.

Reflect

How do you deal with your own fears? Do you use withdrawal and avoidance techniques as well as seeking comfort and security? Do you find that expressing your fears helps you cope with them?

6. Couple the unfamiliar with the familiar. A comforting person or object can help a child cope with a new, potentially frightening situation.
7. Give young children time to adjust to something new.

Consider the following situations. Would knowledge of your own coping techniques help you respond to these children? How would knowledge of the children's temperament help you?

A nine-month-old child has just been left at the center by his mother, who is late to work. Although she did stay with her son a few minutes before handing him over to the caregiver, who happens to be a substitute and new, he started screaming when she hastily said good-bye to him and hurried out the door. He is now sitting on the floor, terrified, alternately screaming and sobbing. What is the probable meaning of this child's behavior? How would you respond if you were the substitute?

A two-year-old is looking through a stack of books lying near at hand. She is on a soft cushion looking very relaxed. Next to her a caregiver holding another child who is also holding a book and looking at the pictures. The child on the cushion picks a book and flips through it. She comes to a picture of a clown, slams the book shut, and sits looking terrified. How would you interpret this child's behavior? How would you respond if you were the caregiver?

A two-and-a-half-year-old is making an enclosure out of large plastic blocks. She stands inside looking very proud of herself, saying, "Look at my house, teacher." A siren screams outside in the street. She freezes. Then she races to the stack of cots and crawls under the bottom one, squeezing her body almost out of sight. What do you make of this behavior? How would you respond if you were the caregiver?

In your responses, did you acknowledge the children's feelings? Did you have the urge to rescue them, or could you find ways to give them some help in discovering their own methods for relieving their feelings? Can you see what purpose the fear might serve in each of these situations?

In general, fear protects the individual from danger. In infants, it is fairly easy to see how fear functions, because infants react to falling, to harsh assaults on their senses, and to separation from the person primarily responsible for their well-being. Fear can protect them from danger. Toddlers have more complex fears because their cognitive development allows more to go on inside. When they are frightened, both infants and toddlers often protect themselves by withdrawing, as contrasted to angry infants and toddlers, who more often lash out.

Helping Infants and Toddlers Cope with Anger

Anger, like fear, may make life hard for caregivers. Take another look at the opening scene of this chapter. Remember Tara and her frustrations with the infant and with her caregiver? Review how the adult dealt respectively with both children. The caregiver protected the infant, but in doing so made Tara angry. Nevertheless, the adult treated her anger with respect by accepting the fact that she was angry and by acknowledging that fact to her. However she did not allow Tara to act on her anger by hurting Trung.

Toddlers find a variety of ways of coping with their feelings.

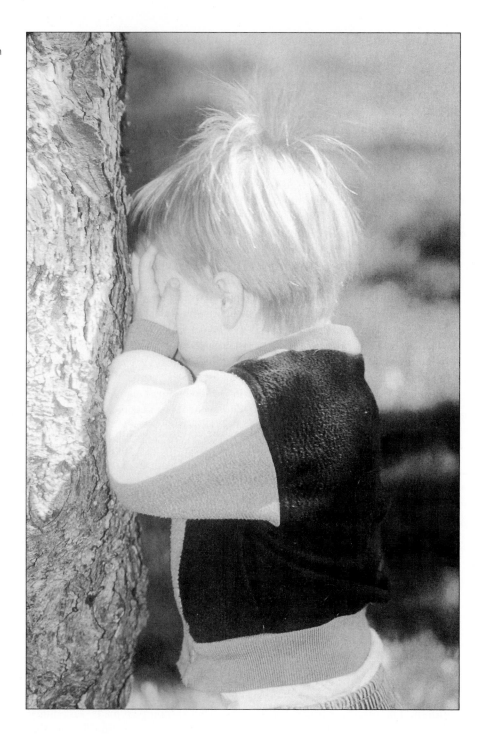

Although the cause of this toddler's anger seemed to be being thwarted, causes are sometimes not related to the immediate situation and come from some deeper place. It is harder to accept a young child's feelings as real and valid when *you* do not see any good reason for them. When the cause for anger is not as obvious or is not considered valid by adults, they tend to make remarks like, "Oh, that's nothing to get mad about" or "Oh, come on now, you're not really mad." But feelings are real even when the cause isn't obvious or doesn't seem valid. Respectful caregivers treat them as such. They do not contradict the feelings an infant or a toddler expresses, even if their own experience is otherwise. They *pay attention* and try to *reflect* what they perceive coming from the child. They neither tease nor distract the child by changing the subject. This approach says to the child, "What you feel is important." Nothing is done to discount or minimize the importance of recognizing and accepting feelings. One should not have to justify feelings—that they are present is enough.

Caregivers must manage somehow to be serene, tolerant, and self-controlled if they are to accept and reflect feelings. They must be able to be empathetic. But, at the same time, they must not deny their own feelings. Just as principle 6 in Chapter 1 states, *caregivers should be honest about how they feel* and be able to decide when it is appropriate to express their feelings. Good caregivers also learn how to set aside their own feelings when appropriate in order to understand what a child is feeling. This is the empathetic relationship. It is important in order to help children recognize, accept, and then cope with their own feelings.

In addition to responding by accepting a child's feelings and expressing their own when appropriate (which teaches by modeling), caregivers can deal with infants' and toddlers' anger in several other ways, including prevention which is sometimes possible. Be sure that infants and toddlers do not confront too many frustrating problems during their day. Toys should be age-appropriate and should also be in good repair. Toys that don't work or have missing parts can be frustrating. Don't remove all sources of frustration, however, because that eliminates problem solving.

Provide for infants' and toddlers' physical needs. A tired or hungry child is more easily angered than one who is rested and full. Short tempers hinder problem solving because the child gives up in unproductive anger.

Think about how you deal with your own anger. You might even list the ways you express and cope with it. Are you satisfied with how you cope? Can you teach infants and toddlers to cope with their anger in some of the same ways? A difficulty arises when the built-in responses to emotions are inappropriate and a person cannot use the energy that rises with the anger. Then the feelings, and the energy, are blocked, and that energy is released through action or expression. Some adult ways of directly expressing anger are through words and actions. Some indirect ways are through physical activity, such as jogging or chopping wood, or through some artistic pursuit, such as painting, music, or writing poetry.

Young infants have limited resources for expression. Crying may be their only option. However, crying is a good release for infants because it involves both sound and physical activity. The early crying can later become refined physical

Reflect

How do you express your anger? Do you do it in different ways? Do you find that you often do not express anger when you feel it, especially when you cannot act upon it?

VIDEO OBSERVATION 10

Child Trying to Get Her Turn in a Swing

See Video Observation 10: Child Trying to Get Her Turn in a Swing for an example of a child who wants something and has some feelings about not getting it. Pay attention to your own feelings as you watch this scene. Are you affected by what you perceive the child's feelings to be?

Questions

- What do you think this child is feeling? What tells you? How do you know?
- What would you feel if you were in this child's situation?
- Is she coping well with her feelings? If yes, how? How would you cope in this situation?
- What does the use of the swing tell you about this program's philosophy on independence or interdependence?

To view this clip, go to www.mhhe.com/itc7e. Click on Student Edition, select Chapter 10, and click on Video Observation.

activity and words as infants grow in their ability to use their body and language. Caregivers who allow infants to cry in anger are also able to direct angry toddlers' energy to pounding clay, throwing beanbags, and telling people how they feel. This way neither infants nor toddlers learn to deny or cover up their anger in an unhealthy way.

Look at the following situations and think about how the caregiver might respond. Here's a situation with an angry two-year-old:

The boy is playing with a plastic rake next to a low fence in the yard of an infant-toddler center. He sticks the rake through the fence and twists it. When he tries to pull it out again, he finds it stuck. He pulls and twists, but the rake doesn't come loose. He shows frustration on his face. His little knuckles are white from holding on to the rake handle. His face is getting red with anger. He kicks the fence, then sits down and cries.

Here is another two-year-old who is angry for a different reason:

The girl is dragged into the center screaming and kicking. Her exasperated mother gives the unwilling little hand to a caregiver, tells her daughter good-bye, and walks briskly out the door. The child runs after her mother, begging her not to go. As the door shuts, she grabs the handle and tries to open it. When she finds she cannot, she lies on the floor right in front of it screaming and kicking.

Sometimes anger mobilizes extra energy for problem solving or provides motivation to keep on trying. Not all problems have satisfactory solutions, and in such cases anger is only as an expression of the frustration felt. This expression can be seen as an aspect of asserting independence.

A Caution: Some cultures have different ideas about expressing anger and do not see independence as a goal. It is important to consider what each parent wants for his or her child.

The Principles in Action

Principle 6 Be honest about your feelings around infants and toddlers. Don't pretend to feel something that you don't or not to feel something that you do.

The caregiver believes part of her job is to help children with their feelings. She models being congruent—that is, showing what she really feels rather than pretending everything is okay when it's not. Not that she shows strong feelings in such a way that babies are frightened, but she believes if you are annoyed you shouldn't pretend not to be. One of the mothers in the program who is of a different culture from that of the caregiver always has a little smile on her face no matter what happens. The caregiver never can tell what she is feeling. The caregiver tells her about principle 6 and asks if she believes in it. She explains that in her culture equanimity is always the goal. Showing emotions is bad because it disrupts group harmony. She says that she wants her baby to learn to control expression of feelings and she's working on teaching him. The caregiver worries that she might be doing harm to the baby, but at the same time she believes in cultural sensitivity. The caregiver's goal is to bridge cultures. She seeks to understand the mother's point of view so they can together figure out what is best for the baby.

1. What do you think?
2. Is there a way you can see both points of view—the caregiver's and the mother's?
3. Is there one point of view that is more comfortable than the other for you?
4. Do you think these two will be able to understand each other and figure out what's best for this baby in this situation? What would it take for that to happen?
5. Can the baby learn both ways of expressing his feelings and eventually operate in two cultures equally well? If yes, what would it take for that to happen? If no, why not?

Self-Calming Techniques

Most infants discover ways to calm themselves and use these devices into toddler-hood and beyond. It is important that children not rely solely on others to settle their emotional upsets. Most infants are born with varying degrees of abilities to do this. These abilities are called **self-calming devices.** At first the techniques are quite simple, just as the infants' emotions are also simple (though intense). The most commonly seen self-calming device is thumb sucking, which may start at birth (or even before). As infants' emotions become more complicated, so do their abilities to deal with them. The variety of self-calming behaviors seen in an infant-toddler child care setting will give you an idea of how these behaviors work.

Twelve children are engaged in various activities. Two infants are asleep in their cribs in a blocked-off corner of the room. One six-month-old is on the lap of a caregiver, taking her bottle. Two three-month-olds are lying on their backs in a fenced-off corner of the room watching two toddlers who are poking toys through the slats of the fence. These children are being watched by one adult, who also has her eye on a toddler who is headed for the door, apparently intent on some outdoor activity. In another corner of the room, four toddlers are eating a snack, seated at a table with another adult. Suddenly, a loud bang from the next room interrupts all activity.

One infant wakes up, starts to cry, then finds her thumb, turns her head down into the blanket, and goes back to sleep. The other sleeping infant startles without waking up, twists around slightly, and goes back to sleep.

The six-month-old taking her bottle stops, looks intensely at the caregiver, gropes with her free hand for something to hang on to, and hangs on tight.

The two infants on their backs start to cry. One struggles to change his position, gets involved in his effort, and stops crying. The other continues to cry.

The two toddlers who have been watching them stop their activity. One sits down and starts twisting her hair. The other heads for his cubby, where he knows he will find his special blanket. The child who was headed to the door runs to the caregiver, picking up a doll on the way. He stands by the caregiver, stroking the smooth satin dress of the doll.

Of the children who were having a snack, one cries and cannot comfort himself until the caregiver's voice soothes him saying, "Yes, that was a loud noise, and it scared you." One cries for more food, one cries for mommy, and one climbs under the table, whimpering.

Some self-calming behaviors are learned; others, like thumb sucking, appear to be innate. A newborn who is tired or frustrated will suck even when no nipple is present. When children are a bit older, thumb or finger sucking still serves in times of stress. Knowing that someone they trust is nearby and checking in with them by glancing toward them or calling to them helps children calm themselves.

This growth of self-calming behaviors, from one as simple as sucking to one as complex as sharing important feelings, is a process influenced and supported by social relationships.

What do you do to settle yourself down when you are upset? Are you aware of your own self-calming devices? How are your self-calming behaviors similar to or different from those of the infants and toddlers in the previous scene?

Developing Self-Direction

Emotions, and the resultant attempts at self-calming, are related to a sense of self-direction. Each of us has within us a force that provides the natural thrust toward maturity, guides growth, and gives direction to our life (both in the long term and from day to day). This force guides growth toward health and whole-ness, the integration of all aspects of development.

C. G. Jung described this force as "an inner guiding factor that is different from the conscious personality. . . . It is a regulating center that brings about a constant extension and maturing of the personality."[6]

Abraham Maslow also recognized this self-directing force. He saw it as a process and called it **"self-actualization."** He argued that healthy people are always in the process of self-actualizing. That means they are aware of their potential and, at least at times, make choices that move them toward it instead of away from it. Maslow said that self-actualizing people perceive reality clearly; are open to experience; tend to be spontaneous and expressive; have a sense of alive-ness; function well; are able to be objective and detached; tend to be creative; have the ability to love; and, above all, have a firm identity, autonomy, and uniqueness—a strong sense of self.[7] (Chapter 13 contains more about helping children develop a sense of self and self-concept.)

Maslow made it very clear that people acquire these characteristics only when their physical, emotional, and intellectual needs are met. He sets out five levels of needs (see Figure 10.3). Only when the needs on one level are satisfied can a person move on to the next level.

What implications does Maslow's levels of needs have for caregivers? Levels 1 and 2 are of primary concern in an infant-toddler child care program. The needs of those levels are usually regulated by licensing requirements (in states that have licensing requirements). Levels 3, 4, and 5 are more often left up to the staff of the center or the caregiver(s) in a family child care home. This book has taken as its primary focus the top three levels. A look at the principles in Chapter 1 shows little focus on the physical needs of infants, but rather assumes that caregivers will provide for these needs first. They are, after all, the obvious needs. The aim here has been to bring out the needs that must be met after the basic ones have been satisfied. The aim in Chapter 2 was to show how to serve physical needs in ways that respond to higher needs at the same time.

Although Maslow stressed the importance of meeting needs, he also pointed out that overindulgence is not good. That means if most of the time children's needs are met promptly, sometimes they can wait a bit. He said, "The young child needs not only gratification; he needs also to learn the limitations that the

Figure 10.3 Maslow's Hierarchy of Physical, Emotional, and Intellectual Needs
Source: Abraham H. Maslow, *Motivation and Personality* (New York: Harper & Row, 1970), p. 72.

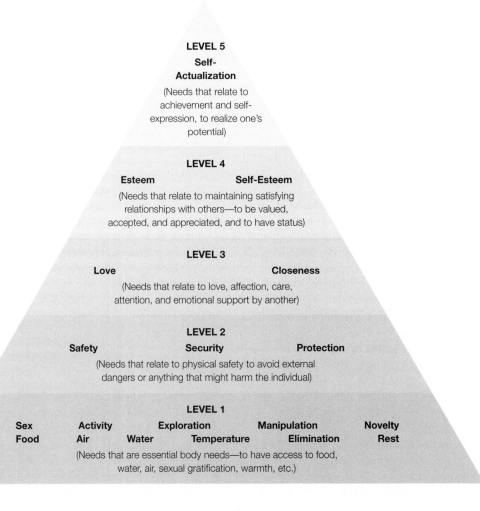

LEVEL 5
Self-
Actualization
(Needs that relate to
achievement and self-
expression, to realize one's
potential)

LEVEL 4
Esteem   **Self-Esteem**
(Needs that relate to maintaining satisfying
relationships with others—to be valued,
accepted, and appreciated, and to have status)

LEVEL 3
Love   **Closeness**
(Needs that relate to love, affection, care,
attention, and emotional support by another)

LEVEL 2
Safety   **Security**   **Protection**
(Needs that relate to physical safety to avoid external
dangers or anything that might harm the individual)

LEVEL 1
Sex   **Activity**   **Exploration**   **Manipulation**   **Novelty**
Food   **Air**   **Water**   **Temperature**   **Elimination**   **Rest**
(Needs that are essential body needs—to have access to food,
water, air, sexual gratification, warmth, etc.)

**NAEYC Program
Standard 1**
Relationships

physical world puts upon his gratifications. . . . This means control, delay, limits, renunciation, frustration-tolerance, and discipline."[8]

All creatures have a need for stress, for problems. A lack of problems creates deficiencies. *Optimum* (not maximum or minimum) stress gives children an opportunity to try out their own powers, to develop their strength and will by pushing against something. Problems, obstacles, even pain and grief, can be looked upon as beneficial for development of a sense of self-direction. What else can caregivers do to help a child develop a sense of self-direction? Here are some suggestions. First, help children pay attention to what their perceptions, feelings, and bodies tell them. As stated earlier, don't contradict their perceptions with statements like, "That soup is not hot!" or "That didn't hurt, now, did it?"

Second, don't interrupt when children are obviously deeply involved in something. When you break in, you are asking them to pay attention to *you*. Children have the ability to get the most out of whatever it is they experience, so let them fully experience it. Be sure to allow periods without stimulation. Let children have peace and quiet so they can hear their inner music, feel their inner urges, and see their inner images.

Third, don't push development. Provide a prepared environment and good relationships, and then trust that children's sense of self-direction will ensure that they will do what they need to do when it comes to conquering developmental tasks like crawling, walking, or talking. When they have very thoroughly done what they need to do at one stage, they will become bored and will move on. When pushed, children lose touch with their own inner sense of direction.

Fourth, give choices. Maslow said, "In the normal development of the healthy child, it is now believed that, much of the time, if he is given a really free choice, he will choose what is good for his growth. This he does because it tastes good, feels good, gives pleasure or *delight*. This implies that he 'knows' better than anyone else what is good for him."[9]

Fifth, encourage children to develop independence and become self-sufficient. Growing means letting go. One learns to walk only when one is willing to let go, to take risks. Caregivers can help children let go by allowing them to take reasonable risks and by providing warmth, confidence, reasonable safety, and a home base. The choice of when to let go is up to the child.

You may notice that these suggestions are related to and in some cases restatements of the principles of caregiving listed in Chapter 1. All of them involve *respecting the child*, which is what the principles are based on. The child's sense of self-direction is nourished by the respectful child-adult relationship that these principles promote.

The Emotional Brain

Many of the findings related to brain development clearly validate the caregiving principles that are the philosophical core of this book. Understanding what is happening to the brain from an early developmental perspective can sharpen our awareness of just how important sensitive, responsive care is to a young child's healthy growth. We know that the brain is impressionable; it has plasticity and clearly responds to a variety of experiences. The brain is resilient; it can compensate for some negative experiences if they are not unduly prolonged. And the brain is *emotional*! It reacts to, and processes, emotions.

Before language develops, early emotional exchanges between babies and their parents or caregivers serve as the basis for communication. These early emotional exchanges actually foster brain growth. When a responsive relationship has been established, an infant experiences delight in seeing that person. Visual emotional information is processed through the neurons in the right hemisphere of the cortex and brain activity increases. This arousal in the brain usually causes an increase in the infant's physical activity. And if the cues that result from this behavior are responded to correctly by the parent or caregiver, brain growth is encouraged. A sensitive adult influences not only an infant's expression of emotion, but also the neurochemistry of that young brain.[10]

Earlier in this chapter we noted that optimum stress can provide growth opportunities for young children. Stress may be necessary for development, but how much is too much? What happens to the brain when a very young child experiences too much stress for too long?

Frequent and intense early stress experiences (poverty, abuse, neglect, or sensory deprivation) actually cause an infant's brain to reorganize itself. The infant's "stress regulation mechanism" is set to a higher level to help him or her cope more effectively (related to the "fight or flight" experience often referred to in psychology), and certain chemicals are released in the brain. One of the best understood neurochemicals is the steroid hormone called cortisol. It can be measured in saliva. During times of stress, cortisol is released in the brain. It alters brain functioning by reducing the number of synapses in certain parts of the brain. If these neural connections continue to be destroyed by cortisol, developmental delays in cognitive, motor, and social behavior result. The good news is that very young children who have warm, nurturing care in the first year of life are less likely to produce high levels of cortisol in times of stress.[11] The attachment experience acts as a protective buffer against stress.

So much of the current information about the brain emphasizes the importance of attachment and nurturing responsive care for healthy neural development. We've acknowledged what can happen if a child receives too much stimulation, or too much stress. But what happens when a baby is with a depressed parent, and the infant's cues for emotional interactions are ignored? Over time the baby also develops depressive behavior and is less active and more withdrawn. The young child may also begin to turn inward for self-stimulation and self-soothing. When tested, these babies had elevated heart rates, elevated cortisol levels, and reduced brain activity. Infants whose parent(s) are depressed are at greatest risk for long-term developmental delays from the age of 6 to 18 months. This is also the prime time for emotional attachments. An important note to add is that when the parent was treated and went into remission, the baby's brain activity returned to normal.[12] This is clearly an example of how important family support is when considering the overall healthy development of young children.

For all of us, and especially for young infants, emotions amplify experience. Strong troublesome emotions need a supportive context if an infant is to learn to tolerate and adapt to such feelings. Don't forget that joy and delight are also strong emotions and can create an attitude that the world is full of wonderful things to discover. Respectful relationships are prerequisites for healthy emotional growth.

 ## Children with Special Needs: Emotional Disorders

Sometimes, however, no matter how respectful a caregiver is, a child may not seem to be developing a sense of self-direction. The child seems to lack the ability to self-calm and remains upset for long periods in spite of the comfort he or she is given. It is important to recognize that some infants and toddlers may have particular emotional difficulties. These may be organic, inborn, or environmental. The caregiving principles within this text certainly still relate to most of these children, but their special needs require some additional comment.

Whenever discussing *special needs*, it is important to try to clarify and describe the abilities and limitations a child may have as quickly as possible. If this has not already been done for a child in your program (for example, in the IFSP—the individualized family service plan), you need to work in partnership with the parents to do so. Remember that labels should be applied carefully; the significance of doing this was discussed in previous chapters. Trying to determine if a child may have an emotional disorder is particularly difficult for several reasons.

NAEYC Program Standard 4 Assessment

First, there is no clear definition of "normal" emotional health. The earlier you look at behavior (in this text, under three years), the more you look at a *wide range* of behaviors. Each infant and toddler is unique, and his behavior may be perfectly appropriate for where he is at that moment. You have to get to know a baby (at least for a short time) to determine emotional health.

It is also difficult to determine the cause of an emotional disorder, especially in a very young child. It may be genetic or environmental. What we consider a "disorder" might be the child's unique way of coping with stress. She may have had to learn very early how to adjust to an unhealthy parent or to an unsupportive environment. If a child has another disabling condition (for example, deafness or retardation), the definition of an emotional concern for that child is further confused. Which disability is the "primary" one?

Current efforts to define "emotional disorder" focus on behavior that has several common features, including the following, and for our purposes, can be applied to young children:

- Behavior goes to an extreme (not just a little different from the usual).
- The problem is long-lasting or chronic.
- The behavior is unacceptable (for social or cultural reasons).
- The child's inability to learn cannot be explained by intellectual, sensory, or health factors.
- The child cannot build or maintain a satisfactory relationship.
- The child's mood is generally unhappy or depressed.[13]

The specific behaviors most frequently referred to include distractibility, short (or no) attention span, hypersensitivity, anxiousness, repetitive speech or repetitive behavior, and extreme restlessness. A caregiver or parent will no doubt immediately realize that any one of these behaviors could be perfectly appropriate at a particular time. If a child is upset or has a mild illness, any of these behaviors could be seen. It is when these behaviors (usually two or three together) go on and on that a parent or caregiver should seek the assistance of a specialist.

It is also important for adults to realize the impact of stress on a young child and the subsequent impact on emotional health. As noted earlier in this chapter, having too many stress hormones in the brain affects its ability to function and to adapt to "normal" stress. Hypervigilance (always on the alert) or total indifference (sad or angry) are examples of emotional disorders caused by an overproduction of stress hormones and abnormal brain growth in infancy.

Infant temperament inclines babies to express themselves in particular ways. We now know, however, that temperament characteristics at birth often don't last. Such characteristics don't necessarily predict later behavior. But the temperament research has shown us (again) the importance of attachment. Personality is shaped by the constant interaction of temperament and environment. A difficult baby requires a lot of extra effort and patience. Parents and caregivers may be at risk for "care burnout" with such babies, especially if they do not understand their developmental needs or are threatened by them. Any baby with a possibly difficult temperament may be at risk for developing attachment problems. Attachment problems often lead to emotional disorders.[14]

The issue here is prevention. If parents and caregivers know that a baby may be difficult, but otherwise healthy, they should be more sensitive and responsive to that baby's demands. Caregivers and parents, working together and being supportive of each other, can help a difficult baby develop self-calming skills. Sensitivity to attachment needs and early intervention are the important concepts to be appreciated.

Review some of the points about attachment made earlier in this text. Attachment provides the base for trust, security, and emotional health. Infants and toddlers with special needs often have additional attachment issues and concerns. If they are slow in their responses, caregivers may assume that they are unresponsive and may not interact as much with them. If they cannot hear or see adult signals, they may miss vital cues for interaction. In all cases, their emotional needs may remain unmet.

Some very young children today have special attachment needs. A chronically ill child or any child forced to remain in the hospital for long periods runs a risk of emotional deprivation. Helping such children experience as full a life as possible is a current concern. *Morning Glory Babies: Children with AIDS* by T. McCarroll is a particularly sensitive account of caregiving. This gentle story demonstrates how wisdom, strength of spirit, and unconditional love can be part of any child's life.

Reflect

Think for a moment about an infant or toddler in your care who was *difficult*. Describe the child's behavior. What were your reactions? What would you try to do if you were in the same situation today?

The following general guides may help caregivers work with children who have emotional concerns. Be sure you are aware of additional community resources and specialists in your area who may assist you.

- Be sensitive to the child's environment. Limit the noise level and visual stimuli when necessary.
- Become a good observer. Watch for behavior that may indicate a child's growing irritability.
- Provide free play times for impulsive children. Choices for these children may need to be limited.
- Maintain physical closeness or a gentle touch to help children maintain control.
- Do not permit aggressive behavior. Firm consistency helps children develop trust in you and in themselves.

Help all children feel good about themselves. Even when children have emotional concerns and behavioral problems, they need opportunities to develop self-direction. Sensitive caregivers reassure children that they are worthy human beings. They give all children the opportunity to express their feelings appropriately and socialize with others.

DEVELOPMENTAL PATHWAYS

Behavior Showing Development of Emotions

Young infants **(up to 8 months)**	• Express discomfort and comfort or pleasure unambiguously • Can usually be comforted by a familiar adult when distressed • Laugh aloud (belly laugh) • Show displeasure or disappointment at loss of toy • Express several emotions clearly: pleasure, anger, anxiety or fear, sadness, joy, excitement
Mobile infants **(up to 18 months)**	• Show pride and pleasure in new accomplishments • Express negative feelings • Continue to show pleasure in mastery • Assert self, indicating strong sense of self
Toddlers **(up to 3 years)**	• Frequently display aggressive feelings and behaviors • Exhibit contrasting states and mood shifts (stubborn versus compliant) • Show increased fearfulness (of the dark, monsters, etc.) • Are aware of their own feelings and those of others • Verbalize feelings more often, express feelings in symbolic play

Source: S. Bredekamp and C. Copple, *Developmentally Appropriate Practice in Early Childhood Programs* (Washington, D.C.: National Association for the Education of Young Children, 1997).

(continued)

DEVELOPMENTAL PATHWAYS

Behavior Showing Development of Emotions *(continued)*

Diverse Developmental Pathways

What you see	Jacob always arrives with a smile on his face. He's flexible and easygoing—even when things don't seem to go his way. He enjoys playing in small groups, and you're even seen him being empathic with others (patting and comforting a crying child).
What you might think	At almost three years of age, Jacob is a pleasure to be around, but on busy days you almost forget about him. Sometimes you feel guilty that you don't spend more time with him.
What you might not know	Jacob is a middle child—he has a brother two years older, and there is a new baby at his house. There is some financial stress at home—his dad is working two jobs, and his mom is doing a catering business out of the home (while caring for the new baby). There isn't much attention time at home for Jacob.
What you might do	Try to check in more with Jacob—it may be just a smile when you catch his eye, or sitting near him while holding another child. Try to set aside some special time with him doing his favorite things. Let him *help* you put the napkins out for snack. Remember that all children need special attention. Just because Jacob doesn't demand it doesn't mean he doesn't enjoy it. Don't allow yourself to overlook him because you are busy.
What you see	Megan is an active and intense two-and-a-half-year-old. She lets everyone know when she is happy or not! She's fussy and often gets into conflicts with other children over a toy or other object.
What you might think	Megan is a handful! You appreciate her zesty temperament, but you don't like her aggressive tendencies. She often seems frustrated, even *before* she begins activities.
What you might not know	Megan *is* a feisty child. She loves the rough and tumble play she often gets into with her five-year-old brother. She does receive subtle, and not-so-subtle, mixed messages from her parents: her father (from another culture) disapproves of her active behavior and often reprimands her; her mother has just started working outside the home and loves her new job—she sees Megan's behavior as a sign of her daughter's growing independence.
What you might do	Help Megan with her intense reactions. Empathize with her when things don't go her way, but place firm limits on any aggressive behavior. Try to give her extra time for transitions; let her know that a snack is coming and that then she will be going outside. Help her manage her frustrations better by providing lots of active play opportunities. Remember that her feisty behavior today could set the stage for leadership skills tomorrow.

Summary

Emotions are the affective response to an event.

The Development of Emotions and Feelings

- Young infants have emotional responses that are not very refined; stirred-up states begin to differentiate themselves in a few months into the emotions of pleasure, fear, and anger.
- Toddlers express pride, embarrassment, shame, and empathy; adults need to support toddlers' efforts to learn to use coping techniques to deal with everyday frustrations.

Temperament and Resiliency

- Temperament, or an individual's behavioral style, can be discussed in terms of *traits*, and understanding these traits can help caregivers respond to children in caring, supportive ways.
- Resiliency, or the ability to overcome adversity, is viewed as a dynamic process; research related to it indicates that there are caregiving strategies to promote its development and to foster lifelong coping skills.

Helping Infants and Toddlers Cope with Fear

- A common fear in the first year is stranger anxiety. Fears become more complex in toddlerhood and can be related to imaginary creatures, animals, the dark, and threat of harm.
- It is important to accept fears as valid and to give young children time to adjust to new experiences.

Helping Infants and Toddlers Cope with Anger

- Respectful caregivers accept and reflect a young child's anger; they do not contradict what the child is feeling while they protect the child (and others) as she learns to develop coping skills.
- Anger can mobilize extra energy to solve problems or release frustration. It is important to remember that some cultures have different ideas about expressing anger.

Self-Calming Techniques

- Learning to settle personal emotional upsets is an important skill. Some of these *self-calming* behaviors may be innate (for example, thumb sucking) and others can be learned (for example, sharing feelings).
- The growth of self-calming behaviors is influenced by the development of trust and supported by caring, social relationships.

Online Resources

Go to the Online Learning Center at **www.mhhe.com/itc7e** to access the student study guide that includes quizzes, practice with key terms, and a review of chapter content; links to websites related to the chapter; and additional resources.

Developing Self Direction

- Implications from the work of Abraham Maslow and others indicate how important it is for caregivers to meet the primary needs of very young children in respectful ways if higher level needs are to be fulfilled.
- A child's sense of self direction is nourished by respectful adult–child relationships.

The Emotional Brain

- Early emotional exchanges (before language) between infants and their caregivers foster brain growth. Respectful relationships strengthen brain pathways and are the prerequisites for healthy emotional growth.
- Frequent and intense early stress experiences can cause an infant's brain to reorganize itself. Stress hormones are released causing a reduction of the number of synapses in certain areas of the brain.

Children with Special Needs: Emotional Disorders

- It is important to clarify and describe the abilities and limitations a child may have as quickly as possible. Identifying and determining the cause of any emotional disorder may be particularly challenging.
- The development of attachment and the impact of stress on a young child are of specific importance when considering emotional disorders in early childhood.

Key Terms

conditioning 212
emotion 206
feeling 206
resiliency 209

self-actualization 219
self-calming devices 218
temperament 207

Thought/Activity Questions

1. Review your definition of attachment. What role does it play in emotional development?
2. How does knowing about temperament help you interact more effectively with very young children?
3. How would you help calm a fearful eight-month-old infant? How would your behavior change if a two-year-old was fearful?
4. How would you help a toddler cope with anger? Describe a recent experience with an angry toddler and what you did in response.
5. How can you respond to infants and toddlers in ways that promote individuality? Consider special-needs children, too.

6. How would you describe your own temperament? Do you think you are a resilient person? Consider how the answers to these questions influence your interactions with very young children.

For Further Reading

D. Bergen, D. Reid, and L. Torelli, *Educating and Caring for Very Young Children: The Infant/Toddler Curriculum* (New York: Teachers College Press, 2000).

E. Elliot, "Challenging Our Assumptions: Helping a Baby Adjust to Center Care," *Young Children* 58(4), July 2003, pp. 22–28.

Magda Gerber, "Helping Baby Feel Secure, Self-Confident and Relaxed," *Educaring* 1(4), Fall 1980, p. 4.

Daniel Goleman, *Emotional Intelligence* (New York: Bantam Books, 1995).

Jim Greenman, *What Happened to the World? Helping Children Cope in Turbulent Times* (Washington D.C.: National Association for the Education of Young Children, 2001).

C. Kalb, "When Does Autism Start?," *Newsweek magazine* 145(9), February 28, 2005, pp. 45–53.

K. C. Kersey and C. R. Malley, "Helping Young Children Develop Resiliency: Providing Supportive Relationships," *Young Children* 60(1), January 2005, pp. 53–58.

S. Landry, *Pathways to Competency: Promoting Healthy Social and Emotional Development in Young Children* (Baltimore, Md.: Paul H. Brooks, 2002).

J. LeDoux, *The Emotional Brain: The Mysterious Underpinnings of Emotional Life* (New York: Simon & Schuster, 1996).

Alicia Leiberman, *The Emotional Life of the Toddler* (New York: Free Press, 1993).

R. Novick, "Learning to Read the Heart: Nurturing Emotional Literacy," *Young Children* 57(3), May 2002, pp. 84–89.

L. Plattner, "Granting Children their Emotions," *Child Care Information Exchange*, July/August 2003, pp. 34–36.

M. E. Schreiber, "Time-outs for Toddlers: Is Our Goal Punishment or Education?," *Young Children* 54(4), July 1999, pp. 22–26.

chapter 11

Social Skills

Focus Questions

After reading this chapter you should be able to answer the following questions:

1 What are some examples of early social behaviors?

2 Erikson named three stages of psychosocial development for the early years, which he thought of as issues to resolve. What are the names of these stages and what happens if the issues aren't resolved in each stage?

3 Learning to cope with fears and other feelings around separation is an important social skill.

4 Guidance and discipline involve setting limits. Two other specific issues are discussed in this chapter related to discipline. What are they?

5 The other side of discipline involves teaching prosocial behavior. What are some examples of prosocial behaviors that adults can teach or encourage in children?

6 What seven gifts can adults give infants and toddlers to promote healthy brain growth?

What Do You See?

A mother enters the infant center carrying a child who has a tense look on her face. The child has both arms around her mother's neck and is hanging on tight. Her mother puts her diaper bag into a cubby by the entrance, then speaks briefly to the caregiver, then says to her daughter, "I have to go pretty soon, Rebecca. You're going to stay here with Maria. She'll take care of you while I'm gone. She bends over to try to put her daughter down. Maria has come over near the couple and kneels down, waiting. Rebecca clings tighter and refuses to be put down, so her mother sits down on the floor with Rebecca still in her arms. They both sit there for several minutes. The child begins to relax a bit. She reaches for and takes hold of the handle of a push toy and rolls it back and forth across the rug while still in her mother's arms. She gets absorbed in this and gets off her mother's lap and moves slightly away. With that her mother gets up, leans down and kisses her daughter. She says, "It's time for me to go now. Good-bye." She walks over to the door. Rebecca follows, looking distressed. At the door her mother turns once briefly, waves, throws a kiss, turns back, opens the door, and is gone. At the sound of the door closing, Rebecca lets out a wail, then collapses in a heap, sobbing.

One of the most important sets of social skills that all people have to learn is how to separate from those they care about. Rebecca is working on this skill. Later in this chapter you'll see how Maria helped Rebecca handle her feelings about being left behind.

NAEYC Program Standard 1
Relationships

Socialization, the subject of this chapter, includes the skills that connect us to other people and those that help us be away from them as well. It is the learning process by which we become acceptable members of our society. Social skills foster cooperation and interdependent relationships. Human beings have to learn social skills; we aren't born with them, and they don't just unfold as do gross motor and language skills. Social skills are specific to each individual's culture, and they are learned only from other people.

The development of social skills in infants and toddlers is dependent on other areas of development. A secure attachment base allows a child to trust and therefore separate from parents with some degree of ease. Muscle and motor development provide for social skills that range from toilet training to self-feeding. Cognitive and language skills combine to help young children solve problems and make their needs clearly known to others. A sense of self and a growing ability to manage feelings provide the base for the development of empathy. And it is through empathy, this feeling with another, that we become a connected and caring society.

Of course, parents play a big role in teaching and supporting the development of social skills. It is up to child care providers to understand what social skills the parents emphasize at home so that child care doesn't jar them with contradictory messages. This involves caregiver–family partnerships, which is explored more fully in Chapter 14. We need to provide experiences for young children that will foster the social skills we value as a culture. Children learn these skills from responsible adults who care about them and consistently show them respect.

This chapter looks at the progression of social development from infancy through toddlerhood. Special emphasis is given to Erik Erikson's stages of trust, autonomy, and initiative. Practical applications of his theory are discussed as they relate to discipline and prosocial behavior. Practical applications are also included for healthy brain growth. The special needs of all children are reviewed in a summary set of guidelines for caregivers and parents.

At no time in history has the development of social skills been so important. We can't afford to raise a generation to believe that might is right. We need to teach young children how to resolve conflicts without resorting to force. This teaching starts with infants.

Emmi Pikler's first book, *Peaceful Babies, Contented Mothers* (printed in Hungarian in 1940), focused on the issue of raising peaceful people. She carried that theme over into her work in setting up and maintaining the Pikler Institute where children were, and still are, being reared in a residential setting. Indeed observers are surprised at the social skills such young children show.

Another socialization issue is illustrated in The Principle in Action feature. When adults focus so heavily on intellectual skills that they don't notice a child's lack of social skills, development can be lopsided and the child gravely disadvantaged. Pikler's and Gerber's approaches stress the importance of focusing on the whole child.

The Principles in Action

Principle 4 Invest time and energy to build a total person (concentrate on the "whole child"). Don't focus on cognitive development alone or look at it as separate from total development.

Cody is 26 months old and the caregivers in his toddler program marvel at him. As the only child of two professional parents, he talks like an adult, using big words and complex sentences. He knows the words to many songs he has heard on the radio and enjoys telling everybody about the latest video he has seen. He seems to be trying to teach himself to read, and he is already a whiz at number concepts. He seldom pays attention to the other children and spends most of his time showing off his many skills to adults or else by himself. He doesn't seem to know how to enter into the play of others or even play close to them in a parallel way. He has so entranced the caregivers that they seem blind to his need to learn social skills so he can connect with his peers. Nobody is worried about Cody.

1. Do you see a reason to worry?
2. If you worked in that program, what might you do to help Cody become interested in other children and want to learn to relate to them?
3. If you see Cody's development as lopsided, how might you approach the parents to talk about what you perceive?
4. Why do you think Cody seems to need so much attention from the adults?
5. What other ideas do you have about Cody?
6. What would you want to know more about?

Early Social Behaviors

Infants come equipped with a set of social behaviors that start to work right from the beginning to involve the people around them in the socialization process. In fact, just hours after birth, you can see babies interact with synchrony by moving their bodies to the rhythm and body movements of anyone who talks to them. The dancelike movements are minute, but they are present, in spite of the fact that the speaker is usually unaware of them. They occur only in response to language (any language, not necessarily that of the baby's family) but do not show up in response to other kinds of rhythms.[1]

Another early social behavior is imitation. Babies' inclination to imitate serves the socialization process well as they copy or imitate adult social behavior (which means, of course, the adult must be aware of modeling prosocial behaviors). This imitating behavior starts very early. In the first weeks, babies will imitate such behavior as opening their eyes wide or sticking out their tongues.

Another evidence of early social behavior that seems by nature designed to involve the adult in the socialization process from the beginning is smiling. Whether the first smiles are "real" smiles—social smiles—is still debated. Whether truly social or not, smiles almost always elicit a social response from the adult smiled at.

By the time they are a few months old, most babies are effective at nonverbal communication with the people to whom they are attached. As they get better and better at communication with particular people, they develop fear when around people who don't know their unique communication systems. This fear, called **stranger anxiety,** often appears around the sixth month. It seems to be strongest in babies who have excellent communication with their partner(s). The fear is intensified when the stranger tries to communicate with the babies. Often the fear is lessened when the stranger remains silent and non-communicative. If you think of how you would feel when confronted with someone speaking a foreign language who seems most anxious to tell you something, you may understand the infant's upset when faced with a communicative stranger.

By the second year of life, babies are already making communicative social gestures that predict to some extent which of them will be well-liked preschoolers and which will have difficulty with peer relationships. The infants who will probably become well-liked preschoolers already have a number of *friendly* gestures that they exhibit regularly, such as offering toys, clapping hands, and smiling. Infants who regularly use threatening or aggressive gestures or a mixture of friendly and unfriendly gestures to their peers are more likely to grow into less-liked preschoolers.[2]

Attachment is the prime factor in the development of social skills. From a primary relationship come the skills for developing other relationships.

Stages of Psychosocial Development

The theorist who has the most to say about social development is Erik Erikson. In *Childhood and Society,* he describes three stages of what he calls psychosocial development that apply to children under three. (See Table 11.1 on page 235.)

Trust

Reflect
Are you a person who has a basic sense of trust? If yes, what do you think gave you that trust? If no, what happened to you?

The first stage of psychosocial development is **trust.** Sometime during the first year of life, if infants find that their needs are met consistently and gently, they decide that the world is a good place to be. They develop what Erikson calls a "sense of basic trust." If infants' needs are not met consistently, or are met in a harsh manner, they may decide that the world is unfriendly and develop mistrust instead of trust. Such infants can carry this outlook into adulthood if nothing happens to change their view of life.

If infants are in child care, the adults in the program have some responsibility for ensuring that the children in their care come to gain a sense of basic trust.

Table 11.1 Erikson's First Three Psychosocial Stages of Development
(Bold stages relate to children under three years of age.)

Age	Stage	Description
0–1	**Trust versus mistrust**	**Children come to trust the world if their needs are met and they are cared for in sensitive ways. Otherwise they see the world as a cold and hostile place and develop a basic sense of mistrust.**
1–3	**Autonomy versus shame and doubt**	**Children work at becoming independent in areas such as feeding and toileting. They can talk and assert themselves. If they don't learn some degree of self-sufficiency, they come to doubt their own abilities and feel shame.**
3–6	Initiative versus guilt	Children thrust themselves into the world, trying new activities and exploring new directions. If their boundaries are too tight and they continually overstep them, they experience a sense of guilt about these inner urges that keep leading them into trouble.

That means that their *needs* must be a primary concern of everyone from the director down. There is no way to run an infant program that emphasizes anything but individual needs—infants are not like older children, who can put group needs before their own and wait for lunch or snack or wait an hour to go to the bathroom.

The importance of developing a sense of basic trust also means that infants in child care need small groups with consistent caregivers. Stability in programs contributes to the infants' well-being and building sense of trust.

Part of developing trust means coping with separation. As attachment strengthens, so does the pain of being away from the person(s) to whom the child is attached. Child care workers spend a lot of time and energy helping children manage the feelings separation brings forth. The opening scene provided an example. Go back to that scene. There is Rebecca collapsed on the floor in a heap, sobbing.

NAEYC Program Standard 1
Relationships

She looks up as a hand touches her shoulder. She sees, kneeling beside her, Maria, the caregiver. She moves away from the touch. Maria continues to stay close by her. "I see you're upset that your mom left, Maria says." Rebecca begins to scream again.

Maria remains close, but silent. Rebecca's screams subside, and she goes back to quiet sobbing. She continues to sob for a while; then she spots her diaper bag where her mother left it in her cubby. She reaches for it; her tear-stained face has a look of expectancy on it. Maria gets it out for her. Rebecca clings to it. Maria reaches inside and pulls out a stuffed bear wrapped in a scarf. Rebecca grabs the bear, hugging it fiercely. She strokes the scarf, holding it to her nose periodically and smelling it. Her face gets more and more relaxed.

Maria moves away from her. Rebecca doesn't seem to notice. Maria comes back with a box of dolls and blankets, which she arranges on the floor near Rebecca. Rebecca crawls over immediately, tips the box over, and crawls inside. The scene closes as Rebecca is wrapping a doll in a blanket and putting it to bed in the box next to her bear, which is covered with the scarf.

Notice how Maria helped Rebecca cope with separation. She stated the situation and the feelings. She was available but not pushy. She was sensitive to Rebecca's responses to her touch and to her words. She encouraged Rebecca to find solace in familiar belongings. She set up the environment to entice Rebecca.

NAEYC Program Standards
2 Curriculum
3 Teaching

Helping Children Through Separation   Here are some more ideas about how to help children through the process of temporary separation as they say good-bye to parents.

1. Be honest. State the facts, including the emotional facts. Say something like Maria did or something like this: "Your mom had to go to work, and you're unhappy about being left." If the feeling you perceive is anger, you can state that.

2. Handle the situation with the appropriate degree of seriousness. If the suffering is minor, don't make it more serious than it is. But don't make light of it either. Don't underplay the importance of the child–parent relationship and the degree of suffering the child may be experiencing. You may think to yourself, "This is nothing—you'll be taken care of. There's nothing to be afraid of here." But the child doesn't know that and in spite of your reassurance may not believe it. It will take time for the child to discover that is the situation—there really is nothing to be afraid of. In the meantime, if the child is terrified, accept that fact.

3. Provide a balance of kindly concern and matter-of-fact confidence. Somehow convey the attitude that it hurts now, but you'll survive it and grow from it. Be careful about being overly reassuring. If you make promises, the child may begin to wonder if you're really positive that his or her parent will return.

4. Offer support and help with coping. Physical closeness may help. Some infants and toddlers do better with an adult close by; others move from parent to a toy or interesting material put out to be enticing. Sometimes children will play out their feelings with a toy.

5. Welcome things from home. Some children find comfort in a link to home provided by a familiar object. This may be some special attachment object such as a blanket or stuffed animal, or it may be something that has no emotional significance other than the fact that it came from home. One toddler felt great comfort in the fact that his mother left her purse (an empty purse) by his diaper bag. It seemed that he wasn't sure she would come back for him, but he *knew* that she would come back for her purse!

6. Allow children individual ways of feeling comforted. Some children refuse to remove a sweater, hat, or other piece of clothing. Something about wearing it seems to make them feel more secure when away from home. Or maybe it has to do with feeling the stay is only temporary as

long as they don't take off the piece of clothing—something like the message adults give when they enter a room and keep their car keys in their hands the whole time they are there.

It is important to deal with separation even with a child who is not terribly upset. Coping with loss and separation is a lifetime task, not something we get over when we are babies after the first separation from parent(s). All our lives we lose those we are close to as friends and family grow away from us (or we from them), move to another city, or die. The coping skills we develop in our first years serve us for the rest of our lives. When children learn to cope with fears of loss and separation, they get feelings of mastery. When they don't learn to cope, they feel failure and mistrust.

Adult Issues with Separation   Sometimes it is difficult for adults to deal with infants' and toddlers' feelings about separation because of their own experiences. They may have old issues about separation—unfinished business, so to speak—that they aren't ready to deal with. So they may prefer not to reopen old wounds. In that case, they may feel uncomfortable around children who are suffering a sense of loss. Instead of trying to understand the feelings and help the children cope, they wish the feelings would just go away. They may distract children from their feelings, hoping they will forget the pain. But the pain doesn't just "go away." Children need to learn to cope with the feelings. Separation skills are a competency infants and toddlers build; they don't usually arrive in a program already competent. So when separation is an issue, separation is the curriculum, and that's where the adult focus should be.

Recognizing the range of feelings that comes with separation can be helpful for caregivers. The feelings of loss may range from mild discomfort and anxiety to sadness or even grief. Fear and anger are other reactions common to a separation situation. A feeling of loneliness is another reaction. A child may be feeling all of these at once or may feel just one. All of these feeling words have been used by adults to describe their reaction to a loss that came from being apart, temporarily or permanently, from someone they were attached to. Though infants and toddlers aren't necessarily competent at describing feelings, it is easy to detect that they feel the same range of emotions that adults feel.

An additional issue that caregivers often have to face is that of parental behaviors around separation. It is common to hear caregivers complain that parents magnify separation problems and even create additional ones. This happens when parents have as much (or more) pain at leaving their children as their children have at leaving them. Because of these feelings, parents may act in ways you don't approve of. Some prefer to sneak away because they can't stand saying good-bye. Others prolong the good-byes until everyone is in pain, though the child has already shown he or she is better off with a quick, uncomplicated departure. Some parents suffer because the child cries when they leave; others suffer because he or she *doesn't* cry. Be sensitive to parent feelings and realize that separation is hard on them too. The parents' difficulties may be compounded by a

Reflect

What do you remember about a time in your life that you were separated from someone you were attached to? What feelings do you remember? What helped you cope with them? Did someone help you cope?

Reflect

Are you a person with issues around separation? Do children's feelings upset you more than other people you know? If yes, what can you do about your own separation issues? If no, how do you think you learned to cope with separation?

sense of guilt at leaving their children. Give them all the support and help you can. (There's more on this subject in Chapter 14.) One easy thing caregivers can do is to encourage parents to call during the day to check on how the child is doing, sometimes just such a simple thing eases parents' minds considerably.

An additional factor to consider when looking at separation in infant-toddler day care is that of children's attachment to caregivers. As shifts change, personnel changes, and adults come and go, infants and toddlers may have to deal with separation from a beloved caregiver before they say hello once again to a beloved parent. In fact, a day in a child care center may be full of hellos and good-byes because of breaks, lunches, and assorted responsibilities that may call a particular caregiver out of the room. These comings and goings are usually less of a problem for infants and toddlers in a family child care home.

Autonomy

Erikson's second stage of psychosocial development, **autonomy,** occurs as the growing infant reaches the second year and begins to move around in the environment. When infants become toddlers, they begin to perceive themselves as separate individuals, not just a part of the person(s) they are attached to. They discover the power they possess, and they push toward independence. At the same time, their developing capabilities allow them to do more for themselves. They learn self-help skills.

Readiness for toilet learning, discussed in Chapter 3, is an example of the coming together of increased capabilities and the push for independence. The necessary capabilities lie in three separate domains—the physical (control), the cognitive (understanding), and the emotional (willingness). The goal is to get the movement toward independence working for you and not against you. If you get too demanding or pushy, you may find yourself in a power struggle over toilet learning, and then the child, in the name of independence, feels the need to oppose you. Independence becomes linked in the child's mind with diapers or "accidents." It is far better for the child to see you as a support and an aid rather than as an obstacle to his or her own developing capabilities and independence.

Language provides clues about another area of autonomy. The "NO!" for which toddlers are so famous is a further clue to the push for separateness and independence. They differentiate themselves from others by what seems to be contrariness. If you want them to go in, they want to stay out. If you want them to stop, they want to start. If you're serving milk, they want juice.

Granted, caregivers don't usually see as much of this kind of behavior as parents do. The tie between parent and child is a much stronger, more passionate one. Many children feel more secure and therefore free to express themselves in words and actions at home than they do in child care. It is important not to make parents feel they are doing something wrong because more defiant and rebellious behavior comes out when they are present. Rejecting behaviors are normal, and even good, for toddlers to exhibit. They show that the child's growing sense of autonomy and separateness is strong.

Reflect

Do you react strongly to the behaviors toddlers show when working on issues of autonomy? If yes, why? If no, why not? Do you think your culture has anything to do with your answer?

Demanding only "good" behavior in toddlers may cause a great deal of frustration for children. If a toddler program does not allow children to feel normal rejecting behaviors, what do they do with those feelings? Are they getting their needs met in child care? What might it do to their relationship with their parents if they have to concentrate all their rejecting behaviors into the few hours they spend with them?

Language provides further clues about other areas of autonomy that are part of the toddler period. "Me do it!" shows that drive for independence. By capitalizing on this drive, you can promote the development of self-help skills. When children want to "do it," set up the situation so they *can.*

Because we want children to grow up being cooperative and sharing individuals, we sometimes push them to share before they are ready. Children who have no sense of possession can't understand the concept of sharing. Children who have some sense of possession still may not be ready to share. Some take a long time to develop a feeling that something *belongs to them.* If they spend most of their waking hours in an environment where everything belongs to everybody or to the program, it may take a good deal longer.

Sometimes, in the name of fairness, children are constantly asked to give up a turn or a toy before they are finished with it. When this occurs in an environment where there are no private possessions, rather than learning to be a sharing person, some children learn just not to care. It doesn't matter to them whether they play with this toy or that one or for how long. They learn to stay uninvolved rather than face the pain of being constantly interrupted and sidetracked. Think what it would be like to be a child who never gets a chance to play out a fantasy or an interest or reach a point of satisfaction by being allowed to have a toy or material in your possession until you are really through with it. How would this situation affect attention span? Do some children learn to have short attention spans because some caregivers overstress sharing?

Initiative

Erikson's term for the stage of older toddlers as they approach preschool age is **initiative.** The focus on autonomy eventually passes. The energy that has previously gone into separating and striving for independence, and which often results in defiance and rebellion, is now available for new themes. This energy pushes children to create, invent, and explore as they seek out new activities. At this new stage, toddlers become the initiators of what happens in their lives and gain enthusiasm from their newfound power.

The caregiver should respond to this need to initiate by providing information, resources, freedom, and encouragement. Although older toddlers still very much need limits, the caregiver can set and keep the limits in such a way that toddlers don't feel guilty about this powerful push they feel to take initiative. People with initiative make valuable citizens. They gain this quality early in life when the people around them encourage them to be *explorers, thinkers,* and *doers.*

Guidance and Discipline

NAEYC Program Standard 3
Teaching

The socialization process in infants comes about as adults meet their needs. Infants require no guidance or discipline. Limits come naturally from their own limitations. Control may be a minor issue at times. Usually, meeting a specific need will take care of their lack of control, or they may need to be held close and tight. An example of providing control when an infant needs it is when newborns cry in distress that is not hunger. Sometimes they quiet down when wrapped tightly in a blanket. The blanket seems to provide the control that they do not have as their legs and arms hang free under loose covers.

This same theme—tightness providing control the infant lacks—looks different in the toddler stage. Toddlers may also appreciate a "feeling of tightness" when control comes from the outside, in situations when their own underdeveloped ability to control themselves gives way. Holding out-of-control toddlers tightly usually enables them to regain inner control.

Limits for Toddlers

Toddlers need to feel that there are **limits** even when they do not need the tightness of outside control. Think of limits—rules of behavior—as invisible fences or boundaries. Because they can't see these boundaries, children need to test in order to discover them. And they have little faith in words alone. Just as most of us are compelled to touch the surface behind the "wet paint" sign, so are toddlers compelled to bump up against a limit to see if it is really there and to make sure it will hold. Some children will do more testing than others, but all children need to know that there are limits. The limits provide a sense of security, just as the tight blanket does for the newborn.

To illustrate the security that limits provide, think of yourself driving across a high bridge. You probably have done that more than once in your life. The limits on the bridge are the rails on the sides. Can you imagine yourself driving across that bridge if the rails were removed? You don't physically need those rails, you know. After all, how often have you actually bumped the rails while driving across a bridge? Yet the thought of the bridge without the rails is terrifying. The rails provide a sense of security, just as the limits set for toddlers provide security in their lives.

Any discussion of limits, guidance, and discipline in toddlers quickly brings forth a discussion of what to do about such behaviors as biting, hitting, throwing things, and negativism. No single answer covers all behaviors in all situations with all children. The only single answer that applies is "It depends . . . ."

Biting

Let's look at biting. Start by asking, "Why is this child biting? What is behind the behavior?" If children are very young, they may be biting out of love. Sometimes when adults model playful nibbling, chewing, or "eating up" as a way of demonstrating affection, infants imitate their actions by biting those they love. This is not hard to understand if you relate to feelings implied in the expression "to sink your teeth into something." Mouths are expressive organs, and when a child is too small to convey the intensity of a feeling with words, biting may do it.

Of course, not all biting is done for love; some is done for power. When a child is small, physical power is minimal. But the jaws have powerful muscles, and little teeth are sharp. Even a very young child can do real damage with a bite. Some children learn this as a means of getting their own way with children who are bigger than they are.

Some biting may be done out of curiosity. Just as infants mouth and bite objects, so may they mouth and bite people. They do this with no malice intended—they are merely exploring.

Some biting is done as an expression of anger. Adults clench their jaws and grind their teeth; infants and toddlers sink their teeth into any available arm.

Some biting may be a means of gaining attention. Imagine yourself a toddler in a program where adults are available but are spread thin, and you get focused attention from one of them rarely and then only briefly. Or imagine that you do get focused attention, but the adult tends to be cold and rather vacant—more of a shell than a real person. No matter what you do, you can't seem to tap the real person inside the shell. Then one day you discover that by merely putting your teeth into a child's leg, you can get an adult to come over and touch you—even pick you up, hold you tight, look you right in the eye, and talk at length to you. This adult, who was all fluff before, becomes hard and real as the exchange provides passion and intensity. The message is that you finally did something that *mattered!*

Some young children need this kind of strong interaction. It tells them that you care what they do, that their behavior matters to you. If they can't provoke an intense interaction any other way, they may continue to bite just to get it.

The way to stop biting is to prevent it, not try to deal with it after it happens. Biting is too powerful a behavior to allow to continue. It's too painful for the person bitten, and it's too frightening for the biter to have that much power to do harm. When biters can't control their own behavior, it's up to you to control it. A useful technique after waylaying the biting is to redirect the urge. Give these children something to bite on that is made for biting—teething rings, cloth, or rubber or plastic objects. Offer these as choices, saying something like, "I can't let you bite Craig, but you can bite the plastic ring or this wet washcloth." Don't do this in a punitive way.

What else you do besides control the behavior and offer biting alternatives depends on the origins of the biting. If it is being modeled, try to cut off the modeling. If it is an expression of a feeling (love, frustration, or anger), teach alternative means for expression. Help children redirect their energy into positive ways of expressing the feelings. Redirecting the biting to objects is a start, but you should go beyond that. If a power issue is involved, teach children other techniques for getting what they need and want. If it is an attention issue, find ways to give children the attention—the intense interactions they need—without biting being the trigger. None of these is an easy solution, and it may take a good deal of brainstorming, discussion, cooperation, and teamwork even to identify the origins of the behavior and the appropriate approach.

Biting is an example of an aggressive (intent to harm) behavior. Other aggressive behaviors that cause toddler caregivers problems are hitting, kicking, shoving, pulling hair, throwing objects, and destroying toys and materials. To figure out what to do about these behaviors, you must go through a problem-solving process, looking at the particular child, the possible origins of the behavior, the message behind the behavior, the way the environment may contribute to the behavior, the way adult behavior may trigger the aggression, and the resources the child has for expressing feelings. Beware of advice that advocates any one simple solution. Behavior is complex, as are children. No one approach is right for everyone all the time.

Negativism

Another category of difficult behaviors that caregivers of toddlers must deal with is negativism. A frequent complaint from caregivers is "They won't do what I say." Part of the problem may be that toddlers can't always translate word messages into physical control, even when they understand what you want. Another part of the problem is that when toddlers are faced with demands or commands they often do the opposite.

The secret to dealing with negativism is to stop issuing challenges. Stay out of power struggles. Try not to be boldly confronting. If you approach a toddler who is outside a limit, say a girl climbing on a table, start by being calm and matter-of-fact rather than confrontive. Don't issue a challenge (such as "Get off the table"). State the limit in positive terms, such as "The ramp is for climbing" or "Feet belong on the floor." One particularly talented teacher simply says, "You can put your feet right here," patting the appropriate place. Nine times out of ten the feet go directly to where they belong! Something about the way she says it conveys such a confident and positive attitude that there is no challenge issued.[3]

Teaching Prosocial Behavior

There is another half to discipline and guidance besides setting limits—that is, developing **prosocial behavior.** Prosocial behavior doesn't just automatically occur by putting infants and toddlers in groups and setting limits. You have to plan for it to happen. You have to *make* it happen.

Some children have natural inclinations toward kindness and compassion from the early years, but most have to be taught. We used to think that the egocentricity of preschool-age children kept them from seeing another person's perspective. We know now this is not true. Even infants cry in empathy for other infants, and many toddlers will offer a toy or a pat to a child in pain, obviously trying to comfort or help. Here are some ideas about how to promote and teach prosocial skills.

1. Whenever you set a limit, explain *why*. Let children know the effects of their behavior on others—that hitting hurts, that grabbing toys causes unhappiness.
2. Notice children who show they care about other children. Mention the behaviors. Call attention to the behaviors you wish to occur more often. Use such simple statements as "I see how you are being very careful with the doll," "I liked the way you gave Chelsea her blanket when she was crying," "I noticed you tried to help Joanie solve that problem," or "I bet you feel good about giving that toy to Sammy when he asked you for it." Remark about specific behaviors rather than making global judgments (such as "Good girl!").
3. Model prosocial behaviors yourself. Say thank-you when someone shares something with you. Be kind and considerate not only to the children you work with but also to other adults they see you with.
4. Take a problem-solving view rather than a power stance when there is a conflict. You will want not only to model conflict resolution with other adults but also to help the children in their dealings with one another. Encourage them to talk to one another rather than to you. Give them the words to use if they need them—for example, say, "Tell Jesse you don't like it when he takes the toy away from you." Then turn and see what Jesse says in response. Help him make himself understood if he needs help. Help the children see one another's points of view and come to

VIDEO OBSERVATION 11

Girls Playing Together

See Video Observation 11: Girls Playing Together for an example of children so-
cializing with each other and enjoying each other's company as they move around
through a play structure set up. Note that the adult is not teaching them or interfering in any way. She remains quietly nearby in case they need her.

Questions

- Are you surprised to see children this young interact so positively with each
  other? Why or why not?
- What is your experience with children interacting in the early toddler stage?
- What social skills are these children showing?

To view this clip, go to www.mhhe.com/itc7e. Click on Student Edition, select
Chapter 11, and click on Video Observation.

some kind of conclusion. Don't solve their conflicts for them; teach them
to solve conflicts themselves.

5. Encourage cooperation. One effective way to teach cooperation that we
discussed in Chapter 3, is to make caregiving tasks, especially diapering
and dressing, a cooperative effort. Once a cooperative spirit is established, cooperation can become the norm. In addition to cooperative
approaches to caregiving, have cooperative activities where children do
things together rather than separately. Instead of individual art projects,
try taping butcher paper to a table, making felt pens or crayons available,
and letting children create a group picture.

6. Pay special attention to children who are constantly picked on or rejected
by their peers. They need extra help with social skills. Both aggressor and
victim need your extra attention (but not when they are aggressing or
being victimized). Teach aggressors other ways of getting what they need
or want, and teach victims how to stand up for themselves.

7. Avoid punishment. Punishment may work to curb antisocial behaviors, but it works against teaching prosocial ones. And it is never appropriate to inflict pain on a child.

Promoting social development and teaching social skills are not easy. Often you end up undoing what you've been trying to do. Some undesirable behaviors are impossible to ignore, but by paying attention to them, you ensure that they will continue. You're also bound to model behavior you don't want the child to pick up. The message is far stronger if you model the behavior you are after. As human beings, we can't be perfect, which in itself is an important message to infants and toddlers. As you forgive your own less-than-perfect social skills, so, perhaps, you can forgive theirs.

Promoting Healthy Brain Growth

The importance of early social contact has been emphasized a great deal by the current information on the brain. Social development discussed in this chapter has its beginnings in the early attachment experiences, and these cause an amazing sequence of activity related to brain function.

Ron Lally, a pioneer in planning environments for infants and toddlers, has been a leader in interpreting brain research as it relates to quality care for very young children. He has identified seven "gifts" that are vital for healthy social growth.

1. *Nurturance* is caring and giving. Because each infant is unique, nurturance means responding to every baby individually. When a baby feels a caregiver's responsive nurturance, comfort and security are established. It is the comfort of this connection that is vital for attachment.
2. *Support* is the context of care that a child receives. To support a young child means that the caregiver must respect a child's various feelings. Caregivers offer support by acknowledging a child's frustrations, by encouraging curiosity, and by enforcing rules that promote social interactions with others.
3. *Security* is related to both nurturance and support, and it is what makes a child feel safe. Caregivers provide security when they provide reliable, responsive care and when they enforce safety rules consistently.
4. *Predictability* is the "gift" that is vital for a child's sense of security and mental growth. Predictability is both social and environmental. A child needs to be able to rely on people and to be able to find things and places. Predictability avoids both confusion and rigidity. It allows a child to feel secure and to seek challenges.
5. *Focus* supports very young children's attention in their environment. An infant or toddler's attention span will increase if there are not too many toys, too many interruptions, or too many other people. Their opportunity to focus on meaningful experiences needs to be respected.
6. *Encouragement* from a knowledgeable caregiver tells a young child, "I appreciate your efforts; you are becoming a competent person." A child's own learning is reinforced through encouragement. It is a response that

**NAEYC Program
Standard 9**
Physical Environment

understands the importance of a child's imitation, experimentation, and discovery as critical links to learning.

7. *Expansion* of a child's experience involves "bathing (not drowning) the child in language." Watch for the young child's cues and build on his or her unique experiences. Involvement in fantasy play, talking along with a child, and responding to activities are all ways to demonstrate to young children the value of learning.[4]

The child-care setting that offers these seven gifts provides a base for the practical application of brain research and for the secure social development of a child. The current research has emphasized just how early neural circuitry is formed and how critical social development is to that formation. The healthy brain is a social brain!

The Special Need of All Children: Self-Esteem

Considerations involving children with special needs have been included at the end of the chapters in Part 2, "Focus on the Child." Children with special needs can have a variety of conditions that influence their interactions with people and things. Their specific challenges may place extra demands on parents and caregivers who are trying to promote healthy interaction and social skills. The unresponsive child, or the one with a sensory impairment or with delayed, inconsistent communication, needs a caregiver who understands the vital significance of interpersonal relationships.

Although the study of children with special needs seems to be a study of "differences," it is also a study of "similarities." Children with special needs are more similar to other children than they are different. The most important characteristics of children with special needs are their *abilities*. And a very important need for all children is that they *feel good* about their abilities. This sense of inner positiveness is a prerequisite for mental health and competent social interaction.

Social skills and the socialization process have been the focus of this chapter. As noted numerous times in this text, the foundation for interacting with others is attachment. From a nurturing attachment experience, children learn to value themselves and others. This valuing of self is called "self-esteem." **Self-esteem** is vital for *all* children. And it is important for caregivers creating quality experiences for children to appreciate it.

The definition of self-esteem is complex. As we grow and develop, it is being constantly reshaped while we interact and experience our world. It is a personal assessment of positive worth. But it is not the "me, my, mine" sense of worth. An individual with self-esteem is confident, optimistic, and sensitive to the feelings and needs of others. The roots of this lifelong process are clearly taking hold in infancy and toddlerhood.

Two types of experiences are most significant to the development of self-esteem. As an infant experiences attachment that is secure and nurturing, his self-concept begins to develop. Self-concept is formed by the infant's feelings about himself as they are reflected in his interactions with others. When a baby is responded to and is part of a loving relationship, his self-concept is positive and trusting.

The second important experience that contributes to self-esteem is the successful accomplishment of tasks. As a toddler explores and interacts with her world, her self-image is growing. Self-image is a more personal assessment of an individual's experience. If a toddler lives in a world with lots of "No's" and has little opportunity to test her skills, her image of herself may be low. Her inexperience limits her view of her own competence.

Very young children need secure relationships (with others) and opportunities to actively explore the world (on their own). When the self-concept is positive and trusting and the self-image is vital and active, children experience life as accepting and meaningful. This is the beginning of self-esteem. Children's ability to feel themselves as loving and competent allows them eventually to see others in a similar way.

Pause for a moment and think about how the work of Erikson, Piaget, and Vygotsky relates to children's positive feelings about themselves. Erikson emphasized the establishment of trust (through relationships with others) and autonomy (through experiences with everyday events) as vital to healthy development. Piaget and Vygotsky viewed children as active participants in their own world. And this physical activity leads to cognitive activity, eventually resulting in coping skills. Individuals with self-esteem tend to have good coping skills.

As young children experience the challenges and limits of life, they need the stability of a personal base within themselves. This is important for all children; it may be even more important for children with special needs. We all need a place to "come home to," a place that is accepting and renewing. The ability to create such a place is the essence of self-esteem.

How can adults help children develop self-esteem? The importance of a secure attachment has already been mentioned. Adults who feel good about themselves tend to pass that feeling on to their children. It is important that caregivers and parents see self-esteem as a lifelong process and that they are contributing to their own needs for nurturance and challenge.

Certainly the 10 principles on which this book is based promote self-esteem. The principles support independence while providing a loving base. They respect individual needs and stress appreciation of problem-solving efforts.

Adult feedback to children should be authentic. Persistently positive information, like persistently negative information, does not prepare children for the *real* world. They will not be ready for the challenges of peers and school if caregivers and parents have not given them honest information. Remember to trust their competence and encourage their resiliency.

No doubt every adult has had the experience of not feeling respected by others. Your self-respect and self-esteem are as valuable as your attitude toward children. Cultivating your own self-worth and getting to know yourself better are worthy goals (for children and for all of us). The following poem by Kahlil Gibran, with its appreciation of uniqueness and individual growth, provides a summary for this chapter and for the developmental section of this book.

Your hearts know in silence the secrets of the
days and the nights.
But your ears thirst for the sound of your
heart's knowledge.
You would know in words that which you have
always known in thought,
You would touch with your fingers the naked
body of your dreams.
And it is well you should.
The hidden well-spring of your soul must
needs rise and run murmuring to the sea;
And the treasure of your infinite depths
would be revealed to your eyes.
But let there be no scales to weigh your
unknown treasure;
And seek not the depths of your knowledge
with staff or sounding line.
For self is a sea boundless and
measureless.
Say not, "I have found the truth," but
rather, "I have found a truth."
Say not, "I have found the path of the
soul," say rather, "I have met the soul walking upon my path."
For the soul walks upon all paths.
The soul walks not upon a line, neither
does it grow like a reed.
The soul unfolds itself, like a lotus of
countless petals.[5]

DEVELOPMENTAL PATHWAYS

Behaviors Showing Development of Social Skills

Young infants (up to 8 months)	• See adults as objects of interest and novelty; seek out adults for play • Smile or vocalize to initiate social contact • Anticipate being lifted or fed and move body to participate • Try to resume a knee ride by bouncing to get adult started again
Mobile infants (up to 18 months)	• Enjoy exploring objects with another as the basis for establishing relationship • Get others to do things for their pleasure (wind up toys, read books) • Show considerable interest in peers • Indicate a strong sense of self through assertiveness; direct actions of others (for example, "sit here!")

Toddlers **(up to 3 years)**	• Gain greater enjoyment from peer play and joint exploration • Begin to see benefits of cooperation • Identify self with children of the same age or sex • Exhibit more impulse control and self-regulation in relation to others • Enjoy small group activities; show empathic concern for others

Source: S. Bredekamp and C. Copple, *Developmentally Appropriate Practice in Early Childhood Programs* (Washington, D.C.: National Association for the Education of Young Children, 1997).

Diverse Developmental Pathways

What you see	Makayla spends a lot of time getting very close to children's faces, which annoys them and gets in the way of her making connections. At 18 months she doesn't move around as much as the other children her age, and when she does she sometimes trips and falls.
What you might think	She lacks social skills. She needs more practice with using her motor skills.
What you might not know	The parents have been hearing concerns from their pediatrician and yet are hesitant to follow up on the testing that she advises.
What you might do	Observe Makayla to see if she just needs to learn social and motor skills or if there is something else going on. Build a relationship with the parents. If they come to trust you, you may be able to support them in ways that will bring them around to following the pediatrician's advice.

Cultural Diversity and Developmental Pathways

What you see	Xavier is crying and clinging to his mother as she is trying to walk out the door.
What you might think	This is typical behavior and to be expected. This is a step toward Xavier becoming an independent individual. He is expressing his feelings openly.
What his mother might think	This is embarrassing because it shows a lack of proper upbringing.
What you might not know	This family is not interested in their child becoming an independent individual; instead, they are more worried that he is unmannerly and is disrespecting his elders, both of which are moral mandates for the group-oriented behavior they want their child to learn.
What you might do	Learn more about the family's perspective and share yours, but not in a "parent-education mode." Work on supporting Xavier and helping him develop the behaviors his family expects.

Summary

Social skills are learned behaviors that connect us, help us to be independent, and foster cooperation and interdependent relationships.

- Early Social Behaviors
  - o Infants interact with synchrony by moving their bodies to the rhythm of someone who talks to them.
  - o Infants imitate or copy adult social behavior such as opening their eyes wide or sticking out their tongue.
- Stages of Psychosocial Development
  - o Erikson's stages of psychosocial development are stated in terms of issues that children must resolve at different stages. They are
  - o Trust versus mistrust for age 0 to 1
    - o Learning to separate is an important social skill that reflects trust
  - o Autonomy versus shame and doubt for ages 1 to 3
  - o Initiative versus guilt for ages 3 to 6
- Guidance and Discipline
  - o Limits for Toddlers are important and can be thought of as fences or boundaries.
  - o Some behaviors, such as biting, demand that adults do something.
  - o Negativism is associated with a group of behaviors that many adults find difficult.
- Teaching Prosocial Skills
  - o Promoting positive interactions is the other half of discipline and limits.
- Promoting Healthy Brain Growth
  - o Ron Lally, a leader in interpreting brain research, has identified seven "gifts" to promote healthy, social brain growth.
- The Special Need of All Children: Self Esteem
  - o All children need adults who respect them for their unique growth patterns.

 Online Resources

Go to the Online Learning Center at **www.mhhe.com/itc7e** to access the student study guide that includes quizzes, practice with key terms, and a review of chapter content; links to websites related to the chapter; and additional resources.

Key Terms

autonomy 238
initiative 239
limits 240
prosocial behavior 242

self-esteem 246
stranger anxiety 234
trust 234

Thought/Activity Questions

1. Why shouldn't caregivers use distraction as a primary strategy for children showing feelings about being separated from their parents?
2. What do you think are the most important social skills in our society? How would you begin to teach them to infants and toddlers?

3. How can caregivers respond to infants and toddlers in ways that promote individuality? That promote cooperation?
4. You are writing a brochure for your new infant-toddler child care program. In it you want to include a statement about your philosophy on "discipline." What do you want to share with parents on this topic? Try writing several statements.
5. List behaviors that you think indicate positive social development. How can caregivers and parents encourage these behaviors in the first three years?

For Further Reading

L. Brault and T. Brault, *Children with Challenging Behavior: Strategies for Reflective Thinking* (Phoenix: CPG Publishing, 2005).

P. M. Butterfield, C. A. Martin, and A. P. Prairie, *Emotional Connections: How Relationships Guide Early Learning* (Washington, D.C.: Zero to Three, 2004).

Renatta M. Cooper, "Child Care as Shared Socialization," *Child Care Information Exchange*, July 2002, pp. 58–60.

S. Crockenberg, "How Children Learn to Resolve Conflicts in Families," *Zero to Three*, April 1992.

Erik Erikson, *Childhood and Society*, 2nd ed. (New York: Norton, 1963).

P. Greenberg, *Character Development: Encouraging Self-Esteem and Self-Discipline in Infants, Toddlers, and Two-Year-Olds* (Washington, D.C.: National Association for the Education of Young Children, 1990).

Hermine H. Marshall, "Cultural Influences on the Development of Self-Concept," *Young Children* 56(6), November 2001, pp. 12–25.

R. Parlakian, *How Culture Shapes Social-Emotional Development: Implications for Practice in Infant-Family Programs* (Washington, D.C.: Zero to Three, 2004).

M. Pratt, "The Importance of Infant/Toddler Interactions," *Young Children* (54)4, July 1999, pp. 26–29.

J. J. Shirilla and D. J. Weatherston, *Case Studies in Infant Mental Health: Risk, Resiliency, and Relationships* (Washington, D.C.: Zero to Three, 2002).

G. Gordon Williamson and M. Anzalone, *Sensory Integration and Self-Regulation in Infants and Toddlers: Helping Very Young Children Interact with their Environment* (Washington, D.C.: Zero to Three, 2001).

part three

Focus on the Program

chapter 12

The Physical Environment

Focus Questions

After reading this chapter you should be able to answer the following questions:

1 What needs to be done to make a safe environment for infants and toddlers?

2 How can you create a healthy environment for infants and toddlers?

3 What areas need to be provided for in the layout of an infant-toddler program?

4 How does the developmental appropriateness of the environment relate to safety and to learning?

5 What should be in the play environment?

6 When assessing the quality of an infant-toddler environment what five dimensions should you consider? What are four other considerations?

What Do You See?

Olivia is sitting on the floor next to Kai who is lying on his back. He turns onto his side, and then onto his stomach. He stops, pushes up and smiles at Olivia, who smiles back and then squeals. Kai rolls onto his side again and over quickly onto his back. He looks around for Olivia and discovers he has moved to a new place. He looks pleased with himself. Olivia now throws herself onto all fours and is crawling toward a low platform nearby. She climbs up easily and sits back down, looking at the room from her new vantage point. She watches Kai continuing to roll until he is almost on the other side of the room. She quickly crawls down from the platform and over to Kai who is now lying on his back waving a scarf in the air. Olivia crawls over to another scarf and brings it to him and now he has one in each hand. She settles back into a sitting position and picks up a soft ball that is close to her foot. She squeezes it several times, then crawls over and puts it in a bucket, which already has another ball in it. She empties both out on to the floor and watches them roll in opposite directions. Kai laughs out loud at the sight.

Compare that scene to this one.

Savannah is the same age as Olivia and Travis is Kai's age. Savannah is strapped into a baby swing and Travis is on the floor strapped into an infant seat. When the swing stops Savannah fusses until a caregiver comes over and gives her another push. Travis has a toy in his hand, but he drops it and now he can't reach it. He cries and a caregiver comes over and gives it to him. She puts three more toys on his lap and leaves. He throws all the toys on the floor and cries again. In the meantime Savannah has stopped swinging and started fussing. On her way over to push Savannah the caregiver says to her teammate, "I think we should get one of those motorized swings." Then she walks over to Travis who is screaming now. "Young man," she says. "I think you are throwing those toys out on purpose just to get me over here to pick them up." She brings a frame of hanging toys and sets them across Travis, who reaches out and grabs a ring and tries to pull it off. "Now those toys are going to stay put!" she says as she goes off to push Savannah again.

What did you see? Did you notice that Olivia and Kai were able to move around and experience the environment on their own? They were absorbed in what they were doing and also able to interact with each other. What about Savannah and Travis? They could see what was in the environment, but they couldn't get to anything. They were dependent on the caregiver to interact with them and keep them interested.

Both environments were safe—a primary consideration. We'll return to these two scenes later in the chapter to explore other environmental qualities they exhibit. The Child Development Associate (CDA) assessment process defines quality settings for infant and toddler care as those that are safe environments that promote health and learning.

This chapter examines each of those components and then goes on to use an assessment tool called "dimensions of teaching/learning environments" created by Betty Jones and Liz Prescott.[1]

A Safe Environment

NAEYC Program Standard 9
Physical Environment

Safety is a first consideration in planning for infants and toddlers. Group size and adult-child ratio are important factors in creating a safe environment. The WestEd Center for Child and Family Studies, in conjunction with the California Department of Education, has created the guidelines shown in Table 12.1.

Creating a Safe Physical Environment: A Checklist

- Cover all electrical outlets.
- Cover all heaters so children are kept well away from them.
- Protect children from all windows and mirrors that aren't shatterproof.
- Remove or tie up all drapery cords. (Long strings, cords, and ties of any kind should be eliminated to prevent strangling.)
- Get rid of all slippery throw rugs.
- Get some instructions from your local fire department on how to put together a plan in case of fire. Consider the number and location of fire extinguishers, easy exit, and methods for carrying children who can't walk. Then schedule periodic fire drills.

Table 12.1 Guidelines for Group Size and Adult-Child Ratios

Group Size Guidelines (Same-Age Groups)			
Age	Adult-Child Ratio	Total Size	Minimum Number of Square Feet per Group*
0–8 months	1:3	6	350
8–18 months	1:3	9	500
18–36 months	1:4	12	600
Mixed-Age Guidelines (Family Child Care)			
Age	Adult-Child Ratio	Group Size	Minimum Number of Square Feet per Group*
0–36+ months	1:4**	8	600

*The space guidelines represent minimum standards of adequate square footage per group; the amounts shown do not include space used for entrance areas, hallways, diapering areas, or napping areas.

**Of the four infants assigned to a caregiver, only two should be under 24 months of age.

Developed by Far West Laboratory for Educational Research and Development and the California Department of Education. Reprinted by permission of J. Ronald Lally.

- Make sure there are no poisonous plants in the environment. (Many common house and garden plants are deadly poison. If you don't know which ones are, find out!)
- Make sure all furniture is stable and in good repair.
- Remove lids from toy storage boxes to prevent accidents.
- Make sure all cribs and other baby furniture meet consumer protection safety standards—that is, slats are close together so babies can't get their heads stuck, and crib mattresses fit tightly so babies can't get wedged between mattress and side and smother.
- Keep all medicines and cleaning materials well out of reach of children at all times.
- Beware of toys with small parts that can come loose and go into mouths (such as button eyes on stuffed animals).
- Remove all broken, damaged toys and materials.
- Be sure no toys or materials are painted with or contain toxic substances.
- Know first aid and CPR.
- Keep a first-aid kit at hand.
- Keep emergency numbers by the phone along with parent emergency information. Update parent emergency numbers frequently.
- Make sure the equipment you have is appropriate for the age group served. For example, climbing structures should be scaled down for toddlers.
- Supervise children well and allow them to take only minor risks but not risks with grave consequences. (Don't differentiate between boys and girls in the degree of risk you allow.)

If you have children with special needs in your program, you have to do a safety check that includes their special circumstances or disabilities. Are there ramps of an appropriate degree of slant for wheelchairs? Is some equipment safely adaptable for their special needs?

A Healthful Environment

NAEYC Program Standard 5
Health

A healthful environment is as important as a safe one. Good light, comfortable air temperature, and ventilation contribute to the health and well-being of the infants and toddlers in the environment.

Creating a Healthful and Sanitary Environment: A Checklist

- Wash hands often. Hand washing is the best way to keep infections from spreading. Wash after coughing, sneezing, wiping noses, and changing diapers and before preparing food. Use dispenser soap instead of bar soap and paper towels instead of cloth. Avoid touching faucets and waste receptacles after washing. (Foot-controlled faucets and trash cans with a foot-control lid opener eliminate the probability of recontaminating clean hands.)
- Wash children's hands regularly also, especially before eating and after diapering or using the bathroom.
- Do not allow children to share washcloths or any other personal items.
- Clean toys and play equipment daily for any group of children who are young enough to mouth objects.
- Wear socks or slippers rather than street shoes in areas where infants lie on the floor.
- Vacuum rugs and mop floors regularly.
- Be sure each child has his or her own bed, cot, or pad, and change sheets regularly.
- Take routine precautions in changing diapers to prevent the spread of illness. Provide a clean surface for each changing by washing down the waterproof diaper changing area with disinfectant solution and/or provide fresh paper each time. Wash hands carefully after each changing.
- Take routine precautions in food preparation, serving, and cleaning up. Wash hands before handling food. Store food and bottles in refrigerator until right before using them. To wash dishes and bottles, use extra hot water. (Dishwashers with the hot water heater turned to high help eliminate germs.) Use a weak bleach solution if you don't have a dishwasher. Date all stored food. Clean out the refrigerator regularly, and throw away old food.
- Be sure all children in your care are up to date on their immunizations.
- Learn to recognize the signs of common illnesses.
- Make clear policies about which symptoms indicate when a child is too sick to be in your program. Parents' and caregivers' ideas and needs often differ when it comes to this subject.

- Require permission slips before you administer any medicine, and then be sure to give prescriptions only to the child with his or her name on the bottle.

Although you do not want to compromise health practices, be aware that cultural differences may arise concerning health matters. Try to be sensitive to parents who have ideas different from accepted practice about the paths to good health.

Also be sensitive to the special needs of chronically ill children, who sometimes have immunity problems. They may need extra protection from the spread of virus and bacteria that other children in your program carry. Examine your health and sanitary practices carefully to be sure you give these children the protection they need. Resist criticism from those who accuse you of being overprotective.

Nutrition

Caregivers must pay careful attention to what to feed infants and toddlers and how. Food must be appropriate to the child's age, physical condition, and cultural or religious traditions. The tastes and habits children develop in the first three years can influence them throughout their lifetimes. Because obesity is such a concern in the United States, child care programs should be concerned about dietary habits. Feeding a well-rounded variety of wholesome foods can make a difference, especially if the program also has discussions with families. The goal should be for children to grow up eating mostly wholesome and nutritional food and eat sugary or fatty foods as only an occasional treat, not an every day menu. French fries, donuts, and candy are not appropriate foods for children. The eating environment and interactions with caregivers can create a warm, comfortable feeling about eating that encourages good eating habits and a positive attitude toward food.

Feeding Infants

Babies go through many stages as they move from taking only liquids to learning to chew and swallow solid food, to feeding themselves table food. Babies' first food is either breast milk or formula. Although caregivers don't make the decision about which to use, what they do can encourage or discourage mothers to continue breast-feeding after the child enters child care. Because breast milk has the advantage of being uniquely suited to human infants' growing needs and offers protection against infections, caregivers should make an effort to support breast-feeding mothers. Such a simple device as a comfortable chair in a quiet, private corner for mothers to nurse gives a supportive message. Being aware of arranging for the baby to be hungry when the mother arrives is another way to support breast-feeding. Knowing the details of how to store breast milk safely helps a mother feel secure about continuing to nurse her baby (see Table 12.2).

Table 12.2 Storing and Using Breast Milk
• Expressed breast milk should arrive cold in a clean and sanitary bottle.
• It should be stored immediately in the refrigerator or in the freezer if it arrives frozen.
• All bottles should be clearly labeled with the date of collection and the child's name.
• Any milk remaining after a feeding should be discarded and not used again.
• Refrigerated breast milk should be discarded after 48 hours.
• When warming bottles, use running tap water or place the bottle in a container of warm water for five minutes or less.
• Do not let milk sit at room temperature because bacteria can grow.
• Do not use a microwave to warm breast milk.

For detailed instructions about how to keep food for infants sanitary and safe, see Susan Aronson and Patricia M. Spahr, *Healthy Young Children: A Manual for Programs.* This manual has sample meal patterns for infants in the first year, giving examples of what they can eat and when. It includes such information as how to introduce solid foods, when to introduce cow's milk, how to avoid baby-bottle tooth decay, how to wean, and many more details. Of course, understanding each family's approach to feeding infants is vital, especially if there are cultural differences, food restrictions, or pertinent taboos. Infants with special needs may have a specific diet or ways of being fed that caregivers need to know about. Parents are the source for this information.

Offer good individualized infant nutrition, or ask the parents to provide nutritious food and bottles. Some guidelines agreed upon by most pediatricians are to wait on solids until the child is three to six months old, then introduce them slowly, one at a time, working up from a spoonful to a reasonably sized infant helping. Most pediatricians have a favorite order in which they advise introducing solids, starting with cereal. Most advise waiting to introduce those solids that may trigger allergies, such as egg white and orange juice. Stay away from mixtures like casseroles that contain several foods, because if one ingredient causes an allergic reaction, you won't know which one. Stay away from all additives—salt, sugar, and artificial colors and flavors. Infants need pure, natural, unseasoned food. Don't serve honey or corn syrup to infants under a year old, because these foods may contain a certain kind of spore that causes a food poisoning only infants are susceptible to. Avoid foods that infants can choke on, such as raw carrots and popcorn.

Feeding Toddlers

Infants who opened their mouths so happily for whatever the caregiver wanted to put into it can sometimes become toddlers who are picky eaters. The growth rate in the first year of life is so great that food intake must be plentiful. Toddlers'

VIDEO OBSERVATION 12

Feeding Routine

See Video Observation 12: Feeding Routine for an example of an environment that is developmentally appropriate and works well for the children in it. Watch this remarkably calm and civilized feeding scene.

Questions

- Why do you think this program has children sitting together in low chairs at the table instead of using in high chairs? Does the environment tell you anything about the philosophy of the program?
- How safe does this environment seem to be? Can you see any hazards?
- How comfortable and secure do the children seem to feel in this environment? What might be contributing to their comfort and sense of security?

To view this clip, go to www.mhhe.com/itc7e. Click on Student Edition, select Chapter 12, and click on Video Observation.

growth rate takes a plunge and, often, so do their appetites. If adults aren't aware of the change, their worries or behavior can create eating problems. It's common for worried adults to urge and cajole in ways that fan the flames of toddlers' natural resistance. It's important to offer a nutritious variety of foods, but it's also important to let toddlers decide how much and what they will eat. Small portions help encourage toddlers to eat up!

Many of the guidelines for infant feeding also apply to toddlers. Choose food that is pure and natural—not processed with additives. Toddlers (and infants too) enjoy finger food. They need a break from purees and cereals. Give fruit or vegetable snacks rather than cookies or highly salted crackers. Give apple slices and carrot sticks (and then be cautious of apple peels) only when children have enough teeth and the ability to chew them. Avoid such foods as popcorn, nuts, peanut butter, hot dog rounds, grapes, and other foods on which toddlers might choke. Cut hot dogs lengthwise and then in small pieces—avoid rounds! Cut grapes at least in half, and cut big ones in fourths. This particular caution goes double for those children with special needs whose reflexes may not be totally developed and who may be more prone to choking or breathing difficulties.

The Learning Environment

NAEYC Program Standards 2 and 3
Curriculum and Teaching

Much of the **structure** of an infant-toddler program comes from a well-planned environment. According to Louis Torelli, "A well-designed environment . . . supports infants' and toddlers' emotional well-being, stimulates their senses and challenges their motor skills. A well-designed group care environment promotes children's individual and social development.[2]

If you think about how learning at this age depends on emotional well-being, sensory experiences and free movement, you may wonder about the environment that Savannah and Travis are in back at the beginning of the chapter. Go back to the two scenes that open this chapter. Read them again and recall what you read in Part 2 about motor development and its connection to perception and cognition. Think about the experiences of Olivia and Kai who were moving all over the environment in the first scene as compared to Savannah and Travis who were strapped in a swing and an infant seat. What discoveries are they making? They are learning how to attract adult attention, but that's about all. Olivia and Kai don't need adult attention while they are exploring and learning many other things, including their own increasing capabilities.

Research shows that behavior is influenced by environment.[3] A structured environment gives us clues about how to behave in it. Just compare the library with the workout room in the gym. Or think of how the grocery store communicates what's expected, with carts at the door and open shelves and checkout stands, compared with a jewelry store, where you sit at a glass counter and someone offers you things from behind lock and key.

Infants and toddlers also get messages from the environment if it is well planned and consistent. In fact, learning to receive those messages is an important part of their socialization process as they learn about expectations for various behavior settings.[4]

Reflect

Look around the environment you are in right now. What messages does it send about the way you are supposed to behave in it? Think about a contrasting environment you have been in recently. What different messages did it send?

Children with physical limitations will get specific messages if the learning environment isn't adapted to their special needs. For example, if a child in a wheelchair isn't able to go outside or across a thick carpet, his experiences in the program will be limited. If toys or equipment aren't at his level, he gets the message that they're not for him to play with. Make accommodations in the environment for *all* the children in the program, including those with special needs.

Although much learning goes on in the play area of the infant-toddler environment, it is not confined to that space. The whole environment, including caregiving areas, is the learning environment in an infant-toddler program. See the sample classrooms in Figures 12.1, 12.2, and 12.3.

Figure 12.1 Infant Classroom

Figure 12.2 Toddler Classroom

Figure 12.3 Infant-Toddler Classroom

Layout

There are some general rules for setting up an environment for infant-toddler care, whether in a center or family child-care home. You should have a designated place for arrivals and departures. Near this area should be storage for children's belongings. The sleeping area should be apart from the play area and should have a subdued atmosphere that has restful colors and is quiet and nonstimulating. The eating area also should be somewhat separate from the play area, though the two may overlap at times because you use eating tables for various other kinds of activities. The eating area should, of course, be close to a kitchen or other warming or cooking facility. The diaper area should be away from the eating area and close to a bathroom, or at least a sink. The indoor play area should be cheerful and well lighted and should invite exploration. There should be an outdoor play area as well that is equally inviting to explore. At the Pikler Institute in Budapest, eating and sleeping are also done outdoors, and the environment is set up appropriately for these two activities. The children have two sets of beds—one set that stays outdoors. Storage and office space (at least a desk and phone) are also usually a part of the environment. Infants and toddlers come to learn what is expected in each space if the spaces are distinct from one another.

The furniture, equipment, and materials for caregiving activities vary somewhat with the philosophy and goals of the program. The following corresponds to the philosophy of this book.

Eating

A refrigerator and provision for warming food either in the room or very nearby are essential. A sink and counter also are essential. A dishwasher is handy. Tools and utensils for food preparation are needed as well as unbreakable dishes, cups, and spoons, in addition to bottles and nipples (which the parents may send with the children). The eating and food preparation area needs storage for food, dishes, and utensils. Small, low tables and chairs that children can get in and out of themselves add to feelings of independence. (Some children eat better in smaller groups because small groups are less stimulating, which is something to consider when choosing tables.) Although some programs feel high chairs are a necessity, we advocate using low tables and chairs for children who are able to get into them themselves. It takes some training on the part of the caregivers to get the children to eat at the table if children have a choice to leave. Provision should be made for adults to eat in comfort—whether in the room or somewhere else—so they feel more at home than if they always have to stand at a counter or squat in tiny chairs.

Sleeping

The sleeping furniture depends on the ages of the children. The youngest infants are more secure in bassinets or cradles; the older infants need cribs.

Toddlers can sleep on cots or pads on the floor. Children should not share cribs, cots, or bedding; each child should have his or her own.

Although sleeping separately is standard practice in infant-toddler care, for cultural reasons and for health considerations, it is important to recognize that some cultures do not consider separate sleeping arrangements for infants or toddlers either normal or healthy.

Diapering

The diapering area needs counters or tables to change diapers. Diapering counters usually have children laying sideways to the adult. At the Pikler Institute, the diapering areas are arranged so that the child lies perpendicular to the edge and facing the adult. The adult then bends straight over instead of twisting to one side. All supplies needed for diapering should be stored within arms reach of the diapering counter. Supplies include diapers, cleaning products for disinfecting the changing surface after each diapering, and sanitary storage or disposal for soiled diapers. A sink with warm water, soap, and towels must be in the diapering area and cannot be located where food is prepared or dishes are washed.

Toileting

Toddlers appreciate child-size toilets, and they need access to sinks with soap and paper towels (or a sanitary way to use cloth towels). This area should be convenient to play space, both indoors and outdoors.

Developmental Appropriateness

The most important factor in a learning environment is that it be developmentally appropriate for the age group. Infants are not served in an environment planned only for toddlers, just as toddlers do not behave the same in an environment designed solely for infants or for preschoolers. Developmental appropriateness is vital.

Often you have to be extremely flexible when you have infants and toddlers in the same room. The environment not only has to respond to the needs of the particular age constellation but also must respond to changes as the children grow and develop over time.

Jim Greenman illustrates this notion of flexibility in an interview in *Child Care Information Exchange:*

> *Flexibility comes from rethinking the usual, like a couch. For infants, a couch provides a perfect space for two caregivers to sit and hold babies. As children learn to crawl, the couch can be moved out from the wall to create an interesting path. When children want to practice walking, the same couch provides a soft walking rail. Once toddlers become fascinated by more complex kinds of spatial games like hide-and-seek, the couch can become the base for a slide or*

Reflect

How is the sleeping place in your own life different from the "play space"? Are there any implications for setting up appropriate infant-toddler sleeping and play spaces?

for tunnels made from blankets. This process of designing and redesigning an environment creates a caring and a working space which keeps pace with changes in the children.[5]

Another example of flexibility is what one caregiver did with a set of shelves that holds toys. She found the children constantly dumping the toys on the floor and trying to climb up the empty shelves, so she laid the unit down on its back, and it became a piece of gross motor equipment as children crawled in and out, curled up between the shelves, and "drove" in it like a truck. This supine bookcase provided wonderful opportunities for the imaginations of the young children in this program.

Appropriate Environments for Infants

How is the environment different for the infant and for the toddler? Partly it is size. The younger the child, the smaller the group and the space around should be. For the newborn, space can be frightening, and very confined space is appropriate—like a bassinet. The older immobile babies need expanded space, but not enormous space. They need to be on the floor but protected from walking feet that might step on or trip over the helpless infants. This is the age for which playpens are most appropriate. As babies begin to move around, by either rolling or crawling, they need even more space. The standard playpen is too small. When they first get upright, children need support for cruising—rails or furniture to hang onto. In a home environment, coffee tables, end tables, chairs, and couches provide this support. An infant center must have other provisions. (The *outside* of the playpen will work for this purpose.)

A word about cribs: Cribs are not good learning environments; they are sleeping environments. When the message is consistent about what cribs are for, some babies learn early to associate them with sleeping and have less difficulty going to sleep when put down. But if the crib is lined with toys and hung with mobiles, music boxes, and bags of goldfish, a mixed message is given. The environment is stimulating, not conducive to sleep. It is better to give the message that playing happens outside the crib. Cribs are too small for all but the youngest babies to play in anyway. It is better to use them only to confine tired children, not alert, awake ones. Awake children need a different environment.

Appropriate Environments for Toddlers

Toddlers, of course, need even more space and gross motor challenges appropriate to their age level. They also need an environment that encourages independence—steps up to the sink so they can wash their hands, swings they can get in and out of themselves, pitchers to pour their own milk and juice, cloths so they can wipe up their own spills, a dishpan at hand so they can bus their own dishes. Toddlers also need an environment that invites them to explore using gross and fine motor skills and all their senses.

The play space should contain a variety of age-appropriate toys and equipment that encourage active, creative, whole-body play as well as manipulative skills. It should suit the mood of all children at any given time on any given day—those who feel energetic, those who feel mellow, those who want to be alone, and those who feel sociable.

Family Child Care and Mixed-Age Groups

Setting up a child care environment for children of varying ages in a home is different from center-based program environments where children are grouped by age. Family child care homes have some distinct advantages that centers find hard to come by. There is less likely to be an "institutional feel" to them. The small scale of a home environment can be a great comfort to children who are easily overstimulated. There is a richness in a home that results from the greater variety found in an environment set up for mixed-age groups as well as adult family members. A home naturally provides a variety of textures, sounds, and activities as life in the home continues in the presence of the children. Some of the advantages of being in a home are also some of the challenges that providers face as they try to make their homes safe, comfortable learning and care environments for children. Seeing how family members use their time may be a wonderful experience for children as they watch the teenage family member fix her car or grandma sort her stamp collection. But the activities the family members engage in may not necessarily be good for children. For example, if the same teenager comes in and plops down in front of the television, that may be a problem the provider will have to deal with.

The Principles in Action

Principle 8 Recognize problems as learning opportunities, and let infants and toddlers try to solve their own. Don't rescue them, constantly make life easy for them, or try to protect them from all problems.

A family child care provider has her home set up so that children can explore freely. She's pleased at the way they make discoveries, run into problems, and take steps to solve them. Recently she enrolled a two-year-old named Austin, who is physically challenged, and she's trying to provide opportunities for him to explore, make discoveries, and solve problems. Austin is not able to move from one place to another, so the provider helps him experience new sights and orientations by changing him from place to place in the room. He can reach out if he is securely positioned so he's not in danger of falling over. The provider has figured out ways to get him close enough to the toys so that he can make his own choices about what to play with. She either puts him close to the shelves or takes one of the baskets of toys and lays it on its side so he can reach in. She also has modified some of the toys so they work more easily. She watched him try to turn the pages of a cardboard book, and he struggled so hard that he finally gave up. That time she rescued him, put him in her lap, and turned the pages for him as they read the book together. Later she came up with the idea of gluing Popsicle sticks to the pages, so he can get his hand around a stick and open up the cover. Using the sticks on the other pages, he can go through the whole book. He's delighted that he can do it himself, though he still looks to her to enjoy books with him. She's investigating how to use a computer to provide even more opportunities for Austin to play with toys that he can easily have an effect on. Making something happen is one of the inner urges of all toddlers, and Austin too is intrigued with creating an effect. The provider is working hard to give him many opportunities.

1. What other ideas do you have to help this child explore in the environment even though he can't get around by himself?
2. Imagine yourself at this moment physically challenged in the environment where you are right now. What kind of help would you need to make use of your limited reach and grasp if you had a strong desire to make an effect on something in this environment?
3. Think about the various ways this caregiver could move Austin from place to place in her home or make it possible for him to move himself.
4. What might be some barriers in the average home that would prevent this child from exploring the environment more fully?

Unlike the carefully designed center layouts shown in Figures 12.1, 12.2, and 12.3, family child care depends on a preexisting floor plan that is for family living rather than specifically for child care (see Figure 12.4). Providers make choices about which rooms to use for children's activities. Some choices are obvious, like bathrooms for washing and toileting, kitchens for cooking and perhaps eating. In the other chosen rooms, furniture may need to·be rearranged to make space for play. Some providers create play spaces in the living room, family room, dining room, a spare room, a basement, a converted garage, or a combination of rooms. Furniture may be moved back to make room for children to move around, or it may be rearranged as dividers to create sections for storage and use of specific children's toys and materials. Area rugs also can be used to define **play spaces.** Good use can be made of loft beds as spaces where older children can go to be away from younger ones. On the other hand, cutting off the legs of a loft bed to a safe height makes a low climbing space for younger children as well as perhaps a small area to crawl under. Low shelves make toys accessible to everybody, so in **mixed-age groups,** care must be taken to put only appropriate and safe toys and materials on them that are suitable for even the very youngest child. Mixed-age groups present a special set of challenges. The provider must be diligent about providing a safe environment that allows play and exploration for all ages. That means putting things at different levels for different age groups. Infants and toddlers who still explore by mouthing must be protected from small parts and fragile toys. Activities not suitable for the youngest children can be done at the kitchen table or counter to keep them out

Figure 12.4 Family Child Care Setting

of reach of little hands. The materials must be stored up high. Nobody wants a toddler pulling out the hundred-piece puzzle and chewing on the cardboard pieces. Storage for toys is important so everything isn't out every day. Rotating toys ensures novelty when stored toys are brought out for use and create new interest in old things. Some toys should be rotated and others should be left out all the time to give children a sense of consistency.

What Should Be in the Play Environment

NAEYC Program Standard 2
Curriculum

Age appropriateness is again the key to what toys, equipment, and materials should be in the play environment (see Appendix B). Newborns and very young infants need little in their play environment. A few things to look at are enough. The most interesting object in their environment is the live human face. Recognize that fact, and don't try to replace it with toys, pictures, or even television. Infants need responsive people more than they need any animate or inanimate object. (They also need lots of peace and quiet and minimal stimulation.)

As infants get older, they need a limited variety of soft, washable, brightly colored toys to be looked at or sucked on. Bright scarves and soft beach balls are easy to grip and wave around. Rattles, squeeze toys, plastic keys, and large plastic beads are interesting to babies who are learning reaching and grabbing skills. Toys that are responsive and make noise encourage babies to try different kinds of manipulations.

By nine months of age, infants enjoy a wide variety of objects, including cloth or cardboard books, a variety of hats and other head gear, dolls, plastic or wooden cars and trucks, play telephones, and nesting toys. They also like objects from the adult world—wooden spoons, pots and pans, and real telephones. Crawlers are very interested in exploring, manipulating, and testing the world of objects.

Beginning walkers enjoy push-and-pull toys in addition to all the things already mentioned. They spend more time walking around carrying and dropping toys than manipulating them at this stage, when they are practicing their walking skills. Large, very lightweight blocks are a hit. Children enjoy hauling them around, stacking them, and building enclosures.

By 18 months, toddlers are still enjoying all of the objects mentioned above in addition to playing with more dress-up clothes (besides hats), as well as using available objects for playing pretend, also called **dramatic play.** By making available such things as housekeeping tools and equipment, toy stoves, brooms, plastic dishes, dolls, and steering wheels, you encourage their dramatic play.

Two-year-olds are even more sophisticated in dramatic play and need a larger variety of objects to encourage it. They enjoy small figures, doll houses, snapping blocks, and beads to string. Two-year-olds also enjoy books and can use real ones as well as babyproof ones. Simple puzzles, **lock-and-latch boxes,** button and zipper boards, and other manipulative devices appeal to them. The closer to three the child is, the more the environment can resemble a typical preschool environment.

Toys and Materials for Inside

The list of appropriate toys and materials in the inside environment can be almost endless. Practically anything you can think of that is safe and interesting can become a **learning tool** for infants and toddlers. Here is a general list of things for the inside environment you might not have thought of:

- Beanbags. They can be hauled around, put in things, dumped and thrown. They don't fall off when stacked. (They do sprout when sucked on, though.) Do inspect them every time to be sure there are no holes the beans can leak out. A loose bean can be a safety hazard around a child who is too young to know that they should not go in the mouth.
- Plastic margarine tubs with damp sponges cut in different shapes.
- Blocks of all sizes, especially large, lightweight, plastic-covered foam ones that allow even the youngest toddlers to build, stack, and produce structures and enclosures with them.
- Shoe boxes with lids. Children love to take lids off and put them on again. You can put a surprise inside such as bubble packing or a piece of white tissue paper. *A Safety Hint:* Be sure the bubble packing is safe because it is lightweight plastic. Plastic bags, of course, should be kept away from children at all times, because they can put them over their heads and suffocate. Balloons are another dangerous item. If they burst and children put the pieces in their mouths, they can choke.
- Scarves are fun for all ages, even the very youngest child.
- Books, books, books. Babyproof ones are needed for the youngest children; regular ones are fine for older toddlers.
- Muffin pans with a ball in each cup (a beginner's "puzzle" that even the very youngest child can be successful with).
- Water. The possibilities are endless: scooping, pouring, straining, floating objects (soap, sponges), and washing dolls are a few ways to use water as a learning medium. Remember that children should never be left alone with water. They can drown in just an inch of it.
- Flannel boards with felt pieces. Make them available to toddlers, and watch them explore, experiment, and talk as they move the pieces around.
- Paper to tear. Toddlers have very long attention spans when paper tearing is an activity.[6]

Toys and Materials for Outside

The outside environment should give infants a feeling of being safe and should give toddlers plenty to do. Younger infants need a shaded, grassy, protected place to lie on a blanket. Crawlers need safe spaces to crawl and explore, with textures to feel that don't hurt their knees. A hint for protecting knees comes from a reviewer of this text. Take adult-size tube socks and cut off the toes. Double them and pull them up over crawler's knees to create instant, cheap, knee pads! Crawlers need safe objects to manipulate and mouth. Beginning walkers need smooth surfaces that aren't too challenging as well as push-and-pull toys. Wheel toys are good for this age group, too.

Here are some ideas of what to have in the outside environment for toddlers:

- Truck inner tubes. These are usually free. Don't inflate fully. They make great bouncers.
- Knotted ropes to swing on.
- Trapezes made of a dowel suspended from ropes. Wrap the ends of the dowel with duct tape.
- Sling swings hung very low for the child to swing on belly down.
- Milk crates, big wooden boxes, thick planks, sawhorses, and ladders to make whatever climbing structure strikes your fancy.
- Wheel toys, including riding toys, push toys, and wheelbarrows and wagons to haul things around.
- Small slides they can go down head first.
- Various elevations—especially a hill. The hill is always fairly dry, even after a rain, and it's a challenge to walk up and down it. If you can get grass to grow on the hill, it makes a good place to roll.
- Rocking toys that children can get off and on by themselves.
- A sandbox with all sorts of containers and shovels and funnels, big and small.
- Water in all sorts of containers—little plastic swimming pools, big saucers, cement-mixing pans, baby bathtubs. Make available containers, funnels, hoses, sponges, cloths, and paintbrushes. Painting with water is always a favorite. Remember to always watch children around water— even a small amount can be dangerous.
- Straw provides additional softness for outside. Children can jump into it and haul it around.[7]

Assessing the Quality of an Infant-Toddler Environment

**NAEYC Program
Standard 4**
Assessment

Besides looking at age appropriateness, there are other ways of assessing the quality of a learning environment.

In their book *Dimensions of Teaching-Learning Environments II: Focus on Day Care*, Elizabeth Jones and Elizabeth Prescott defined five dimensions of a learning environment: soft-hard, intrusion-seclusion, high mobility–low mobility, open-closed, simple-complex.[8]

Balancing Soft and Hard

The soft-hard dimension is fairly self-explanatory. Assess this dimension of an infant-toddler environment by asking the question, Is the learning environment full of softness? In their indoor environment, infants and toddlers need thick rugs, soft blankets, stuffed animals, cozy furniture, mattresses, pads, cushions, and laps. In the outside environment, they need grass, sand, water, soft balls, pads, and laps. A soft environment is *responsive*. Many centers tend to have less softness than infants and toddlers need—partly because it is harder to clean soft materials and surfaces and partly because they tend to wear out. Child care homes usually do better than centers regarding providing enough softness, because a home usually has the stuffed furniture and curtains that centers lack.

Is there also some hardness, or is there carpet on every inch of the floor and grass on every inch of the yard? Hard floors and smooth cement present a different feel to the crawler, are easier to walk on for the beginning walker, and make nice noises for the older toddler. Some hard surfaces and hard toys and materials belong in infant-toddler care, but the emphasis should be on softness.

Providing for Intrusion and Seclusion

The environment should provide for both optimum intrusion and seclusion. Desirable intrusion comes as the outdoor environment comes inside, providing interest and novelty. Low windows allow children to see what is happening outside, in back or on the street but protect them from the dangers and noise. Desirable intrusion also occurs as outsiders come into the infants' and toddlers' environment—the telephone repair person, parents picking up children, visitors. Caregivers should maintain an optimum level of intrusion.

Seclusion should be provided so children who need to be alone or with one other child can find spaces to do that. Of course, supervision must always be a concern, but there are ways to make private spaces that adults can still see into. One simple way is to move a couch out from the wall. One center has a series of topless wooden boxes against one wall, with holes to crawl into. The sides screen the crawlers and toddlers from the rest of the room, but adults can see into them.

Louis Torelli talks about the importance of being able to break away from the larger group:

> *A multi-level design, for example, varies the floor height with appropriately scaled platforms, lofts, "nests" and canopies. These mini learning environments set up a landscape for safe exploration in which infants can handle a toy, look at a book, stack blocks, crawl up steps, or simply watch the adults and other children from a cozy, semi-enclosed "private space."* [9]

For some children with special needs, a place to escape what may be for them too much stimulation is imperative. Be aware of these children's needs for seclusion and minimal stimulation and provide for those needs.

Encouraging Mobility

High mobility and low mobility should both be encouraged in an environment for infants and toddlers. Children who are old enough should be able to move around freely. Children should not have to wait for outdoor time to engage in vigorous movement. That means, of course, that group size must be on the small side. Eight is big enough for an infant-toddler group. Two- to three-year-olds can manage in a slightly larger group—twelve, if the environment is well planned. Children with special needs may benefit from being in even smaller groups than other children.

The Open-Closed Dimension

The open-closed dimension has to do with choices. An example of openness in the environment is low open shelves that display toys to choose from. Closed storage is also appropriate to regulate or reduce choices and to get rid of a cluttered atmosphere.

Openness also has to do with the arrangement of furniture and dividers. A good arrangement is to have openness from your waist up so you can supervise, but some feeling of closed space below so infants and toddlers aren't overwhelmed by large expanses.

The open-closed dimension also has to do with whether a toy or material has one right way to do it (like a puzzle, form board, or graduated stacking rings) or whether it encourages all kinds of exploration. A stuffed animal and play dough are both open, as is water play. Children under three need many more open materials and toys than closed ones. Older toddlers may enjoy some closed materials and tasks, but younger ones and infants disregard their intended use and make everything open. They find ways to use all toys and materials (closed ones as well as open ones) that adults never dreamed of. For an infant, the concept of the wrong way to use a toy doesn't exist.

The Simple-Complex Dimension

Simple toys and materials are the best for infants. Ruth Money in "The RIE Early Years 'Curriculum'" says to provide passive toys for active children such as simple, open-ended toys—toys that need to be acted upon for a reaction to happen, not vice versa. "We offer simple objects such as a sturdy cotton scarf that an infant can maneuver . . . empty plastic bottles or lightweight colanders that an infant can lift and look through."[10] Some play materials aren't even toys. An observer at the Pikler Institute reported seeing a basket of children's clothes brought in and put on the floor for the children to play with. They spent a good deal of time trying things on, working on buttoning, exploring and enjoying the clothes.

The complex end of the simple-complex dimension is more of a concern for caregivers with older toddlers. The more complex a material or toy (or combination of materials and toys), the more things toddlers can think of to do with them. Sand, water, and utensils combined present lots more possibilities for action than any one of the three by itself. Caregivers who explore this dimension find that children's attention spans increase when complexity is introduced into the environment.

In "Designing Infant/Toddler Environments," Jim Greenman mentions some additional dimensions to consider when planning learning environments for infants and toddlers.[11]

Scale

Greenman points out that just as adults feel small in environments designed to promote that feeling (such as courtrooms or cathedrals), so infants and toddlers feel small in any environment designed for other age groups. Even a preschool environment will add to the infant's and toddler's feeling of smallness. When they sit in chairs that leave feet dangling, swing in swings they can't get into or out of, or play at chest-high tables, they feel smaller than they need to feel. Infants and toddlers need rooms, ceilings, furniture, and spaces scaled down for them. You want them to feel big and capable, not small and inadequate. The physical environment can make a difference in their self-concept.

Aesthetics

Infants and toddlers should spend their time in a place that is visually appealing. Lighting is an important factor in visual appeal. If possible, avoid the overlit and even effect of fluorescent lighting. Natural and incandescent lighting give variety and add warmth. Color and its different emotional qualities should be considered, as should visual noise. In most infant-toddler environments, there is so much going on—so much to see—that the background should be calm, warm, and neutral. Greenman suggests avoiding the usual riots of color and design when planning walls, surfaces, curtains, and other fabrics. With a neutral backdrop, the people, toys, and materials stand out better, allowing children to find them and focus on them. The children are less distracted.

Acoustics

Noise can be a real problem where infants and toddlers are together in a group. Every effort should be made to lower the noise level and protect the children who need quiet from those who are shouting, crying, or engaging in noisy activities. Group size has a lot to do with noise level, which is an important reason to keep groups small. Dividing the space helps, too, as does providing plenty of softness to absorb sound (carpets, stuffed furniture, pads and cushions, curtains, and acoustical ceilings). Be aware of background noises and their effect on the children and adults as a group and individually. Some lights emit a high-pitched sound that irritates sensitive ears. Noise from fans or other machinery can be soothing or irritating, depending on the sound and the room. When the group contains one or more children with hearing impairments, even greater attention must be given to acoustics if those children are to be able to use whatever residual hearing they have.

Order

Relating to both aesthetics and acoustics is a sense of order. Because infants and toddlers create constant disorder as they spread toys and materials around, pull things apart, and dump and rearrange everything they can get their hands on, the environment needs to provide a sense of basic order that is a contrast to the constant mess on the floor. Room arrangement should contribute to the sense of order. Using furniture, shelves, and screens to divide play space into small

Reflect

Think about the place where you are most comfortable and happy. What are the characteristics of this place? Can you learn anything from your own experience about how to set up an environment for infants and toddlers? Would any of those characteristics be appropriate for that age group?

modules just large enough for two or three children (or slightly more for older toddlers) helps them focus and cuts down on noise (visual as well as auditory). Clear pathways should lead to these play spaces, and each space should contain shelves of toys. In addition, if entrances to spaces offer some motor challenge, such as stepping up or crawling through, children spend less time wandering.

Of course, the room only needs to be divided below the three-foot level, so the whole room is in view at the adult level. That's an important point to make: there are two environments in the room—below three feet and above three feet. To fully understand the children's environment, you need to get down at their level. When you're down there, you'll discover things like baseboards, of which you are probably totally unaware. It is good to get low and take the children's perspective regularly when planning and maintaining an environment for them. Order and accompanying consistency are vital qualities of an environment in which children with visual impairments are served. If the walking paths are cluttered, or the furniture is moved around, a child who has memorized the environment will feel insecure and hesitate to move around in it.

NAEYC Program Standard 4
Assessment

The environment is never determined once and for all. Planning, arranging, evaluating, and rearranging is an ongoing process as caregivers strive for quality and find what works best for them and for the children.

Appropriate Practice

Overview of Development

According to the National Association for the Education of Young Children, a feeling of security allows young babies to use their senses and physical abilities to explore and learn about what's around them, including objects and people. For young infants, security has to do with attachment and trust. The same is true for mobile infants; however, safety becomes a huge concern for babies constantly on the move spurred on by curiosity. They need a safe and rich environment for their quest to learn all they can about the world. Toddlers too need a safe and interesting environment for their explorations, which take on new dimensions as they are constantly trying to discover who they are, what they can do, and who is in charge. Throughout the first three years, the sense of security that was a major issue in early infancy combines with the urge

to explore, and children develop increasing purposefulness in their explorations.

Developmentally Appropriate Practice

Following are samples of developmentally appropriate practices that relate to the physical environment:

Health and Safety

- Adults follow health and safety procedures, including proper hand washing methods and universal precautions to limit the spread of infectious disease. There are clearly written sanitation procedures specific to each area. Instructions on the proper diapering sequence (including use of protective gloves), cleaning cribs and play areas, and food storage and preparation (including dish washing) are displayed on the walls as visual reminders to adults.

- Health records on infants' well-baby checkups, immunizations, and particular health problems are filed separately and confidentially for every infant. Clear policies alert parents to when infants must be excluded from child care for health reasons.
- Caregivers do safety checks of all areas, inside and out, several times a day.
- Emergency evacuation plans are posted on the wall near the infants' daily record charts; a bag of emergency supplies and child emergency forms are immediately accessible. Evacuation drills are practiced on a regular basis.

For Infants

- Adults provide infants with an auditory environment that is not overstimulating or distracting. They choose music and other recordings that infants enjoy.
- Space is arranged so children can enjoy moments of quiet play by themselves, have ample space to roll over and move freely, and can crawl toward interesting objects. Areas for younger infants are separated from those for crawlers to promote the safe interactions of infants in similar stages of development.
- Toys provided are responsive to the child's actions: a variety of grasping toys that require different types of manipulation; a varied selection of skill-development materials, including nesting and stacking materials, activity boxes, and containers to be filled and emptied; a variety of balls, bells, and rattles.
- A variety of safe household items that infants can use as play materials are available, including measuring cups, wooden spoons, unbreakable bowls, and cardboard boxes.
- Mobile infants have an open area where balls, push-and-pull toys, wagons, and other equipment encourage free movement and testing of large-muscle skills and coordination. Low climbing structures, ramps, and steps are provided. Structures are well padded and safe for exploration.
- Open shelves within infants' reach contain toys of similar type, spaced so that infants can make choices. Caregivers group materials for related activities on different shelves.
- An outside play space adjacent to the infant area includes sunny and shaded areas. It is enclosed by protective fencing. The ground around climbing structures and in some of the open space is covered with resilient, stable surfacing for safety, making it easy for mobile infants to push wagons and ride on toys. There are soft areas where young infants can lie on quilts.

For Toddlers

- The environment and schedule have enough predictability and repetition to allow toddlers to form expectations, repeatedly practice emerging skills, and feel the security of a familiar routine.
- Caregivers organize the space into interest or activity areas, including areas for concentrated small-group play, being alone, art/water/sand and other messy activities, dramatic play, and construction. The activity areas are separated by low partitions, shelves, or sitting benches, making it difficult for running toddlers to disturb toddlers engaged in concentrated play, and creating clear traffic patterns.
- Children have daily opportunities for exploratory activity, such as water and sand play, painting, and clay or play dough manipulation.
- A child-size sink with a good supply of paper towels is located near areas designated for messy activities, so toddlers learn that cleaning up and washing their hands follow any messy activity.
- Children have many opportunities for active, large-muscle play both indoors and outdoors.

(continued)

Appropriate Practice (continued)

- Each toddler has a cot and bedding that are personally labeled. Getting his or her own blanket or special stuffed toy is part of the child's nap routine.

Individually Appropriate Practice

Following are samples of individually appropriate practices that relate to the physical environment:

- Adults ensure that every child receives nurturing, responsive care.
- Adults create an "inclusive" classroom, making sure that spatial organization, materials, and activities enable all children to participate actively.

Individualizing is a vital requirement if each and every child is to receive what he or she needs from the environment and people in it. For some children, environmental adaptations and adult interventions are necessary for caregiving routines as is encouraging free play.

Culturally Appropriate Practice

Following are samples of culturally appropriate practice that relate to the physical environment:

- Caregivers work in partnership with parents, communicating daily to build mutual understanding and trust and to ensure the welfare and optimal development of the infant.
- Caregivers listen carefully to what parents say about their children, seek to understand parents' goals and preferences, and are respectful of cultural and family differences.
- Caregivers and parents confer in making decisions about how best to support children's development or handle problems or differences of opinion as they arise.

Much of the way the environment is set up in this chapter has to do with stressing independent exploration and self-help skills. In families where interdependence is more important than independence, the setup of the environment may not make much sense. It is not okay to just use parent education to get parents to see the approach in this book as the only right way. Remember that developmentally appropriate practice mandates that professionals work in partnership with parents and work to build mutual understanding and trust. The goal is to ensure the welfare and optimal development of the child. Identity issues can be at stake, so it is imperative that caregivers seek to understand and respect cultural differences as well as involve parents in decisions about what's best for their child.

Source: S. Bredekamp and C. Copple, eds., *Developmentally Appropriate Practice in Early Childhood Programs*, rev. ed. (Washington, D.C.: National Association for the Education of Young Children, 1997).

Appropriate Practice in Action

Look back on The Principles in Action scene on page 269 in terms of appropriate practice.

- Go through the items under the "Developmentally Appropriate Practice" section for toddlers and think about the scene. Obviously you don't have the whole picture, but from what you have read, which practices are compatible with what the family child care provider is doing?
- What about the items under the "Individually Appropriate Practice" section? How many of those are compatible with what you read the provider is doing?
- After reading the last paragraph under the "Culturally Appropriate Practice" section, consider that all parents may not have the same goals as the family child care provider for free exploration, making discoveries, and problem solving as independently as possible. If Austin's parents don't have the same goals, what can or should the provider do?

Summary

- A number of factors need to be considered to create a safe and healthy environment for infants and toddlers, including:
  - o Nutrition
  - o Feeding infants
  - o Feeding toddlers
- The learning environment is made up of a play area plus the spaces for caregiving activities such as:
  - o Eating
  - o Sleeping
  - o Diapering
  - o Toileting
- Developmental appropriateness is important for safety reasons but also to facilitate learning.
  - o What is appropriate for infants is different from what is appropriate for toddlers.
  - o Mixed-age groups, which in family child care homes provide a special set of challenges for making the environment work for everybody.
  - o The toys and materials that are developmentally appropriate vary for each age group.
  - o What should be in the play environment?
- Assessment of any infant toddler environment is an ongoing process and requires taking into consideration the factors already mentioned plus looking at five dimensions and four additional considerations, including:
  - o Soft-hard dimension
  - o Intrusion-seclusion dimension
  - o High mobility–low mobility dimension
  - o Open-closed dimension
  - o Simple-complex dimension
  - o Scale
  - o Aesthetics
  - o Acoustics
  - o Order

Online Resources

Go to the Online Learning Center at **www.mhhe.com/itc7e** to access the student study guide that includes quizzes, practice with key terms, and a review of chapter content; links to websites related to the chapter; and additional resources.

Key Terms

dramatic play 272
learning tools 273
lock-and-latch boxes 272
mixed-age groups 270
play spaces 270
structure 262

Thought/Activity Questions

1. Using the checklists in this chapter, evaluate an infant-toddler environment.
2. Make your own checklist using the key points under the section on assessing the quality of an infant-toddler environment. Use that checklist to observe an infant-toddler program.
3. Figures 12.1, 12.2, and 12.3 show center-based program environments. Draw a layout of a home (it could be your own home) and design spaces in it that would accommodate a group of children of varying ages, including infants and toddlers.

For Further Reading

S. Aronson, "Sudden Infant Death Syndrome," *Exchange* 153, September/October 2003, p. 67.

Susan Aronson and Patricia M. Spahr, *Healthy Young Children: A Manual for Programs* (Washington D.C.: National Association for the Education of Young Children, 2002).

C. Coughlan, "Using the RIE Approach in a Family Day Care Home," in *Authentic Relationships in Group Care for Infants and Toddlers: Resources for Infant Educarers (RIE) Principles into Practice*, edited by S. Petrie and S. Owen (London and Philadelphia: Jessica Kingsley Publishers, 2005), pp. 69–82.

D. Curtis and Carter, M. *Designs for Living and Learning: Transforming Early Childhood Environments*. (St. Paul, MN: Redleaf, 2003).

Magda Gerber and Andrea King, "Modifying the Environment to Respond to the Changing Needs of the Child," *Educaring* 6(1), Winter 1985, pp. 1–2.

Jim Greenman, *Caring Spaces, Learning Places: Children's Environments That Work* (Redmond, Wash.: Exchange Press, 1988).

J. Ronald Lally and Jay Stewart, *Infant/Toddler Caregiving: A Guide to Setting Up Environments* (Sacràmento, Calif.: Far West Laboratory for Educational Development and California Department of Education, 1990).

J. Lumeng, "What Can We Do to Prevent Childhood Obesity?," *Zero to Three* 25(3), January 2005, pp. 13–19.

S. A. Mulligan, "Assistive Technology: Supporting the Participation of Children with Disabilities," *Young Children* 58(6), November 2003, pp. 50–52.

Anita R. Olds, "Places of Beauty," in *Play as a Medium for Learning and Development*, edited by D. Bergen (Olney, Md.: Association for Childhood Education International, 1998), pp. 123–127.

Louis Torelli and Charles Durett, *Landscapes for Learning: Designing Group Care Environments for Infants, Toddlers, and Two-Year-Olds* (Berkeley, Calif.: Spaces for Children, 1998).

F. R. Vokmar and L. A. Wiesner, *Healthcare for Children on the Autism Spectrum: A Guide to Medical, Nutritional and Behavioral Issues* (Bethesda, Md: Woodbine, 2004).

L. Wessel and J. Span, "The Chronic Care Model: A Collaborative Approach to Preventing and Treating Asthma in Infants and Young Children," *Zero to Three* 25(3), January 2005, pp. 20–27.

L. C. Whitehead and S. I. Ginsberg, "Creating a Family-Like Atmosphere in Child Care Settings: All the More Difficult in Large Child Care Centers," *Young Children* 54(2), 1999, pp. 4–10.

chapter 13

The Social Environment

Focus Questions

After reading this chapter you should be able to answer the following questions:

1 What makes up the social environment in an infant-toddler program and how can you *see* it?

2 Why is identity formation of special concern in infant-toddler programs?

3 What is self-image and what factors contribute to a positive self-image?

4 What are the influences on gender identity?

5 Why is it important to use positive approaches to discipline and guidance, and what are some examples of positive approaches?

6 Why is a section called "Modeling Self-Esteem by Taking Care of Yourself" included in a chapter on the social environment?

What Do You See?

The caregiver is new to the early childhood field and this is her first day in the infant room. She goes around and introduces herself to the children starting with Brian. "Oh what a big strong boy you are," she says and she picks him up and holds him high in the air. When she notices that he doesn't look scared, she compliments his bravery. Next she approaches Brianna and leans over her smiling gently. "What a pretty little girl," she says, lightly stroking her cheek. "And look at that outfit you have on!" The teacher watching her wonders what she will say when she approaches the next baby who is dressed in green and there is no way to tell gender.

Maybe you too are wondering. What did you notice about the interactions this adult had with these two babies? She is tremendously focused on gender. It's hard to imagine how she will be able to have a conversation with a baby if she doesn't know the gender. Maybe she will ask. Gender identity is one of the components of the social environment and will be discussed later in the chapter when we revisit this scene.

**NAEYC Program
Standard 2 and 3**
Curriculum and
Teaching

The social environment is harder to talk about than the physical environment because it is far less visible. You can stand and look around the physical environment to evaluate it. But you have to catch behaviors as they happen in order to see the social environment.

A good deal of Part 1 and some of Part 2 focus on the social environment without calling it that. The environmental chart in Appendix B outlines the social environment. This chapter discusses aspects of the social environment that haven't been discussed elsewhere.

Identity Formation

Because in the past most infants and toddlers were at home or in kinship care, not much thought was given to their identity formation. It was a process that just happened naturally. Times have changed; great numbers of infants and toddlers are now in out-of-home care, and their identity development has begun to be a concern. In the past, identity formation wasn't such an issue because children didn't usually go into child care until after they were three. Families sent children off to preschool programs where no one talks about identity formation, because by age three children have a working sense of self. They can state what they like and what they don't like. They have inclinations and attitudes that are part of their identity. Infants and toddlers are a different matter, because their identity has not yet begun to jell. They are in the process of forming a sense of self. They aren't quite sure yet who they are, what they like, and where they belong. Their identity formation comes as they absorb the images of themselves they see reflected in their caregivers' eyes. They learn by identifying with their caregivers and imitating them. They can pick up their caregivers' personal traits and attitudes. Infants and toddlers learn from caregivers' perceptions of how people act in different situations and how people act toward them. They observe how emotions are expressed. From all these observations, infants and toddlers figure out how they appear to others. They begin to develop attitudes about how they and others should be treated. They also learn what to feel under what circumstances. From countless daily little interactions with their caregivers, infants take in numerous impressions and incorporate them into their identity. For the first time in history, great numbers of those caregivers are not family members.

The Principles in Action

Principle 1 Involve infants and toddlers in things that concern them. Don't work around them or distract them to get the job done faster.

Kaleb is the only dark-skinned child in the toddler center. The director is most worried about his identity formation, and staff members have had several antibias trainings. She is pleased to see how staff members are working with their various biases and how equitably they treat all the children. Today, however, there is a substitute who has had no training, and while the director is watching her, she picks up what she assumes are some unconscious behaviors. First, she notices that when children need a tissue, the substitute gets one and wipes their noses, that is, until Kaleb needs one. She takes the box to Kaleb, offers a tissue, and suggests he wipe his nose. Then she holds out the wastebasket for him to throw the used tissue in. After seeing the tissue episode, the director decides to stay in the room and pay closer attention to the substitute. Diapering presents another scene that disturbs the director. The substitute diapers the children she is supposed to, all but Kaleb. When it's his turn, she says she needs to take her break. The director asks her to diaper Kaleb first. When she does, she hands him a toy to play with and diapers mechanically, ignoring the child and focusing only on the task. She doesn't say a word to him and takes half the time that she took with the other children. The director asks another caregiver to take primary responsibility for Kaleb the rest of the day.

1. What messages do you think Kaleb might have been picking up from the substitute?
2. How might the substitute's behaviors have influenced Kaleb's ideas about himself, his body, and its products?
3. Should the director have done more than she did?
4. If she had confronted the substitute with her observations, how do you think the substitute might have responded?
5. Do you have some feelings about this scene?

According to J. Ronald Lally, the following are lessons that infants and toddlers learn from their caregivers that may become part of the sense of self.[1]

- What to fear
- Which behaviors are appropriate
- How messages are received and acted upon
- How successful they are at getting their needs met by others
- What emotions and intensity level of emotions they can safely display
- How interesting they are

The responsibility for caregivers, administrators, and policy makers is enormous. No one can afford to ignore the effect of caregivers on infants' and toddlers' sense of self. The society may see those who care for the youngest children as just baby-sitters, but the reality is that they are, as Virginia Satir, author and therapist, used to say, "people-makers." If caregivers are untrained, underpaid, and working in substandard programs, there's no telling what the results of their people-making might be.

Identity is made up of many facets, one of which is **self-concept.** An important reason for studying the emotional environment is to bring clarity to the way a child's identity is formed by the people with whom the child interacts. We start with a look at the environmental influences on self-concept. The self-concept, which relates to attachment, is made up of the child's perceptions of and feelings about himself or herself. Self-concept comes from body image as well as cultural and gender identification. The social environment, the way a child is treated by adults and children, affects self-concept and influences the degree of self-esteem.

Attachment

NAEYC Program Standard 1
Relationships

The prerequisite for high self-esteem in infants and toddlers is attachment. From attachment comes the feeling "I matter to somebody; who I am and what I do is important because somebody cares." All the self-esteem activities in the world won't make a difference if the child's basic attitude is "Nobody cares about me."

"Caring" in the sense of attachment has to happen at home, but it is important in day care, too. It seems as though "caring" is what infant-toddler programs are all about because of all the caregiving focus. But "caring" the feeling is different from "caring" the action (taking care of). You can care for a child, wash his bottom, feed his face, without really caring for him. And you can't *make* yourself care for him (in the feeling sense). You can make yourself respect the child, and that may help the caring feeling come. Respecting the child will help you deal with all of him, not treating him as a bottom or a face, and in turn he may feel better about himself and reveal more of himself to you. That may help the caring feeling come.

What If You Don't Feel Attached? But what can you do if you are respectful and you still find a child doesn't "matter to you"? First of all, don't blame yourself. Perhaps you and the child just don't hit it off—you have personality differences; you clash. If you're in a center, it's possible that another caregiver has a different feeling about this child, and that's all that's needed. Someone cares about him. It doesn't have to be you, as long as you continue to be respectful.

If you're the only caregiver of a child you don't care about, that's a real problem, but it's not unsolvable. Here are a couple of ideas for what to do.

Observe the child. Step back and really pay attention to her every move. Try to understand her. See if you can view the world from her perspective. Do a "child study" in which you make a series of short observations over a period of time, and then put them together and examine them for evidence of growth. Carry a notebook around in your pocket, and every chance you get make notes about what you see this child doing. Be very detailed and specific. Note body posture, quality of movement, facial expressions, and tone of vocalizations. Try hard to be very objective—don't judge; just observe. If you get good at stepping into and out of an **observation mode,** you can do it quickly and effectively many times during the course of a day. In addition, at the end of the day, write some anecdotal records—notes about what you remember about the child that day and what you remember about your interactions with her. These reflection records as well as on-the-spot observations will provide you with material for your child study in the course of a few months. Observations alone may help your feeling for this child grow.

Observation can have powerful effects. One student who was required to do an extensive child study chose a child she didn't like very much. She reported that it was the best choice she could have made because after she really got to know this child and began to understand him better, her feeling for him changed.

Studying a child is a very rational approach to take—a left-brain way of approaching the problem. Here's another idea—a right-brain approach—to help you increase your ability to care about a particular child. Use visualization. Spend some quiet time each day visualizing yourself interacting with this child in a truly caring mode. If she has behaviors that get in your way, try imagining the child without those behaviors. See her not as she *is* but as she *could be*. Here's a sample of how a visualization can work:

You work with a two-and-a-half-year-old who doesn't appeal to you at all. She is very verbal, and she has a loud, piercing voice that becomes even louder when she is angry, which is 90 percent of the time. She is bossy to the other children and reports every little misdeed to any nearby adult. When you ask her to do something, she's very likely to say no. If you try to persuade her, she stands with her feet apart and screams, "You can't make me." All of those behaviors bother you, and the more you try to change them, the worse they get. The days she is absent are a big relief. You notice a big difference not only in you but also in the other children.

One day you decide you have to do something about your feelings about this child. You've heard about visualization—a form of meditation. You're dubious, but at this point you'll try anything. It can't hurt.

You take 10 minutes before bedtime to sit quietly, in a relaxed position, and clear your mind. As a person who is used to meditating, this part is easy. But then it gets harder.

First you try to visualize the child without the behaviors that bother you so much, but nothing comes. You just can't seem to disconnect her from the way she behaves. So you try a different tack. You decide if you can't even *imagine* her different, you'd better work on yourself first.

So you spend your 10 minutes imagining the little girl as she behaves every day, but you visualize yourself not reacting to her. It's hard. At first you are like a statue, standing still and cold. You don't like that image very much. After a short time of cold silence, you notice that your image has become more like a wooden puppet. In your mind's eye, you watch as the child screams, tattles, defies you, and bosses, and you just dangle from your strings with a blank smile on your face. You don't like that image very much either, but you continue to let your visualization lead where it will. You watch in surprise as the wooden puppet changes before your eyes to a strong, sturdy tree. Now you're in a comfortable image (though it seems a little weird to you). You feel good as you respond to the wind of the little girl's voice—your leaves rustle, your branches bend, but it doesn't affect you. She tries harder to affect you. She seems to want to blow you over, but your roots are deep and your trunk is strong. You bend slightly, but you come back upright as soon as she stops. She tries harder. She gives up and walks away. You end the visualization.

For the next few nights you try the same visualization. You're a tree and she's herself. You practice withstanding her onslaught without getting caught up in it. You do nothing different during the day, but for some reason her behavior isn't bothering you so much. You wonder if it is changing or if you just feel it less.

One night after you have been doing this for a few days, 10 minutes at a time, a change in your visualization surprises you. The child has been frantically trying to get to you, trying to do damage, but all is in vain. She is kicking your trunk (which you can't feel because of your thick bark) when suddenly she throws her arms around your trunk, slides to the ground, and lies there sobbing pathetically, one little hand clutching at an exposed root. The little girl who rises off the ground is a different child—though she looks the same. Now at last you can imagine her without the behaviors that were so much a part of her before. You change out of your tree shape and sit down on the ground and hold her.

The next time your visualization is very different. You can now imagine yourself interacting with her during the day, and the behaviors are gone. Sometimes it's hard to see her, but other times the images come quite easily. You notice that she is very insecure at times, and other times she seems to need attention very badly. At one point you are astounded to take a close look at her face and discover your own!

Meanwhile, during the day you've gained a deeper understanding of her behavior, seeing the scared, uncertain, powerless little girl who's behind the defiant, bossy one. Her behavior hasn't changed much, but yours has. No longer do you react so strongly. No longer do you dislike her so intensely.

Eventually you begin to find ways to help her both gain social skills and feel better about herself. You've learned something about this child—and something about yourself too. You give up the visualization, satisfied that it has done its job.

Of course, visualization doesn't work for everyone, but we all carry around in our heads unconscious images that influence our expectations of others as well as our own behavior toward them. These images can be very powerful, and visualization is one way of clarifying them in order to change them.

Self-Image

Children are influenced not only by the images of them that adults carry around but also by the image they have of themselves. Part of self-concept is **self-image**—that is, one's own perception of oneself that relates to body image and awareness. **Body awareness** is a major task of infants and toddlers and grows as their motor skills develop. As they learn what capabilities their bodies have, they develop an image of themselves. You can watch a nine-month-old backing down off a couch he has crawled up on and get an idea of his body awareness. The child with good body awareness knows where he is in space and how far to back before putting his feet over the edge of the couch. He can guess how far it is to the floor, so he is able to slide off and remain in control.

When working with children who have physical disabilities, it is important to take their body awareness and self-image into account. If you focus only on their lack of skills, they'll have some difficulties with self-concept. Pay special attention to whatever abilities they have, emphasizing what they *can do* rather than concentrating on what they can't do.

As children develop competence, their self-concept expands. They take pride in each accomplishment. Thus the thrust for independence and the development of self-help skills relate to body image and the growth of self-concept.

NAEYC Program Standard
Curriculum

Cultural Identity

Cultural identity is also a part of self-concept. The culture we come from influences every detail of every action of our lives, including how close we stand to people, where we touch them, gestures we make, what we eat, how we talk and think, how we regard time and space—how we look at the world. You bring your culture to your work with infants and toddlers. You also absorb the culture of the program itself, or if you don't absorb it, you are influenced by it. You are teaching infants and toddlers culture every day in everything you do. In a program where the children and caregivers are of the same culture, and it is compatible with the culture of the program, there is real consistency. Those children don't think about culture—it's so much a part of them.

In fact, few of us think about culture until we encounter someone who comes from a different one. This can happen to infants and toddlers quite early when they go into day care. The question is, How does exposure to different cultures affect infants and toddlers? What do they do with a second or third set of cultural messages? This is no new phenomenon: Throughout history members of one culture have been involved in raising the children of another. A modern example, outside of child-care programs, is the au pair system popular among some well-off American families. A young woman, the au pair, comes from another country to live with the family and be a nanny. Her culture may be similar to or very different from that of the parents.

One theory is that children who are raised biculturally or multiculturally have a greater understanding and acceptance of differences in people. They may also be more willing to see beyond cultural differences and relate to people as individuals, regardless of their cultural differences. This is the theory behind the push at present for multicultural education. The goal in multicultural education is to help children appreciate their own culture and cultural differences. The advocates of multicultural education see it as a way to fight bias of all kinds and racism in particular.

A Multicultural Infant-Toddler Curriculum But what is a **multicultural curriculum** in an infant-toddler center? It is easier to talk about what it is not than what it is. It is not pictures stuck on walls, rotating ethnic foods, or celebration of holidays. Infants and toddlers do not gain much understanding of culture from those devices, though you may choose to include those components in your

Part of self-concept is the awareness the child has of herself.

program for various reasons, including your own enjoyment and satisfaction or that of the parents.

A more meaningful multicultural approach comes from learning from parents how their culture is different from yours and/or that of the program. Some of this you may be able to just observe. It helps to ask. By asking, you may open up a dialogue about cultural differences. All of this may turn out to be very interesting and valuable to you.

However, none of this makes a real difference to the infants and toddlers in your care. What does matter when you care for children from a culture different from your own is that you listen to what their parents want for them in their day-to-day care. This means discussion of caregiving practices. It also means potential conflict when your beliefs and values clash with those of the parents. For example, take a parent who does not understand your goals for each child to become independent. She may insist on spoon-feeding her child way beyond an age you feel is appropriate. Or take a parent who stresses independence beyond your own goals. She may ask you to allow a toddler to sleep or eat whenever or wherever he or she wants without regard to any kind of schedule. Or a parent may want to keep siblings together even though the age difference makes your environment inappropriate for one or the other. Or a parent may ask you to help her with toileting her child even though the child is far younger than you think appropriate. Or a parent may ask you to dress or not to dress his or her child in a certain way, or in certain kinds of clothes you don't approve of. All of these can be cultural issues.

A true multicultural infant-toddler approach in such cases would be to invite parent input and then figure out what to do with it. Some requests are easy to respond to immediately; others take more talking, clarifying, understanding, and perhaps negotiating. Still others go against your very deeply held values and beliefs, and no amount of talking or negotiating will convince you to comply with the parent's wishes. Sometimes when a serious conflict like this occurs, the parent has other choices for child care, in which case he or she may find someone who is more able to comply. But often the parent has no other choice, so difficulties arise.

One way some caregivers get around these difficulties is to stop discussing the issue, pretend to go along with the parent just to keep peace, and then keep doing what they believe in when the parent leaves. That approach can leave the child in the position of coping with a culturally assaultive environment while in child care. Imagine yourself in a culturally assaultive environment. How would that feel?

It is much better to work continually toward resolving the conflict. It's good practice for all of us to open up and expand our cultural awareness by being persistent in resolving difficult dilemmas that arise when parent beliefs and practices conflict with caregiver beliefs and practices. It may be that you and the parent will come to an agreement that it won't hurt the child if day care is one way and home is another way. Or it may be that together you'll find some middle ground. It may even be that you'll change your practices once you understand the parent's point of view, or she will change hers when she understands your point of view.

Gender Identity

Part of self-concept is **gender identity.** Most children are aware quite early whether they are a boy or a girl, and their feelings about their gender influence how they perceive themselves. You can see one way they learn about gender if you recall the behavior of the newcomer in the scene at the beginning of the chapter. Adults influence children's ideas of how they are supposed to be according to their gender, and this influence starts early. Remember that Brian was mainly noticed for his size, strength, and bravery, while Brianna was only acknowledged for her sweetness and appearance. Even without the words, the differential way each was touched and handled gives a strong message.

> **Reflect**
>
> Imagine yourself in a culturally assaultive environment. If you can't imagine such an environment, pick an environment you feel most comfortable in and imagine its opposite. How would it feel to spend a good part of your waking hours in such an environment? What relationship do your own imaginings and experience have to caring for culturally diverse children?

Throughout this book we have mentioned sex role stereotyping. The information has come mostly in the form of questions designed to heighten your awareness of sex role stereotyping.

Children can grow up with a severely limited view of their capabilities and potentials by being taught narrow sex roles. These teachings start early, as shown in the opening scene. The expectations even at birth can be very different for a boy baby than for a girl baby. Those expectations influence a child's self-concept. If you expect boys to grow to be strong, brave, unemotional, and capable, you act differently toward them than you do toward girls. If you expect girls to be sweet, kind, attractive, emotional, and not too smart, they are likely to live up to your expectations.

Reflect

Observe yourself interacting with infants and toddlers. Do you treat boys differently from girls? If yes, why? If no, why not?

You can see for yourself how people treat boys differently from the way they treat girls with a simple observation. Just keep track of what adults, especially strangers, say to very young children. They are much more likely to comment to girls on appearance and clothes. Boys are noticed for their deeds and less often for appearance.

Children learn about what is expected of their gender by such simple, innocent remarks. They also learn from the clothes they are given to wear. (It's hard to crawl and climb in a dress.) Toys give messages too. When boys are encouraged to play with tools, construction sets, and doctors' kits, they get one message. When girls are given dolls, play dishes, and makeup kits, they get another message. Children learn about expected gender roles from television, books, and above all, role models. If the family child care provider waits until her husband gets home to fix the screen door and makes it clear that she never touches tools, she is giving a message. When centers leave their tricycles unrepaired until a man comes on the scene, they too are giving a message.

If current trends continue, the children in infant and toddler programs today will grow up into a world of a variety of job opportunities for both sexes. The days when men and women were restricted from certain jobs are mostly in the past. Yet if children grow up with a limited view of their capabilities because of the narrow sex roles taught to them, their freedom to qualify for these jobs will be limited.

Figure 13.1 offers four ideas about how to offer both the boys and the girls you work with a broad view of their gender roles. First, be aware of treating boys and girls differently. Do you offer more support and sympathy to girls when they get hurt and expect boys to "tough it out"? Do you help girls when they need it

Figure 13.1 Strategies for Expanding Children's Ideas about Gender Roles

1. Be careful not to treat boys and girls differently. Observe yourself carefully!

2. Model expanded gender roles yourself.

3. Avoid exposing children to media messages that show stereotyped gender roles.

4. Watch your language so you don't link occupations to gender.

and wait for boys to figure things out on their own? Do you offer girls dolls and boys blocks, or do you encourage and support both sexes to play with all the toys? Do you touch girls more than boys (or vice versa)? Do you talk to girls more than boys (or vice versa)?

Second, model expanded gender roles. If you're a woman, how often have you tried to fix something, or do you just put it aside, convinced you don't know how? Can you check your own oil? (Learn—it's easy.) If you're a man and you're reading this book, you've already expanded your gender role. Can you think of ways to expand it further?

Third, avoid exposing children to media messages that teach narrow gender roles. We hope the infants and toddlers in your program aren't watching any television, so you don't need to worry about that medium. Find books and pictures that show strong, capable women as well as nurturing men in a variety of occupational roles.

Finally, avoid linking occupations to gender—say "police officer" rather than "policeman," "firefighter" rather than "fireman." These are simple changes, but they make a difference.

Self-Concept and Discipline

The way you guide and control behavior can influence children's ideas of and feelings about themselves. The discussion here will center around ways to discipline that don't tear down self-esteem.

Much of what is appropriate discipline for infants and toddlers comes about naturally through meeting individual needs in a timely fashion and through setting up an environment that is appropriate to their age level. If they can't get to hot stoves, they won't touch them. If they can't reach radio knobs, they won't turn them. If they have no access to steep stairs, you don't have to find ways to prevent them from climbing them. To a great extent, the environment sets the limits.

However, you do have to protect the children from hurting each other, and sometimes you do have to prevent them from ruining toys and furniture by banging, chewing, and throwing. You can do this by using a strategy called **redirection.** You redirect the child from what he shouldn't be doing to something similar that is okay to do. For example, if a child is throwing a toy car, give her a ball to throw. The closer the action is to what she is already doing, the easier it is to redirect. Redirection is close to distraction but not quite the same. Distraction is often used to keep a child from feeling emotion, while redirection is more about using the energy in an acceptable rather than an unacceptable way. Distraction is manipulative in a way that redirection is not. Sometimes redirection doesn't work and you must firmly but gently physically restrain the child (if a word won't do it) and removing the object or the child if he or she threatens to continue this behavior. If you remain calm and gently persistent, you won't be as apt to trigger rebellion as you would if you issue sharp warnings or commands. You do need persistence because older infants and young toddlers continually

Reflect

What do you remember about the way you were disciplined as a young child. Can you remember a situation that hurt your self-esteem?

VIDEO OBSERVATION 13

Child in Sandbox (Redirection)

See Video Observation 13: Child in Sandbox (Redirection) for an illustration of a situation where guidance is needed. You'll see a girl sitting in the sand who keeps trying to put a sand-filled spoon in her mouth. Watch how the adult handles this situation. This is an example of redirection.

Questions

- How did you feel about the kind of redirection the adult was using? Would you have done it differently?
- What other kinds of approaches could have been used in this situation?
- What effect do you think this kind of redirection might have on the child's self-concept? How about the other approaches you came up with—might they have had a different effect on the child's self-concept?

To view this clip, go to www.mhhe.com/itc7e. Click on Student Edition, select Chapter 13, and click on Video Observation.

test limits. That's how they find out about you and the world they live in. Once they're satisfied you really mean it, the test is over—until the next situation anyway. The way to preserve their good feelings about themselves as well as their sense of power while you enforce the limits is to avoid shaming, belittling, blaming, or criticizing them.

Don't Punish or Scold Punishment, scolding, and anger have no place in the discipline of infants and toddlers. You may, of course, feel and express anger at times when you are not able to control the behavior of the children you care for. That's normal and doesn't hurt anything. However, recognize that the anger is personal. Don't blame the children for it, and don't use anger to control their behavior. Find other ways to get the effect you want from them. When you use anger to get your way, the children will quickly pick up this behavior, and you'll find them trying it on you.

Punishment damages self-esteem. There are other ways to change undesirable behavior that not only leave self-esteem intact but that also actually enhance self-concept as children learn to control their own behavior and feel good about getting attention for staying within the limits and exhibiting prosocial behavior.

Define Unacceptable Behavior   Before you consider ways of changing behavior, you must first define what is undesirable behavior. The child's age will influence your definition. For example, the screams of a young infant are not undesirable behavior; they are communication and must be attended to. Touching and mouthing objects are not undesirable behaviors in older infants; they have a need to touch and mouth. Experimentation and exploration are not undesirable behaviors in toddlers; that's how they learn about the world.

No One "Right" Way   When considering alternatives to punishment, you have to realize that no one approach works for all the children all the time. What works depends on the child, the situation, and the origins of the behavior. For example, if a certain toddler behavior has in the past been rewarded by adult attention, it has been learned. Therefore, the approach is to "unlearn" it by removing the reward. At the same time, you must be sure to replace the attention the child has been receiving when you remove it from its connection with a particular behavior. Sometimes adults forget that there must be two parts to this approach of removing the reward from undesirable behavior. The children *need* the attention you're denying them. Find other ways to give it to them. Also be sure before you try this approach that you determine whether this behavior is communicating some other unfulfilled need. If that is the case, don't ignore the behavior; regard it as communication and fulfill the need.

Some behaviors are expressions of feelings. Accept the feelings. Help the child learn to express them in socially acceptable ways. What is considered an acceptable expression of feelings varies with the culture. Some people see screaming in anger as healthy; others find screaming unacceptable.

Changing Behavior in Toddlers   Here is a summary of six approaches to changing undesirable behavior in toddlers:

1. Teach socially acceptable behavior. Modeling is one of your most effective teaching methods. Children naturally pick up your behavior, so make sure it is the behavior you want to teach.
2. Ignore the behavior you want the child to change. Often it is being done for your benefit. (But of course don't ignore behavior that threatens safety or communicates a need—a hungry, crying baby needs to be fed, not ignored.)
3. Pay attention to behavior that is socially acceptable. Praise children publicly for being gentle with one another, for taking care of toys and

NAEYC Program Standard 2
Curriculum

equipment. Make a big fuss over desirable behavior (not undesirable behavior).

4. Restructure the situation. Perhaps there are too many choices of things to do, or not enough. Either situation can cause infants and toddlers to act in less than desirable ways. Maybe two children need to be separated for a while.

5. Prevent harmful behavior from happening. Stop the hitting before it occurs. Catch the biting before the teeth sink in. The strong reaction children get from the children they hurt can be very rewarding. That reward is cut off when the action is not allowed to happen. Such behaviors will decrease if you stay on your toes instead of letting them happen and then dealing with them afterward.

6. Redirect the energy when appropriate. When you must restrict a child, give several other choices of things he or she can do. ("I won't let you throw the block, but you can throw the pillow or the soft ball." "I won't let you bite Maria, but you can bite this washcloth or this plastic ring.")

"Time-Out"? A word about **time-out.** Time out—that is removing the child who is misbehaving—is sometimes used as a blanket approach by caregivers who don't know any other methods of guiding behavior. Marian Marion (*Guidance of Young Children*, Columbus, OH: Merrill, 1999) sees time out as punishing and inappropriate. It is controversial because it is misunderstood and often overused. Removing a child from a situation he can't handle is different from time out. Sometimes toddlers are out of control because they are being overstimulated. Removing an out-of-control toddler to a quieter place for a short time helps him or her regain composure and control. Confining children, even by making them sit in a chair, as a punishment for an infraction of a rule is not the same as helping them gain control when they need to.

Once you perceive that a particular child has this need occasionally, you can help her learn to judge the situation and make the decision to leave on her own. The ultimate goal of discipline, after all, is to turn it over to the individual. Your approaches to discipline should lead eventually to self-discipline—the establishment of inner controls.

Cultural Notes Feelings for or against the use of time-out can relate to cultural differences. When privacy is a cultural value, a child may be taken away from the group, (whether it is called time out or not) so the child can have time and space alone to gather himself or herself back together and regain control. This approach is used by those who stress independence and individuality. Not all cultures see the benefits of stressing those two characteristics. For some, belonging in the group is more important than the notion of individuality. From a collectivist orientation, time-out is like shunning and is an extreme punishment. No matter how kindly it is done, and with what intentions, cutting the

Talking is part of guiding behavior and can strengthen the link between positive self-concept and discipline.

child off from the group is punishment. It's important to be sensitive to differences in perspective.

Another difference in perspective relates to notions of authority. In her book *Other People's Children*, Lisa Delpit discusses the problem of the way some European-Americans speak to children as compared with how some African-Americans speak to them.[2] The soft-spoken request for a certain behavior is not recognized by some children as a command. They are more used to hearing the command form of the verb (tempered or not): "Sit down, please." "Stop banging your cup." These children may not pay attention to other forms of guiding behavior. A pleasant voice saying "It's not safe to stand up" or "I don't like it when you bang your cup" is ignored. Children who ignore adults whose tone or words don't convey authority can end up being labeled as problems. That isn't fair! Caregivers should be sensitive to children's differing backgrounds and learn to speak their language, even if it's just another form of English. That doesn't mean that those adults can't continue to behave in authentic ways that feel comfortable to them. It does mean that they have to *teach* children in their care that they mean it when they make a soft-spoken statement that sounds indirect. They teach by following up with action when the words alone don't work, which is a good approach to use with anybody's children!

One last point about self-concept and discipline: Not all cultures see the goal of discipline as establishing **inner controls.** From some perspectives, discipline always comes from an outside authority, whether it's a person or group pressure. Discipline is not something that is inside but is external to the individual.[3] Children who expect to be monitored may feel justified in misbehaving if no one is paying attention. Again, this difference in views of controlling behavior (internal control or external control) may result in a situation where children from diverse backgrounds end up labeled as problems unless caregivers are aware of the difference.

Modeling Self-Esteem by Taking Care of Yourself

NAEYC Program Standard 6
Teachers

It may seem strange to find a section on taking care of yourself in a book that focuses on caring for infants and toddlers. But many caregivers are very poor models for the children they work with. The job demands sacrifice, it is true, and you need to put your own needs last quite often. But the job also demands high self-esteem. Children need to be around adults who see themselves as worthy, who respect and care for themselves. The opposite of the worthy adult is the adult whom everyone tramples on—the children, the parents, and the coworkers.

No one can tell you how to increase your worth in your own eyes, but Figure 13.2 presents some advice on how to take care of yourself. First, take care of your needs. You have the same range of needs that the children have (that is, physical, intellectual, emotional, and social needs). Don't neglect yourself. Eat right, exercise, pamper your body regularly with a swim, a hot bath, a walk, whatever it enjoys most. Take regular breaks at work, even if that's hard to arrange. Find a way. Stimulate your mind with a good book, a class, a game of chess. People who work with children sometimes feel as if their minds are decaying. Don't let that happen to you. Feel your feelings; don't ignore them. Learn to express them in ways that are healthy for you and the children. Find ways to use anger to help you solve problems or gather needed energy for making changes. Nurture your social life. Build relationships. Build a broad base of support. Don't depend on just one person to support and nurture you—spread that function out to several people. The more choices you have, the less chance you'll be let down. And don't hide your relationships from the children. It's good for the children to be with an adult who relates to other adults.

Second, learn to be assertive. Say no when appropriate. Family child care providers are especially famous for saying yes, yes, yes, until everyone in their lives is taking advantage of them. Don't let that happen to you.

Reflect

How do you feel about yourself? On a scale of 1 to 10, what is the level of your self-esteem? What do you do to increase your self-worth in your own eyes?

Figure 13.2 Some Hints about Nurturing Your Own Self-Esteem

1. Take care of your needs; don't neglect yourself. Take care of your physical, intellectual, emotional, and social needs.

2. Learn to be assertive. Don't let anybody take advantage of you.

3. Learn conflict management.

4. Learn time management.

5. Feel proud of what you do. You have an important job. Let people know that.

6. Play. Play renews energy and brings out your creative spirit.

Third, learn conflict management. Negotiation and mediation skills are important, in working not only with children but also with adults.

Fourth, learn time management. This set of skills helps you immeasurably by teaching you to use the time you have in ways that benefit you most.

Fifth, find ways to explain the importance of your job so that you can be proud of it. Don't apologize for what you do. The first years are the most important ones. The high school teacher or the college professor touches lives minimally and makes little difference compared to the impact you have. The people who rear children (that is, you and the parents) are the people responsible for the future of their country.

And finally, play. Adults need to play just as children need to play. You may even be able to find a way to play at work and do your job at the same time. Play renews energy and brings out a creative spirit.

This chapter has covered a lot of territory—from *caring about* each child that you *care for* (and how to work toward that goal if it doesn't happen naturally) to *taking care of* yourself, with stops along the way to look at self-concept from the view of culture, gender, and discipline. The social environment is made up of all these factors and more! The next chapter examines another programmatic issue: adult relationships. Although it is in a chapter by itself, this topic is part of the social environment.

Appropriate Practice

Overview of Development

According to the National Association for the Education of Young Children, attachment is a foundational building block for identity formation. In young babies attachment brings a sense of belonging, which gives them security to use their senses and physical abilities to explore. Seeing himself or herself as an explorer and investigator becomes part of the child's early identity. Mobile infants come to see themselves as expert explorers if they are supported and encouraged. All this exploration relates to the identity issues of toddlers as they deal with the dual issues of independence and control.

Source: J. Ronald Lally, Abbey Griffin, Emily Fenichel, Marilyn Segal, Eleanor Szanton, and Bernice Weissbourd, "Development in the First Three Years of Life," in

Developmentally Appropriate Practice in Early Childhood Programs, rev. ed. (Washington, D.C.: National Association for the Education of Young Children, 1997).

Developmentally Appropriate Practice

Following are samples of developmentally appropriate practices that relate to the social environment:

- Adults respect infants' individual abilities and respond positively as each baby develops new abilities. Experiencing caregivers' pleasure in their achievements, infants feel competent and enjoy mastering new skills.
- Adults know that infants are curious about each other. At the same time, caregivers help ensure that children treat each other gently.

(continued)

Appropriate Practice (continued)

• Pictures of infants and their family members are hung on walls at heights where infants can see them.

Source: S. Bredekamp and C. Copple, eds., *Developmentally Appropriate Practice in Early Childhood Programs*, rev. ed. (Washington, D.C.: National Association for the Education of Young Children, 1997).

Individually Appropriate Practice

Following are samples of individually appropriate practices that relate to the physical environment:

• Adults ensure that every child receives nurturing responsive care. In order to be individually appropriate and give nurturing responsive care to promote positive identity formation in all children, caregivers must know how to meet the specific needs of each child rather than take a general age and stage approach. They must give positive messages to the children (both verbal and nonverbal) that what they need is okay.
• Adults create an "inclusive" classroom, making sure that spatial organization, materials, and activities enable all children to participate actively. Adaptations need to be made in a way that indicates to the child that who they are is just fine and they will be welcomed here.

Source: S. Bredekamp and C. Copple, eds., *Developmentally Appropriate Practice in Early Childhood Programs*, rev. ed. (Washington, D.C.: National Association for the Education of Young Children, 1997).

Culturally Appropriate Practice

Following are samples of culturally appropriate practices:

• Caregivers work in partnership with parents, communicating daily to build mutual understanding and trust and to ensure the welfare and optimal development of the infant. Caregivers listen carefully to what parents say about their children, seek to understand parents' goals and preferences, and are respectful of cultural and family differences.
• Some cultures find photographs uncomfortable or distasteful. As one mother said, "I was shocked when the teacher pulled out pictures of her family. In my country we only have pictures of people who have died, and we don't carry them around with us." In such a case, Bredekamp and Copple suggest that caregivers and parents confer in making decisions about how best to support children's development or how to handle problems or differences of opinion as they arise.

Source: S. Bredekamp and C. Copple, eds., *Developmentally Appropriate Practice in Early Childhood Programs*, rev. ed. (Washington, D.C.: National Association for the Education of Young Children, 1997).

Appropriate Practice in Action

Looking back at The Principles in Action on page 286, consider the care the caregiver is giving Kaleb. Then look at the first item under the "Individually Appropriate Practice" section of the Appropriate Practice box and answer the following questions.

1. Is Kaleb receiving nurturing, responsive care?
2. Is the caregiver following principle 1?
3. From what you read in The Principles in Action, can you tell anything for sure about Kaleb's culture?
4. Do you think the caregiver's treatment of Kaleb relates to his culture?
5. How would you write an additional item under the "Individually Appropriate Practice" section that would address the risk to Kaleb's self-identify formation?

Summary

- The social environment is made up of the less visible parts of an infant-toddler program and relates to attachment as it affects the following interrelated characteristics of children:
  - o Identity formation
  - o Self-image
  - o Cultural identity
  - o Gender identity
  - o Self-concept
- The social environment is seen through the behaviors of the adults and children in it.
- Identity formation is of special concern in infant-toddler programs because children under age three are in the beginning stages of learning who they are, what they can do, and where they belong.
- Self-image is how children see themselves and includes the following characteristics:
  - o Body awareness, which increases as movement develops
  - o Cultural identity, which grows when the program regards families as partners and pays attention to cultural differences in ideas about what infants and toddlers need from adults
- Gender identity relates to children's feelings about their gender as well as the following factors:
  - o How their gender influences how they perceive themselves
  - o How adults interact with them based on their gender
  - o How adults model gender roles
- Self-concept can be deeply affected by the adult's approach to discipline and guidance. It is important that adults do the following to positively impact children's self-concepts:
  - o Use positive ways to guide behavior, such as redirection
  - o Define what is acceptable behavior in terms of developmental ages and stages
  - o Be aware of cultural differences in ideas about discipline
- Modeling Self-Esteem by Taking Care of Yourself
  - o If children are to grow up knowing how to take care of themselves, they need role models who meet their own physical, mental, emotional, and social needs.

Online Resources

Go to the Online Learning Center at **www.mhhe.com/itc7e** to access the student study guide that includes quizzes, practice with key terms, and a review of chapter content; links to websites related to the chapter; and additional resources.

Key Terms

body awareness 290
cultural identity 291
gender identity 293
inner controls 299

multicultural curriculum 291
observation mode 288
redirection 295
self-concept 287

self-image 290
time-out 298

Thought/Activity Questions

1. What is the difference between self-concept, self-image, and body awareness?
2. Explain some of the issues around using time-out as a guidance strategy.
3. Try using visualization to see a child differently. Pick a child whose behavior bothers you and try the exercise outlined in this chapter.
4. Imagine yourself working in a toddler program using the principles of this book and the ideas about discipline outlined in this chapter. You are confronted with a hard-to-handle child whose parent thinks she acts that way because you aren't behaving the way her daughter expects an authority to behave. Create a dialogue between you and this parent.

For Further Reading

Amy Ruth Baker, "Why Should You Document the Everyday Experience in Your Infant or Toddler Room?" *Focus on Infants and Toddlers*, 15(1), Fall 2002, pp. 1–5.

Adam Bryand and Erika Check, "How Parents Raise Boys and Girls," *Your Child, Newsweek* special edition, Fall and Winter 2000, pp. 56–63.

Grace Careri, Paola Collini-Martins, and Patricia Rego, "Research Update: Are Children Being Treated the Same?" *Interaction* 12(2), Summer 1998, pp. 34–36.

Renatta M. Cooper, "Child Care as Shared Socialization," *Child Care Information Exchange*, July 2002, pp. 58–60.

Lorraine DeJong and Barbara Hansen Cottrell, "Designing Infant Child Care Programs to Meet the Needs of Children Born to Teenage Parents," *Young Children* 54(1), January 1999, pp. 37–45.

Amy Laura Dombro, Laura J. Colker, and Diane Trister Dodge, *Creative Curriculum for Infants and Toddlers* (Washington, D.C.: Teaching Strategies, 1997).

P. Elam, "Creating Quality Infant Group Care Programs," in *Authentic Relationships in Group Care for Infants and Toddlers: Resources for Infant Educarers (RIE) Principles into Practice*, edited by S. Petrie and S. Owen (London and Philadelphia: Jessica Kingsley Publishers, 2005), pp. 83–92.

Daniel Gartrell, "Replacing Time-Out: Using Guidance to Maintain an Encouraging Classroom," *Young Children* 57(2), March 2002, pp. 36–43.

M. Gerber, "RIE Principles and Practices," in *Authentic Relationships in Group Care for Infants and Toddlers: Resources for Infant Educarers (RIE) Principles into Practice*, edited by S. Petrie and S. Owen (London and Philadelphia: Jessica Kingsley Publishers, 2005), pp. 35–49.

Janet Gonzalez-Mena, "Working with Cultural Differences: Individualism and Collectivism," *The First Years* (New Zealand Journal of Infant and Toddler Education) 4(1), 2002, pp. 13–15.

M. Marion, *Guidance of Young Children* (Columbus OH: Merrill, 1999).

S. L. Odom, T. Teferra, and S. Kaul, "An Overview of International Approaches to Early Intervention for Young Children with Special Needs and their Families," *Young Children*, September 2004, pp. 38–43.

chapter 14

Adult Relations in Infant-Toddler Care and Education Programs

Focus Questions

After reading this chapter you should be able to answer the following questions:

1 What are the stages of caregiver development in relating to parents and other family members? Which is the stage to aim for and why?

2 If you have a service plan that focuses on the child, why do you also need one that focuses on the family?

3 What blocks communication with parents and what are some ways to open up communication?

4 What is parent education and involvement and how is it different if parents are partners instead of merely consumers of a service?

5 How are caregiver relations different for center staff than for family child care providers?

What Do You See?

A mother arrives to pick up her daughter. She is obviously in a hurry. Her daughter runs toward her, arms outstretched. The mother starts to smile, then takes a look at the knees of her little pink pants, which are bright green with grass stains. A big frown takes over the smile. She picks her daughter up a little brusquely. Muttering to herself, she strides over to the nearest caregiver. "How did this happen?" Her voice sounds strained.

How will the caregiver react in the face of this upset mother. You will find out later in the chapter. Her response is important. What she conveys to the mother has implications for whether it's a relationship-building response or one that breaks down the relationship. Although relationships don't usually hinge on just one response or one set of interactions, the goal of each interaction should be to help these two important people in this child's life have a positive relationship with each other.

Parent-Caregiver Relations

Even though we have left it until the end, the subject of parent-caregiver relations is very important. Every professional who provides a service to others must develop a relationship with his or her clients. In the field of infant-toddler care, this relationship with the client—that is, the parent(s)—is vital because it affects the relationship of the children to the caregiver.

Although the term *parent* occurs throughout the chapter, it is important to recognize that in many cases it is the *family* to whom the staff or provider must relate. It is worthwhile to understand lines of authority and responsibility within each family.[1]

Caregiver Stages of Relating to Parents

There are three stages that caregivers commonly go through when they start working with children. It is important to recognize these in yourself and realize that you can move to the next stage when you realize that your attitudes, feelings, and behaviors relate to being new in the field. (Of course, some people get stuck in a stage and don't move forward.)

Stage 1. Caregiver as Savior   Sometimes caregivers forget that their client is the parent(s) and not the child alone. They make their own decisions about what to do for the child without consulting parents as to their goals and desires. They may even have feelings of competition with the parent. If these competitive feelings are strong enough, they result in a **"savior complex,"** when caregivers see their role as rescuing children from their parents. The savior complex is a stage many of caregivers go through when they first find themselves in charge of someone else's children.

The caregiver as savior is an interesting phenomenon. Not only is she out to save each child in her care from his parents (with a few exceptions, of course), but she plans to save the whole world through what she is doing with children! Stage 1 caregivers ride around on their high horses looking down on parents.

Stage 2. Caregiver as Superior to Parent   Most people move out of that stage when they realize that their charge is only part time and temporary. They may influence children for part of the day while they are in child care, but the parents are the predominant and permanent force in the children's lives. It is the parents who give the child a sense of connection with the past and a view of the future. At about the same time caregivers come to see the importance of parents in children's lives, they also begin to see individual parents' points of view. Caregivers in this second stage have more understanding about what influences the parents' child-raising practices.

During the second stage, caregivers come to see parents as the client. While still in the glow of the savior complex, caregivers work to change parents—to educate them. The difference between a stage-one and a stage-two caregiver is the perception of who the client is. The savior effect is still in operation as caregivers see themselves as superior substitutes for parents.

Stage 3. Caregiver as Partner to Parent and/or Family   The final stage comes when caregivers see themselves as partners—as supplements and supports to parents rather than substitutes. The parent and caregiver *share* in the care of the child. This stage brings on a mutual relationship in which the caregiver and parent communicate openly, even when conflicts arise. In this stage, the caregiver is clear about how important it is to do nothing that weakens children's sense of belonging to their own family.

Being a support, a surrogate, a supplement doesn't make you any less professional. Look at architects. Their job is not to impose ideas on the client but rather to take the client's ideas and needs and, using professional expertise, come up with something that works as well as pleases. Communication is an important part of the process.

The Principles in Action

Principle 3 Learn each child's unique ways of communicating (cries, words, movements, gestures, facial expressions, body positions) and teach yours. Don't underestimate children's ability to communicate even though their verbal language skills may be nonexistent or minimal.

Emily has cerebral palsy. It is her first day in the family child care home, and her provider is trying to get to know her. She realized in the first five minutes that it would be a challenge to learn to read Emily's facial expressions and body language. Happily, her mother realized the difficulty the provider would have, so she offered to stay with her daughter the first few times so she could teach her the unique ways Emily has of communicating. The provider paid close attention to Emily and listened to her mother's interpretations of what she was seeing and hearing. Otherwise, the provider never would have known what pleased Emily and what didn't. Her facial expressions weren't what the provider was used to. Several times she guessed, but she was wrong. "She's hungry," her mother decided, based on when Emily had last eaten and her present agitation. "Let me show you how to feed her," she offered. Feeding didn't look so hard, but reading the hunger signs did. Now Emily has eaten, but she has started whimpering. The provider turns to the mother to understand what Emily is trying to convey.

1. Would this scene be different in any way if it were in a center rather than in a family child care home?
2. Some providers and caregivers ask parents not to stay very long because they want the child to get used to them. What do you think of that approach? Would that have worked in this case?
3. What about a child who doesn't have diagnosed special needs—should a parent stay the first few times to help the provider or caregiver get to know the child?
4. How would you feel about taking care of a child with Emily's condition?

The architect's responsibility is considerably less than that of a caregiver. The architect's goal is merely a structure; the caregiver is dealing with human lives.

Communication with Parents and/or Family Members

Communication should be a major concern from day one. It's not just a matter of helping the parent understand the policies and practices of the center and finding out more about the child and family. It's even more important to use communication to start building a relationship with the family. So even though there may be a set procedure for the intake interview, including forms to fill out, if you keep your eye on the goal of creating a relationship, you'll have more success both at the beginning and down the line. One early job is to find out the needs of the child and family and then decide on a service plan.

Service Plan: Focus on the Child

What kinds of information should be discussed in the development of a **needs and services plan?** Parents should make caregivers aware of their children's habits, special needs, ways of communicating, and daily routines. Such information should include when and how much the child sleeps; how the child goes to sleep; and the child's eating habits, needs, likes and dislikes, bowel function, liquid intake and output, cuddling needs, **comfort devices,** and so on. These should be discussed when the child enters the program and on a daily basis thereafter. It may be hard to find "talking time," and shift changes may mean the child's caregiver is not present when the parent arrives, but simple written records give the information that may be of great importance to the parent. (Did he just have a snack, or is he crying because he is hungry?)

Although it is difficult to find time to do it, writing down anecdotes is also useful because some parents appreciate hearing about what went on that day. But be careful about leaving a parent feeling guilty about the child's behavior. It's up to you to guide behavior while you are with the child. If you had a hard time that day, don't blame the parent for it. Also, when you're relating positive anecdotes, be careful that you don't make parents feel left out because of all the cute things the child did that they missed. If the child took a first step that day, you want to weigh your own excitement with the parents' possible disappointment of not having been there to see it. Of course, not all reports are happy ones. If a child has a significant fall, scrape, or bite, the parent needs to be called and the details need to be reported on an accident or incident form by someone who observed it. A copy of the report goes in the files and another one should be sent home. Minor bumps and scratches call for a simpler "ouch" report.

Be sure that while you're conveying information you are also listening. You need information too—about what happens in the other part of the child's life. Is she particularly fussy this week because something is going on at home? Is he tired today because he didn't sleep much last night, or might he be coming down with something? Are her bowels loose because of something she ate that didn't

Figure 14.1 A Summary of the Principles under which PSP Programs Operate

- The way to ensure the health and well-being of children is to ensure the health and well-being of their parents.

- Parents are the child's primary teachers, and they know the child best.

- The relationship between parents and staff is one of equality and respect.

- Parents make their own choices about the services they want.

- Programs and services are voluntary.

- Programs build on parents' strengths and are ethnically relevant and community-based. Each community sets its own reality based on what is good for it.

- Social support networks are a crucial element in the happiness, healthiness, and productivity of people.

agree with her, or might she have picked up an infection? Listening is half of communicating.

Service Plan: Focus on the Family

The Parent Services Project (PSP), which was started by Ethel Seiderman and is now nationwide, addresses the development of the child and family together. Each participating program has a plan that includes services to the parents, not just a service plan for the child. The idea is to ensure the well-being of the parents as a way of caring for their children. One way to promote well-being is to bring parents together in ways that foster community building as parents make connections and develop social networks.

NAEYC Program Standard 7
Families

Staff in the national headquarters of the PSP organization train child care professionals to focus on positive attitudes about working with parents and practical activities to serve the family. The program builds on family strengths and resources and regards cultural sensitivity and inclusion an important part of the work. What kinds of activities are written into the service plan? The activities differ from program to program depending on what the families in the particular program need and want. Each PSP program is tailor-made, so no two are exactly alike. A typical sampling might include a menu of adult activities, such as support groups, classes, workshops, leadership opportunities; family fun activities, such as Friday night pizza parties with a rented video for entertainment; field trips on weekends to the beach, to an amusement park, to the zoo; specialized child care such as respite care, sick child care; programs for men, for grandparents, for foster parents; multicultural experiences; mental health activities.

See Figure 14.1 for a summary of the principles under which the PSP programs operate. They should be guiding principles for *all* child care programs. The full set of PSP principles is listed in Appendix C.

Communication Blocks

Sometimes it's hard to listen when you are angry with a parent. The source of your anger can be something as simple as a personality conflict or as deep as a basic attitude toward parents who leave their children to go off to work, especially when it seems there is no financial reason to do so. Ironically, some caregivers feel ambivalent about child care and whether or not it is good for children. Some family child care providers decide it is better for them to stay home with their children than go out to work, so they go into the business of caring for the children of other mothers who leave home to work. If a woman who made this choice sees it as a sacrifice, she may resent a mother who arrives in the morning well dressed, happy, and about to embark on what the caregiver perceives to be a more socially or intellectually stimulating day. This is an unfortunate situation and can cause hard feelings between caregivers and parents. A first step to solving this problem comes when the caregiver faces such feelings squarely, recognizing that anger or annoyance over child or parent behavior really springs from this particular source. What to do about it will become clearer once the feelings are acknowledged.

Sometimes it's hard to listen because a parent is angry. Parental anger is often misplaced, centering on some minor issue instead of the real source. Parents may cover their insecurities, their conflicting feelings, their feelings of guilt and stress with anger. Parents may sense uncomfortable competition—real or not—between themselves and the caregiver. Parents often feel threatened by competent caregivers. They worry that they are losing their children as they see them express affection for the caregiver. Parents who feel insecure about parenting skills may hide that insecurity by acting extra wise or knowledgeable—even pushy. If you listen carefully enough, you may be able to detect the real message behind the words. Just as when children feel insecure you try to bolster their confidence in themselves, point out their strengths and competencies, and steer them toward successes, so you can take the same approach with an insecure parent.

Some parents actually need parenting themselves. They look to you as wise and capable and lean on you for support. You have to decide how much of this need you can fulfill. You can't be everything to everyone, and this parent's needs may be one burden too many for you. Then you have to decide whether you can put the energy into supporting the parent while you help him or her become self-sufficient, whether you have to redirect the parent to someone else, or whether you have to just set a limit and say no. Sometimes you can get parents together with each other, and they will form a mutual support system.

Sometimes it's hard to listen when you feel you're being attacked. You end up defending yourself instead of allowing the other person to really express what is on his or her mind. For example, a parent may say that all her child does is play in your program, and she wishes he were learning something. If you get defensive, show anger, and close down communication, you may never have a chance to create the kind of **dialogue** or conversation using nondefensive language in which you can listen to each other's points of view. But if you are able to listen,

Reflect

Suppose you are a caregiver and a parent is very angry about something you did with her child. How would you handle this situation. Would it make a difference if it were a father who was angry with you?

eventually you'll have a chance to point out all the child is learning through the caregiving and free play.

Opening Up Communication

You can open the communication by letting the parents know you heard them. This can be done by simply restating the parent's own words, which allows them to correct you or explain further. This approach is called active listening and also includes stating what the other person seems to be feeling. The idea is to really listen and let the other person know that you are listening. Adults who use this strategy all the time with children sometimes have a harder time remembering that it works with adults as well. As you establish a dialogue, you'll be able to get a better picture of what parents want as well as explain your approach and what you believe in.

Conferences   Besides day-to-day informal encounters, **conferences** are important for communication. Setting aside time when parents and caregivers can sit down to talk to each other helps to develop relationships. When parents and caregivers have a warm and trusting relationship, infants and toddlers benefit. The first conference, called an **intake interview,** can set the pattern for communication, especially when the caregiver makes the family feel comfortable and at home. It's called an interview, but it should be thought of as a two-way conversation. Although it can be informal and warm, it is important that some matters be made clear from the beginning. One issue is that child care personnel are mandated to report any suspected child abuse. If such a situation should arise, parents who know about this requirement ahead of time won't feel betrayed or deceived when the caregiver files a report. Of course, this is a touchy subject and not one anyone wants to talk about. But from a legal point of view and for the protection of the child, the cards must be put on the table. Some programs have parents read a short statement concerning the mandate to report child abuse; they are asked to sign it to show they have read it. It's even possible that this policy acts as a prevention device.

Besides the initial intake interview, periodic informal conferences help parents and caregivers develop their partnership, gain insights, and set long-range goals. It is important to help parents feel secure about such a conference. They may perceive themselves as being in the "hot seat." Some parents arrive at conferences with all the old feelings left from report card sessions in their elementary or high school days. In such situations, you need to do all you can to help them relax and feel comfortable so you have real communication.

Helping Parents Feel at Home   Start by looking at the environment in which you will conduct the conference. If you sit behind a desk with a file folder in front of you and a wall of reference books behind you, that gives the proceedings the tone that you are an expert, removed from the amateurs—the parents. Any insecurities they arrive with will be magnified in this setting.

Reflect

What are your experiences with conferences? Do you remember parent-teacher conferences as a child? Are you a parent? Do you have experiences in the parent chair of parent-teacher conferences? Do any feelings come to you as you think about conferences?

Because you are in your own territory, it is especially important that you make the parents feel welcome and at home. If you know educational, psychological, or developmental jargon, try not to use it. That gets harder as you begin to see yourself as a professional. After all, professionals have their own way of talking that sets them apart. But just think how you appreciate the doctor who can explain your symptoms without sending you off to a medical encyclopedia. At the same time, don't talk down to parents. It's hard to communicate openly when one party is being patronizing.

If you have a specific goal for the conference, state it at the beginning. If it is to be just an informal give and take session, state that. Don't leave parents wondering why they have been asked to this conference. Use conferences to examine issues between you, explore problems and questions concerning the child, decide on ways to approach behavior that needs changing, exchange information, and develop goals. If the child is present at the conference, don't talk around him or her. Include the child in the conversation (even babies).

♚ ♛ Issues of Parents of Children with Special Needs

Recognize that parents of children with special needs may have an extra set of issues that other parents don't have when they come to a conference with you. They may be in denial about their child's condition. Denial is a normal stage in coming to grips with something as serious as giving birth to a baby with special needs. Be gentle and understanding with parents in denial and be patient about helping them beyond this stage. It may take some time.

Some parents of children with special needs carry a heavy burden of guilt. They may not show this guilt to you, but it may affect your relations with them, especially if they have a sense that you blame them.

Anger may also be present in these parents. Though it may come out at you, it may well have nothing to do with you personally. Approach the parents' anger the way you do children's anger. Allow them to express their feelings without getting defensive or angry back.

Realize that these parents may have had a number of dealings with "experts" before they met you, and they may bring the issues from these experiences to their conference with you. Of course, not all parents of infants and toddlers with special-needs will bring anger, guilt, or unresolved issues to their conferences with you. Some will have had positive experiences in working together with "experts" and will be ready to establish a partnership with you, their child's caregiver. But others will come with a load on their back, and if you recognize this fact, you can deal with it.

When Just Listening Is Not Enough Sometimes parents and caregivers have disparate needs or differences of opinion that put them in conflict with one another. Just listening isn't enough; what is needed is a problem-solving or conflict-resolution approach. When this happens, it is important both to listen and to express your own feelings and position. When you have defined the problem, then brainstorm potential solutions. It may be that there is a cultural difference that troubles both you and the parent. You don't see eye to eye on something such as toilet training, for example. If in the parent's culture the time to start toilet training is much earlier than you believe it should be started or than is the policy of your program, this is an issue about which you need to communicate. It may be hard to keep from arguing with the parent, but you'll get further if you try to understand each other. That's where dialoguing comes in. Instead of trying to convince the parent that one way is right and the other wrong, you need to sort out the differences. It may even come down to some basic conceptual differences. For example, at the Pikler Institute they never use the word toilet training. Instead they call it sphincter control, because it is only a matter of the child gaining the muscle strength to manage their own elimination process. Because diapering, dressing, bathing, and feeding have been cooperative processes, sphincter control is all children need to take the next step, which is to use the toilet. That is very different from the kind of conditioning process that is involved in toilet training babies.

Reflect

What are your experiences with cross cultural encounters? Do you have feelings or ideas about those experiences?

Communicating with parents whose culture is different from yours may be very difficult; yet it is important that you accept the parents' ways of doing things as much as possible and try to carry out their wishes. That is easy to do when the ways and the wishes don't tread on your theories of what is good for children. It's much harder when what the parents want is in conflict with what you think is right. The problem is that theories are culturally bound. There is no one right answer—no one truth. It is easy to forget that and get carried away telling people what is good for babies. You have to remember to listen to their ideas rather than just sell yours. For that reason, when you are deciding what is good for babies and toddlers, you have to take culture into consideration.

And while you are looking at culture, you also have to look at the difference in generational perspectives. The generation gap is real. If you are a grandmother and the parents of the children in your care are much younger, they may well have a different way of looking at what's good for children, even if they are of your same culture. The experience differential doesn't explain all the differences; you have to consider the times in which the person grew up. Or if you are 20 and many of the parents are twice your age, you have to recognize that they may have a different view. One isn't right and the other wrong; they are just different.

A gender difference may create a communication gap. The way a father perceives his child may be different from the way a mother does. Male caregivers' responses, reactions, and understandings of children may be different, because of their gender, from those of female caregivers.

Let's revisit the scene at the beginning of this chapter and see how the caregiver handled the situation. Remember, the mother who arrived to find her child had grass stains on the knees of her pink pants? The mother was in a hurry and was upset as she walked over to the nearest caregiver and demanded an explanation. We can't tell whether this is a cross-cultural, cross-generational, or cross-gender situation or not. It could be. But even if it is not, the goal is the same—to create a dialogue with the parent rather than getting defensive. Let's look at the rest of that scene. Try to keep out of a blaming mode and in a problem-solving mode.

"How did this happen?" The mother's voice sounds strained. The caregiver looks concerned.

"We were outside this morning—it must have happened then. I'm sorry. I can see that you're pretty upset about it."

"You bet I am!" the mother says angrily.

"It's going to be hard to get out," the caregiver says understandingly.

"Yes, it is." There is a pause in the conversation. The caregiver waits, still attentive to the mother—maybe to see if the mother wants to say more. Then the caregiver adds, "You must be pretty mad at us."

At that the mother explodes. The words rush out on top of one another, first about her anger and then about how she is going to meet her fiancé's mother, and it's important that her daughter look her very best. She talks about how insecure she feels around the new family that she's about to become a part of. When she's finished, she looks a lot better. The frown is gone, replaced by a slightly nervous look.

"Do you have time to sit down for a minute?" the caregiver asks kindly.

"Not really," replies the mother, sitting down anyway. She's holding her daughter with tenderness now, and the child plays with her hair.

"I'm just wondering how we could keep this from happening next time," says the caregiver tentatively.

"You could keep her inside," says the mother immediately.

"I hate to do that," says the caregiver. "She loves to be outside."

"Yes, I know," admits the mother.

"Besides," continues the caregiver, "there are times when we are all outside, and there's no one inside to watch her."

"Well," says the mother hesitantly, "I suppose I could send her in jeans—but she looks so cute in her little outfits. . . . When I'm going someplace after work, like today, I want her to look nice." She thinks for a minute. "I guess it makes more sense to dress her up when I pick her up than to expect her to keep an outfit nice all day."

"It would sure make us feel better to have her in jeans instead of trying to keep her from getting her clothes dirty."

"Yes, I guess I can understand that. Well," she says, standing up, "I really do have to go. Thanks for listening to me."

This problem was resolved quickly and easily by the caregiver listening and not getting defensive and angry herself. This particular problem of clothes is not always solved so easily. Some parents do not want their children to be away from home in anything but good clothes. They won't be persuaded so easily that it's better for everybody if the child arrives in play clothes with sturdy knees. Sometimes this reflects a cultural attitude about school and has to do with the family wishing to retain a certain image.

Whether communication comes easily or not because of age, gender, or cultural differences or just individual differences, there are some ways that you can facilitate it. Here are some tips for opening and maintaining lines of communication with parents:

- Regard communication as a two-way process. If you're having problems with a child's behavior, the parent probably is too. Make it easy to exchange information.
- Develop your listening skills. Learn to listen for the feelings behind the words and discover ways to encourage parents to express those feelings without offending you.
- Develop a problem-solving attitude, and learn techniques of communication, mediation, and negotiation to use during conflict management and resolution.
- Keep records so you can report specifics.
- Make time available when it is clear that a parent needs to talk. It helps to have a comfortable place to sit.
- Try to talk to each parent every day at arrival and pickup, even if you're busy.
- Try to make parents feel welcome whenever they are around, even if they pop in and disturb your program. In some teen parent programs on high school campuses, mothers come by between classes. It is hard on some of the children for a while because they have to learn to handle the more frequent hellos and good-byes. But it is important for the staff to be understanding about these parents' needs even though it makes their job harder.

Parent Education

Your job is not only infant and toddler education but **parent education** as well. Education involves not just knowledge, but knowledge along with attitudes and skills. If you build a relationship, parents will be influenced by you in all these areas. But if you set yourself up as an expert and try to teach them directly, you may run into trouble. Knowledge alone doesn't change attitudes. They change over time with exposure to different people's values, ideas, methods, and attitudes. Most parents leave a program knowing more and feeling different from when they first enrolled, even if they never attend any kind of formal lecture on parenting or child development. If you can involve parents, over time they will pick up knowledge of child development by watching other children and seeing what is common behavior, by reading what you make available, and by asking questions and having discussions with you. Parent involvement works best when parents feel welcome to take part in the program and help out on the side. Mandatory involvement moves parents away from a partnership role, unless the program is set up especially for parent participation and parents choose it. In that case the main purpose of the program is parent education and it comes about through

NAEYC Program Standard 7
Families

VIDEO OBSERVATION 14

Girl Crawling through Low Window (Parent Ed Program)

See Video Observation 14: Girl Crawling through Low Window (Parent Ed Program) for an example of a parent participation program. This particular one happens to have been started by Magda Gerber. Although you don't see the educarer (as Magda called caregivers), only the father, you can hear her voice encouraging and supporting his actions with his daughter. Think back to Chapter 2 and the emphasis on problem solving. This is a good example of an infant solving a problem.

Questions

- This father is obviously nervous about leaving his daughter alone to solve the problem she had set up for herself. Do you think the caregiver was wrong in encouraging him not to help his daughter?
- What might be a cultural issue in this scene? Is it cultural to allow, and even encourage, babies to solve problems by themselves?
- What would you have done if you had been the caregiver in this scene watching the father and his daughter?

To view this clip, go to www.mhhe.com/itc7e. Click on Student Edition, select Chapter 14, and click on Video Observation.

actively working with the children, through discussion groups, parent meetings, and guest speakers. This model is the ideal way to augment the knowledge building that happens naturally when parents spend time around a center, even just for short drop-off and pickup sessions.

 Parents of Children with Special Needs

Parents of children with special needs may need to learn different things than do other parents. If these parents have not been exposed to other children before they come to your program, at first they may learn more than they want to know about typical development. It can come as a great shock to some parents to compare their children for the first time with children who don't have special needs. Be extra sensitive to their feelings.

Most parents are eager to learn more if they don't feel threatened or pushed. An invitation to observe or participate either occasionally or regularly is welcomed by many parents and is a further means to parent education. In a family child care home, a father regularly stayed an extra half hour in the afternoon when he had time. He would sit and play the piano and interact with the children who approached him. He not only contributed to the program but also gained knowledge just by being there.

Skill building comes gradually too. Parents come to you with varying degrees of parenting skills. Most will gain more by being exposed to professional caregivers. However, a danger lurks when caregivers present themselves as models for parents.

Early Care and Education Professionals

The parent role is different from your role as a professional caregiver, though it may look very similar at times. You don't have the parent's involvement or commitment. You don't have the shared history, nor will you be part of the child's future. You don't have the intensity of interest that brings about passionate exchanges. If the child "behaves just fine" with you and becomes a tyrant when the parent arrives, don't brag or feel superior. The explanation for the contrast is more likely to relate to the normal parent-child relationship and strong attachment than to your seemingly superior competence.

Children need competent caregivers, but they also need totally human, emotional, and connected parents. What you see as poor handling of a situation is more likely a parental handling rather than a professional handling. The two are different, though each should have many elements of the other. Parents operate (and should operate) more spontaneously from the gut level, reacting emotionally rather than responding reasonably. Of course, parents should also use their heads, should be objective now and then, and should build some of the competencies you have (which will happen to some extent through observing you). They should also gather information about child development and caregiving so they can *think* about what they are doing. But they should still parent mostly from gut reactions rather than from thought-out approaches. Parents should be far more human than competent. Caregivers also should be human and step out of their usual role now and then and interact intensely and passionately with children; but they should mostly be fairly objective and thoughtful in goals and reactions.

If you are both a parent and a caregiver, you can probably understand when you think about those times you handled things differently as a parent of your own child than you would have as the caregiver of someone else's. Perhaps at the time you felt guilty. But if you look at role differences, you can be glad that you are a normal parent. Your children deserve a real parent, not a professional caregiver. And other people's children deserve professional caregivers, not more parents.

That doesn't mean a professional caregiver should be cold and detached. If you've read this far in this book, you know that the message throughout has been to be real, to get connected, to feel your feelings. The point is balance. The balance swings more to feelings and spontaneity in the parenting role and more to thoughtfulness, objectivity, and planning in the caregiver role.

Relating to the Parents of a Child Who Isn't Doing Well

Sometimes, in spite of all your efforts in the parent relations and parent education department, you may have a child in your care who isn't doing well. He or she may be disrupting your whole program, taking a large portion of your time so that you have to worry about neglecting the other children. If you're in a center, the first step is to talk to other staff members (and the director). If you're in a family child care home, you may not have such a clearly defined problem-solving support group with which to discuss issues like this, but it is important that you find somebody—another child care provider perhaps.

You'll also want to talk to the parent(s)—not to place blame, but to get additional perspectives on the problem and further ideas for strategies to find ways to meet this child's needs. Teamwork and cooperation at home and in the program may work.

Or nothing may work. After trying and assessing various strategies, you may find that the child's behavior is still causing considerable turmoil. You'll probably also come to the conclusion that the situation isn't good for you, the other children, *or* the child. It is hard to realize that you can't meet every child's needs to the fullest extent. You may resist the idea that you can't be everything this particular family needs.

The next step is a **referral.** Perhaps some outside source can be of assistance to this family. Often that works. With specialized help the situation becomes tolerable, and you find you can meet the child's needs. But sometimes you have to realize that you've done all you can for a particular child, and it's time to ask the family to find care elsewhere. This is an extremely painful process for all concerned, but sometimes a necessary one.

Caregiver Relations

Staff relations are of extreme importance in a job as demanding as child care. In a family child care home, you don't have staff relations; instead, the issue is family relations, which is somewhat different. We'll deal with this subject briefly before discussing center staffs.

The Family Child Care Provider

Getting support is valuable if you are a family child care provider. But if the rest of your family is resentful, it may be hard to get their support. One family child-care provider sat down and wrote out a contract with her family—husband and two preteen children—before she went into business. She felt it was important to be clear about the use of the house, which belonged to all four, and about what was or was not expected of each family member regarding the children in care. This contract was not something she forced them into; it was an agreement that they built together, considering everyone's ideas and feelings. In this family, the children were old enough to understand the contract, their rights, and their obligations. The contract saved the family a good deal of conflict.

In many child care families, conflict is the name of the game. If the children are younger, it's hard for them to understand why they have to share room, toys, even "mommy." Usually the agreements are less clear than a written and negotiated contract. As a result, a good deal of resentment, tension, and friction can arise. Some friction is, of course, normal but may be unexpected when a provider first goes into business. But in most families the advantages outweigh the disadvantages, and the friction falls into place with the other ordinary family conflicts.

Family child care providers also should look for support outside their own families. It is hard because you're tied to your home all day every weekday, but if you look, you can find other family child care providers to talk to. The provider who worked out the contract with her family found another family child care provider in her own neighborhood through attending local support meetings. The two meet regularly at the park with their children (it is a short walk), so they have adult company as well as an outing for the children. No one can listen with more understanding to a family child care provider than another family child care provider. Find someone to talk to if you haven't already.

Center Staff

In a center setting, staff relations are different because you work together and are not related to one another. It's a strange situation to be around adults all day but seldom focus on them. That can create problems because you have little time to sit down and talk things out. Most child care staffs have staggered schedules, so the only time all the staff is there together is during the busiest time of the day, when the adults have little time to relate to each other. Some staffs working with older children are able to get together during nap time, but that won't work for most infant center staffs. In many centers, even breaks are staggered so that no two staff members are off the floor at the same time.

If child care were like other fields, there would be built-in time for staff meetings, for staff training, even provisions for staff renewal. But for many programs on a tight budget, those are unaffordable luxuries.

Obviously, staff members can seldom get off and talk to each other without the children around. And they need to talk to establish relationships, to settle conflicts, to share information on children and families, to set goals, to evaluate, and to share resources. Most of all they need adult contact to alleviate the isolation that adults who spend many hours a day with children commonly feel.

If you are new to the field and in a training program where you learn to focus almost exclusively on the children, you may be surprised to come into a center

Staff relations are important in a job as demanding as infant-toddler caregiving.

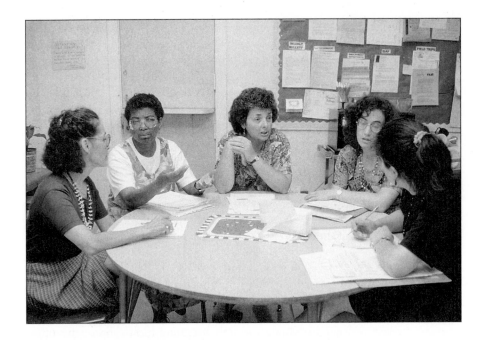

and see adults sitting around talking to each other while the children play. You may be quite critical if your training has made it sacrilege to focus on anything but the children when you are working (except on break). But over time, you may come to realize that those talks are important to staff members who work all day every day with very young children. And they are important to the children. How else are children to see adults relating to adults if their daily contact consists only of adults who focus on them and ignore the other adults present? Children need to see adults exhibit a wider range of behavior than what they see when the adults relate only to them.

In a three-hour program, it is still preferable to see adults concentrate mostly on the children, but that expectation is neither realistic nor desirable in all-day care. Of course, it isn't good policy to focus on adult relationships to the exclusion of the children and to the point of neglecting their needs. But if each child gets plenty of wants-nothing quality time, when the caregiver is available to him or her during free play, as well as wants-something quality time during caregiving activities when the focus is on the individual child, the adult can relate to other adults while the children are present without neglecting the children.

Respect as the Key to Adult Relationships

Although the term respect has not be used so far in this chapter, that quality should underlie all the interactions adults have with each other—whether parent, family member, fellow staff member, or administrator—as well as with the children. Magda Gerber's influence should be felt through out the program, not just in the interactions between adults and babies. Polly Elam writes about her experiences with Magda Gerber as her mentor where she experienced mutual respect and trust.[2]

When Magda started talking about respectful care back in the 1970s her ideas were new to those focused on infants and toddlers. She was proud of being some-what of a rebel. Nobody was using the word *respect* when talking or writing about infants and toddlers. Respect back then was something that young children had to learn to give elders. Gerber turned that around so that giving respect became a two-way process. By the end of the 1990s Magda was lamenting that she had lost her rebel status. Her ideas were everywhere and were no longer thought of as strange or new. The word *respect* is commonly used in the field of infant-toddler care. But from observations of how some caregivers treat parents and fellow caregivers, perhaps more attention should be paid to using the 10 principles when working with adults. Just consider these points:

- Principle 1 is about teamwork and applies to adults as well as infants and toddlers. Do adults cooperate with each other, or do they work around each other to get the job done?
- Principle 2 is about quality time. How often do adults spend quality time with one another? This question isn't about blaming anybody. The child care field makes it very hard to find time to really relate to each other in ways that build relationships. We need to advocate for our field to provide for adult relationships. We also need to take advantage of the opportunities that do arise.
- Principle 3 is about communication. How hard do adults work to learn each other's unique ways of communicating? This is a big question if more than one language is spoken in the program. It's a smaller question if it means being sensitive to body language and getting to know each person well enough to be able to "read" him or her.
- Principle 4 is about investing time and energy to appreciate the whole person. Do adults value some people more than others for particular qualities they have or do they appreciate each one for who he or she is?
- Principle 5 warns not to objectify people. How often does one adult treat another as an object? It may be harder to see how principle 1 applies to adults because they are the same size, but when you consider status differences, prejudice, and bias, that may make principle 5 more meaningful.
- Principle 6 is about authentic feelings. How honest are the adults in the program about their feelings? Do they hide them even from themselves, or do they bring their authentic selves to the relationships with the people they serve and work with?
- Principle 7 is about modeling. Notice how many adults criticize others for particular behaviors that they themselves exhibit, although often they are not aware of that fact. Are you aware that we are more like our worst

enemy than our best friend? Being consciously aware of behaviors and working on them is a worthwhile pursuit for all adults.

- Principle 8 is about recognizing problems as learning opportunities and applies to adults just as it does to children. Infant-toddler programs are full of problems and working to solve them is part of the job and is good for the brain!
- Trust is the issue in principle 9. Trust is an issue between caregivers and the families they serve, but it is also an issue among caregivers. Being trustworthy is a valuable trait and one to aim for.
- Principle 10 is about quality of development and maybe brings us back to respect—self respect. Caregivers need to develop an appreciation for adult development and learn ways to facilitate it rather than pushing it or criticizing other caregivers' or parents' shortcomings.

This chapter has been about adult relations and their importance to the children in child care. Children need to see their caregivers as full human beings, and they can't if they don't see them in relation to other adults—their parents as well as other staff members.

Appropriate Practice

Overview of Development

Each baby is different. No matter how well trained caregivers are, they need to learn about the babies in their care from the babies' families. Certainly, well-honed observation skills help caregivers get acquainted with each baby's needs, interests, and preferences, but no firsthand experience or training replaces what the family knows. Building a solid relationship from the time a child enters the program helps caregivers learn from the experiences and knowledge of the family. They also need to learn about the culture of the family, their goals, and their child-rearing beliefs. When caregivers value the family, the relationship becomes one of mutual support and learning. They are able to create an alliance. They maintain that alliance through regular and ongoing two-way communication between family and caregiver. The alliance is important when the infant is young and becomes a further source of strength and support when babies begin to move around. At that time babies enter a new stage of development mixed with feelings about separation and attachment. Working together, family and caregiver can support each other in discovering how to keep the infant feeling secure as they discuss safety issues and the need for changes in the environment both at home and possibly in the program as well. Babies grow into toddlers whose feelings become more complex as they feel a conflict between independence and dependence, pride and shame, anger and tenderness—to name a few of the emotions toddlers experience. All these feelings challenge parents and caregivers. The adults can offer each other support through what can be a difficult time. Finally, toddlers are in the midst of their identity formation, which is rooted in the family and community. Only when caregivers know and understand can they support healthy identity formation.

Source: J. Ronald Lally, Abbey Griffin, Emily Fenichel, Marilyn Segal, Eleanor Szanton, and Bernice Weissbourd, "Development in the First Three Years of Life," in *Developmentally Appropriate Practice in Early Childhood Programs*, rev. ed. (Washington, D.C.: National Association for the Education of Young Children, 1997).

Developmentally Appropriate Practice

Following are samples of developmentally appropriate practices that relate to the adult relations, particularly the family-caregiver alliance:

- Caregivers work in partnership with parents, communicating daily to build mutual understanding and trust.
- Caregivers help parents feel good about their children and their own parenting by sharing with them some of the positive and interesting things that happened with their children during the day.
- Caregivers and parents confer in making decisions about how best to support children's development or to handle problems or differences of opinion as they arise.

Source: S. Bredekamp and C. Copple, eds., *Developmentally Appropriate Practice in Early Childhood Programs*, rev. ed. (Washington, D.C.: National Association for the Education of Young Children, 1997).

Individually Appropriate Practice

Following are samples of individually appropriate practices that relate to the adult relations:

- Caregivers and parents confer in making decisions about how best to support children's development or how to handle problems or differences of opinion as they arise.
- The key to meeting all children's needs is to individualize. Parents are the ones who know their children best. If children have special needs, it is even more important to talk to the parents and find out what they know and with what specialists they may be connected.

Source: S. Bredekamp and C. Copple, eds., *Developmentally Appropriate Practice in Early Childhood Programs*, rev. ed. (Washington, D.C.: National Association for the Education of Young Children, 1997).

Culturally Appropriate Practice

Following are samples of culturally appropriate practice:

- Caregivers work in partnership with parents, communicating daily to build mutual understanding and trust and to ensure the welfare and optimal development of the infant. Caregivers listen carefully to what parents say about their children, seek to understand parents' goals and preferences, and are respectful of cultural and family differences.
- Cultural and family differences can create goals and priorities that conflict with those of the center or family child care program. Toilet training in some families' traditions occurs in the first year of life instead of the second or third, for example. When caregivers set themselves up as experts on child development and judge families without understanding cultural issues, they put up barriers to working in partnership with families.

Source: S. Bredekamp and C. Copple, eds., *Developmentally Appropriate Practice in Early Childhood Programs*, rev. ed. (Washington, D.C.: National Association for the Education of Young Children, 1997).

Appropriate Practice in Action

Look back at The Principles in Action on page 309. Then return to this page and read the first item in the "Developmentally Appropriate Practice" section of the Appropriate Practice box and both items under the "Individually Appropriate Practice" section.

1. Do you think Emily's provider is showing evidence of a partnership with her parent's attitude?
2. What if the provider had felt insecure around the mother and, to keep her status as a professional provider, had pretended she was an expert in children with cerebral palsy? How might this scene have turned out very differently?
3. Is it more important to learn to read the signals of children who have special needs than it is to learn to read the signals of all children in your care?

Summary

- An important aspect of adult relationships in infant toddler programs is realizing that caregivers tend to go through stages of relating to parents.
  - o Caregivers in stage 1 focus on the child alone and sometimes can be said to have a "savior complex."
  - o Caregivers in stage 2 tend to focus on both parent and child, but they have a strong urge to educate parents so they learn how to better handle and rear their children.
  - o Caregivers in stage 3 aim to create a partnership with the parent and family.
- Communication with parents involves the following:
  - o A first task when enrolling a child in a child care program is to jointly create a service plan for the child and also for the family.
  - o Understanding what blocks communication can help to open it up so parents are comfortable in both informal conversations and also during more formal conferences.
  - o Parents who have children with special needs may have additional issues that you may need to understand when communicating with them.
  - o Sometimes just listening is helpful, but other times, caregivers and parents must negotiate with each other.
- Parent Education and Involvement
  - o Parent education can occur informally as parents and other family members see what is going on in the program. Parent involvement can help them feel welcome and encourage them to spend more time in the program, but it should be voluntary.
  - o The goal of parent education should not be to make the parent into a professional caregiver. Caregivers and parents have different roles and that is as it should be.
- Caregiver relations take on different meanings depending on whether the caregiver is a family child care provider or a member of a center-based staff.
- Respect is a key component of all relationships—both those that adults have with children and those that adults have with each other.

Key Terms

comfort device 310	intake interview 313	referral 320
conference 313	needs and services plan 310	savior complex 308
dialogue 312	parent education 317	

Thought/Activity Questions

1. Caregivers are mandated reporters. What does that term mean?
2. What are some ways to make parents feel comfortable during a conference with their child's caregiver?

3. Interview caregivers to see if you can tell in which stage of development they are. Is there anything to indicate that they are saving children from their parents, educating the parents to be as good as they are, or seeing parents as partners?
4. When thinking about communicating with and supporting parents, what additional issues may be present with a parent whose child has a disability or special need?
5. Suppose you work with someone from a culture different from your own who has very different ideas about childrearing and caregiving. What steps would you take to open up communication between the two of you?

For Further Reading

Amy Ruth Baker, "Why Should You Document the Everyday Experience in Your Infant or Toddler Room?" *Focus on Infants and Toddlers* (Association for Childhood Education International) 15(1), Fall 2002, pp. 1–5.

H. E. Bruno, "Hearing Parents in Every Language," *Exchange* 153, September/October 2003, pp. 58–60.

Renatta M. Cooper, "Child Care as Shared Socialization," *Child Care Information Exchange*, July 2002, pp. 58–60.

P. Elam, "Creating Quality Infant Group Care Programs," in *Authentic Relationships in Group Care for Infants and Toddlers: Resources for Infant Educarers (RIE) Principles into Practice*, edited by S. Petrie and S. Owen (London and Philadelphia: Jessica Kingsley Publishers, 2005), pp. 83–92.

J. Gonzalez-Mena, *Diversity in Early Care and Education: Honoring Differences* (New York: McGraw-Hill, 2005).

A. M. Ingalls, R. Greenberg, and Jeanine Jeffers-Woolf, "A Journey of Hope: Forming Partnerships with Families and the Community," *Zero to Three* 24(6), July 2004, pp. 26–32.

S. Lawrence-Lightfoot, *The Essential Conversation: What Parents and Teachers Can Learn from Each Other* (New York, Random House, 2003).

Glenn W. Olsen and Steven W. Shirley, "Resolving Staff Conflict," *Child Care Information Exchange* 141, September/October 2001, pp. 22–25.

J. H. Pawl and A. L. Dombro, *Learning and Growing Together with Families: Partnering with Parents to Support Young Children's Development* (Washington D.C.: Zero to Three, 2001).

H. Seploch, "Family Ties: Partnerships for Learning: Conferencing with Families," *Young Children* September 2004, pp. 96–100.

K. Stephens, "Sometimes the Customer *Isn't* Always Right: Problem Solving with Parents," *Exchange* 158, July/August 2004, pp. 68–74.

Quality in Infant-Toddler Programs: A Checklist

1. Look for evidence of a *safe* environment:
   - ☐ No obvious safety hazards, such as electric cords, open sockets, broken equipment, toys with small parts, cleaning supplies within children's reach, unsecured doorways
   - ☐ No hidden safety hazards, such as toxic paint or toys stuffed with toxic materials
   - ☐ Fire and disaster plan that includes how adults will get babies outside
   - ☐ Emergency numbers posted by telephone
   - ☐ Parents' emergency cards on file indicating what to do when the parents can't be reached in an emergency
   - ☐ Safe ratios maintained at all times (California law reads no more than four infants [children under two] to one adult.)
   - ☐ Children allowed optimum risk-taking opportunities ("Optimum" means failure involves learning but not injury.)
   - ☐ Interaction allowed, but children protected from hurting materials or one another

2. Look for evidence of a *healthy* environment:
   - ☐ Sanitary diaper-changing process
   - ☐ Consistent hand-washing after diapering and before eating
   - ☐ Proper food preparation and storage
   - ☐ Staff recognizes symptoms of common illnesses
   - ☐ Health policies that indicate when children are to be excluded from the program because of illness
   - ☐ Health records, maintained on all children, showing evidence that their immunizations are up to date
   - ☐ Regular washing of sheets and toys
   - ☐ Staff knowledge of infant and toddler nutritional needs
   - ☐ Food allergies posted prominently

3. Look for evidence of a *learning* environment:
   - ☐ Optimum amount of age-appropriate toys, materials, and equipment
   - ☐ Caregivers consider caregiving times as "learning times"
   - ☐ Free play valued above exercises, directed play activities, group times
   - ☐ Environment includes plenty of softness, some seclusion, provisions for high mobility
   - ☐ Environment developmentally appropriate for all children present any given day

4. Look for evidence that the staff's goal is to advance physical and intellectual competence:
   - ☐ Staff's ability to explain how the environment, the free play, the caregiving activities, and the staff's relationship with the children make up the curriculum
   - ☐ Staff's ability to explain how the curriculum promotes development of fine and gross motor skills and cognitive skills, including problem-solving and communication skills

5. Look for evidence that the program supports social and emotional development and that staff members provide positive guidance and discipline:
   - ☐ Staff members encourage children to develop a sense of themselves through body awareness, by using their name, and through promoting cultural identification.
   - ☐ Staff members recognize and accept children's feelings and encourage appropriate expression.
   - ☐ Staff members control and guide behavior without using either physical or verbal punishment.
   - ☐ Staff members encourage creative social problem solving when children experience conflict with another child.
   - ☐ Staff members teach respect by showing respect.

6. Look for evidence that the program strives to establish positive and productive relationships with families:
   - ☐ Regular and ongoing communication with parents at pickup and dropoff times emphasizing an *exchange* of information
   - ☐ Friendly atmosphere
   - ☐ Conferences and parent meetings
   - ☐ Mutual problem-solving approach to conflicts

7. Look for evidence that the program is well run and purposeful and responds to participants' needs:
   - ☐ Good record keeping
   - ☐ Attention to infants' individual needs
   - ☐ Attention to parents' needs
   - ☐ Responsible program management

8. Look for evidence that the staff is professional:
   - ☐ Well trained
   - ☐ Respect confidentiality

appendix B

Environmental Chart

This chart shows how to set up both the physical and the social environments to promote development. Remember that rates of development vary a great deal among children. These age guides may not fit individual children, but the chart as a whole does reflect the *sequence of development.*

Level I: Development After Birth

Area of Development	Physical Environment	Social Environment
Physical *Large Muscles* Infants' primary task is head control • Lifts head briefly • Can turn head to clear nose for breathing • Most arm and leg movements are reflexive and are not under infants' conscious control *Small Muscles* • Cannot control hands—often keep them clenched • Grasp whatever is put into hands because of reflexive action • Stare at objects, especially faces; begin to coordinate eyes	**Appropriate Toys and Equipment** • Crib or bassinet, a place to feel secure while sleeping • Mat, rug, or blanket in a safe space to lie unencumbered with room to move around • Few toys needed yet because environment is stimulating enough • Faces are interesting, and so is a bright-colored scarf • Don't put rattles or toys into hands because they can't let go of them	**Adult Role** • Use sensitive observation to determine infants' needs • Provide a feeling of security when necessary (wrap infants in a blanket and place in a small enclosed space) • Let infants experience wide open space, like the floor, at times • Provide peace and quiet and a minimal amount of stimulation—people infants associate with (caregiver and other children) provide enough stimulation • Put infants in a safe spot where they can be part of the center but not overstimulated • Call infants by name • Encourage infants to focus on caregiving tasks
Emotional/Social *Feelings and Self-Awareness* • Infants show only satisfaction or dissatisfaction • Infants do not differentiate self from the rest of the world *Social* • May smile • Make eye contact	• Infants need to be where safe and secure and needs can be easily met • Large playpen provides safety from more mobile toddlers (should be large enough to hold both adults and children)	• Respond to infants' messages and try to determine real needs (remember that dissatisfaction is not always due to hunger) • Provide for attachment needs by having a consistent caregiver • Hold during feeding

Level I: Development After Birth (*continued*)

Area of Development	Physical Environment	Social Environment
Emotional/Social • Are soothed by faces • Respond to being held	**Appropriate Toys and Equipment**	**Adult Role** • Provide for infant-to-infant contact • Minimum adult interference—infants should be free to develop at their own rates
Intellectual • Can coordinate eyes and follow objects or faces as they move • Respond to faces or objects they see • Suck and gum objects that come near the mouth • Display reflexes that are the beginnings of the sensory skills, which in turn provide the basis for the development of intellectual skills	• Infants need an interesting yet safe environment with a limited variety of soft, washable, colorful toys to be looked at or sucked on (be sure there are no small parts to come off and be swallowed) • Allow space for infants to move freely (though they can't yet go anywhere) • Don't prop in infant seat or other restrictive device	• Give them faces to look at (especially that of the primary caregiver) and opportunities to see, touch, and gum objects • Don't force anything on them • Place them on their backs so they can have a broader view, both ears can hear, and they can use their hands
Language • Listen • Cry • Respond to voices	• At this level, people are more important for language development than is physical environment • Set up environment so that infants' needs are easily met and they don't have to wait for long periods of time	• Listen to infants • Try to interpret their cries • Talk to infants, especially during caregiving times; tell them what will happen; give time for a response; tell them what is happening as it happens

Level II: Month 3

Area of Development	Physical Environment	Social Environment

Physical
Large Muscles
- Beginning to lose reflexes and have voluntary control of arms and legs
- Can lift head and control it better when held in upright position

Appropriate Toys and Equipment
- Large playpen, big enough for caregivers and several infants
- Variety of washable objects within reach of infants for them to look at and stretch for
- Rug or mat for infants to lie on
- Avoid restrictive devices

Adult Role
- Sit with children periodically and watch attentively
- Respond when called for
- Don't continually distract with unnecessary noise or talk; entertainment isn't necessary
- Allow infants freedom to explore through looking, sucking, stretching, and reaching

Small Muscles
- Grasp reflex no longer takes over hands all the time
- Reach for objects with both arms but with hands fisted
- Swipe and miss

- Same as above

- Same as above

Emotional/Social
Feelings and Self-Awareness
- Show wider variety of feelings and use voice to express them
- Begin to see hands and feet belong to them and begin to explore them, as well as face, eyes, and mouth, with hands
- Begin to recognize primary caregiver
- Respond differently to different people
- Coo and babble when talked to

- People are more important than objects

- Provide for attachment needs because infants need to develop a primary relationship
- Recognize and respect infants' feelings: talk about what infants seem to be expressing, especially during caregiving

Intellectual
- Respond to what they see
- Attend longer than at first
- Look from one object to another
- Can hold object on their own and manipulate to some extent
- Give signs of remembering
- When they hear a noise, they look for the source
- Look and suck at the same time but have to stop sucking to listen

- Some interesting toys and objects for infants at this level of development include bright scarves, soft balls, rattles, squeeze toys, plastic keys, and large plastic beads

- Encourage exploration and curiosity by providing a variety of objects of different textures, shapes, and sizes
- Allow children freedom and peace to explore by putting them on their back in a safe area large enough for them to move freely
- Provide for interaction with other infants

Language
- Listen attentively
- Coo, whimper, gurgle, and make a variety of other sounds
- Cry less often
- "Talk" to themselves as well as to others, particularly primary caregiver

- People are still more important than equipment or objects for language development
- Some toys to give auditory experiences—let them try making noise with bells, rattles, and squeaky toys

- Talk to infants, especially during caregiving routines; prepare them ahead of time for what is going to happen
- Respond to babbling and cooing—play sound games with infants

Level III: Month 6

Area of Development	Physical Environment	Social Environment
Physical *Large Muscles* • Have control of head • Turn from back to stomach and stomach to back • May move from place to place by rolling • May creep or inch forward or backward • May almost get to sitting while rolling over *Small Muscles* • Reach with one arm and can grasp at will • Hold objects and manipulate them • Can grasp with thumb and forefinger but not well yet • Change objects from one hand to the other	**Appropriate Toys and Equipment** • Need more open space and freedom than before • Need a variety of textures under their body—hard floor, rugs, grass, wooden deck, etc. • Need a variety of interesting objects to move and reach toward	**Adult Role** • Place objects far enough from them so that infants must work to get them • Provide plenty of room and motivation for moving around as well as manipulating and grasping objects • Provide for interaction with other infants • Keep infants in positions they can get in by themselves
Emotional/Social *Feelings and Self-Awareness* • Display a wider variety of feelings • Becoming aware of body parts • See difference between self and rest of the world • Respond to name • Have taste preferences • May want to start self-feeding *Social* • May respond with fear to strangers • Call to primary caregiver for help • Enjoy games with people (peek-a-boo)	• Space large enough for exploration and social interactions will promote relationships	• Talk to infants, especially during caregiving; place special emphasis on naming body parts • Call children by name • Encourage children to take over self-help skills as they are able
Intellectual • Visually alert a good part of waking hours • Recognize familiar objects • Can see and reach for objects they want • Can pick up and manipulate objects • Look for dropped objects • Can use several senses at once • Memory is developing	• Infants continue to enjoy all the toys and objects listed in Level II under Intellectual Development • Can now appreciate a wider variety of objects at once • Place objects around a safe area so that infants have reason to move around and reach for them	• Provide for attachment needs and let children use primary caregiver to provide security in presence of stranger • Play games like peek-a-boo • Allow children freedom to explore • Change or rearrange objects in the environment periodically • Provide for interaction with other infants
Language • Respond to different voice tones and inflections • More control over sounds produced • Use a variety of sounds to express feelings • Imitate tones and inflections	• Cloth or cardboard books	• Respond to children's communication • Talk to children, especially during caregiving routines • During playtimes, comment on what children are doing if appropriate (be careful not to interrupt so the words get in the way of the experience)

Level IV: Month 9

Area of Development	Physical Environment	Social Environment
Physical	**Appropriate Toys and Equipment**	**Adult Role**
Large Muscles	• Infants need more room to explore and a greater variety of objects, textures, experiences, toys	• Watch for children who stand up but can't sit back down; help when they indicate they are stuck
• Crawl	• Plastic or wooden cars and trucks, play or real telephones, blocks, dolls, balls of different sizes, nesting toys	• Be sensible about helping children who get stuck; don't rescue them but promote problem solving
• May crawl stiff-legged		
• May crawl while holding object in hand		
• Pull to stand on furniture	• Pillows and low platforms (or steps) can be added to the environment to provide a variety of levels for children to explore	• Provide open spaces and safe climbing opportunities
• May stand alone		• Allow children to explore with little adult interference
• May or may not be able to get back down from standing	• Rails or low furniture needed for standing or cruising	• Encourage infants to use manipulative skills, such as pulling off socks, opening doors, taking apart nesting toys
• Get into sitting position		
• May move along holding on to furniture		
Small Muscles		
• Can pick up small objects easily with thumb and forefinger		
• Explore and manipulate with forefinger		
• Growing in eye-hand coordination		
Emotional/Social		
Feelings and Self-Awareness		• Provide enough of a schedule for infants to come to anticipate the sequence of events
• Clearly attached to primary caregiver and may fear separation		
• Reject things they don't want		• Allow opportunities for uninterrupted concentration
Social		
• Feed selves biscuit	• Need the tools for self-help, such as cup and spoon	• Encourage problem solving
• Drink from cup holding handle		• Don't help until they're really stuck
• Usually a willing performer if asked		• Allow them to discover the consequences of their behavior whenever it is safe to do so
• Becoming sensitive to and interested in the moods and activities of others		
• Tease		
• Anticipate events		
Intellectual		
• Remember games and toys from previous days	• The objects and toys listed under Physical Development are also appropriate for promoting intellectual development	• Provide the opportunity for infants to become assertive
• Anticipate people's return		• Help children interpret the effect of their actions on others
• Can concentrate and not get interrupted	• Also provide interesting and safe objects from the adult world—pots, pans, wooden spoons, and junk such as discarded boxes, both big and little (infants appreciate real objects as much as toys)	• Give plenty of opportunities for children to develop self-help skills
• Pull cover off toy they have seen hidden		• Help children express separation fears, accept them, and help them deal with them
• Enjoy taking things out of container and putting them back		• Provide for attachment to primary caregiver
• Solve simple manipulative problems		• Provide good models for children (adults who express honest feelings, neither minimized nor exaggerated)
• Interested in discovering the consequences of their behavior		

Level IV: Month 9 (*continued*)

Area of Development	Physical Environment	Social Environment
Language • Pay attention to conversations • May respond to words other than own name • May carry out simple commands • Use words such as "mama" and "dada" • Have intonation • May repeat a sequence of sounds • Yell	**Appropriate Toys and Equipment** • Appreciate a greater variety of picture books	**Adult Role** • Include infants in conversations • Don't talk about them if they're present unless you include them (especially important at this stage) • Promote interactions with other infants • Respond to infants' sounds • Encourage use of words • Ask questions infants can respond to

Level V: Month 12

Area of Development	Physical Environment	Social Environment
Physical	**Appropriate Toys and Equipment**	**Adult Role**

Physical

Large Muscles
- Can stand without holding on
- May walk but probably prefer to crawl
- Climb up and down stairs
- May climb out of crib

Small Muscles
- May use both hands at the same time for different things
- Use thumbs well
- Show preference for one hand
- May undress self or untie shoes

Appropriate Toys and Equipment
- Need lots of space both indoors and outdoors to enjoy crawling and practice walking
- Need lots of objects to manipulate, explore, experiment with, and carry around

Adult Role
- Provide for safety and plenty of movement
- Don't push children to walk—allow them to decide when they are finished with crawling

Emotional/Social

Feelings and Self-Awareness
- Show wide variety of emotions and respond to those of others
- Fear strangers and new places
- Show affection
- Show moods and preferences
- May know difference between their possessions and others'

- Provide an environment that encourages and facilitates self-help skills

- Provide for self-help skills
- Acknowledge infants' possessions and help protect them
- Give approval
- Set reasonable limits
- Accept uncooperative behavior as a sign of self-assertion
- Give choices
- Give and return affection
- Accept and help infants deal with fears and frustrations

Social
- Feed self
- Help dress self
- Obey commands
- Seek approval but are not always cooperative

- Provide needed tools and equipment for self-help skills

- Encourage self-help skills

Intellectual
- Good at finding hidden objects
- Increased memory
- Solve problems
- Use trial-and-error method effectively
- Explore new approaches to problems
- Think about actions before doing them (sometimes)
- Imitate people who are not present

- Children at this level enjoy most of the toys and household objects already mentioned but use them in more sophisticated ways
- Also enjoy large beads to string, large Lego blocks, small building blocks, stacking cones, wooden snap trains, etc.

- Promote active problem solving
- Provide for interaction with other children
- Set up environment so children see new and more complex ways to use toys and equipment

Language
- Know words stand for objects
- Begin to sound like they speak the language of their parents (use same sounds and intonations)
- Use gestures to express self
- May say two to eight words

- Toy telephones, dolls, and books promote language development at this level
- Any toy can become a reason to talk as children play
- Music promotes language development

- Promote interaction among children; children learn to talk from adults, but they practice as they play with other children
- Give simple instructions
- Play games with children
- Sing songs and do finger plays
- Encourage expression of feelings
- Fill in missing words and expand utterance for children when responding

Level VI: Month 18

Area of Development	Physical Environment	Social Environment
Physical	**Appropriate Toys and Equipment**	**Adult Role**
Large Muscles	• Need room to walk and run	• Keep the environment full and
• Walk fast and well	• Enjoy taking walks if adult isn't too	interesting; may need to change
• Seldom fall	goal-oriented	arrangement periodically and intro-
• Run, but awkwardly	• Enjoy plenty of sensory experiences	duce new toys
• Walk up stairs holding a hand	such as water play and sand	• Promote interactions among
Small Muscles		children
• Can use crayon to scribble as well		• Allow for enough physical exercise
as imitate marks		
• Better control at self-feeding		
Emotional/Social		
• Imitate adults in dramatic play	• Provide the tools for dramatic play,	• Allow children to help as they are
• Interested in helping with chores	such as dress-up clothes, dolls,	able
• Interested in dressing process; can	housekeeping equipment, dishes	• Set limits and gently but firmly
undress to some extent		enforce them
• May be beginning to get some		• Encourage self-help skills
bladder and bowel control		• Help children with their interaction
		and talk them through aggressive
		situations
Intellectual		
• Can begin to solve problems in their	• Provide a variety of toys available	• Provide a number of choices
head	on low shelves for children to	• Help children work on a problem
• Rapid increase of language	choose from—small people,	uninterrupted
development	animals, doll houses, containers	• Encourage use of language
• Beginning of ability to fantasize and	filled with small objects, measuring	
role-play	cups, spoons, etc.	
Language		
• May use words to gain attention	• Books with clear, simple pictures	• Provide a variety of experiences
• Can use words to indicate wants		and help children put language to
• May know 10 words		them
• Enjoy picture books		• Ask questions and encourage
		children to ask them too
		• Read aloud

Level VII: Month 24

Area of Development	Physical Environment	Social Environment

Physical

Large Muscles
- Run headlong, have trouble stopping and turning
- Walk up and down stairs (may hold on)
- Throw a ball
- Kick a ball forward

Small Muscles
- Put on some easy clothing
- Hold spoon, fork, cup but may still spill
- Can use a paintbrush but doesn't control drips
- Can turn the pages of a book

Appropriate Toys and Equipment
- Low climbers and slides
- Large balls, both lightweight and heavier
- Low three- and four-wheeled, steerable, well-balanced vehicles both with pedals and without
- Swings children can get into and out of themselves
- Hills, ramps, low stairs
- Space to run
- Large, lightweight blocks
- Wooden puzzles with two to four large pieces
- Pegboards
- Stacking toys
- Big beads to string
- Construction sets (easy to put together)
- Play dough
- Rhythm instruments
- Texture matching games
- Feely boxes
- Sand and water and toys to play with in them
- Dolls to dress and mostly *undress*
- Books
- Felt pens, crayons, finger paint

Adult Role
- Encourage freedom to move in any way they like (within limits, of course)
- Allow for plenty of physical and sensory experiences
- Encourage children to find new ways to combine and use familiar toys and equipment
- Offer choices
- Allow loving chases or loving wrestles
- Play circle games and sing songs with movements (but not with the whole group as a circle time compulsory activity)
- Encourage small-muscle use by offering a wide variety of choices
- Offer a number of sensory activities
- Allow children to use toys and materials in creative ways (within limits, of course)
- Allow children to combine materials and toys in unique ways (within limits, of course)
- Facilitate problem solving when children get stuck

Emotional/Social
- May understand personal property concepts ("That's mine"; "That's Daddy's")
- May tend to hoard possessions; may resist sharing
- Assert independence ("Me do it!")
- Take pride in accomplishments
- May say "no" even to things they want

- Provide space for personal possessions (cubbies or boxes)
- Provide duplicates of favorite toys so sharing isn't such an issue
- Provide plenty of things to do so sharing isn't such an issue
- Hand puppets sometimes allow children to express their feelings
- Art, music, and dramatic play experiences (listed under Small Muscles) allow children to express their feelings
- Large muscle experiences also allow children to express their feelings

- Respect children's need to hold on to their possessions
- Model sharing rather than require it
- Allow children to try things by themselves, even when you know you can do them better or faster
- Help them have accomplishments they can take pride in

Level VII: Month 24 (*continued*)

Area of Development	Physical Environment	Social Environment

Intellectual

- Can identify parts of a doll—hair, ears, etc.
- Can fit forms into a form board
- Can solve many problems on their own
- Can work simple puzzles

Appropriate Toys and Equipment

- Provide books, puzzles, records, in addition to toys listed above, that allow choices and provide opportunities for concept development and for problem solving

Adult Role

- Provide a variety of choices of materials to use and ways to spend time
- Give freedom to use materials in creative ways
- Encourage problem solving
- Allow exploration

Language

- Use personal pronouns (I, me, you) but not always correctly
- Refer to themselves by name
- Use two- and three-word sentences
- May know as many as 50 to 200 words
- Talk about what they are doing

- Provide a good variety of books (children can use them carefully now)
- Pictures at child's eye level around the room, changed often, give children something to talk about
- Allow and set up "happenings"— experiences that give children something to talk about
- Provide for music experiences

- Encourage conversation both between children and between child and adult
- Help children speculate ("I wonder what would happen if . . .")
- Go places and talk about what you do and see
- Encourage verbalization of feelings and wants
- Help children begin to talk out differences instead of relying on hitting, kicking, and other negative physical behaviors

Level VIII: Month 36

Area of Development	Physical Environment	Social Environment

Physical

Large Muscles
- Walk, run with control, climb well, throw a ball with aim
- Jump in place
- Balance on one foot for a second or two
- May pedal tricycle

Small Muscles
- Put on shoes but don't tie laces
- Put on clothing except for buttoning
- Feed self alone and well
- Scribble with more control
- Draw or copy a circle
- Use paintbrush and control drips
- Use construction toys imaginatively
- Exercise bowel and bladder control

Appropriate Toys and Equipment

Need all the toys and equipment listed for the 24-month-old, but larger versions that provide more challenges. The 36-month-old can begin to use the equipment designed for preschoolers and is probably ready to move on from the toddler program.
- May enjoy some large wooden blocks, balance boards, planks, boxes, ladders for building
- Unit blocks and accessories to go with them
- Construction sets with more and smaller pieces
- Small-wheeled vehicles to go with blocks
- Sensory table
- Puzzles
- Objects to sort
- Flannel board and figures
- Small beads to string
- Wide range of art materials, including paint, collage, scissors, glue, crayons, felt pens, chalk
- Dolls and accessories
- Doll house
- Extensive dramatic play equipment
- Puppets

Adult Role

- Offer choices
- Can move gross motor equipment outside for this age group and expect them to be slightly more restrained inside
- Be careful about encouraging gross motor experiences in boys more than in girls (they should get equal encouragement; indeed, girls should get extra encouragement if they are reluctant)
- Allow plenty of choices
- Encourage children to use toys and materials in creative ways
- Find ways that older children can become involved in small-muscle, manipulative activities without being interrupted by younger children who want to dump rather than build
- Keep small parts from younger children, who might put them in their mouths
- Encourage fine motor activities in both boys and girls (if boys are less interested, find materials that entice them)

Emotional/Social

- May show regard for people or possessions
- Play with sustained interest
- Play and interact with another child
- Willing to use toilet
- Can conform to group for short periods

- Provide space for personal possessions
- Provide plenty of materials to allow children to share feelings and to role-play, such as dramatic play equipment, dress-up clothes, puppets, dolls, small figures, musical instruments and experiences, art materials
- Books that children can identify with also help them express their feelings
- Have toilet readily available

- Begin to encourage sharing and cooperative play
- Help children get involved and stay involved in play activities by preventing interruptions by other children
- Can expect children to participate in short active group times, such as circle time
- Encourage interaction among children

Level VIII: Month 36 (*continued*)

Area of Development	Physical Environment	Social Environment

Intellectual

- May count to two or three
- May draw face or very simple figure
- Can work simple puzzles
- More sophisticated problem solving
- Call self "I" and other people "you"
- Know he is a boy or she is a girl
- Know most of the parts of the body
- Compare sizes

Appropriate Toys and Equipment

- The variety of construction materials, manipulative toys, dramatic play, and art materials listed above all contribute to intellectual development
- Objects to sort
- Plenty of puzzles
- Parquetry blocks
- Simple games such as lotto
- Simple, hands-on science displays and experiments

Adult Role

- Provide plenty of choices
- Encourage peer interaction during problem solving
- Encourage absorption, involvement with materials, activities, and people
- Encourage an inquiring attitude
- Encourage creative thinking
- Encourage children to think about past experiences as well as future ones
- Encourage development of number concepts in a natural context

Language

- Use plurals
- Converse in short sentences, answer questions, give information, use language to convey simple ideas
- Name pictures and label actions
- May have 900-word vocabulary
- Articulate fairly clearly

- Setting up the environment for gross motor, fine motor, social, emotional, and intellectual experiences should provide plenty for the children to talk about
- Add to variety and complexity of books and pictures provided for two-year-olds
- Music experience
- Simple hands-on science displays and experiments

- Encourage comparisons of size, weight, etc., of objects in a natural context
- Read books, tell stories, sing songs
- Embed language in all experiences
- Encourage questioning
- Encourage conversations
- Encourage speculation
- Encourage verbal conflict resolution
- Encourage verbalization of feelings
- Help children listen to one another
- Play language games such as lotto

Guiding Principles of the Parent Services Project

The Parent Services Project Philosophy

The Parent Services Project (PSP) recognizes that the well-being and sense of significance of parents are of central importance to the development of the child. Parents who possess a sense of fulfillment will enrich their children's lives, take more active roles in their communities, and strengthen their families, adding to the overall quality of life.

Partnership

The relationship between families and staff is one of equality and respect, resulting in the creation of a mutually beneficial partnership. Success comes from promoting the excellence of all partners.

Empowerment

Families are their own best advocates. They are decision makers on a collaborative team. Parents who are confident and competent empower their children to achieve success and foster their well-being.

Family Strengths

Families are assets, not barriers to overcome or work around. They are a vital resource to themselves and to one another. Programs build on these family strengths. Seeking services is considered a sign of strength.

Cultural Competence

Respect is possible when each family's culture is valued and recognized. Programs are community-based and are culturally and socially relevant to the families they serve.

Participant-Driven

Program services are best determined by participants. Parents make choices to participate in activities that reflect their own needs and interests.

Social Support

Support is important to all families. Social support networks reduce social isolation and promote the well-being of the child, the family, and the community. Programs are a bridge between families and other services.

Notes

Chapter 1

1. We use the word *caregivers*, but others prefer *infant care teacher* or *infant-toddler teacher*, or *teacher*, or in the case of family child care, *provider*. Magda Gerber's Resources for Infant Educarers (RIE) used the term *educarer*. At the Pikler Institute the term is *nurse*, though the caregivers there have not studied medicine.
2. Linda Acredolo and Susan Goodwyn, *How to Talk with Your Babies Before They Can Talk* (Lincolnwood, Ill.: Contemporary Books, 1996).
3. See further explanation in Gonzalez-Mena, *Multicultural Issues in Child Care* (Mountain View, Calif.: Mayfield, 2001).
4. Although expression of anger has been used as an example of relating in a respectful way to infants and toddlers, it is important to note that this particular example is culture bound. Not all cultures believe in the individual's right to express feelings unless that expression somehow serves the group.
5. Bradley Wright Films, 1 Oak Hill Drive, San Anselmo, California 94960.
6. Jerome S. Bruner, "The Organization of Action and the Nature of Adult-Infant Transaction," in *The Analysis of Action*, edited by M. von Cranach and R. Harre (Cambridge: Cambridge University Press, 1982).
7. This hands-off approach is a cultural issue. In some cultures, children are taught that graciously receiving help is a skill to be learned and is more important than standing on their own two feet. See further explanation in Gonzalez-Mena, *Diversity in Early Care and Education: Honoring Differences* (New York: McGraw-Hill, 2005).
8. From the video, *The Next Step: Including the Infant in the Curriculum*, developed by the WestEd Program for Infant Toddler Caregivers (PITC), 2001.

Chapter 2

1. Miriam David and Genevive Appell,. *Lóczy: An Unusual Approach to Mothering*. Translated from *Lóczy Ou Le Maternage Insolite* by Jean Marie Clark; revised translation by Judit Falk (Budapest: Association Pikler-Loczy for Young Children, [1973, 1996] 2001).
2. Magda Gerber and Allison Johnson, *Your Self Confident Baby* (New York: Wiley, 1998). Magda Gerber, *Dear Parent: Caring for Infants with Respect* (Los Angeles: Resources for Infant Educarers, 1998).
3. Nel Nodding, *Educating Moral People: A Caring Alternative to Character Education* (New York: Teachers College Press, 2002). Nel Nodding, *Starting at Home: Care and Social Policy* (Berkeley: University of California Press, 2002). Nel Nodding, *The Challenge to Care in Schools* (New York: Teachers College Press 1992).
4. J. Ronald, Lally, "Brain Research, Infant Learning, and Child Care Curriculum" *Child Care Information Exchange*, May 1998, pp. 46–48.
5. Personal letter from Patti Wade, October 1978.
6. Abraham H. Maslow, *Toward a Psychology of Being*, 2nd ed. (New York: Van Nostrand, 1968), p. 51.

7. Albert Bandura's social learning theory is behind the idea that modeling is a powerful teaching tool. Bandura's research showed that people are influenced by each other's behaviors. Later researchers became fascinated with how infants, starting at a very young age, imitate others. A. Bandura, *Social Learning Theory* (Englewood Cliffs, N.J.: Prentice-Hall, 1977).

Chapter 3

1. J. Ronald Lally, "The Impact of Child Care Policies and Practices on Infant/Toddler Identity Formation," *Young Children* 51(1), November 1995, pp. 58–67. In this article, Lally makes a compelling case for the importance of such practices as primary caregiving systems.
2. Miriam David and Genevive Appell, *Lóczy: An Unusual Approach to Mothering.* Translated from *Lóczy Ou Le Maternage Insolite* by Jean Marie Clark; revised translation by Judit Falk (Budapest: Association Pikler-Loczy for Young Children, 2001).
3. Anne Morrow Lindbergh, *Gift from the Sea* (New York: Pantheon, 1955), p. 104.
4. For the complete study results, look for the "Feeding Infants and Toddlers Study" in the *Journal of the American Dietetic Association,* January 2004.
5. What you saw in that scene was based on an observation at The Pikler Institute in November 2003. The description is adapted from an article by Janet Gonzalez-Mena, "What Can an Orphanage Teach Us? Lessons from Budapest," *Young Children,* 58(5), 2004, pp. 27–30. There, the idea of caregiving as curriculum is taken very seriously. Adults are trained in specific ways to carry out each caregiving routine and the result is that the infants and toddlers in this residential nursery are trusting and secure in the relationships they have with their caregivers. Fulfilled with the kind of individual attention they get during those times of the day, they then are able to explore freely the rest of the time, playing alone and with each other with little or no adult interruptions. Granted this is a very specific curriculum coupled with a good deal of training, and nothing is done casually. The approach has been developed, studied, and refined since 1946. We aren't suggesting that you adopt the model, but we are suggesting that the fact they created their own unique curriculum through observation and research can inspire others to do the same.
6. The suggestions in this chapter fit the overall philosophy of the book, which is based on a value of independence and individuality. It's important to note that not all cultures have these values. Therefore these approaches to caregiving should be discussed with the families and some agreement should be reached. See Gonzalez-Mena, *Diversity in Early Care and Education* for more information on how to communicate with parents regarding cultural issues. Also see the videos on the subject: *Early Childhood Training Series: Diversity,* Magna Systems, 1995.
7. S. M. Beal and C. F. Finch, "An Overview of Retrospective Case Control Slides Investigating the Relationship Between Prone Sleep Positions and SIDS," *Journal of Pediatrics and Child Health* 27, 1993, pp. 334–339.

Chapter 4

1. S. Rosenkoetter and L. Barton, "Bridges to Literacy: Early Routines that Promote Later School Success," *Zero to Three* 22(4), February/March 2002, pp. 33–38.
2. Seymour Papert, *Mindstorm: Children, Computers, and Powerful Ideas* (New York: Basic Books, 1980), p. vi.
3. Elena Bodrova and Deborah Leong, *Tools of the Mind: The Vygotskian Approach to Early Childhood Education* (Columbus, Ohio: Merrill, 1996).
4. Janet Gonzalez-Mena, "What Can an Orphanage Teach Us? Lessons from Budapest," *Young Children,* September, 2004, pp. 26–30.
5. Magda Gerber, "From a Speech by Magda Gerber," *Educaring* 16(3), Summer 1995, p. 7.
6. J. McVicker Hunt, *Intelligence and Experience* (New York: Ronald Press, 1961), p. 267.
7. Judith Van Horn, Patricia Monighan Nourot, Barbara Scales, and Keith Rodriquez Alward. *Play at the Center of the Curriculum* (Columbus, OH: Merrill, 2003).
8. Abraham H. Maslow, *Toward a Psychology of Being,* 2nd ed. (New York: Van Nostrand, 1968), pp. 55–56.
9. Jerry Ferguson, "Creating Growth-Producing Environments for Infants and Toddlers," in *Supporting the Growth of Infants, Toddlers, and Parents,* edited by Elizabeth Jones (Pasadena, CA: Pacific Oaks, 1979.)

Chapter 5

1. Rima Shore, *Rethinking the Brain: New Insights into Early Development* (New York: Families and Work Institute, 1997), pp. 16–18.
2. M. Klaus and J. Kennell, *Parent-Infant Bonding* (St. Louis: Mosby, 1982), p. 2.
3. R. Isabella and J. Belsky, "Interactional Synchrony and the Origins of Infant-Mother Attachment," *Child Development* 6, 1991, pp. 373–384.
4. M. Ainsworth, M. Blehman, E. Waters, and S. Wall, *Patterns of Attachment: A Psychological Study of the Strange Situation* (Hillsdale, N.J.: Erlbaum, 1978), pp. 333–341.
5. O. Mayseless, "Attachment patterns and their outcomes," *Human Development*, 39, 1996, pp. 206–223.
6. Harry Harlow, "The Nature of Love," *American Psychology* 13, 1958, p. 386.
7. John Bowlby, *Attachment*, vol. 1 of *Attachment and Loss* (New York: Basic, 2000), p. 343.
8. J. Ronald Lally, "Brain Research, Infant Learning, and Child Care Curriculum," *Child Care Information Exchange* 121, May/June 1998, pp. 46–48.
9. C. P. Edwards and H. Raikes, "Relationship-Based Approaches to Infant/Toddler Care and Education," *Young Children* 57(4), July 2002, pp. 10–17.
10. David Kaplan, "Fetal-Infant Crack Addiction," *Foster Parent Training*, conference notes, Daly City, Calif., 1990.
11. T. M. Roebuck, S. Mattson, and E. Riley, "Prenatal Exposure to Alcohol: Effects on the Brain," in *Alcohol and Alcoholism*, edited by J. H. Hannigan and L. P. Spear (Mahwah, N.J.: Erlbaum, 1999), pp. 1–16.

Chapter 6

1. J. M. Mandler and L. Douglas, "Concept Formation in Infancy," *Cognitive Development* 8, 1993, pp. 291–318.
2. Robert Samples, *The Metaphoric Mind* (Menlo Park, Calif.: Addison-Wesley, 1976), p. 95.
3. T. G. R. Bower, *Development in Infancy*, 2nd ed. (San Francisco: W. H. Freeman, 1982), pp. 87–99.
4. P. W. Jusczyk and R. N. Aslin, "Infants' Detection of the Sound Patterns of Words in Fluent Speech," *Cognitive Psychology* 29, 1997, pp. 1–23.

5. D. R. Mandel, P. W. Jusczyk, and D. B. Pisoni, "Infants' Recognition of the Sound Patterns of Their Own Names," *Psychological Science*, 1995, 6, pp. 314–317.
6. J. E. Steiner, "Human Facial Expressions in Response to Taste and Smell Stimulation," in *Advances in Child Development and Behavior*, Vol. 13, edited by H. W. Reese and L. P. Lipsitt, pp. 257–295.
7. S. W. Porges and L. P. Lipsitt, "Neonatal Responsivity to Gustatory Stimulation," *Infant Behavior and Development*, 1993, 16, pp. 487–494.
8. K. Simons, ed., *Early Visual Development: Normal and Abnormal* (New York: Oxford University Press 1993), pp. 439–449.

Chapter 7

1. S. J. Fomon and S. E. Nelson, "Body Composition of the Male and Female in Reference to Infants," *Annual Review of Nutrition*, 22, 2002, pp. 1–17.
2. P. M. Thompson and J. N. Giedd, "Growth Patterns in the Developing Brain," *Nature*, 404, 2000, pp. 190–192.
3. P. Casaer, "Old and New Facts About Perinatal Brain Development," *Journal of Child Psychology and Psychiatry*, 34, 1993, pp. 101–109.
4. M. A. Bell and N. A. Fox, "Brain Development over the First Year of Life," in *Human Behavior and the Development of the Brain*, edited by G. Dawson and K. W. Fischer (New York: Guilford, 1998), pp. 314–345.
5. E. Thelen and L. B. Smith, "Dynamic Systems Theories," in *Handbook of Child Psychology*, vol. 1, edited by W. Damon (New York: Wiley, 1998), pp. 563–633.
6. Emmi Pikler, "Data on Gross Motor Development of the Infant," *Early Development and Care*, 1, 1972, pp. 297–310. Also, S. Petrie and S. Owen, *Authentic Relationships in Group Care for Infants and Toddlers: Resources for Infant Educarers (RIE) Principles into Practice*, (London and Philadelphia: Jessica Kingsley Publishers, 2005).
7. Adapted from "Parents: Do You Know the Early Warning Signs of Children with Special Needs?" National Easter Seal Society (2023 W. Ogden Ave., Chicago, IL, 1989).
8. S. Krog, *The Integrated Early Child Curriculum* (New York: McGraw-Hill, 1990) pp. 6–41.

Chapter 8

1. J. H. Flavell, "On Cognitive Development," *Child Development* 53, 1982, pp. 1–10.
2. L. Berk and A. Winsler, *Scaffolding Children's Learning: Vygotsky and Early Childhood Education* (Washington, D.C.: National Association for the Education of Young Children, 1995), p. 22.
3. J. Schickendanz, K. Hansen, and P. Forsyth, *Understanding Children* (Mountain View, Calif.: Mayfield, 1990), p. 196.
4. R. Lalley, "Brain Research, Infant Learning, and Child Care Curriculum," *Child Care Information Exchange* 121, May/June 1998, pp. 46–48.
5. M. Diamond, *Magic Trees of the Mind* (New York: Plume, 1998), pp. 112–120.
6. Stephen Rushton, "Applying Brain Research to Create Developmentally Appropriate Learning Environments," *Young Children* 56(5), September 2001, pp. 76–82.
7. P. H. Brooks and C. McCauley, "Cognitive Research in Mental Retardation," *American Journal of Mental Deficiency* 88, 1984, pp. 479–486.

Chapter 9

1. L. Vygotsky, "Play and Its Role in the Mental Development of the Child," in *Play: Its Role in Development and Evolution*, edited by J. Bruner, A. Jolly, and K. Sylvia (New York: Basic Books, 1976).
2. A. L. Woodward and E. M. Markman, "Early Word Learning," in *Handbook of Child Psychology: Vol. 2. Cognition, Perception and Language*, 5th ed., edited by William Damon (series ed.), Deanna Kuhn and R. S. Sieger (vol. eds.) (New York: Wiley, 1998), pp. 371–420.
3. S. Begley, "How to Build a Baby's Brain," *Newsweek*, Spring/Summer 1997, 28–32.
4. D. L. Mills, S. A. Coffey-Cornia, and H. J. Neville, "Variability in Cerebral Organization During Primary Language Acquisition," in *Human Behavior and the Developing Brain*, edited by G. Davidson and K. W. Fischer (New York: Guilford, 1994), pp. 427–455.
5. Amy Wetherby, "First Words Project: An Update. Florida State University," in *Proceedings of the NAEYC* (Portland, OR: National Institute for Early Childhood Professional Development, 2003).

6. S. B. Heath, *Ways with Words: Language, Life, and Work in Communities and Classrooms* (Cambridge: Cambridge University Press, 1983).
7. G. Stiames and H. Rubin, eds., *Stuttering: Then and Now* (Columbus, Ohio: Merrill, 1986).

Chapter 10

1. Frederick Leboyer, *Birth Without Violence* (New York: Random House, 1978).
2. Stella Chess and Alexander Thomas, *Temperament: Theory and Practice* (New York: Brunner/Mazel, 1996).
3. Alexander Thomas and Stella Chess, *Temperament and Development* (New York: Brunner/Mazel, 1977).
4. M. K. Rothbart, B. A. Ahadi, and D. E. Evans, "Temperament and Personality: Origins and Outcomes," *Journal of Personality and Social Psychology* 78, 2000, pp. 122–135.
5. S. C. Luthar, D. Cicchetti, and B. Becker, "The Construct of Resilience: A Critical Evaluation and Guidelines for the Future," *Child Development* 74, 2000, pp. 543–562.
6. M. L. von Frantz, "The Process of Individuation," in C. G. Jung et al., *Man and His Symbols* (New York: Doubleday, 1964), p. 162.
7. Abraham H. Maslow, *Toward a Psychology of Being* (New York: Van Nostrand, 1968), p. 157.
8. Ibid., pp. 163–164.
9. Ibid., p. 198.
10. L. Gilkerson, "Brain Care: Supporting Healthy Emotional Development," *Child Care Information Exchange* 121, May 1998, pp. 66–68.
11. Rima Shore, *Rethinking the Brain* (New York: Families and Work Institute, 1997), pp. 28–30.
12. Ibid., pp. 41–43.
13. D. Hallahan and J. Kauffman, *Exceptional Children, Introduction to Special Education*, 5th ed. (Englewood Cliffs, N.J.: Prentice Hall, 1991), pp. 176–178.
14. B. Egeland and E. A. Farber, "Infant-Mother Attachment: Factors Related to Its Development and Changes over Time," *Child Development* 55, 1984, pp. 753–771.

Chapter 11

1. T. G. R. Bower, *Development in Infancy*, 2nd ed. (San Francisco: W. H. Freeman, 1982), p. 256.

2. Jaipaul L. Roopnarine and Alice S. Honig, "The Unpopular Child," *Young Children*, September 1985, p. 61.

3. Doyleen McMurtry, early childhood instructor, Solano College, Suisun, California.

4. R. Lally, "The Art and Science of Child Care," *Program for Infant/Toddler Caregivers*, WestEd, 180 Harbor Drive, Suite 112, Sausalito, Calif.

5. Kahlil Gibran, *The Prophet* (New York: Alfred A. Knopf, 1923).

Chapter 12

1. "Together in Care: Meeting the Intimacy Needs of Infants and Toddlers in Groups," in *Child Care Video Magazine* (Sacramento, Calif.: Far West Laboratory and California Department of Education, 1992), pp. 7–8.

2. Louis Torelli, "The Developmentally Designed Group Care Setting: A Supportive Environment for Infants, Toddlers and Caregivers," *Zero to Three*, December 1989, pp. 7–10.

3. Elizabeth Prescott, "The Physical Environment— Powerful Regulator of Experience," *Child Care Information Exchange*, Reprint #4, C-44, Redmond, Wash. 98052.

4. Roger G. Barker, *Ecological Psychology: Concepts and Methods for Studying the Environment of Human Behavior* (Stanford, Calif.: Stanford University Press, 1968).

5. Dennie Wolf, "An Interview with Jim Greenman," *Child Care Information Exchange*, September 1987, p. 19.

6. Thanks to Maggie Cole for these ideas that she has used with infants and toddlers at Napa Valley College Child Care Center.

7. These ideas come from Molly Sullivan, who used them in her family day-care home in Berkeley, California.

8. Elizabeth Jones and Elizabeth Prescott, *Dimensions of Teaching-Learning Environments II: Focus on Day Care* (Pasadena, Calif.: Pacific Oaks, 1978).

9. Torelli, "The Developmentally Designed Group Care Setting."

10. Ruth Money, "The RIE Early Years 'Curriculum'," in *Authentic Relationships in Group Care for Infants and Toddlers: Resources for Infant Educarers (RIE) Principles into Practice*, edited by S. Petrie and S. Owen (London and Philadelphia: Jessica Kingsley Publishers, 2005), pp. 51–68.

11. Jim Greenman, "Designing Infant/Toddler Environments," in *Caring for Infants and Toddlers: What Works, What Doesn't*, vol. 2, edited by Robert Lurie and Roger Neugebauer (Redmond, Wash.: Child Care Information Exchange, 1982).

Chapter 13

1. J. R. Lally, "The Impact of Child Care Policies and Practices on Infant/Toddler Identity Formation," *Young Children* 51(1), November 1995, pp. 58–67.

2. Lisa Delpit, *Other People's Children* (New York: New Press, 1995).

3. In *Black Children: Their Roots, Culture, and Learning Styles*, Janice Hale-Benson discusses how discipline works in the black community. Every adult in the community is expected to firmly correct undesirable behavior even when someone else's child is the one misbehaving. Any misbehavior is not only immediately corrected but reported to the parent as well. In other words, in the black community, there is a social control network that takes responsibility for all the children in that community. Children aren't on their own; they're always being watched by somebody. Hale-Benson says that this approach is different from that in schools, where the teachers don't watch so closely because they expect the children to develop inner controls. Therefore, children who are used to being diligently observed and controlled find themselves more on their own than they're used to. Parents who expect to be notified immediately of any misbehavior may find school a lax place where there seem to be fewer external pressures to keep children behaving properly. See Janice E. Hale-Benson, *Black Children: Their Roots, Culture, and Learning Styles* (Baltimore: Johns Hopkins University Press, 1986), p. 85.

Chapter 14

1. A teenage parent may rely on her mother or may at least need to consult with her mother. A wife may need her husband's approval to make decisions. Sometimes the grandmother, rather than the parents, makes decisions concerning her

grandchildren. Some families have joint decision making. It's of no use to discuss a problem with a mother if she has no authority to make any decision. The family structures in some cultures leave someone other than the mother, or even the father, as the ultimate decision maker.

2. P. Elam, "Creating Quality Infant Group Care Programs," in *Authentic Relationships in Group Care for Infants and Toddlers: Resources for Infant Educarers (RIE) Principles into Practice*, edited by S. Petrie and S. Owen (London and Philadelphia: Jessica Kingsley Publishers, 2005), pp. 83–92.

References

Chapter 1

Acredolo, L., and S. Goodwyn. *How to Talk with Your Babies Before They Can Talk.* Lincolnwood, Ill.: Contemporary Books, 1996.

Bruner, J. S. "The Organization of Action and the Nature of Adult-Infant Transaction." In *The Analysis of Action,* edited by M. von Cranach and R. Harve. Cambridge: Cambridge University Press, 1982.

Coughlan, C. "Using the RIE Approach in a Family Day Care Home," in *Authentic Relationships in Group Care for Infants and Toddlers: Resources for Infant Educarers (RIE) Principles into Practice,* edited by S. Petrie and S. Owen. London and Philadelphia: Jessica Kingsley Publishers, 2005, pp. 69–82.

David, M., and G. Appell. *Lóczy: An Unusual Approach to Mothering.* Translated from *Lóczy ou le Maternage Insolite* by Jean Marie Clark; revised translation by Judit Falk. Budapest: Association Pikler-Loczy for Young Children, 2001.

Edwards, C., and L. Gandini. "Research as a Partnership for Learning Together." In *Bambini: The Italian Approach to Infant-Toddler Care,* edited by L. Gandini and C. P. Edwards. New York: Teachers College Press, 2000, pp. 181–199.

Elam, P. "Creating Quality Infant Group Care Programs," in *Authentic Relationships in Group Care for Infants and Toddlers: Resources for Infant Educarers (RIE) Principles into Practice,* edited by S. Petrie and S. Owen. London and Philadelphia: Jessica Kingsley Publishers, 2005, pp. 83–92.

Ferraro, P. "Supporting Competence in Children." *Educaring* 8(2), Spring 1993, pp. 1–3.

Garcia, R. *Home Centered Care: Designing a Family Day Care Program, a Guide for Caregivers and Parents.* San Francisco: Children's Council of San Francisco, 1985.

Gerber, M. *Resources for Infant Educarers.* Los Angeles: Resources for Infant Educarers, 1991.

Gerber, M. "Respecting Infants: The Loczy Model of Infant Care." In *Supporting the Growth of Infants, Toddlers and Parents,* edited by E. Jones. Pasadena, Calif.: Pacific Oaks, 1979.

Gerber, M. "RIE Principles and Practices," in *Authentic Relationships in Group Care for Infants and Toddlers: Resources for Infant Educarers (RIE) Principles into Practice,* edited by S. Petrie and S. Owen. London and Philadelphia: Jessica Kingsley Publishers, 2005, pp. 35–49.

Gonzalez-Mena, J. *Diversity in Early Care and Education.* New York: McGraw-Hill, 2004.

Gonzalez-Mena, J. "What Can an Orphanage Teach Us? Lessons from Budapest." *Young Children,* 59(4), September 2004, pp. 26–30.

Greenough, W., R. N. Emde, M. Gunnar, R. Massinga, and J. P. Shonkoff. "The Impact of the Caregiving Environment on Young Children's Development: Different Ways of Knowing." *Zero to Three* 21(5), April/May 2001, pp. 16–24.

Honig, A. S. *Secure Relationships: Nurturing Infant/Toddler Attachment in Early Care Settings.* Washington, D.C.: National Association for the Education of Young Children, 2002.

Klass, C. S. "Childrearing Interactions within Developmental Home- or Center-Based Early Education." *Young Children*, March 1987, pp. 9–13.

Money, R. "The RIE Early Years 'Curriculum'," in *Authentic Relationships in Group Care for Infants and Toddlers: Resources for Infant Educarers (RIE) Principles into Practice*, edited by S. Petrie and S. Owen. London and Philadelphia: Jessica Kingsley Publishers, 2005, pp. 51–68.

National Research Council and Institute of Medicine, Board on Children, Youth, and Families, Commission on Behavioral and Social Sciences and Education. *From Neurons to Neighborhoods: The Science of Early Childhood Development*. Washington, D.C.: National Academy Press, 2000.

Nguyen, T. D. "Honey, the Baby Is Wet!" *Educaring* 16(2), Winter-Spring 1995, pp. 10–12.

Petrie, S. "The Work of Emmi Pikler and Magda Gerber." In *Authentic Relationships in Group Care for Infants and Toddlers: Resources for Infant Educarers (RIE) Principles into Practice*, edited by S. Petrie and S. Owen. London and Philadelphia: Jessica Kingsley Publishers, 2005, pp. 17–34.

Pinto, C. "Is Faster Better?" *Educaring* 16(2), Winter-Spring 1995, pp. 4–6.

Pinto, C. "Supporting Competence in a Child with Special Needs: One Child's Story." *Educaring* 22(2), Spring 2001, pp. 1–6.

Schall, J. "Rites of Passage." *Educaring* 23(1), Winter 2002, pp. 1–5.

Shonkoff, J. P., and D. Phillips. "From Neurons to Neighborhoods: The Science of Early Childhood Development—An Introduction." *Zero to Three* 21(5), April/May 2001, pp. 4–7.

Solter, A. "Listening to Infants." *Educaring* 15(1), Winter 1994, pp. 1–4.

Sterling Honig, A. "Quality Infant/Toddler Caregiving: Are There Magic Recipes?" *Young Children*, May 1989, pp. 4–10.

Szanton, E. S. "For America's Infants and Toddlers, Are Important Values Threatened by Our Zeal to 'Teach'?" *Young Children* 56(1), January 2001, pp. 15–21.

Vinson, B. M. "Fishing and Vygotsky's Concept of Effective Education." *Young Children* 56(1), January 2001, pp. 88–89.

Vygotsky, L. S. *Mind in Society: The Development of Higher Psychological Processes*. Cambridge: Harvard University Press, 1978.

Chapter 2

Bandura, A. *Social Learning Theory*. Englewood Cliffs, N.J.: Prentice-Hall, 1977.

Bernhard, J. K., and J. Gonzalez-Mena. "The Cultural Context of Infant and Toddler Care." In *Infants and Toddlers in Out-of-Home Care*, edited by D. Cryer and T. Harms. Baltimore: Brookes, 2000, pp. 237–267.

Bower, T. G. R. *Development in Infancy*. San Francisco: W. H. Freeman, 1982.

Brazelton, T. B., and S. Greenspan. *The Irreducible Needs of Children*. Cambridge, Mass.: Perseus, 2000.

Cook, R. E., A. Tessier, and M. D. Klein. *Adapting Early Childhood Curricula for Children in Inclusive Settings*. Columbus, Ohio: Merrill, 2000.

David, M., and G. Appell. *Lóczy: An Unusual Approach to Mothering*. Translated from *Lóczy ou le Maternage Insolite* by Jean Marie Clark; revised translation by Judit Falk. Budapest: Association Pikler-Loczy for Young Children, [1973, 1996] 2001.

Flyer, J. "Profound, I Say!" *Educaring* 15(2), Spring 1994, pp. 1–4.

Gerber, M. "Conflict Resolution with Infants." *Educaring* 4(4), Fall 1983, p. 3.

Gerber, M. *Dear Parent: Caring for Infants with Respect*. Los Angeles: Resources for Infant Educarers, 1998.

Gerber, M., and A. Johnson. *Your Self Confident Baby*. New York: Wiley, 1998.

Gibran, K. *The Prophet*. New York: Alfred A. Knopf, 1965.

Goffin, S. G., with C. Tull, "Problem Solving: Encouraging Active Learning." *Young Children*, March 1985, pp. 28–32.

Gonzalez-Mena, J. "Praise with a Purpose Is Sneaky and Manipulative." *Educaring* 14(4), Fall 1993, pp. 1–4.

Gonzalez-Mena, J. "Toddlers: What to Expect." *Young Children*, November 1986, pp. 47–51.

Greenberg, P. "Do You Take Care of Toddlers?" *Young Children*, January 1991, pp. 52–53.

Greenspan, S. I. *Building Healthy Minds*. Cambridge, Mass.: Perseus, 1999.

Greenspan, S. I., and S. Wieder. *The Child with Special Needs: Encouraging Intellectual and Emotional Growth*. Reading, Mass.: Perseus, 1998.

Grey, K. "Not in Praise of Praise." *Child Care Information Exchange* 104, July/August 1995, pp. 56–59.

Honig, A. S. "Quality Infant/Toddler Caregiving: Are There Magic Recipes?" *Young Children*, May 1989, pp. 4–10.

Lally, J. R. "Brain Research, Infant Learning, and Child Care Curriculum." *Child Care Information Exchange,* May 1998, pp. 46–48.

Levine, S. "Stimulation in Infancy." *Scientific American,* May 1960, pp. 436, 624.

Love, J., H. Raikes, D. Paulsell, and E. E. Kisker. "New Directions for Studying Quality in Programs for Infants and Toddlers." In *Infants and Toddlers in Out-of-Home Care,* edited by D. Cryer and T. Harms. Baltimore: Brookes, 2000, pp. 117–162.

Maslow, A. H. *Toward a Psychology of Being,* 2nd ed. New York: Van Nostrand, 1968.

Musatti, T., and S. Mayer. "Knowing and Learning in an Educational Context: A Study in the Infant-Toddler Centers of the City of Pistoia." In *Bambini: The Italian Approach to Infant-Toddler Care,* edited by L. Gandini and C. P. Edwards. New York: Teachers College Press, 2001.

Nodding, N. *The Challenge to Care in Schools.* New York: Teachers College Press, 1992.

Nodding, N. *Educating Moral People: A Caring Alternative to Character Education.* New York: Teachers College Press, 2002.

Nodding, N. *Starting at Home: Care and Social Policy.* Berkeley: University of California Press, 2002.

Paretto, H. P., Jr., N. S. Dunn, and D. R. Hoge. "Low-Cost Communication Devices for Children with Disabilities and Their Family Members." *Young Children* 50(6), September 1995, pp. 75–81.

Reinsberg, J. "Reflections on Quality Infant Care." *Young Children* 50(6), September 1995, pp. 23–25.

Segal, M., W. Masi, and R. Leiderman. *In Time and with Love: Caring for Infants and Toddlers with Special Needs.* New York: New Market Press, 2001.

Widerstrom, A. H. "Educating Young Handicapped Children." *Childhood Education* 63(2), December 1986, pp. 78–83.

Chapter 3

Beal, S. M., and C. F. Finch. "An Overview of Retrospective Case Control Slides Investigating the Relationship Between Prone Sleep Positions and SIDS." *Journal of Pediatrics and Child Health* 27, 1993, pp. 334–339.

Bergen, D., R. Reid, and L. Torelli. *Educating and Caring for Very Young Children: The Infant/Toddler Curriculum.* New York: Teachers College Press, 2001.

Bernhardt, J. L. "A Primary Caregiving System for Infants and Toddlers: Best for Everyone Involved." *Young Children,* 55(2), March 2000, pp. 74–80.

Butterfield, P. M. "Child Care Is Rich in Routines." *Zero to Three* 22(4), February/March 2002, pp. 29–32.

Cook, R. E., A. Tessier, and M. D. Klein. *Adapting Early Childhood Curricula for Children in Inclusive Settings,* 5th ed. Columbus, Ohio: Merrill, 2000.

Cortez, J., ed. *Infant-Toddler Caregiving: A Guide to Culturally Sensitive Care.* Sacramento: California Department of Education, 1991.

David, M., and G. Appell. *Lóczy: An Unusual Approach to Mothering.* Translated from *Lóczy ou le Maternage Insolite* by Jean Marie Clark; revised translation by Judit Falk. Budapest: Association Pikler-Loczy for Young Children, 2001.

Educaring, published quarterly by Resources for Infant Educarers.

Elam, P. "Creating Quality Infant Group Care Programs," in *Authentic Relationships in Group Care for Infants and Toddlers: Resources for Infant Educarers (RIE) Principles into Practice,* edited by S. Petrie and S. Owen. London and Philadelphia: Jessica Kingsley Publishers, 2005, pp. 83–92.

Garcia, R. *Home-Centered Care: Designing a Family Day Care Program, a Guide for Caregivers and Parents.* San Francisco: Children's Council of San Francisco, 1985.

Gerber, M. *Resources for Infant Educarers.* Los Angeles: Resources for Infant Educarers, 1991.

Gerber, M. "Respecting Infants: The Lóczy Model of Infant Care." In *Supporting the Growth of Infants, Toddlers and Parents,* edited by E. Jones. Pasadena, Calif.: Pacific Oaks, 1979.

Gerber, M. "RIE Principles and Practices," in *Authentic Relationships in Group Care for Infants and Toddlers: Resources for Infant Educarers (RIE) Principles into Practice,* edited by S. Petrie and S. Owen. London and Philadelphia: Jessica Kingsley Publishers, 2005, pp. 35–49.

Gonzalez-Mena, J. *Diversity In Early Care And Education.* New York: McGraw-Hill, 2004.

Gonzalez-Mena, J. *Infant-Toddler Caregiving: A Guide to Routines.* Sacramento: California Department of Education, 1990.

Gonzalez-Mena, J. *Multicultural Issues in Child Care.* Mountain View, Calif.: Mayfield, 1996.

Gonzalez-Mena, J. "Working with Cultural Differences: Individualism and Collectivism."

The First Years: Nga TauTuatahi 4(2), September 2002, pp. 13–15.

Gonzalez-Mena, J. "What Can An Orphanage Teach Us? Lessons from Budapest." *Young Children*, 59(4), September 2004, pp. 26–30.

Gonzalez-Mena, J., and A. Stonehouse. "In the Child's Best Interests." *Child Care Information Exchange*, November/December 1995, pp. 17–20.

Greenspan, S. I., and S. Wieder. *The Child with Special Needs: Encouraging Intellectual and Emotional Growth.* Reading, Mass.: Perseus, 1998.

Honig, A. S. "Quality Infant/Toddler Caregiving: Are There Magic Recipes?" *Young Children*, May 1989, pp. 4–10.

Honig, A. S. *Secure Relationships: Nurturing Infant/Toddler Attachment in Early Care Settings.* Washington, D.C.: National Association for the Education of Young Children, 2002.

Josephs, Z. "Reducing the Risk of SIDS." *Educaring* 14(4), Fall 1993, p. 5.

Kaiser, B., and J. S. Rasminsky. "Opening the Culture Door." *Young Children* 58(4) July 2003, pp. 53–56.

Lally, J. R. "The Impact of Child Care Policies and Practices on Infant/Toddler Identity Formation." *Young Children* 51(1), November 1995, pp. 58–67.

Mangione, P., ed. *Infant-Toddler Caregiving: A Guide to Culturally Sensitive Care.* Sacramento, Calif.: Far West Laboratory and California Department of Education, 1995.

Martini, Mary. "How Mothers in Four American Cultural Groups Shape Infant Learning During Mealtimes." *Zero to Three* 22(4), February/March 2002, pp. 14–20.

Money, R. "The RIE Early Years 'Curriculum'," in *Authentic Relationships in Group Care for Infants and Toddlers: Resources for Infant Educarers (RIE) Principles into Practice*, edited by S. Petrie and S. Owen. London and Philadelphia: Jessica Kingsley Publishers, 2005, pp. 51–68.

O'Brien, M. *Inclusive Child Care for Infants and Toddlers: Meeting Individual and Special Needs.* Baltimore: Brookes, 1997.

O'Sullivan, E. "See How They Sleep." *Educaring* 22(3), Summer 2001, pp. 1, 5.

Petrie, S. "The Work of Emmi Pikler and Magda Gerber," in *Authentic Relationships in Group Care for Infants and Toddlers: Resources for Infant Educarers (RIE) Principles into Practice*, edited by S. Petrie and

S. Owen. London and Philadelphia: Jessica Kingsley Publishers, 2005, pp. 17–34.

Phillips, C. B., and R. M. Cooper. "Cultural Dimensions of Feeding Relationships." *Zero to Three* 7(5), June 1992, pp. 10–13.

Provence, S. "Feeding Problem." *Zero to Three* 7(5), June 1992, pp. 18–19.

Raver, S. A. *Intervention Strategies for Infants and Toddlers with Special Needs*, 2nd ed. Upper Saddle River, N.J.: Prentice-Hall, 1999.

Satter, E. "The Feeding Relationship." *Zero to Three* 7(5), June 1992, pp. 1–9.

Segal, M., W. Masi, and R. Leiderman. *In Time and with Love: Caring for Infants and Toddlers with Special Needs*, 2nd ed. New York: New Market Press, 2001.

Widerstrom, A. H. "Educating Young Handicapped Children." *Childhood Education* 63(2), December 1986, pp. 78–83.

Chapter 4

Chang, H. *Affirming Children's Roots: Cultural and Linguistic Diversity in Early Care and Education.* San Francisco: California Tomorrow, 1993.

Clark, A. L., ed. *Culture and Childrearing.* Philadelphia: F. A. Davis, 1981.

Cook, R. E., A. Tessier, and M. D. Klein. *Adapting Early Childhood Curricula for Children in Inclusive Settings.* Columbus, Ohio: Merrill, 2000.

DeLoache, J. S. "Cognitive Development in Infants: Looking, Listening, and Learning." In *Infants and Toddlers in Out-of-Home Care*, edited by D. Cryer and T. Harms. Baltimore: Brookes, 2000, pp. 7–47.

Division of Research to Practice, Office of Special Education Programs. *Synthesis on the Use of Assistive Technology with Infants and Toddlers.* Washington, D.C.: U.S. Department of Education, 2001.

Eckerman, C. O., and H. Whitehead. "How Toddler Peers Generate Coordinated Action: A Cross-Cultural Exploration." *Early Education and Development* 10, 1999, pp. 241–266.

Feeney, S., and M. Magarick. "Choosing Good Toys for Young Children." *Young Children*, November 1984, pp. 21–25.

Fromberg, D. P. *Play and Meaning in Early Childhood Education.* Boston: Allyn & Bacon, 2002.

Frost, J., S. Wortham, and S. Reifel. *Play and Child Development.* Upper Saddle River, NJ: Merrill/Prentice Hall, 2001.

Galardini, A., and D. Giovannini. "Pistoia: Creating a Dynamic, Open System to Serve Children, Families and Community." In *Bambini: The Italian Approach to Infant-Toddler Care*, edited by L. Gandini and C. P. Edwards. New York: Teachers College Press, 2000.

Gandini, L., and C. P. Edwards, eds. *Bambini: The Italian Approach to Infant-Toddler Care*. New York: Teachers College Press, 2000.

Gerber, M. "Good Play Objects for Babies." *Educaring* 7(3), Spring 1986, pp. 4–6.

Gonzalez-Mena, J. *A Caregiver's Guide to Routines in Infant-Toddler Care*. Sacramento, Calif.: Child Development Division, Center for Child and Family Studies, Far West Laboratory for Educational Research and Development, California Department of Education, 1990.

Gonzalez-Mena, J., "Cultural Sensitivity in Routine Caregiving Tasks." In *Infant/Caregiving: A Guide to Culturally Sensitive Care*, edited by Peter Mangione. Sacramento, Calif.: Far West Laboratory and California Department of Education, 1995.

Gonzalez-Mena, J. "What can an orphanage teach us? Lessons from Budapest." *Young Children*, September 2004, 26–30.

Greenspan, S. I., and S. Wieder. *The Child with Special Needs: Encouraging Intellectual and Emotional Growth*. Reading, Mass.: Perseus, 1998.

Handler, J. *Infants and Toddlers as Members, Makers, Interpreters*. Dubuque, Iowa: Kendall/Hunt, 2003.

Hatcher, B., and K. Petty. "Visible Thought in Dramatic Play." *Young Children* November 2004, pp. 79–82.

Kelly, J. F., and C. L. Booth. "Child Care for Children with Special Needs: Issues and Applications." *Infants and Young Children* 12(1), 1999, pp. 26–33.

Lally, J. R. "Infants Have Their Own Curriculum: A Responsive Approach to Curriculum and Lesson Planning for Infants and Toddlers." In *Headstart National Training Guide: Curriculum, a Blueprint for Action*. Washington, D.C.: Administration for Families, Children, and Youth, 1999.

Monighan-Nourot, P., B. Scales, J. Van Horn, and M. Almy. *Looking at Children's Play: A Bridge Between Theory and Practice*. New York: Teachers College Press, 1987.

Morelli, G., B. Roqoff, and D. Oppenheim. "Cultural Variation in Infants' Sleeping Arrangements: Questi Independence." *Developmental Psychology* 28(4), 1992.

Petrie, S., and S. Owen. *Authentic Relationships in Group Care for Infants and Toddlers: Resources for Infant Educarers (RIE) Principles into Practice*. London: Jessica Kingsley, 2005.

Phillips, C. B., and R. M. Cooper. "Cultural Dimensions of Feeding Relationships." *Zero to Three* 12(5), June 1992, pp. 10–13.

Pinto, C. "Supporting Competence in a Child with Special Needs: One Child's Story." *Educaring* 22(2), Spring 2001, pp. 1–6.

Rosenkoetter, S., and L. Barton. "Bridges to Literacy: Early Routines That Promote Later School Success." *Zero to Three* 22(4), February/March 2002, pp. 33–38.

Segal, M., W. Masi, and R. Leiderman. *In Time and with Love: Caring for Infants and Toddlers with Special Needs*. New York: New Market Press, 2001.

Tardos, A. "Facilitating the Play of Children at Loczy." *Educaring* 6(3), Summer 1985, pp. 1–7.

Tonge, M. J. "Hanging Out with Babies at Play: Vignettes from Participant-Observer." In *Supporting the Growth of Infants, Toddlers and Parents*, edited by E. Jones. Pasadena, Calif.: Pacific Oaks, 1991.

Van Hoorn, J., P. Monighan Nourot, B. Scales, and K. Rodriquez Alward. *Play at the Center of the Curriculum*. Columbus, Ohio: Merrill, 2003.

Williams, C. K., and C. Kamii. "How Do Children Learn by Handling Objects?" *Young Children*, November 1986, pp. 23–26.

Chapter 5

Ainsworth, M. D., and B. A. Wittig. "Attachment and Exploratory Behavior of One-Year-Olds in a Stranger Situation." In *Determinants of Infant Behavior*, vol. 4, edited by B. M. Foss. New York: Barnes and Noble, 1969.

Beginnings Workshop: "Working with Parents of Children with Differing Abilities." *Child Care Information Exchange* 88, November 1992.

Bowlby, J. *Attachment and Loss*, vol. 1 of *Attachment and Loss*. New York: Basic, 2000, p. 332.

Brazelton, T. B., and B. Cramer. *The Earliest Relationships*. New York: Addison-Wesley, 1990.

Caldwell, B. M., C. Wright, A. S. Honig, and J. Tannenbaum. "Infant Care and Attachment." *American Journal of Orthopsychiatry* 40, 1970, pp. 397–412.

Colin, V. *Human Development*. New York: McGraw-Hill, 1996.

Cosentino, H. E., R. Menel, J. Money, A Lansbury, J. Johnson, A. Tardos, and R. Hammond. "How Attached Should We Be? RIE Reflections on Attachment." *Educaring* 20(4), Fall 1999, pp. 1–7.

Dozier, M., D. Dozier, and M. Manni. "Attachment and Biobehavioral Catch-Up: The ABC's of Helping Infants in Foster Care Cope with Early Adversity." *Zero to Three* 22(5), April/May 2002, pp. 7–13.

Goodnough, G., and L. Goodnough. "Mothers Returning to the Workforce: The Father's Role in the Transition." *Focus on Infants and Toddlers* 14(2), Winter 2001, pp. 1–2, 5–6.

Harlow, H. "The Nature of Love." *American Psychology* 13, 1958, pp. 59–86.

Harwood, M., and J. S. Kleinfeld. "The Value of Early Intervention for Children with Fetal Alcohol." *Young Children* 57(4), July 2002, pp. 86–90.

Honig, A. S. *Secure Relationships: Nurturing Infant-Toddler Attachment in Early Care Settings.* Washington, D.C.: National Association for the Education of Young Children, 2002.

Howes, C. "Social Development, Family, and Attachment Relationships of Infants and Toddlers: Research into Practice." In *Infants and Toddlers in Out-of-Home Care*, edited by D. Cryer and T. Harms. Baltimore: Brookes, 2000, pp. 87–113.

Kagan, J., R. B. Kearsley, and P. R. Zelazo. "The Effects of Infant Day Care on Psychological Development." *Education Quarterly* 1(1), February 1977, pp. 143–158.

Karen, R. "Becoming Attached." *Atlantic* 265, February 1990, pp. 35–70.

Klaus, M., and J. Kennell. *Parent-Infant Bonding.* New York: Mosby, 1982.

Lally, J. R. "The Impact of Child Care Policies and Practices on Infant/Toddler Identity Formation." *Young Children* 51(1), November 1995, pp. 58–67.

Lamb, M. *The Father's Role: Cross-Cultural Perspectives.* Hillside, N.J.: Erlbaum, 1987.

McCracken, J. "So Many Goodbyes." Brochure #573, National Association for the Education of Young Children, Washington, D.C., 1986.

Portnoy, F. C., and C. H. Simmons. "Day Care and Attachment." *Child Development* 49, 1978, pp. 239–242.

Rubenstein, J. "Caregiving and Infant Behavior in Day Care and in Homes." *Developmental Psychology* 15(1), 1979, pp. 1–24.

Stern, D. *The Interpersonal World of the Infant.* New York: Basic Books, 1985.

Thomas, E., and S. Browder. *Born Dancing: How Intuitive Parents Understand Their Baby's Unspoken Language and Natural Rhythms.* New York: Harper & Row, 1988.

Chapter 6

Abbott, C. F., and S. Gold. "Conferring with Parents When You're Concerned That Their Child Needs Special Services." *Young Children*, May 1991, pp. 10–15.

Bornstein, M., and M. Lamb. *Development in Infancy: An Introduction*, 3rd ed. New York: McGraw-Hill, 1992.

Bower, T. G. R. *Development in Infancy*, 2nd ed. San Francisco: W. H. Freeman, 1982.

Bower, T. G. R. *A Primer of Infant Development.* San Francisco: W. H. Freeman, 1977.

Choudhury, N., and Gorman, K. "The Relationship Between Attention and Problem-Solving in 17–24-Month-Old Children." *Infant and Children* 9, 2000, pp. 127–146.

Dannemiller, J. L. "Brain-Behavior Relationships in Early Visual Development." In *Handbook of Developmental Cognitive Neuroscience*, edited by C. A. Nelson, and M. Luciana. Cambridge, MA: MIT Press, 2001, pp. 221–235.

De Haan, M. "The Neuropsychology of Face Processing During Infancy and Childhood." In *Handbook of Developmental Cognitive Neuroscience*, edited by C. A. Nelson and M. Luciana. Cambridge, MA: MIT Press, 2001, pp. 381–398.

Field, T. M. *Touch.* Cambridge, MA: MIT Press, 2001.

McCarty, M. E., and D. H. Ashmead. "Visual Control of Reaching and Grasping in Infants." *Developmental Psychology* 35, 1999, pp. 620–631.

Mennella, J. A., Jagnow, C. P., Beauchamp, G. K. "Prenatal and Postnatal Flavor Learning by Human Infants." *Pediatrics*, 107, 2001, pp. 1–12.

Mondloch, C. J., T. Lewis, and D. R. Budreau. "Face Perception During Early Infancy." *Psychological Science* 10, 1999, 419–422.

Patton, J. R. *Exceptional Children in Focus*, 5th ed. New York: Merrill, 1991.

Rose, S. A., J. Jankowski, and G. J. Senior. "Infants' Recognition of Contour-Deleted Figures." *Journal of Exceptional Psychology: Human Perception and Performance* 23, 1997, pp. 1206–1216.

Samples, R. *The Metamorphic Mind.* Menlo Park, Calif.: Addison-Wesley, 1976.

Sherman, T. "Categorization of Skills in Infants." *Child Development* 56, 1985, pp. 1561–1573.

Slater, A., and S. P. Johnson. "Visual Sensory and Perceptual Abilities of the Newborn: Beyond the Blooming, Buzzing Confusion." In *The Development of Sensory, Motor, and Cognitive Capabilities in Early Infancy*, edited by A. Slater and S. P. Johnson, pp. 121–141. Hove, U.K.: Sussex Press, 1999.

Stern, D. *Diary of a Baby.* New York: Basic Books, 1990.

Turaati, C., F. Simon, I. Miloni, and C. Umilta. "Newborns' Preferences for Faces: What Is Crucial?" *Devlopmental Psychology*, 38(6), 2002, pp. 875–882.

Warren, D. H. *Blindness and Early Childhood Development*, 2nd ed. New York: American Foundation for the Blind, 1984.

Weiss, W., J. Salomon, and P. Zelazo, eds. *Newborn Attention: Biological Constraints and the Influence of Experience.* Norwood, N.J.: Ablex, 1991.

Chapter 7

Adolph, K. E. "Learning in the Development of Infant Locomotion." *Monographs of the Society for Research in Child Development* 3(251), 1997.

Adolph, K. E., B. Vereijken, and M. A. Denny. "Learning to Crawl." *Child Development* 69, 1998, pp. 1299–1312.

Blenk, A., with D. L. Fine. *Making School Inclusion Work: A Guide to Everyday Practices.* Cambridge, Mass.: Brookline, 1995.

Bower, T. G. R. *Development in Infancy*, 2nd ed. San Francisco: W. H. Freeman, 1982.

Bruer, J. T. *The Myth of the First Three Years: A New Understanding of Early Brain Development and Lifelong Learning.* New York: Free Press, 1999.

Chandler, P. A. *A Place for Me: Including Children with Special Needs in Early Care and Education Settings.* Washington, D.C.: National Association for the Education of Young Children, 1994.

Diamond, M., and J. Hopson. *Magic Trees of the Mind.* New York: Plume, 1999.

Fallen, N. H., and W. Ilmansky. *Young Children with Special Needs.* Columbus, Ohio: Merrill, 1985.

Fogel, A. *Infancy.* Minneapolis: West, 1997.

Gottlieb, Alma. "Luring Your Child into This Life: A Beng Path for Infant Care." In *A World of Babies*, edited by Judy DeLoache and Alma Gottlieb. Cambridge, England: Cambridge University Press, 2000.

Hayslip, W., and L. Vincent. "Opening Doors to Activities That Include ALL Children." *Child Care Information Exchange* 105, September/October 1995, pp. 43–46.

Huttenlocker, P. R. *Neural Plasticity: The Effects of the Environment on the Development of the Cerebral Cortex.* Cambridge, MA: Harvard University Press, 2002.

Kolb, B., R. Gibb, and A. Dallison. "Early Experience, Behavior, and the Changing Brain." In *The Role of Early Experience in Infant Development* edited by N. A. Fox, L. A. Leavitt, and J. G. Warhol. Johnson & Johnson Pediatric Institute, 1999, pp. 41–63.

Krog, S. *The Integrated Early Childhood Curriculum.* New York: McGraw-Hill, 1990, pp. 6–41.

Nelson, C. A. (2002). "Neural Development." In *Handbook of Applied Developmental Science*, vol. 1, edited by R. M. Lerner, F. Jacobs, and D. Wertlieb. Thousand Oaks, CA: Sage, 2002, pp. 31–60.

Pikler, E. "Data on Gross Motor Development of the Infant." *Early Child Development and Care* 1, 1972, pp. 297–310.

Sullivan, M. *Feeling Strong, Feeling Free: Movement Exploration for Young Children.* Washington, D.C.: National Association for the Education of Young Children, 1982.

Tardos, A. "The Pikler/Lóczy Philosophy." *Educaring* 7(2), Spring 1986, pp. 1–7.

Chapter 8

Beginnings Workshop: "Make-Believe Play." In *Child Care Information Exchange* 99, September 1994.

Berk, L. "Vygotsky's Theory: The Importance of Make-Believe Play." *Young Children* 50(1), November 1994, pp. 30–39.

Bono, M. A., and C. A. Stifter. "Maternal Attention-Directing Strategies and Infant Focused Attention during Problem Solving." *Infancy*, 4, 2003, pp. 235–250.

Bower, T. G. R. *Development in Infancy*, 2nd ed. San Francisco: W. H. Freeman, 1982.

Bredekamp, S., ed. *Developmentally Appropriate Practice in Early Childhood Programs Serving Children Birth Through Age 8.* Washington, D.C.: National Association for the Education of Young Children, 1986.

Brooks, P. H., and C. McCauley. "Cognitive Research in Mental Retardation." *American Journal of Mental Deficiency* 88, 1984, pp. 479–486.

Flavell, J. H. "On Cognitive Development." *Child Development* 53, 1982, pp. 1–10.

Gergely, G., Bakkering, H., and I. Kiraly. "Rational Imitation in Preverbal Infants." *Nature*, 415, 2003, pp. 755–760.

Gowen, J. "The Early Development of Symbolic Play." *Young Children* 50(3), March 1995, 75–84.

Gross, T. F. *Cognitive Development.* Monterey, Calif.: Brooks/Cole, 1985.

Hildreeth, K., and C. Rovee-Colier. "Forgetting Functions of Reactivated Memories over the First Year of Life." *Developmental Psychology*, 41, 2002, pp. 227–288.

Hughes, F., J. Elicker, and L. Veen. "A Program of Play for Infants and Caregivers." *Young Children* 50(2), January 1995, pp. 52–58.

Kahana-Kalman, R., and A. S. Walker-Andrew. The Role of Person Familiarity in Young Infants' Perception of Emotional Expressions. *Child Development*, 72, 2001, pp. 352–369.

Kamii, C., and R. DeVries. *Physical Knowledge in Preschool Education.* Englewood Cliffs, N.J.: Prentice-Hall, 1978.

Lagattuta, K. H., and H. M. Wellman. "Think about the Past: Early Knowledge about Links between Prior Experiences, Thinking and Emotion." *Child Development*, 72, 2001, pp. 82–102.

Marzolla, J. *Supertot: Creative Learning Activities for Children One to Three and Sympathetic Advice for Their Parents.* New York: Harper & Row, 1977.

Phillips, J. L., Jr. *The Origins of Intellect: Piaget's Theory.* San Francisco: W. H. Freeman, 1969.

Pugmire-Stoy, M. C. *Spontaneous Play in Early Childhood.* Albany, N.Y.: Delmar, 1992.

Rochat, P. *The Infant's World.* Cambridge: Harvard University Press, 2001.

Rodier, P. H. "The Early Origins of Autism." *Scientific American* 282(2), 2000, pp. 56–63.

Rovee-Collier, C. K. "The Development of Infant Memory." *Current Directions in Psychological Science* 8, 1999, pp. 80–85.

Rovee-Collier, C. K. "Information Pick-up by Infants: What Is It, and How We Can Tell." *Journal of Experimental Child Psychology* 78, 2001, pp. 35–49.

Ryalls, B. Oliver. "Infant Imitation of Adult and Peer Models: Evidence for a Peer Model Advantage." *Merrill-Palmer Quarterly* 46, 2000, pp. 188–202.

Schickendanz, J., K. Hansen, and R. Forsyth. *Understanding Children.* Mountain View, Calif.: Mayfield, 1990, pp. 175–203.

Thompson, R. F. *The Brain*, 3rd ed. New York: Worth, 2000.

Chapter 9

Barclay, K., C. Benelli, and A. Curtis. "Literacy Begins at Birth: What Caregivers Can Learn from Parents of Children Who Read Early." *Young Children* 50(4), May 1995, pp. 24–28.

Bialystok, E. *Bilingualism in Development: Language, Literacy, and Cognition.* Cambridge, England: Cambridge University Press, 2001.

Birckmayer, Jennifer. "The Role of Libraries in Emergent and Family Literacy." *Zero to Three* 21(3), December 2000/January 2001, pp. 24–30.

Bower, T. G. R. *A Primer of Infant Development.* San Francisco: W. H. Freeman, 1974.

Brown, R. *A First Language: The Early Years.* Cambridge: Harvard University Press, 1973.

Cazden, C. B., ed. *Language in Early Childhood Education.* Washington, D.C.: National Association for the Education of Young Children, 1981.

Cook, R., A. Tessier, and V. Armbruster. *Adapting Early Childhood Curriculum for Children with Special Needs*, 2nd ed. Columbus, Ohio: Merrill, 1987.

Espiritu, E., D. Meier, N. Villanzana-Price, and M. Wong. "A Collaborative Project on Language and Literacy Learning: Promoting Teacher Research in Early Childhood Education." *Young Children* 57(5), September 2002, pp. 71–78.

Flom, R., and A. D. Pick. "Verbal Encouragement and Joint Attention in 18-Month-Old Infants." *Infant Behavior and Development*, 26, 2003, pp. 121–134.

Gerber, M. "Babies Understanding Words." *Educaring* 3(4), Fall 1982, pp. 5–6.

Gleason, B., ed. *The Development of Language*, 3rd ed. New York: Macmillan, 1993.

Hakuta, K. *Mirror of Language: The Debate on Bilingualism.* New York: Basic Books, 1986.

Hallahan, D., and J. Kauffman. *Exceptional Children: Introduction to Special Education*, 5th ed. Englewood Cliffs, N.J.: Prentice-Hall, 1991, pp. 217–261.

Hammond, R. A. "Preparing for Literacy: Communication Comes First." *Educaring* 22(4), Fall 2001, pp. 1–5.

Hearne, B. *Choosing Books for Children.* New York: Bantam Doubleday Dell, 1990.

Heath, S. B. *Ways with Words: Language, Life, and Work in Communities and Classrooms.* Cambridge: Cambridge University Press, 1983.

Honig, A. "Singing with Infants and Toddlers." *Young Children* 50(5), July 1995, pp. 72–78.

Lally, J. R., P. L. Mangione, and C. L. Young-Holt, eds. *Infant/Toddler Caregiving: A Guide to Language*

Development and Communication. Sacramento, Calif.: Far West Laboratory for Educational Development and California Department of Education, 1992.

Neuman, S., C. Copple, and S. Bredekamp. *Learning to Read and Write: Developmentally Appropriate Practices for Young Children.* Washington, D.C.: National Association for the Education of Young Children, 2002.

Petitto, L. A., S. Holowka, L. E. Sergio, and D. Ostry. "Language Rhythms in Babies Hand Movements." *Nature,* 413, 2001, pp. 35–36.

Richman, R., Jr., and C. Patterson. "Cultural and Educational Variations in Maternal Responsiveness." *Developmental Psychology* 28, 1992, pp. 614–621.

Salkind, N. *Child Development,* part 2, 6th ed. Fort Worth, Tex.: Holt, Rinehart and Winston, 1990.

Schickedanz, J. *Much More Than the ABCs.* Washington, D.C.: National Association for the Education of Young Children, 1999.

Silven, M. "Attention in Very Young Infants Predicts Learning First Words." *Infant Behavior and Development,* 24, 2001, pp. 229–237.

Stiames, G., and H. Rubin, eds. *Stuttering: Then and Now.* Columbus, Ohio: Merrill 1986.

Tomasello, M. *Constructing a Language: A Usage-Based Theory of Language Acquisition.* Cambridge, MA: Harvard University Press, 2003.

Chapter 10

Abbott, C. F., and S. Gold. "Conferring with Parents When You're Concerned That Their Child Needs Special Services." *Young Children,* May 1991, pp. 10–15.

Belsky, J., and D. Eggebeen. "Early and Extensive Maternal Employment and Young Children's Socioemotional Development." *Journal of Marriage and the Family* 53, 1991, pp. 1083–1110.

Brooks, J. *The Process of Parenting,* 3rd ed. Mountain View, Calif.: Mayfield, 1991.

Calkins, S. D. (2002). "Does Aversive Behavior during Toddlerhood Matter? The Effect of Difficult Temperament on Maternal Perceptions and Behavior." *Infant Mental Health Journal,* 23, 2002, pp. 381–402.

Denham, S. A. *Emotional Development in Young Children.* New York: Guilford Press, 1998.

Egeland, B., and E. A. Farber. "Infant-Mother Attachment: Factors Related to Its Development and Changes over Time." *Child Development* 55, 1984, pp. 753–771.

Eisenberg, N., and R. Fabes. "Emotion and Its Regulation in Early Development." In *New Directions for Child Development.* San Francisco: Jossey Bass, 1992.

Gartstein, M. A., and M. K. Rothbart. "Studying Infant Temperament Via the Revised Infant Behavior Questionnaire." *Infant Behavior and Development,* 26, 2003, 64–86.

Gerber, M. "Helping Baby Feel Secure, Self-Confident, and Relaxed." *Educaring* 1(4), Fall 1980, p. 4.

Hallahan, D., and J. Kauffman. *Exceptional Children: Introduction to Special Education,* 5th ed. Englewood Cliffs, N.J.: Prentice-Hall, 1991, pp. 176–178.

Izard, C. E. *The Psychology of Emotions.* New York: Plenum, 1991.

Kagan, J. *Galen's Prophecy: Temperament in Human Nature.* New York: HarperCollins, 1994.

Kagan, J. *The Nature of the Child.* New York: Basic Books, 1984.

Kahana-Kalman, R., and A. Walker-Andrews. "The Role of Person Familiarity in Young Infants' Perception of Emotional Expressions." *Child Development* 72, 2001, 352–369.

Kauffman, J. *Characteristics of Children's Behavior Disorders,* 3rd ed. Columbus, Ohio: Merrill, 1985.

Kochanska, G. "Emotional Development in Children with Different Attachment Histories: The First Three Years." *Child Development* 72, 2001, pp. 474–490.

Kuebli, J. "Young Children's Understanding of Everyday Emotions." *Young Children* 49(3), March 1994, pp. 36–47.

Leboyer, F. *Birth Without Violence.* New York: Random House, 1978.

Lee, D. *Valuing the Self.* Englewood Cliffs, N.J.: Prentice-Hall, 1976.

Lemery, K. S., H. Goldsmith, M. D. Klinnert, and D. A. Mrazel. "Developmental Models of Infants and Child Temperament." *Developmental Psychology* 35, 1999, pp. 189–204.

Maslow, A. *Toward a Psychology of Being,* 2nd ed. New York: Van Nostrand, 1968.

McCarrol, T. *Morning Glory Babies: Children with AIDS and the Celebration of Life.* New York: St. Martin's Press, 1988.

Rochat, P., T. Striano, and L. Blatt. "Differential Effects of Happy, Neutral, and Sad Still Faces on 2-, 4-, and 6-Month-Old Infants." *Infant and Child Development,* 11, 2002, pp. 289–303.

Sternad, R. "Separation." *Educaring* 1(3), Summer 1980, pp. 1–2.

Sullivan, M. W., and M. Lewis. "Contextual Determinants of Anger and Other Negative Expressions." *Developmental Psychology*, 39, 2003, pp. 693–705.

Thomas, A., and S. Chess. *Temperament and Development.* New York: Brunner/Mazel, 1977.

Thomas, A., S. Chess, and H. Birch. "The Origin of Personality." *Scientific American* 223, 1970, pp. 102–109.

Thomas, A., S. Chess, and S. J. Korn. "The Reality of Difficult Temperament." *Merrill-Palmer Quarterly* 28, 1982, pp. 1–20.

Volling, B. L., N. L. McElwain, P. C. Nortaro, and C. Herrera. "Parents' Emotional Availability and Infant Emotional Competence: Predictors of Parent-Infant Attachment and Emerging Self-Regulation." *Journal of Family Psychology*, 16, 2002, pp. 447–465.

von Franz, M. L. "The Process of Individuation." In *Man and His Symbols*, edited by C. G. Jung and others. New York: Doubleday, 1964.

Witherington, D. C., J. J. Campos, and M. J. Hertenstein. "Principles of Emotion and Its Development in Infancy." In *Blackwood Handbook of Infant Development*, edited by G. Brenner, & A. Fogel. Malden, MA: Blackwell, 2001, pp. 427–464.

Chapter 11

Aronson, S. "Supporting the Development of Infants and Toddlers with Special Health Needs." *Child Care Information Exchange* 147, September/October 2002, pp. 62–66.

Bower, T. G. R. *Development in Infancy*, 2nd ed. San Francisco: W. H. Freeman, 1982.

Brault, L., and T. Brault, *Children with Challenging Behavior: Strategies for Reflective Thinking*. Phoenix: CPG Publishing, 2005.

Butterfield, P. M., C. A. Martin, and A. P. Prairie, *Emotional Connections: How Relationships Guide Early Learning*. Washington, D.C.: Zero to Three, 2004.

Carter, M. "Building Self-Esteem: Training Teachers of Infants and Toddlers." *Child Care Information Exchange* 92, July/August 1993, pp. 59–61.

Cooper, R. M. "Child Care as Shared Socialization." *Child Care Information Exchange*, July 2002, pp. 58–60.

Crockenberg, S. "How Children Learn to Resolve Conflicts in Families." *Zero to Three*, April 1992.

Curry, N., and C. Johnson. *Beyond Self-Esteem: Developing a Genuine Sense of Human Values.* Washington, D.C.: National Association for the Education of Young Children, 1990.

Erikson, E. *Childhood and Society*, 2nd ed. New York: W. W. Norton, 1963.

Freiberg, K., ed. *Educating Exceptional Children*, 7th ed. Guilford, Conn.: Dushkin Publishing Group, 1994.

Gandini, L., and C. P. Edwards, eds. *Bambini: The Italian Approach to Infant-Toddler Care.* New York: Teachers College Press, 2001.

Gibran, K. *The Prophet.* New York: Alfred A. Knopf, 1965.

Gordon, A., and K. Browne. *Guiding Young Children in a Diverse Society.* Boston: Allyn & Bacon, 1986.

Greenberg, P. *Character Development: Encouraging Self-Esteem and Self-Discipline in Infants, Toddlers, and Two-Year-Olds.* Washington, D.C.: National Association for the Education of Young Children, 1990.

Hammond, R. A. "Peaceful Foundations." *Educaring* 22(2), Spring 2001, p. 307.

Hayden, T. "A Sense of Self." *Your Child*, Newsweek special edition, Fall and Winter 2000, pp. 56–63.

Honig, A. S. "Compliance, Control and Discipline." *Young Children*, January 1985, pp. 50–58.

Howes, C., and S. Ritchie. *A Matter of Trust: Connecting Teachers and Learners in the Early Childhood Classroom.* New York: Teachers College Press, 2002.

Lally, J. R. "The Impact of Child Care Policies and Practices on Infant/Toddler Identity Formation." *Young Children* 51(1), January 1995, pp. 58–68.

Marshall, H. H. "Cultural Influences on the Development of Self-Concept." *Young Children* 56(6), November 2001, pp. 19–25.

Meyerhoff, M. "Of Baseball and Babies: Are You Unconsciously Discouraging Father Involvement in Infant Care?" *Young Children* 49(4), May 1994, pp. 17–19.

Miller, C. S. "Building Self-Control, Discipline for Young Children." *Young Children*, November 1984, pp. 15–19.

Miller, K. "Caring for the Little Ones: Continuity of Care." *Child Care Information Exchange* 129, September/October 1999, pp. 94–97.

Money, R. "The Competent Toddler: Neither Bully nor Victim." *Educaring* 21(4), Fall 2000, pp. 1–6.

Parlakian, R. *How Culture Shapes Social-Emotional Development: Implications for Practice in Infant-Family Programs.* Washington, D.C.: Zero to Three, 2004.

Pikler, E. *Friedliche Babys—Zufiedene Mutter*. Pado-gogische Ratschlage einer Kinderartzin. 5. Aufl. Freiburg, Basel, Wien, Herder Verlag. 222 S. (Herder-bucherei.), 1991.

Post, J., and M. Hohmann. *Tender Care and Early Learning: Supporting Infants and Toddlers in Child Care Settings*. Ypsilanti, Mich.: High/Scope Press, 2000.

Reynolds, E. *Guiding Young Children: A Child-Centered Approach*. Mountain View, Calif.: Mayfield, 1990.

Riley, L., and J. Glass. "You Can't Always Get What You Want—Infant Care Preferences Among Employed Mothers." *Journal of Marriage and the Family* 64, 2002, pp. 2–15.

Rochat, P. *The Infant's World*. Cambridge: Harvard University Press, 2001.

Roopnarine, J. L., and A. S. Honig. "The Unpopular Child." *Young Children*, September 1985, p. 61.

Thompson, R. A. "The Legacy of Early Attachments." *Child Development* 71, 2000, pp. 145–152.

Trumbull, E., C. Rothstein-Fisch, P. M. Greenfield, and B. Quiroz. *Bridging Cultures Between Home and School*. Mahwah, N.J.: Erlbaum, 2001.

Williamson, G. G., and M. Anzalone. *Sensory Integration and Self-Regulation in Infants and Toddlers: Helping Very Young Children Interact with their Environment*. Washington, D.C.: Zero to Three, 2001.

Chapter 12

Aronson, S. "Sudden Infant Death Syndrome." *Exchange* 153, September/October 2003, p. 67.

Aronson, S., and P. M. Spahr, *Healthy Young Children: A Manual for Programs*, Washington, D.C.: National Association for the Education of Young Children, 2002.

Caring for Our Children: National Health and Safety Performance Standards: Guidelines for Out-of-Home Child Care Programs. American Public Health Association and American Academy of Pediatrics, 1992.

Coughlan, C. "Using the RIE Approach in a Family Day Care Home." In *Authentic Relationships in Group Care for Infants and Toddlers: Resources for Infant Educarers (RIE) Principles into Practice*, edited by S. Petrie and S. Owen. London and Philadelphia: Jessica Kingsley Publishers, 2005, pp. 69–82.

Curtis, D., and Carter, M. *Designs for Living and Learning: Transforming Early Childhood Environments*. St. Paul, Minn.: Redleaf, 2003.

Fauvre, M. "Including Young Children with 'New' Chronic Illnesses in an Early Childhood Education Setting." *Young Children* 43, 1988, pp. 71–78.

Ferguson, J. "Creating Growth-Producing Environments for Infants and Toddlers." In *Supporting the Growth of Infants, Toddlers, and Parents*, edited by E. Jones. Pasadena, Calif.: Pacific Oaks, 1979.

Forman, G. E., and F. Hill. *Constructive Play: Applying Piaget in the Preschool*. Menlo Park, Calif.: Addison-Wesley, 1984.

Gerber, M., and A. King. "Modifying the Environment to Respond to the Changing Needs of the Child." *Educaring* 6(1), Winter 1985, pp. 1–2.

Godwin, A., and L. Schrag, eds. *Setting Up for Infant Care: Guidelines for Centers and Family Day Care Homes*, rev. ed. Washington, D.C.: National Association for the Education of Young Children, 1996.

Gonzalez-Mena, J. *Infant/Toddler Caregiving: A Guide to Routines*, 2nd ed. Sacramento: California Department of Education with WestEd, 2002.

Gonzalez-Mena, J. "What Can an Orphanage Teach Us? Lessons from Budapest." *Young Children*, September 2004, pp. 26–30.

Greenman, J. *Caring Spaces, Learning Places: Children's Environments That Work*. Redmond, Wash.: Exchange Press, 1988.

Greenman, J. "Designing Infant/Toddler Environments" and "Furnishing the Infant/Toddler Environment." In *Caring for Infants and Toddlers: What Works, What Doesn't*, vol. 2, edited by Robert Lurie and Roger Neugebauer. Redmond, Wash.: Child Care Information Exchange, 1982.

Greenman, J. "Just Wondering: Building Wonder into the Environment." *Child Care Information Exchange*, January/February 1993, pp. 32–35.

Infant/Toddler Caregiving: A Guide to Setting Up Environments. Sacramento: California State Department of Education, 1990.

Jones, E., and E. Prescott. *Dimensions of Teaching-Learning Environments, II: Focus on Day Care*. Pasadena, Calif.: Pacific Oaks, 1978.

Kendrick, A. S., ed. *Healthy Young Children: A Manual for Programs*. Washington, D.C.: National Association for the Education of Young Children, 1988.

Lally, J. R., and J. Stewart. *Infant/Toddler Caregiving: A Guide to Setting Up Environments*. Sacramento, Calif.: Far West Laboratory for Educational Development and California Department of Education, 1990.

Lewis, K. D., B. Bennett, and N. H. Schmeder. "The Care of Infants Menaced by Cocaine Abuse." *Maternal Child Nursing* 14(5), October 1989, pp. 324–329.

Love, J. M., H. Raikes, D. Paulsell, and E. E. Kisker "New Directions for Studying Quality." In *Infants and Toddlers in Out-of-Home Care*, edited by D. Cryer and T. Harms. Baltimore: Brookes, 2000, pp. 117–161.

Lumeng, J. "What Can We Do to Prevent Childhood Obesity?" *Zero to Three*, 25(3), January 2005, pp. 13–19.

Marotz, L. R., M. Z. Cross, and J. M. Rush. *Health, Safety, and Nutrition for the Young Child*, 3rd ed. New York: Delmar, 1993.

Moukaddem, V. "Preventing Infectious Diseases in Your Child Care Setting." *Young Children* 45, 1990, pp. 28–29.

Mulligan, S. A. "Assistive Technology: Supporting the Participation of Children with Disabilities." *Young Children* 58(6) November 2003, pp. 50–52.

Olds, A. R. "Designing Play Environments for Children Under Three." *Topics in Early Childhood Special Education* 2, 1982, pp. 87–95.

Olds, A. R. "Places of Beauty." In *Play as a Medium for Learning and Development*, edited by D. Bergen. Olney, Md.: Association for Childhood Education International, 1998, pp. 123–127.

Prescott, E. "The Physical Environment—Powerful Regulator of Experience." *Child Care Information Exchange*, Reprint #4, C-44. Redmond, Wash. 98052.

Rinaldi, C. "Reggio Emilia: The Image of the Child and the Child's Environment as a Fundamental Principle." In *Bambini: The Italian Approach to Infant/Toddler Care*, edited by L. Gandini and C. P. Edwards. New York: Teachers College Press, 2001, pp. 49–54.

Sahoo, S. K. "Novelty and Complexity in Human Infants' Exploratory Behavior." *Perceptual and Motor Skills*, 86(2), 1998, p. 698.

Setting up for Infant/Toddler Care: Guidelines for Centers and Family Child Care Homes, rev. ed. edited by A. Godwin and L. Schrag. Washington, D. C.: National Association for the Education of Young Children, 1996.

Torelli, L. "The Developmentally Designed Group Care Setting: A Supportive Environment for Infants, Toddlers, and Caregivers." *Zero to Three*, December 1989, pp. 7–10.

Torelli, L., and C. Durett. *Landscapes for Learning: Designing Group Care Environments for Infants, Toddlers, and Two-Year-Olds*. Berkeley, Calif.: Spaces for Children, 1998.

Visions for Infant/Toddler Care: Guidelines for Professional Caregiving. Sacramento, Calif.: Far West Laboratory for Educational Development and California Department of Education.

Vokmar, F. R., and L. A. Wiesner, *Healthcare for Children on the Autism Spectrum: A Guide to Medical, Nutritional and Behavioral Issues*. Bethesda, Md.: Woodbine, 2004.

Wessel, L., and J. Span, "The Chronic Care Model: A Collaborative Approach to Preventing and Treating Asthma in Infants and Young Children." *Zero to Three*, 25(3), January 2005, pp. 20–27.

West, K., ed. *Family Day-to-Day Care*. Mound, Minn.: Quality Child Care, 1979.

Whitehead, L. C., and S. I. Ginsberg. "Creating a Family-like Atmosphere in Child Care Settings: All the More Difficult in Large Child Care Centers." *Young Children* 54(2), 1999, pp. 4–10.

Widerstrom, A. H. "Educating Young Handicapped Children." *Childhood Education* 63(2), December 1986, pp. 78–83.

Wolf, D. "An Interview with Jim Greenman." *Child Care Information Exchange*, September 1987, p. 19.

Chapter 13

Affirming Children's Roots: Cultural and Linguistic Diversity in Early Care and Education. San Francisco: California Tomorrow, 1993.

Baker, A. R. "Why Should You Document the Everyday Experience in Your Infant or Toddler Room?" *Focus on Infants and Toddlers*, Association for Childhood Education International 15(1), Fall 2002, pp. 1–5.

Blimes, J. *Beyond Behavior Management: The Six Life Skills Children Need to Thrive in Today's World*. St. Paul, MN: Redleaf Press, 2004.

Bryand, A., and E. Check. "How Parents Raise Boys and Girls." *Your Child, Newsweek* special edition, Fall and Winter 2000, pp. 56–63.

Careri, G., P. Collini-Martins, and P. Rego. "Research Update: Are Children Being Treated the Same?" *Interaction* 12(2), Summer 1998, pp. 34–36.

Choi, D. H., and K. Liu. "Child Care Practices and Culture: What Caregivers Need to Know When Caring for Asian Infants and Toddlers." Presentation at National Association for Education of Young

Children Annual Conference, Anaheim, California, 2001.

Clark, J. I. *Self-Esteem: A Family Affair.* Minneapolis: Winston Press, 1978.

Cooper, R. M. "Child Care as Shared Socialization." *Child Care Information Exchange,* July 2002, pp. 58–60.

Drifte, C. *Encouraging Positive Behavior in the Early Years: A Practical Guide.* London: Paul Chapman Publishing, 2004.

Eggers-Pierola, C. *Connections and Commitments: Reflecting Latino Values in Early Childhood Programs.* Portsmouth, N.H.: Heinemann, 2005.

Feinman, S., ed. *Social Referencing and the Social Construction of Reality in Infancy.* New York: Plenum, 1992.

Fillmore, L. W. "A Question for Early-Childhood Programs: English First or Families First." *Education Week,* June 19, 1991.

Frable, D. E. S. "Gender, Racial, Ethnic, Sexual, and Class Identities." *Annual Review of Psychology* 48, 1997, pp. 139–169.

Gartrell, D. "Replacing Time-Out: Using Guidance to Maintain an Encouraging Classroom." *Young Children* 57(2), March 2002, pp. 36–43.

Gonzalez-Mena, J. *Diversity in Early Care and Education.* New York: McGraw-Hill, 2004.

Gonzalez-Mena, J. "Observation Involves More Than Just Looking." *Educaring* 5(4), Fall 1994, p. 4.

Gonzalez-Mena, J. "What Can an Orphanage Teach Us? Lessons from Budapest." *Young Children,* September 2004, pp. 26–30.

Gonzalez-Mena, J. "Working with Cultural Differences: Individualism and Collectivism." *The First Years* (New Zealand Journal of Infant and Toddler Education) 4(1), 2002, pp. 13–15.

Greenfield, P. M., B. Quiroz, and C. Raeff. "Cross-Cultural Conflict and Harmony in the Social Construction of the Child." In *New Directions for Child and Adolescent Development* 87, edited by S. Harkness, C. Raeff, and C. M. Super. San Francisco: Jossey-Bass, 2000, pp. 93–108.

Greenspan, S. I. "Emotional Development in Infants and Toddlers." In *Infant/Toddler Caregiving: A Guide to Social-Emotional Growth and Socialization,* edited by J. Lally. Sacramento: California Department of Education, 1990.

Grieshaber, S., and G. S. Cannella, eds. *Embracing Identities in Early Childhood Education: Diversity and Possibilities.* New York: Teachers College Press, 2001.

Hall, E. T. *Beyond Culture.* Garden City, N.Y.: Anchor Press/Doubleday, 1981.

Hayden, T. "A Sense of Self." *Your Child,* Newsweek special edition, Fall and Winter 2000, pp. 56–63.

Hedges, H. "Empowering Infants and Toddlers—and Their Teachers." *The First Years* (New Zealand Journal of Infant and Toddler Education) 4(1), 2002, pp. 3–4.

Jones, E. *Teaching Adults: An Active Learning Approach.* Washington, D.C.: National Association for the Education of Young Children, 1986.

Kilbride, K. M. "Multiracial Children: Testing Our Sensitivity, Enhancing Our Vision." *Interaction* 12(2), Summer 1998, pp. 20–21.

Lally, J. R. "The Impact of Child Care Policies and Practices on Infant/Toddler Identity Formation." *Young Children* 51(1), November 1995, pp. 58–67.

Lee, D. *Freedom and Culture.* Englewood Cliffs, N.J.: Prentice-Hall, 1959.

Lee, D. *Valuing the Self.* Englewood Cliffs, N.J.: Prentice-Hall, 1976.

Leipzig, J. "Helping Whole Children Grow: Non-Sexist Childrearing for Infants and Toddlers." In *Alike and Different: Exploring Our Humanity with Young Children,* edited by Bonnie Neugebauer. Redmond, Wash.: Exchange Press, 1987.

Lieberman, A. F. *The Emotional Life of the Toddler.* New York: Free Press, 1993.

Marion, M. *Guidance of Young Children.* Columbus, Ohio: Merrill, 1999.

Marshall, H. H. "Cultural Influences on the Development of Self-Concept." *Young Children* 56(6), November 2001, pp. 19–22.

Meade, A. "The Dilemmas of Pluralism." *The First Years* (New Zealand Journal of Infant and Toddler Education) 4(1), 2001, p. 2.

Morrison, J. W. "Supporting Biracial Children's Identity Development." *Childhood Education* 77(3), Spring 2001, pp. 134–138.

Myers, B. J., H. Carmichael Olson, and K. Kaltenbach. "Cocaine-Exposed Infants: Myths and Misunderstandings." *Zero to Three* 13(1), June 1992, pp. 1–5.

Ocampo, K., G. Knight, and M. Bernal. "The Development of Cognitive Abilities and Social Identities in Children: The Case of Ethnic Identity." *International Journal of Behavioral Development* 21(3), 1997, pp. 479–500.

O'Connell, V. "Special Needs Inclusion: Five A's of Antibias." *Interaction* 12(2), Summer 1998, pp. 21–22.

Odom, S. L., T. Teferra, and S. Kaul. "An Overview of International Approaches to Early Intervention for Young Children with Special Needs and Their Families." *Young Children*, September 2004, pp. 38–43.

Phillips, C. B., and R. M. Cooper. "Cultural Dimensions of Feeding Relationships." *Zero to Three* 12(5), June 1992, pp. 10–13.

Rata, E. "An Overview to Theories of the Social Construction of the Self." *The First Years* (New Zealand Journal of Infant and Toddler Education) 2(2), September 2000, pp. 34–38.

Reynolds, E. *Guiding Young Children: A Child-Centered Approach*. Mountain View, Calif.: Mayfield, 1990.

Samuels, M., and N. Samuels. *Seeing with the Mind's Eye*. New York: Random House, 1975.

Samuels, M., and N. Samuels. *The Well Baby Book*. New York: Summit Books, 1979.

Thoman, E. B., and S. Browder. *Born Dancing: The Relaxed Parents' Guide to Making Babies Smart with Love*. New York: Harper & Row, 1987.

Trumbull, E., C. Rothstein-Fisch, P. M. Greenfield, and B. Quiroz. *Bridging Cultures Between Home and School*. Mahwah, N.J.: Erlbaum, 2001.

Warrent, J. C., C. Oswald Reed, S. Manker-Seale, and L. A. Comp. "Child-Space—Creating an Environment of Respect for Infants and Toddlers and Caregivers of Children." *Zero to Three* 7(4), April 1992, pp. 21–28.

Williamson, G. G., and M. Anzalone. *Sensory Integration and Self-Regulation in Infants and Toddlers: Helping Very Young Children Interact with their Environment*. Washington, D.C.: Zero to Three, 2001.

Wittmer, D., and S. Petersen. "Social Development and Integration: Facilitating the Prosocial Development of Typical and Exceptional Infants and Toddlers in Group Settings." *Zero to Three* 7(4), April 1992, pp. 14–20.

Chapter 14

Baker, A. R., "Why Should You Document the Everyday Experience in Your Infant or Toddler Room?" *Focus on Infants and Toddlers*, Association for Childhood Education International, 15(1), Fall 2002, pp. 1–5.

Bjorklund, G., and C. Burger. "Making Conferences Work for Parents, Teachers, and Children." *Young Children*, January 1987, pp. 26–31.

Brazelton, T. B. *Working and Caring*. Reading, Mass.: Addison-Wesley, 1987.

Bruno, H. E. "Hearing Parents in Every Language." *Exchange* 153, September/October 2003, pp. 58–60.

California State Health and Safety Code, Title 22 Child Care Facility Licensing Subchapter 2. Infant Care Centers. Section 101423.1, Infant Care Discipline.

Carr, M. *Assessment in Early Childhood Settings: Learning Stories*. London: Chapman, 2001.

Centre for Community Child Health. *The Cornerstone of Quality in Family Day Care and Child Care Centres—Parent-Professional Partnerships*. Melbourne: Royal Children's Hospital, 2001.

Centre for Community Child Health. *The Heart of Partnership in Family Day Care—Carer-Parent Communication*. Melbourne: Royal Children's Hospital, 2001.

Cooper, R. M., "Child Care as Shared Socialization," *Child Care Information Exchange*, July 2002, pp. 58–60.

Elam, P. "Creating Quality Infant Group Care Programs," in *Authentic Relationships in Group Care for Infants and Toddlers: Resources for Infant Educarers (RIE) Principles into Practice*, edited by S. Petrie and S. Owen. London and Philadelphia: Jessica Kingsley Publishers, 2005, pp. 83–92.

Galinsky, E. "Parents and Teacher-Caregivers: Sources of Tension, Sources of Support." *Young Children*, March 1988, pp. 4–12.

Gonzalez-Mena, J. "Do You Have Cultural Tunnel Vision?" *Child Care Information and Exchange*, July 1991, pp. 29–31.

Gonzalez-Mena, J. "Mrs. Godzilla Takes on the Child Development Experts: Perspectives on Parent Education." *Child Care Information and Exchange*, September 1987, pp. 25–26.

Gonzalez-Mena, J. *Multicultural Issues in Child Care*. Mountain View, Calif.: Mayfield, 1996.

Gonzalez-Mena, J. "Raising a 'Gifted' Infant." *Educaring* 8(2), Spring 1993, pp. 4–5.

Gordon, A., and K. Williams Browne. *Guiding Young Children in a Diverse Society*. Boston: Allyn & Bacon, 1996.

Gordon, J. "Child Care Professionalism and the Family." *Child Care Information Exchange*, July 1986, pp. 19–23.

Gordon, J. "Separation Anxiety: How to Ask a Family to Leave Your Center." *Child Care Information Exchange*, January 1988, pp. 13–15.

Greenspoon, B. "Toward Fully Inclusive Child Care Programs: Addressing Gay and Lesbian Issues," *Interaction* 12(2), Summer 1998, pp. 17–19.

Ingalls, A. M., R. Greenberg, and Jeanine Jeffers-Woolf. "A Journey of Hope: Forming Partnerships with Families and the Community." *Zero to Three* 24(6), July 2004, pp. 26–32.

Jones, E. *Teaching Adults: An Active Learning Approach.* Washington, D.C.: National Association for the Education of Young Children, 1986.

Jones, E., ed. *Supporting the Growth of Infants, Toddlers, and Parents.* Pasadena, Calif.: Pacific Oaks, 1990.

Kaplan-Sanoff, M., and K. Fitzgerald Rice. "Working with Addicted Women in Recovery and Their Children: Lessons Learned in Boston City Hospitals Women and Infants Clinic." *Zero to Three* 13(1), August/September 1992, pp. 17–23.

Lane, M., and S. Signer. *Infant/Toddler Caregiving: A Guide to Creating Partnerships with Parents.* Sacramento: California State Department of Education, 1990.

Lawrence-Lightfoot, S. *The Essential Conversation: What Parents and Teachers Can Learn from Each Other.* New York: Random House, 2003.

Lynch, E. W., and M. J. Hanson. *A Guide for Working with Children and Their Families: Developing Cross-Cultural Competence*, 2nd ed. Baltimore, Md.: Paul H. Brookes, 1998.

O'Connell, J. C. "Children of Working Mothers: What the Research Tells Us." *Young Children*, January 1983, pp. 63–70.

O'Connell, V. "Special Needs Inclusion: Five A's of Antibias," *Interaction* 12(2), Summer 1998, pp. 21–22.

Olsen G. W., and S. W. Shirley, "Resolving Staff Conflict," *Child Care Information Exchange* 141, September/October 2001, pp. 22–25.

Pawl, J. H., and A. L. Dombro. *Learning and Growing Together with Families: Partnering with Parents to Support Young Children's Development.* Washington D.C.: Zero to Three, 2001.

Post, J., and Hohmann, M." *Tender Care and Early Learning: Supporting Infants and Toddlers in Child Care Settings.* Ypsilanti, Mich.: High/Scope Press, 2000.

Stephens, K. "Sometimes the Customer *Isn't* Always Right: Problem Solving with Parents." *Exchange* 158, July/August 2004, pp. 68–74.

Trumbull, E., C. Rothstein-Fisch, P. M. Greenfield, and B. Quiroz. *Bridging Cultures Between Home and School.* Mahwah, N.J.: Erlbaum, 2001.

Glossary

Ability to predict The skill to expect or know what will happen.

Accommodation From Piaget's theory, the process of taking new information into the mind/body in such a way as to readjust, refine, or expand previous mental categories.

Adaptive behavior Normal or useful. Adaptive behavior includes the ability to adjust to new situations and apply familiar or new skills or organize behavior to better fit a situation.

Aesthetics Visually appealing. When adults value aesthetics, they demonstrate that value in the way they design environments for infants and toddlers.

Anecdotal records A documentation method that briefly describes an activity, a snatch of conversation, a chant, and so on. Anecdotal records can be based on reflection or written on the spot.

Assimilation From Piaget's theory, the process of taking new information into the mind/body by incorporating it into previously developed mental categories.

Assisted learning Social interaction, according to Lev Vygotsky, supports early language development as well as problem solving. The belief is that children's learning is assisted by their interactions with more knowledgeable people; co-constructed.

Attachment An enduring affectionate bond between a child and a person who cares for the child, giving the child a feeling of safety or security. Building a trusting secure attachment through consistency, responsiveness, and predictability shows children they can trust the caregiver to meet their needs (physical, mental, emotional). Attachment allows children to feel safe in their environment and therefore comfortable to explore and venture out.

Autonomy Being independent and responsible for one's actions. Includes feelings of power and a sense of competence in making choices. The second stage of Erik Erikson's psychosocial development.

Axon A filament extending from a nerve cell from which neural impulses are transmitted.

Bilingualism Having the ability to speak and understand two languages.

Body awareness Knowing where one's body is in space and learning its capabilities. Seen to emerge in infants and toddlers as their motor skills develop.

Body wisdom Children's ability to be in their body, know what it needs, and have confidence in how it works and moves.

Brain plasticity Capacity for regions of the brain and individual neurons within these regions to adapt and take on different functions as a result of experience.

Caregiver presence Two ways of relating to infants that are a part of the two kinds of quality time. In wants-something quality time, the caregiver's presence is active. The caregiver has a task to perform, and though he or she may be gentle and responsive, the caregiver is giving direction to the interaction. The other type of caregiver presence is receptive; that is, the infant is the directive one who initiates the action and the caregiver responds to that action.

Cephalocaudal An organized pattern of physical growth and motor control that proceeds from head to foot.

Cerebral cortex The largest, most complex structure of the human brain; responsible for higher level thinking and intelligence; surrounds the rest of the brain (much like a half-shelled walnut).

Cognitive experience Gathering information, organizing it, and finally using it to further one's understanding and know one's world.

Comfort device An object or action that may be of comfort to the child, also known as a transitional object. May be used during the departure of a parent or before nap time to help the child make the transition into a new routine.

Conditioning A relearning of one's behavioral response to react a certain way when presented with specific stimuli.

Conference A meeting with parents arranged with a goal in mind, such as sharing information, thoughts, questions, and concerns, with the purpose of gaining insights and planning long-range goals collaboratively.

Construct A concept, model, or idea. A mental image of how something looks or works used in building an understanding or new knowledge.

Constructing new knowledge A view based on Jean Piaget's work that suggests that children don't passively receive knowledge through being taught, but rather actively construct it themselves.

Continuity of care A method used in child care to keep infants and toddlers with the same caregiver(s) over a period of time. Desirable for building trust and security through attachment. The time can vary, but two years is a goal, and three years is even better.

Cultural identity Part of self-concept, cultural identity relates to everything we do, how we look, talk, what we eat, where we live, and how we look at the world.

Curriculum A plan for learning that is all-inclusive and centers on connections and relationships with an infant or toddler in a caregiving center or home child care. Focus is on education and care that responds to and respects the child's needs in warm, respectful, and sensitive ways that promote attachment. Respectful and responsive curriculum is based on relationships that occur within planned and unplanned activities, experiences, and happenings.

Dendrites Fibers extending from neurons that receive input from neighboring neurons.

Developmental domains Areas of development—ways of dividing up development as a whole to understand and study it. Simply stated, three developmental domains are the mind, the body, and feelings. More complex labels are physical, intellectual, and social-emotional development. Even more complex labels are psychomotor, cognitive, and affective development.

Dialogue Communication where different points of view are listened to and nondefensive language is used to promote open communication and problem solving.

Distraction Sometimes confused with redirection, distraction is a device to keep a child from continuing an action or behavior. Distraction also can be used to take children's minds off of a strong feeling. Distraction works, but has side effects as children learn that their energy or feelings are not acceptable to adults who distract them. Redirection may look similar, but instead of stopping the energy behind the behavior or the feeling, this guidance approach moves it in a more acceptable direction.

Documentation A variety of records that represent children's learning, skill building, social-emotional development or thought processes. Documentation captures the processes and products of children's daily experiences and can be in the form of written records, but also can include photographs, tape recordings, and videos.

Dramatic play Another name for pretend play. Comes more readily when there is a variety of objects that encourage exploration and pretend. Children under three years of age enjoy having representational objects from their day-to-day life for play, such as, dolls, stove, kitchen, cleaning, groceries, and so on.

Emotion Affective response to an event that is personally relevant. Emotions come from within the individual but may be triggered by an external event. Emotional states include happiness, surprise, anger, envy, and sadness.

Environmental limit A physical barrier that keeps a child or a material out of or inside of a given space. Environmental limits may also be accompanied by a verbal limit, such as "the water stays in the pan."

Exploration Act of discovering and examining one's environment, people, objects, and properties of objects through touching, mouthing, smelling, seeing, and hearing. Providing a safe, developmentally appropriate environment that accommodates the various abilities allows for exploration, which can result in a variety of discoveries.

Fast mapping The speedy (and sometimes not very precise) process of acquiring vocabulary by connecting a new word with an underlying concept after only a brief encounter.

Feeling A physical sense or awareness of an emotional state. An emotional response to an event or interaction.

Five senses Touch, hearing, smell, sight, and taste are all ways stimuli from the environment are taken in to the central nervous system for processing.

Floor time The opposite of time-out, when, instead of having attention removed, a toddler who is exhibiting difficult behavior has an adult who pays full attention to the child (down on the floor) and is responsive rather than directive.

Free play The name given undirected but monitored play when children have choices to pursue their special interests without continual adult control or expected outcome.

Gender identity Part of self-concept, how a child perceives of himself or herself as a boy or girl. Influenced by the messages received from others and the media regarding expectations and relative value of boys and of girls.

Gross motor Physical movement that requires the use of larger muscles such as rolling over, pulling up, climbing, walking, running, jumping.

Gross motor activity An activity using the large muscles of the arms, legs, and trunk, such as climbing, rolling, sliding, running, and so on.

Happenings The preferred word in this book for activities. A broad term intended to encompass the simplest event as well as more prolonged and complicated experiences. The word *activity* is avoided because it tends to put people in a preschool mode.

Imitate To replicate a behavior, language, or interaction that one has observed in another.

Individualized family service plan (IFSP) A written plan for early intervention consisting of child's level of development, the family's strengths and needs, goals for the infant and family, and the specific early intervention services needed to meet the goals. Developed by a team including parents and a variety of infant specialists.

Infant stimulation is an approach to infant education based on the idea that stimulating the senses helps infants develop. What is missing from this approach is the idea that infants left on their own in a rich sensory environment can make choices about what to take in. Having sensory experiences by choice is different from being stimulated by someone. Further, when the stimulation comes from the outside, infants can be overwhelmed and feel powerless.

Initiative Sense of purposefulness and effectiveness. Energy related to creating, inventing, and exploring. Third stage of Erik Erikson's psychosocial development, occurring at the onset of preschool age.

Inner controls Another word for self-control. The goal is to help children learn to control their own behavior instead of depending on someone or something outside themselves.

Intake interview Interview conducted when a child is admitted to a program or center. A service plan for both the child and parent is assessed at this time to help meet their needs through the scope of the curriculum or outside resources.

Intentionally Engaging in an action deliberately in a way that is congruent with one's purpose or goal.

Interactional synchrony Mutually reciprocal behaviors that mesh, seen in caregiver-child interactions.

Language The ability to produce symbols and sounds that represent meaning, influenced by emotional and social development. Development of language is context-dependent. The words (symbols), their pronunciation, and the methods of combining them used and understood by a large group (generalized meaning).

Learning tools Anything that is safe and interesting can be a source of learning for an infant or a toddler. Some examples are books, scarves, flannel boards, cardboard boxes, and blocks.

Limits Boundaries placed on a child's behavior. They can be physical boundaries from the environment, such as gates or locked doors, or verbal boundaries, such as reminding children to sit while they have food in their mouth. Children will test invisible boundaries in order to discover them.

Literacy The ability to listen and speak, and eventually to read and write.

Lock and latch boxes Objects that offer fine motor manipulation to open and close using different kinds of locks, hooks, and pulls. Sometimes lock and latch boxes contain objects inside for sensory exploration.

Locomotion The ability to move independently; related in this text to large or gross motor skill development.

Manipulation The ability to move skillfully with the hands and fingers; related in this text to small or fine motor skill development.

Memory Ability to retain and recall past experience, including images or thoughts.

Mixed-age groups Providing care for children of varying ages, more common in family child care.

Model To model behavior means to set an example by performing behaviors, actions, and interactive styles that others observe and imitate. Infants and toddlers learn from modeled behavior, so modeling can be a conscious teaching strategy and also a means of guidance.

Mouthable A characteristic of a toy or material that makes it appropriate for infants and toddlers, who learn about the nature of objects and their properties by putting them in their mouths.

Multicultural curriculum Gaining an understanding of the families' caregiving practices, listening to how they would like you to be with their child, and incorporating this information into your caregiving with their child. Being respectful and reflective of the various cultures in your community.

Myelinization The building or increasing of the myelin sheath that acts as an insulator around the axon with neural fibers allowing for efficient transmission of messages by the brain. Deterioration of the myelin sheath is caused in part by teratogen ingestion and could lead to delayed processing of information by the brain.

Needs and services plan Information regarding the child and family's routine, habits, special needs, and ways of communicating. Also, any needs, concerns, or requests for social support or intervention. Opening communication between the family and community resources is one important goal of a needs and services plan.

Neural pathways Information highways of the brain. Repeated stimulation strengthens some, and the ones that are neglected weaken and disintegrate.

Neurons Nerve cells that send and receive messages and make up the communication system of the brain.

Neuroplastic Flexible and responsive. In the first few months, a child's brain is very flexible and responsive to all sounds. With time, neural connections are strengthened through repetitious, responsive interactions, therefore making more permanent connections and less plasticity.

Neurotransmitters Electrical impulses that transmit messages to the brain via synapses.

Object permanence The understanding that objects continue to exist even when out of direct perception or sight.

Observation mode A particular state or way of being in which the focus is on paying close attention.

Optimum stress The right amount of stress—that is, enough to energize and motivate the child toward activity, including problem solving, but not so much to hamper or inhibit the child's ability to act or solve a problem.

Overstimulation Too much sensory input. An infant may show signs of being overstimulated by crying, turning away, or falling asleep.

Parent education An approach to working with parents designed to meet parents' needs such as the need for support and help or the need for information about techniques and practices that may be useful in guiding a child's development.

Perception The processing and organizing of information that has been taken in through the senses.

Philosophy of education A set of theories or concepts related to development, the acquisition of knowledge, and learning of skills.

Play spaces Areas set up for play, which should contain a variety of stage-appropriate toys and equipment for whole-body play as well as fine motor manipulative play. Also, space should provide for a range in mood from energetic to mellow, as well as social and solitary.

Positive reinforcement Response to an action or a behavior that strengthens the likelihood of that action or behavior being repeated. Also known as a reward.

Preoperational stage The second stage in Piaget's theory of cognitive development. Marked by symbolic thought, where language and ability to pretend begin to appear, starting at around two years of age until about seven years of age.

Pretend play Using one object, thing, or person to represent or stand for another. First appears around two years of age, when children can represent things through symbols and have the ability to think of their world when not directly experiencing it.

Primary caregiver system A system in which a caregiver takes primary responsibility for several infants or a small group of toddlers. In center settings where there is more than one caregiver per group, the effect is to have a caregiving team. That way children feel a strong bond with one person but also have another one or two adults with whom they are comfortable and familiar.

Prosocial behavior Actions that benefit another person without rewards for oneself.

Proximodistal An organized pattern of physical growth and motor control that proceeds from the center of the body outward.

Redirection A guidance strategy for changing children's unacceptable or disruptive behavior. The idea is to help children move their energy in a different direction and involve them in some positive activity. Redirection may look like distraction, but it is different.

Referral An outside service that has been identified as a source of assistance to meet a particular family's needs.

Reflexes Automatic or involuntary response system to touch, light, sound, and other forms of stimulation.

Reinforce To make more known or to increase understanding of how something happens or works. Often behaviors are reinforced through repetition and imitation.

Release time The time when caregivers in a team situation are released from responsibility for the rest of the group and can focus full attention on one child.

Resiliency The ability to overcome adversity within one's development and continue to develop in a functionally adaptive manner.

Resilient The quality of being able to cope with adversity and adapt in a positive way.

Running records A method of documenting that gives a blow-by-blow, objective, written description of what is happening while it is happening. A running record can include adult interpretations about the meaning of the observed behaviors, but it must separate objective data from subjective comments.

Savior complex A pattern that occurs when caregivers disapprove of parents and feel like they want to rescue the child from the family.

Scaffolding A temporary structure of support provided by adults at an appropriate level to help children increase their competence at a given task or interaction. This structure of support can be seen in the use of words describing actions, questions to expand actions, temporary physical assistance, reflecting emotion, or providing for a challenging opportunity. Sometimes the mere presence of the adult or older peer is all that is needed to help a child to solve a problem, accomplish something, or fulfill a need.

Secure attachment Term used from Mary Ainsworth's research (1970s), the Strange Situation, related to young children's responses to strangers and reunions with mothers. Refers to a relationship of trust and confidence and providing reassurance to enable independent exploration. Today the descriptions have *limited* application because of population diversity and reasons for child care.

Selective intervention Interrupting children who need help to stay safe or interact positively. Selective intervention can also take advantage of teachable moments. Learning when to intervene appropriately is an important skill for caregivers in facilitating infant-toddler play.

Self-actualization Sense of self-direction that brings about an extension and maturing of the personality. According to Abraham Maslow, this happens when one's physical, emotional, and intellectual needs are met. A point where one's needs relate to achievement and self-expression to realize one's potential.

Self-calming devices Techniques, such as thumb sucking, that infants may use to calm themselves, to settle their emotional state, which may be inborn. The ability to calm oneself without relying solely on others.

Self-concept Children's perceptions of the attributes and abilities they possess that they see as defining who they are. Self-concept is influenced by social context, gender identity, and culture.

Self-esteem Personal assessment of positive worth. The aspect of self-concept that involves judgment of one's own worth.

Self-help skills The skills children need to act independently, such as feeding themselves or putting on their shoes.

Self-image The picture a person has of himself or herself. Part of self-concept, one's perception of oneself, relates to body image and awareness.

Sensitivity The degree of responsiveness of an individual to external conditions or stimulation. Some children with extreme sensitivity experience discomfort.

Sensorimotor stage The coordination of sensory perception and muscle movement marked as the beginning of thinking. The first stage in Jean Piaget's theory of cognitive development.

Sensory impairment A delay or problem with receiving information through one or more senses.

Sensory input That which comes in and is received through the eyes, ears, nose, mouth, and skin. This information is used to understand one's environment and interactions. Sometimes called "sensory stimulation."

Sensory integration The process of combining and integrating information across the senses; it is critical to the development of perception.

Social interaction A critical component of language development. Through imitation of the caregiver and the caregiver's response, children reinforce their understanding of how to interact with people in a social context.

Strange situation From the research of Mary Ainsworth (1978), it involves a series of departures and reunions between mother and infant to measure attachment. Today it is considered somewhat dated because of varying family life styles and child care arrangements.

Stranger anxiety Distress an infant exhibits when faced with unfamiliar adults.

Structure A plan or setup of a physical environment that gives a clear message or expectation that influences one's behavior in such a space. It is most important for an environment for young children to be structured in a developmentally appropriate manner.

Synapses Gaps between neurons across which chemical messages are sent via neurotransmitters.

Tactile perception The processing of information that comes through touch.

Temperament An overall personality style based in genetic origin that develops within a social context.

Three R interaction An interaction that is respectful, responsive, and reciprocal. This interaction is a key part of effective caregiving. Interactions are linked together, creating a chain of interactions that build a partnership with the infant and are vital to relationships and therefore growth, development, and learning.

Time-out A guidance approach that involves removing a child from a situation in which he or she is behaving unacceptably.

Toilet learning A method by which children learn to use the toilet independently, usually some time during the third or fourth year of life. Children are old enough to learn to use the toilet when they show that they are physically, mentally, and emotionally ready.

Toilet training A method by which children are helped before the third year to use the toilet through a kind of conditioning method that depends more on cultural traditions than it does on readiness.

Trust To feel confident and secure within a relationship. The first stage of Erik Erikson's psychosocial development, which is the focus of the first year of life.

Wants-nothing quality time Quality time in which the adult is available and responsive to the child but is not directing the interaction, activity, or play.

Wants-something quality time Quality time in which the adult and child are involved in a task the caregiver has set up (diapering, feeding, bathing). The caregiver pays attention and includes the child in the process or task.

Zone of proximal development According to Lev Vygotsky, the gap between a child's current performance and his or her potential performance if helped by a more competent child or adult.

Credits

Text and Illustrations

Chapter 2 Page 39, From Abraham H. Maslow, *Toward a Psychology of Being*, 2nd ed. Copyright ©1968 Litton Educational Publishing, Inc. This material is used by permission of John Wiley & Sons, Inc.; **Chapter 3** Page 53, From THE GIFT FROM THE SEA by Anne Morrow Lindbergh, copyright ©1955, 1975, renewed 1983 by Anne Morrow Lindbergh. Used by permission of Pantheon Books, a division of Random House, Inc.; **Chapter 5** Page 94, From Rima Shore, *Rethinking the Brain: New Insights into Early Development*, p. 18. Copyright ©1997 Families and Work Institute. www.familiesandwork.org. Used with permission; **Chapter 7** Page 140, From *Bayley Scales of Infant Development*, 2nd ed. Copyright ©1993 The Psychological Corporation. Reproduced by permission; Page 146, From *Bayley Scales of Infant Development*, 2nd ed. Copyright ©1993 The Psychological Corporation. Reproduced by permission; **Chapter 9** Page 181, Adapted from *How Does Your Child Hear and Talk?* American Speech-Language-Hearing Association. Copyright ©2002 American Speech-Language-Hearing. www.ASHA.org. Used with permission; **Chapter 10** Page 220, From MOTIVATION AND PERSONALITY, 3rd ed., by Abraham H. Maslow, p. 72. Copyright ©1970 Harper & Row. Adapted by permission of Pearson Education, Inc., Upper Saddle River, NJ.; **Chapter 11** Page 248, From THE PROPHET by Kahil Gibran, copyright ©1923 by Kahil Gibran and renewed copyright 1951 by Administrators C.T.A. of Kahil Gibran Estate and Mary G. Gibran. Used by permission of Alfred A. Knopf, a division of Random House, Inc.; **Chapter 12** Page 257, From Program for Infant/Toddler Caregivers. Reprinted by permission of WestEd Center for Child & Family Studies, Sausalito, CA.; Page 271, From Doris Bergen, Rebecca Reid & Louis Torelli in *Educating and Caring for Very Young Children*, p. 173. Copyright ©2001 Teachers College Press. Reprinted with permission.

Photos

Chapter 1 Page 2, Banana Stock; **Chapter 2** Page 24, Creatas/PunchStock; **Chapter 3** Page 46, Royalty-Free/Corbis; Page 52, Frank Gonzalez-Mena; **Chapter 4** Page 70, Nicola Sutton/Life File/Getty Images; Page 75, Frank Gonzalez-Mena; **Chapter 5** Page 92, Michael Newman/PhotoEdit Inc.; Page 99, Mary Kate Denny/PhotoEdit Inc.; **Chapter 6** Page 112, Olivia Baumgartner/Sygma/Corbis; **Chapter 7** Page 130, Nancy Sheehan/PhotoEdit Inc.; Page 142T, Frank Gonzalez-Mena; Page 142B, Frank Gonzalez-Mena; Page 144, Frank Gonzalez-Mena; **Chapter 8** Page 154, Michael Newman/PhotoEdit Inc.; **Chapter 9** Page 178, Tony Freeman/PhotoEdit Inc.; Page 191, Rich Shulman; **Chapter 10** Page 204, Mary Kate Denny/PhotoEdit Inc.; Page 214, Jane Sapinsky/Corbis; **Chapter 11** Page 230, David Young-Wolff/PhotoEdit Inc.; Page 243, Michael Newman/PhotoEdit Inc.; **Chapter 12** Page 254, Sandi Meschoulam; **Chapter 13** Page 284, Geri Engberg/The Image Works; Page 292, Laura Dwight/Corbis; Page 299, Robert Brenner/PhotoEdit Inc.; **Chapter 14** Page 306, Robert Brenner/PhotoEdit Inc.; Page 322, Michael Newman/PhotoEdit Inc.

Index